Grounded Authority

D1566107

Grounded Authority

The Algonquins of Barriere Lake against the State

Shiri Pasternak

University of Minnesota Press
Minneapolis • London

Portions of the Introduction were previously published as "Jurisdiction and Settler Colonialism: Where Do Laws Meet?" *Canadian Journal of Law and Society* 29 (2014): 145–61; doi:10.1017/cls.2014.5; copyright 2014 Canadian Law and Society Association/Association Canadienne Droit et Société; reprinted with permission. Portions of chapter 6 were previously published as "A Tale of Two Visions for Canada: The Trilateral Agreement versus the Land Claims Policy," in *Aboriginal History: A Reader*, ed. Kristin Burnett and Geoff Read (Don Mills, Ontario: Oxford University Press, 2016). Portions of chapter 9 were previously published as "The Economics of Insurgency: Thoughts on Idle No More and Critical Infrastructure," Rabble.ca (January 14, 2013), online at http://rabble.ca/news/2013/01/economics-insurgency-thoughts-idle-no-more-and-critical-infrastructure, and in Shiri Pasternak and Tia Dafnos, "How Does a Settler State Secure the Circuitry of Capital?" *Society and Space: Environment and Planning D* (2017), Sage Publications.

Published by the University of Minnesota Press
111 Third Avenue South, Suite 290
Minneapolis, MN 55401-2520
http://www.upress.umn.edu

Printed in the United States of America on acid-free paper

The University of Minnesota is an equal-opportunity educator and employer.

22 21 20 19 18 17   10 9 8 7 6 5 4 3 2 1

Library of Congress Cataloging-in-Publication Data
Pasternak, Shiri, author.
Title: Grounded authority : the Algonquins of Barriere Lake against the state / Shiri Pasternak.
Minneapolis : University of Minnesota Press, 2017. Includes bibliographical references and index.
Identifiers: LCCN 2017003542 (print) | ISBN 978-0-8166-9832-5 (hc) | ISBN 978-0-8166-9834-9 (pb)
Subjects: LCSH: Algonquins of Barriere Lake (First Nation)—Land tenure. | Land tenure—Law and legislation—Canada. | Indians of North America—Legal status, laws, etc.—Canada. | BISAC: SOCIAL SCIENCE / Ethnic Studies / Native American Studies. | LAW / Indigenous Peoples. | SOCIAL SCIENCE / Human Geography.
Classification: LCC KIC4396.4 .P37 2017 (print) | DDC 346.7104/32089973—dc23
LC record available at https://lccn.loc.gov/2017003542

Dedicated to Benjamin Benaysi Lamson King,
the Thunderbird who landed for five days then returned to the sky

Contents

Abbreviations

AANDC	Aboriginal Affairs and Northern Development Canada
ABL	Algonquins of Barriere Lake
ADR	alternative dispute resolution
AFN	Assembly of First Nations
AFNQL	Assembly of First Nations of Quebec and Labrador
AIP	Agreement in Principle
ANS	Algonquin National Secretariat
ATIP	Access to Information and Privacy
ATR	Additions to Reserve
BC	British Columbia
BCTC	British Columbia Treaty Commission
BCTP	British Columbia Treaty Process
BLS	Barriere Lake Solidarity
CAAFs	Contrats d'approvisionnement et d'aménagement forestier (Timber Supply and Forest Management)
CBC	Canadian Broadcasting System
CCC	Canadian Chamber of Commerce
CCESP	Conversion to Community Election System Policy
CCPRWG	Comprehensive Claims Policy Reform Working Group
CEAA	Canadian Environmental Assessment Agency
CERD	Committee on the Elimination of Racial Discrimination
CIP	Canadian International Paper Company
CLASSE	Coalition Large de l'ASSÉ
CLCP	Comprehensive Land Claims Policy
COIE	Commission des Œuvres Indiennes et Esquimaudes (Commission on Indian and Eskimo Works)
CSIS	Canadian Security Intelligence Service
CUPW	Canadian Union of Postal Workers
DIA	Department of Indian Affairs
DIAND	Department of Indian Affairs and Northern Development
DISC	Delgamuukw Implementation Strategic Committee

DoJ	Department of Justice
EIMD	Emergency and Issue Management Directorate
EMAP	Emergency Management Assistance Program
FA	Final Agreement
FNPOA	First National Property Ownership Act
FNTC	First Nations Tax Commission
GDP	gross domestic product
GLV	Grand Lac Victoria
GOC	Government Operations Centre
GST	General Sales Tax
HBC	Hudson's Bay Company
IBC	Interim Band Council
ICTMN	Indian Country Today Media Network
IEN	Indigenous Environmental Network
INAC	Indigenous and Northern Affairs Canada
IPSMO	Indigenous Peoples Solidarity Movement Ottawa
IRMP	Integrated Resource Management Plan
JBNQA	James Bay and Northern Quebec Agreement
JIG	Joint Intelligence Group
KI	Kitchenuhmaykoosib Inninuwug
KMK	Kwilmu'kw Maw-klusuaqn
MAO	Mitchikanibikok Anishnabe Onakinakewin
MER	Ministère de l'Énergie et des Ressources (Ministry of Energy and Resources)
MFFP	Ministère des Forêts, de la Faune et des Parcs (Ministry of Forests, Wildlife, and Parks)
MIEA	Mitchikanibikok Inik Education Authority
MLCP	Ministère de Loisir, de la Chasse et de la Pêche (Department of Recreation, Hunting, and Fishing)
MFN	Maa-Nulth First Nations
MNR	Ministry of Natural Resources
MOA	Mermorandum of Agreement
MOMI	Memorandum of Mutual Intent
MOU	Memorandum of Understanding
MP	Member of Parliament
MRC	municipalite régionale de comté (regional county municipality)
MTH	Measures to Harmonize

NAC	National Archives Canada
NDP	New Democratic Party
NFA	Nisga'a Final Agreement
NGOs	nongovernmental organizations
NPE	New Political Economy
NStQ	Northern Secwepemc te Qelmucw
NWAC	Native Women's Association of Canada
OPP	Ontario Provincial Police
PST	Provincial Sales Tax
RCAP	Royal Commission on Aboriginal People
RCMP	Royal Canadian Mounted Police
SAS	sensitive area studies
SÉPAQ	Société des établissements de plein air du Québec (SÉPAQ is the way the organization is referred to in English, as well, which translates roughly to "Quebec Society of Outdoor Recreation Facilities")
SOCs	Senior Oversight Committees
SQ	Sûreté du Québec (Quebec Provincial Police)
TFN	Tsawwassen First Nation
TFSI	Tsawwassen Fee Simple Interest
TMA	Trilateral Management Area
TPM	Third Party Manager; Third Party Management
UBCIC	Union of British Columbia Indian Chiefs
UG	Unités de gestion
UN	United Nations
UNDRIP	United Nations Declaration on the Rights of Indigenous Peoples
VPA	Vancouver Port Authority
ZEC	zone d'exploitation controllée (controlled exploitation zone)

Note on Terminology

In this book, I alternate between several names for describing the department of the Canadian government responsible for Indian Affairs. These alternate names mostly correspond to historical changes to the name of the department. Since the time of confederation, "Indians" have been governed under nine differently named administrative bodies, at times signaling drastic regime changes in jurisdiction or governing strategies, at times merely moving some words around. The earliest incarnation of departmental responsibility for "Indians" was under the Department of the Secretary of the State of Canada (to 1869), followed by the Department of the Secretary of State for the Provinces (1869–73), and the Department of the Interior (1873–80). A long period followed when the Department of Indian Affairs (DIA) (1880–1936) emerged, devoted exclusively to Indians and their intensive management and relocation. Accordingly, the DIA plays a significant role in the early history at Barriere Lake. The intensification of land exploitation in relation to Indian lands is written as plainly as the next department name change to the Department of Mines and Resources (1936–50), as was the attempt to distance land rights from the conceptualization of Indian people in the subsequent incarnation of the Department of Citizenship and Immigration (1950–65). In 1966, the portfolio of the offices of the Minister of Citizenship and Immigration were divided between the new departments of the minister the Department of Indian Affairs and Northern Development (DIAND) and the minister of Energy, Mines, and Resources. The identity of DIAND endured until June 13, 2011, when the department became Aboriginal Affairs and Northern Development Canada (AANDC). For the most part, I continue to call the department DIA throughout the period between 1936 and 1966, when it becomes INAC or DIAND, in order to avoid confusion. Since 2015, the department has become Indigenous and Northern Affairs Canada (INAC, again).

Making sense of the names that non-Indigenous peoples have assigned to Indigenous peoples also necessitates some terminological clarification. Non-Indigenous peoples have sorted the peoples of these lands by appearance, approximate geographic locations, trade relationships, language, racial epithets, misunderstood or mispronounced versions of the names Indigenous peoples call themselves, and political acts of subject-making and subordination. To describe generally the people who have made their homes here since before the settlement of Europeans, I use the term "Indigenous" to refer to the original peoples and governments of these lands.

The term "Indigenous" further links the history of colonization on these lands to the international struggle of peoples to assert their nationhood and jurisdiction over ancestral lands. The United Nations has defined "indigenous peoples" as "communities, peoples and nations . . . having a historical continuity with pre-invasion and pre-colonial societies that developed on their territories, consider themselves distinct from other sectors of societies now prevailing on those territories, or parts of them." It is difficult not to conceive of Indigenous peoples in relation to colonial European conquerors or modern attempts at economic, social, and political restructuring and assimilation, but it is not helpful to think of Indigenous peoples as opposite to an industrial modern society, either. "Indigenous" connotes a *dynamic* people who are ancestrally, spiritually, and politically connected to a territory in a multiplicity of ways.

Another umbrella term to describe all the different "categories" of Indigenous peoples living in Canada is "Aboriginal." Lumping together First Nations (formerly "Indians"), Métis, and Inuit, the Canadian government uses the umbrella term "Aboriginal"; I use "Aboriginal" in this book when the word is attached to government policy—for example, Aboriginal treaty rights or Aboriginal title. I avoid using "Aboriginal" more generally because, as Evelyn Peters points out, assumptions about Indigenous peoples are embedded in such categories of interpolation, rendering it difficult to escape colonial frameworks.[1] The census data, for example, is based on categories of status/nonstatus (depending on whether individuals are registered under the Indian Act) or by colonial categories of race, rather than by Indigenous cultural practices. Recent efforts have been made to use more sensitive terminology, but the categories remain unchanged, because they are subject to federal legislation and any changes in terminology would affect the implementation of all policies toward these respective groups. The term "Indigenous" is free from these colonial categories of race, status, and legislative authority. Occasionally, I use the term "First Nations" to describe those peoples formerly described as "Indians," as the key constituents of the land claims and other policy. In rare cases, I use the term "Indian" to describe Indigenous peoples from the perspective of Canadian governments. The derogatory connotations are purposefully left intact. Regarding the Algonquins of Barriere Lake, while they call themselves the Mitchikanibikok Inik, this name is difficult to pronounce for English readers. I refer to them alternately as Barriere Lakers, Barriere Lake Algonquins, or simple "Algonquins." As I describe in chapter 2, the French-originated name of "Barriere Lake" comes closest to translating Mitchikanibikok Inik, the People of the Stone Weir. The definition of the "Algonquin" Nation has come to take precision for non-Indigenous writers and researchers only in recent years, prompted largely by the incredible work of independent historian James Morrison. Even the common history of the Algonquins must be understood within a broader, dynamic network of relationships between nations. The Mitchikanibikok Inik tend to refer to themselves simply as Anishnabe—"human beings"—in which they are connected, first, to closer cousins who speak dialects of the same language and then to all the other nations on earth.

While *Barrière* is a French word and has an accent in French, the community itself does not use the accent—not for formal reasons, but because by trick of fate (the residential schools they were sent to) the community is English-speaking.

Finally, a note on transcription of *anishnabemowin* (Anishnabe language). Where I refer to my own research interviews, I transcribe phonetically to the best of my ability, though I am not committed to a formalized transcription method. Partially, my inadequacies around transcription are owing to my inexperience with the language. But I was also unavailed of resources on transcription of the Barriere Lake dialect. As Sue Roark-Calnek explained to me, "except for a short glossary of Lac Simon Algonquin (which is very close to Barriere Lake), the dictionaries I have are from Maniwaki (McGregor: Algonquin/English and English/Algonquin) and two from Oblate missionaries (Lemoine and Cuoq). Barriere Lake speech is more rapid, eliding some vowels, nasals, and glide consonants." Sue helped me in parts to interpret what I was hearing based on her knowledge of the language, such as the section where Toby Decoursay is describing the relationship between land and belonging. Wherever problems remain, they are mine alone. Scott Nickels's transcriptions were based on his knowledge of the language derived from Harry Wawatie, so they vary slightly from those of Roark-Calnek, and both researchers add accents occasionally to direct pronunciation. Doug Elias's transcriptions borrow from the work of Nickels and Roark-Calnek.

Preface

An Autobiography of Territory

The Story of Shula: In the Land of Blood and Honey, of Milk and Heavy Artillery

The shacks where my grandparents lived when they first settled in the arid Negev desert were small and flimsy. "We really heard everything from room to room," my Safta laughs. A couple occupied each room of the two-room shacks. The kids lived in the Children's House nearby, raised collectively by a caregiver who made her rounds once per night.

My Saba slept most nights in a tent on the fields he worked by day so the Palestinians would not destroy the irrigation pipes. One late evening, when my Saba was on security patrol with the neighbor's husband, two Palestinian men slipped into the settlement and hid behind a stack of palettes. They had probably come to pilfer food. Safta's neighbor, Shula, picked that moment to stir from her sleep, and went to pee behind the palettes. She startled the Palestinians and they killed her.

Shula was pregnant. When the doctor arrived, he realized that he could save the baby, but he decided not to let it live. "A baby can live without a father, but not without a mother," my Safta says. She heard everything that night—the startled cry, the stabbing, and the hasty retreat. Later, the settlers found where the gate had been cut and repaired the breach. Friends named a grove in memory of Shula at the entrance to the kibbutz and life went on.

Safta is losing her memory, but she remembers this story and repeats it regularly, triggered by my incessant questions about settlement. The first time I heard this story was the first time I asked her why we came to this place. She replied with surprising candor: "They told us God gave us this land. Now I wonder, why would God give us a land where others were already living?" I pressed her on this point and she became annoyed, accusing me of understanding very little about life in Israel: "As a North American, you cannot understand what it means to live in times of war and to fight for your survival." A swift means to annex me to the territory, she tells me the story of Shula.

I've come to wonder about this story of Shula. On the surface, it could be a story about embodiment and social reproduction: death meted out by Palestinian hunger, by a pregnant woman's incessant urination, by the killer instincts of self-preservation. If it is a story about the fog of war, the topography is unconventional. I tell a friend the story of Shula and he rolls his eyes and says, "Isn't colonialism *always* an accident? *Nobody* seems to have *ever* meant for anything bad to happen." His sarcasm is aimed at the Jewish settlers. If we dig deeper and see this story as a metaphor for settlement, then what structures the similarities to the whole? Is this a story of the unborn child? Is it about the stillbirth dream of a Zionist utopia? Is this a warning about hunger for land? How the Halutzim (pioneers) drove Palestinians to starvation, and in the process created their own fearful existence?

My grandparents did not technically steal the lands where Kibbutz Be'eri was built. The Jewish Agency and other individuals bought these lands southwest of Be'er Sheva privately. But whose land was it to sell and how had the deed been authorized? In the desert of al-Naqab—what the Jews called the Negev—all land fell into five categories of legal interest. As Hussein Abu Hussein and Fiona McKay explain, "In practice, it was not always clear under which category a plot of land fell and many rights in land, acquired by long possession and use, were not formally registered."[1] On top of this, Turkish title to much of the land—land that was sold to the Jews—was considered merely nominal, because, despite Ottoman rule that lasted until 1918, Palestinians acquired use of land through long occupation and communal land trusts held by Arab villages for generations.

For the Jewish people ownership meant little without possession, too. So the Jewish Agency for Palestine, along with the Jewish National Fund, the Hagana Defense Forces, and Mekorot Water Company, planned an operation to extend Jewish settlement into Bedouin lands. Be'eri, the kibbutz my grandparents helped to found, was established during a wave of colonization called "Eleven Points" that took place on a single night in October 1946 and resulted in the illegal settlement of as many kibbutzim in al-Naqab—a region sparse with Jewish settlement, excluded from British partition plans for the State of Israel. My grandparents' role was significant in reversing these plans and remapping the territory. As one of "Four Points" including Tekuma, Kfar Darom, and Nirim that bordered the Gaza Strip, Be'eri was also strategically essential for containing Palestinian lands.

To catch the British off guard, the settlers chose the evening of Yom Kippur—the most holy of holy nights for the Jewish people—to settle the southern desert. On the night of October 6, under an immense sweep of darkness hammered by stars, the newcomers—my Saba and a dozen or so men—erected four hasty walls and a makeshift roof. They named the settlement Nahabir and waited in the chilled desert hills for sunrise.

Upon discovery by the British, it was the roof that saved the settlement, despite the illegal nature of their covert occupation. An Ottoman law still on the books stated that any structure with a roof intact could not be torn down. "This is the mind of the Jew," my Safta laughs. She is right, in that a legalistic approach to dispossession would dominate spatial change in Palestine.[2] But the Jewish people's appeal to Ottoman law in 1946 was not to an ethnically blind judicial system. Although the civil courts of Palestine were meant to conform to the Ottoman law in force at the time of British occupation (in a strenuous effort to maintain the image of benevolent stewardship), the British Mandate demonstrated enormous flexibility in their interpretation of these laws.[3] Thus, the Ottoman law regarding roofs likely held up by virtue of British sympathy with Jewish presence in al-Naqab, rather than by a strict adherence to an objective juridical order.

Over the next sixty years, Nahabir was relocated nearby to what became Kibbutz Be'eri, and the shacks turned into small but comfortable modern homes, with wireless Internet, air conditioning, and bedrooms now built for children. Safta says: "And now they call us 'the rich.' . . . Our conditions are better than our neighbors'. We are a big kibbutz; we have a factory that is very profitable. Agriculture became less profitable, and we eventually saw it wasn't worthwhile, and we gave up our dairy. But our printing press is doing well . . ." She begins to sing, "There were days . . ." But she can't remember the words.

While I was writing this Preface, my Safta passed away. I was living in Canada; it was too far away and too expensive and too difficult to travel alone with my infant daughter, and I could not attend the funeral. *A Pan of Young Trees* is a short video my sister made a few years ago that begins with a black screen and just the sound of my grandmother's deep voice

asking, "Will there be something for you to tell?" The film now feels ele-
giac. Grainy shots of a junk forest fade onto the screen, planted in rows
outside the kibbutz. As the camera glances shakily around, we hear the
rest of their Hebrew conversation:

MAYA: About what?

SAFTA: To your grandchildren.

MAYA: About what, though?

SAFTA: You didn't found a kibbutz, you didn't, for example, [do]
special things . . .

MAYA: I hope so.

SAFTA: I'm pleased that although it was hard, I did something
important.

MAYA: I want to say at the end of my life that everything that I
wanted to do, that I thought was important, I did . . . whether big
or small.

SAFTA: But what you've done is for yourself, right? What you've
done—it was for yourself.

MAYA: Good question.

SAFTA: I did it for the people of Israel. There was nothing in the
Negev. What's "Negev"? *Linagev*, "to dry," right? They were *years*
of drought . . .

What Safta did, it is true, was for the people of Israel.

The Negev occupied a special place on the interior frontier of the settler colony. David Ben-Gurion, Zionist leader and first prime minister of
Israel, epitomized this logic in a statement that declared: "[t]he people
of Israel will be tested by the Negev . . ."[4] A geography to be conquered,
the Bedouin people of al-Naqab became the present absences in this version of *terra nullius*.

Like Indigenous peoples in Canada, the Bedouin are what Oren
Yiftachel calls a "trapped minority," a population who fall outside of the
nation-state despite being located geographically within.[5] These populations are governed by complex patterns of integration, segregation,
violence, and partition. The constraints exercised by the trapped minority on the state are prevalent in the production of settler space, for

a major issue with the captured minority is their ongoing potential for disruption to the national order by asserting their unvanquished claims to the land—their jurisdiction. An excessive relationship to the land by Indigenous peoples threatens controlled narratives of conquest and domination.

The terrorization of Bedouins continues today, structured as it is into the Jewish settlement goals of Palestine. Almost half of the Bedouins in al-Naqab live in unrecognized village sites that lack basic services such as running water and electricity. The village of Al Araqib located between the Bedouin town of Rahat and the southern Israeli city of Be'er Sheva has been razed to the ground ninety-six times, most recently in April 2016.[6] In one of the first incidents, in 2010, bulldozers arrived escorted by more than one thousand armed officers, destroying around forty houses and uprooting hundreds of trees.[7] The State of Israel's strategy is to cajole the Bedouin into one of seven government-established towns comprised of prefabricated homes with no access to their traditional Bedouin land base or ways of life. Critical observers have labeled this project the continued "Judaization" process of the Negev.[8]

More than seventy years after the founding of Israel, a shop on Ben Yehuda Street in West Jerusalem sells a T-shirt that depicts a Native American counseling former Prime Minister Ehud Barak. The Indigenous figure, who is holding a peace pipe and dons a headdress, warns the former Israeli leader, "Ehud, let me tell you about trading land for peace!" Like the Native American who has been swindled of his lands, the Jewish people are depicted as fighting an unwinnable battle to negotiate their own lands for a peaceful solution with the Palestinians. Cast as Native Americans, the Israelis are to be understood as those with the rightful, *original* claim to the land—in other words, as the Indigenous peoples of Palestine. In the T-shirt image, Ehud and the Indigenous caricature stand against the backdrop of a map of Israel–Palestine, labeled as Israel. Only five points are marked: Haifa, the Golan Heights, the Kineret, the West Bank, and Jerusalem. It is not a geographically accurate map, but that is obviously not its purpose: highlighted here are contested or cohabited areas of Israel, those that many Israelis are determined not to "trade" away. Producing the semiotics of the colonial present,[9] the map depicts the flat space of Israel–Palestine, the regime of modernization that contains Israel as a settled place in a series of points on a map.[10]

T-shirt at a shop on Jerusalem's Ben Yehuda Street. Photograph by author.

Steven Salaita's book *The Holy Land in Transit* finds multiple meanings and functions of "transit" between Israel and America.[11] He examines these places, not as distinct geographic entities, but rather as colonial imaginaries, linked by the rhetoric of early colonialists in North America and by Zionist immigrants in Palestine of a Promised Land.

For example, Salaita tracks the trail of English pioneer towns in America named for biblical settlements, marking the new land as an ancient journey. The Jewish people claim Canaan as the Promised Land because of their historical connection to the region, though much renaming was also necessary to establish their return to the place that had been governed and inhabited by a succession of regional powers in the intervening centuries since Jewish exodus.

Jodi Byrd takes up Salaita's concept of "transit," theorizing that Indians provide imperialists with conceptual modes for linking places and histories, like Israel and America, deepening a global cacophony of alliance. As Byrd writes, "What it means to be in transit . . . is to be in motion, to exist liminally in the ungrievable spaces of suspicion and unintelligibility."[12] In Byrd's conceptualization, the "transit of Indianness" is a tool of empire because Indigenous peoples are swapped in and out of national narratives for political repurposing. In the United States, the frontier of the American West was depicted as the Orient in an attempt to paint the violent assault against Indigenous peoples in a patriotic light. As Alex Lubin describes: "[n]umerous southwestern landscape paintings after the Mexican-American War dressed Mexicans and Indians in clothing and scenery that turned them into Bedouins."[13] Bedouins, in this fabrication, implied liberation and drew on heroic American narratives of exploration throughout the Ottoman Empire.[14] When Americans are abroad, Byrd observes, "Indianness becomes a site through which U.S. Empire orients and replicates itself by transforming those to be colonized into 'Indians' through continual reiterations of pioneer logics, whether in the Pacific, Caribbean, or the Middle East."[15] In the Second World War, for instance, American soldiers sought to familiarize themselves with those they encountered in North Africa through the figure of the "Indian," containing their fears of the unknown through accustomed racist tropes of a "premodern" subject.[16]

More recently, the U.S. military named its mission to kill Osama bin Laden after Geronimo, an Apache warrior who fought to defend his people's homelands against the United States and Mexico. This was ironic on two levels: first, the Americans waged a genocidal war *against* Geronimo in the mid-nineteenth century; second, the imperial connotations of this "transit of Indianness" mistakenly glorified bin Laden by comparing him to a brave man who fought against brutal invaders to protect his people.[17] What these transits can show us is how the colonial frontier is a socially constructed place of invented history; it is defined relative to what has already been deemed knowable through imperial discovery.

Here I come back to my Safta. My sister dug up an image of her in the Be'eri Archives where she dons a headdress and claps along to costumed children playing against a flat landscape of brown dusty land. It is Purim, 1955. Another photo in the set shows two kibbutz children in redface, also wearing headdresses and feathers. They are not just playing dress-up. The transit of the Indian has figured prominently into Jewish mythology for centuries, playing a range of critical roles. One role has been a means by which to resolve identity crises connected to Jews' outsider status to European and then American society.[18] In one rendering of this relationship, Jews saw the American Indians as a lost tribe of Zion, visualizing Jewish migration to America as a reconnection with their people, rather than as another violent moment of displacement.[19]

Our attachments to place are rarely represented in ways that reflect the tangled ways we come to understand and take our place in the world. But the transit through which we root is the way we take responsibility for how we land. Ella Shohat demonstrates these complexities in her uncanny work on the *two* 1492s. Examining Sephardi Arab-Jewish identity and its historical intersections with other communities, she writes: "[t]riumphant over the Muslims, Spain invested in the project of Columbus, whose voyages were financed partly by wealth taken from the defeated Muslims and confiscated from Jews through the Inquisition."[20] Jewish people inadvertently financed Columbus's expedition through their expulsion, forced conversion, and death long before a single Jewish person had turned up on these Atlantic shores. Moreover, the Inquisition against Jews and Muslims was based on Christian demonology that prefigured the "mammoth apparatus of racism and sexism" that would demarcate life on the "new" continent.[21]

Jews who escaped Spain with their lives settled throughout the Arab world. Today, their dark skin, poverty, and non-European cultures render them second-class citizens to the Ashkenazi Jews in Israel, where many eventually settled. Despite these social divisions, all Canadian Jews, regardless of origin, are relentlessly interpolated to identify with universalist articulations of a Jewish identity, an identity that deepens the paradox of Israeli claims to be both *European* and *indigenous* by claiming to be a civilized *European* bastion in the midst of savage Arab

*Yehudit Rappoport, Kibbutz Be'eri, Purim, circa 1955. Courtesy of the Kibbutz
Be'eri archive.*

states. Most disturbing are recent alliances between prominent Jewish
organizations and the Conservative Party of Canada, which supports
Israel as an exercise in Christian evangelical and eschatological solidarity.[22] As I was writing this, in 2012, Prime Minister Stephen Harper
was pledging support for the nation as the Israel Defense Forces shower

missiles into Gaza, some of which were returned in retaliation for rockets that were landing inside the gates of Kibbutz Be'eri where the funeral of my grandmother was being held.

An only child born in Tel Aviv in 1926, my Safta joined the pioneer movement after high school where she learned to throw a grenade. Today, four of Safta's grandchildren have refused to engage in combat or serve in the army. Upon reflection, it seems to me that Shula represents a particular staging of Israeli memory, one that represses the source of the violent conflict, and therefore dispenses the teller of complicity in its reproduction. Israeli nationhood is premised on a brutal and expanding garrison architecture that endeavors to contain and erode Palestinian life in the face of their refusal to surrender. To accomplish this task, Israel must wipe away the traces of Palestinian belonging that will expose the violence of its occupation.

Yet, I do not—I cannot—detach from my settler-colonial homelands in Israel or Canada: my love for these places is constitutive of my identity, violence and all, and to disavow them is to choke off the attachments that give our lives their rich and challenging meanings and form the anchors that tether our responsibilities. What are the grounds of authority upon which we rely to make sense of our relationship to the world? It is this ground that demands questioning; that is why this book is focused on jurisdiction.

My Anishnabe friend Dawnis Kennedy convinced me to start my book with my grandmother: "Know why you're doing this—why this is the story you want to tell. Your spirit chose this family for a reason." I bought a plane ticket and flew to Israel that summer. To cover my expenses, I received a grant to do comparative research on Israeli and Canadian land-privatization initiatives. Interviews eventually turned to the situation for Indigenous peoples in Canada. Anthropology professor Daniel Monterescu said, "You know, there are a lot of Palestinians migrating to Canada now. I thought you were better."[23] That summer, I stayed in Tel Aviv but visited the kibbutz often, where I tried not to get in the way at my grandmother's house. She had always been cold and aloof and she corrected my Hebrew grammar as I spoke, making me feel self-conscious; I tried to find things she could talk about so that I could just listen.

On my final visit to Safta's tiny flat, filled to the brim with the sculptures, paintings, figurines, and ironwork she loved to collect, we sat over tea and she told stories about how all the objects came to her and why she loved each one in particular. She also collected beautiful books and I found a leather-bound copy of Solomon's *Song of Songs* addressed to her and my late grandfather on the occasion of their wedding. I brought it over to her and she slid it open and ran her crumply fingers across the finely engraved monographs. Then she began to read:

Rise up, my love, my fair one, and come away. For lo, the winter is past, the rain is over and gone. The flowers appear on the earth, the time of singing birds has come, and the voice of the turtle is heard in our land. 2:10.

Introduction

Jurisdiction on Indigenous Land

Boyce Richardson captures a remarkable moment in his 1990 film *Blockade*.[1] Richardson went up to the Algonquin community of Barriere Lake to film the moose hunt, but what he found instead were his documentary subjects lined up on the highway to protest clear-cut logging on their territory. At one blockade, he films a confrontation between customary Chief Jean Maurice Matchewan and an unidentified Sûreté du Québec (SQ; Quebec Provincial Police) officer. The provincial police officer asks Matchewan what his community's intentions are for being on the blockade that day and Matchewan responds that they are there to stop the logging. The officer asks him what is their right to stop the logging. Matchewan responds: "A right to live. To have food on the table." Still unsure, the officer persists: "Do you have some paper about that?" and Matchewan tries to make clear that he is not interested in government paperwork: "We're not talking about dealing with rights to the land. We're talking about food on the table and protecting the natural habitat. The wildlife. We're just trying to bring to the Canadian attention that this is a wildlife reserve that they're raping." Undeterred, the officer again misrecognizes Matchewan's intentions and tries one last time to confirm the Algonquins' right to live on what he clearly understands to be provincial lands: "Do you have some documents to *prove* that you have the right to live here, something like that?" To which Matchewan, exasperated, affixes their conversation into the deep time and space of Algonquin life: "We've been around here for thousands of years. That gives us the right to live off this land."

This encounter distills one moment in a long-standing confrontation over who has the authority to occupy and govern Algonquin lands. But it is not only a moment of conflict; it is also an instance of how legal authority is established—far from the courts, detached from constitutional frameworks, shaping the borders of settler law. The cop wants to see paperwork to prove proprietary rights. Chief Matchewan explains that the Algonquins have a duty to protect the land; it is a "right to live," not a right to property. Fulfilling this obligation is what feeds their families and is also what gives the community the authority to block the logging trucks that will devastate the habitat for all living things that make those lands their home. Because the SQ officer understands the conflict as a dispute over property rights, the issue at hand for him is over who holds the proper deed. His role is to resolve a disagreement over ownership by following the paper trail that leads back to the Crown. But the dispute goes deeper; it is a conflict over the inauguration of law—over whose laws of belonging will apply on those lands—and on what grounds. The conflict is over *the authority to have authority*. The conflict concerns jurisdiction.

Twenty-five years later, I am sitting with Jean Maurice Matchewan's son, Norman Matchewan, at a boardroom table in Toronto waiting for the board of directors of Copper One Inc. to arrive. A small group of company executives file in at ten o'clock and note our presence with a mixture of surprise and resignation. They come up and introduce themselves, then silently take their seats. It takes only fifteen minutes for them to run through the business of the meeting before they open up the floor to questions from shareholders. Norman tells the board of directors that he has traveled from Barriere Lake to let them know that the community has discussed it and that there will be no mining in their territory. He tells them that the Algonquins need the land to hunt, fish, and trap and they have no plans to poison it by approving a mine. He assures them that no amount of money could convince the community otherwise. "The territory," he explains, "is divided up among families, each one is responsible for the care of an area." He conveys that the families of the affected area for the Rivière Doré copper-nickel mine did not give their consent to mining and have serious concerns about its impacts.[2]

Everyone is quiet except for one man, Benoît Gascon, who interrupts Norman to reassure him that the company is about eight to ten years away from any mining in the territory. He admits this is partly owing to the volatile cost of commodities, which means that exploration is not worthwhile at the moment. But when pressed about the Algonquins' rejection of the project, in the past and far into the future, Gascon admits that Copper One Inc. had not done due diligence on the mine and was not informed by Cartier Resources (the company from which it purchased the stake) that Barriere Lake opposed the mine that was in the heart of their unceded territory. Gascon says the company paid $150,000 to Cartier Resources and regretted that it had overpaid, given "the situation."[3] He proposes to Norman that Barriere Lake become partners in the company, but Norman responds by requesting that the company leave them alone. There would be no mining in their territory. If accepted, the partnership proposed by Copper One Inc. could diminish Algonquin authority by transforming Barriere Lake's inherent stake in the territory into commercial rights under settler law. Norman instead reasserted the nature of his community's entitlements against Copper One's prospecting license. He explained the organization of authority on Barriere Lake's territory: the kinship-based tenure system, where families responsible for particular ranges hold the legal decision-making power. Once again, the encounter over Algonquin land is set in the register of jurisdiction: the authority to govern rests in the legal relationship between the political community and the place it inhabits.[4]

This book is an argument to foreground jurisdiction as an approach to understanding how authority is established, exercised, and contested in settler colonies. It examines the gap between the state's assertion of sovereignty over Indigenous peoples and its legal authority to exercise territorial jurisdiction over Indigenous peoples and their lands. If jurisdiction were simply a technicality of state sovereignty, then this argument would reshuffle the colonial deck, but it would remain the same old game where the house always wins. Jurisdiction is not a technicality of sovereignty, though. It is the apparatus through which sovereignty is rendered meaningful, because it is through jurisdiction that settler sovereignty organizes and manages authority.[5] In the settler colonies in particular, sovereignty is asserted against the legal and political authority of Indigenous peoples over their lands and nations; in the absence of legal agreement, a perpetual struggle over jurisdiction defines the terrain.[6]

The story of the Algonquins of Barriere Lake distills and demonstrates this argument. Barriere Lake's territory is located about three hours north of Ottawa—the nation's capital—in the French province of Quebec. Their band is one of ten communities that form the Algonquin Nation, and their territory is largely demarcated by the heart-shaped space between two powerful rivers, the Ottawa and the Gatineau, in the northern boreal region. Barriere Lake is a small band of around four hundred people who still speak their language and are fiercely committed to protecting their economic and social autonomy through traditional activities like hunting, fishing, trapping, and medicine gathering. They were also one of the last bands in Canada to govern themselves under a "customary" system—meaning that the Indian Act elective band council system never applied to them until 2010, when Canada forcefully replaced their traditional government. When I began working with them in 2008, I was more invested in the political struggle they were fighting for their land than motivated by research interests.[7] I knew that the governments—Canada and Quebec—had signed a landmark agreement with them in 1991 to comanage the territory but had reneged on their commitments. I also knew that Barriere Lake refused to negotiate under the federal land claims policy and believed that they were being severely punished for their defiance. But most of all, what I learned with each new visit to the territory—and what inspired me to seek their approval to write this book—was that the assertion of their law, structured by a deeply guarded knowledge of the land, could usurp the authority of a modern nation-state.

What I observed initially as a local phenomenon on the traditional territory of the Algonquins of Barriere Lake I soon came to understand as a global pattern inhering in the Anglophone settler polities.[8] The assertion of sovereignty over Indigenous lands in the British settler colonies was disengaged for centuries from colonial officials' capacity to exercise authority over Indigenous peoples in their territories. Long after the ceremonies of possession, the granting of Royal Charters, and a bewildering haze of imperial legalities that bore only the slightest relevance to their supposed subjects, Indigenous peoples' social and political orders remained intact, even as they adapted to the influx of European and other settlers on their lands. The ongoing exercise of Indigenous jurisdiction over land, resources, and bodies on their homelands today reveals the continuity of this suspended space between settler assertions of sovereignty and the vitality of Indigenous territorial jurisdiction. My book draws an analytic thread through the earlier colonial aperture between sovereignty and jurisdiction to the present day. This continuity, evidenced in the Algonquin watershed of Barriere Lake, marks a dynamic of governance where state jurisdiction over Indigenous lands is an object of constant struggle to exercise effective sovereign control.

This book about Barriere Lake attests to the ongoing nature of this struggle and the state's persistent disability at exercising effective sovereign control over Indigenous peoples and lands. Settler sovereignty can appear to dominate daily life for Indigenous peoples in Canada, but often untold are the ways in which it remains peripheral to the dense social and political formations of Indigenous nations, and furthermore, extraneous to the spiritual and geographic knowledge necessary to govern their lands. As a community member at Barriere Lake once told me, "Canada can have its sovereignty. We just want our jurisdiction."[9] My argument to foreground jurisdiction as an analytic for understanding settler colonialism brings perspicuity to state policy on Indigenous peoples by demonstrating the clear focus of Canada's strategy to replace and undermine inherent Indigenous jurisdiction with a state-delegated form of authority.[10]

One dominant tool the state exercises on bands living on unceded lands to transform the nature of their jurisdiction is to encourage their participation in the federal land claims policy.[11] The Comprehensive Land Claims Policy requires negotiating groups to cede their Aboriginal title and the majority of their territory to the Crown in exchange for "certainty" about their rights. Barriere Lake refused to negotiate under this policy, proposing instead an arrangement that would protect their inherent jurisdiction and the full territorial base, which they have been entrusted since time immemorial. They proposed instead a resource co-management agreement with the provincial and federal governments that would give them a decisive say over resource management on their lands, protect their ways of life, and offer modest resource revenue sharing based on the economic value extracted from their territory. Through a remarkable turn of events, Canada and Quebec signed the Trilateral Agreement in 1991. But for the next twenty-five years, the governments would fail in their commitments to honor and implement the agreement. They would do so using every dirty trick in the book, most significantly targeting the Algonquins' customary government, because of its embodiment of the band's inherent sociolegal order. I narrate Barriere Lake's struggle to protect their lands from ecological destruction, in particular clear-cut logging, which compounded the cumulative effects of encroachment on their land since the advent of white settlement. To defend their lands, the Algonquins have asserted the authority of the Mitchikanibikok Anishnabe Onakinakewin, their sacred constitution, against the delegated authority of the state.

When I say that jurisdiction is the *authority to have authority*, I understand that the very substance of what *authorizes* law is at stake.

Throughout this introductory chapter, I will canvas imperial and colonial legalities as a key source of settler authority asserted on Algonquin lands. But from Indigenous perspectives, the meaning of authority can also be sourced within a range of legal traditions. For some, legal authority circles back to Creation and the myriad forms of intelligence and spiritual force animating life on these lands. According to Edward Benton-Banai, a respected Anishnabe knowledge holder, authority means to carry knowledge from the Creator.[12] The Anishnabe remember the laws of the Creator in ceremony and stories and they are realized in the world when people live in a good relation to the teachings, to each other, and to themselves.[13] Sometimes law is also described as coming from the natural world, as "natural law," rather than emanating solely from the Creator as a sacred law.[14] Still, for other communities, self-preservation, political autonomy, and the collective rewards of territorial stewardship characterize the authority of Indigenous law.[15] My effort here is to understand specifically what authorizes the law at Barriere Lake and to center the Mitchikanibikok Anishnabe Onakinakewin as a source of authority that orders their jurisdiction. I describe this exercise of jurisdiction as an *ontology of care*.

The source of settler authority, on the other hand, has been in flux since first contact, drawing on a diversity of European imperial legalities. It shifted from the early papal bulls of the fifteenth century that divided the world between the Portuguese and Spanish kingdoms, to claims to the North American continent by the British based on its unique configuration of "discovery" grounded in English concepts of possession.[16] It was established through brute conflict between the British, French, Dutch, and Russian nations that lost and gained territory in protracted transatlantic wars and *lawfare*; to French capitulation to the British at Quebec in 1760. By the late nineteenth century, only the British Crown was left standing to defend its jurisdiction over the Dominion of Canada.[17] English colonialism is rooted in a particularity of Norman-derived law, in that the sovereign possessed all underlying title to the land.[18] When Great Britain's Act of Parliament formed modern Canada in 1867 and decreed its independence under the Crown of the United Kingdom, the new nation captured Indigenous peoples in an internal anticolonial struggle that pit Indigenous territorial jurisdiction against the presumed radical title of the state.

The events and dates above mark significant administrative and political changes to forms of governance in the colony. But what they have meant in terms of effective applications of jurisdictional authority on the ground turns out to be a complicated and completely different story. The rich history of indeterminacy concerning settler authority in what is now Canada lies outside the scope of this book. However, fragments of this story can be read and stitched together from legal histories that canvas the limitations of imperial and colonial authority over Indigenous peoples long after settler assertions of sovereignty were claimed.[19] These histories speak to Indigenous peoples' role in state formation and also document how state repression has sought to eliminate Indigenous peoples' challenge to settler jurisdiction over their lands. Moreover, this record provides the historical and theoretical grounds on which to undertake a study on the present-day legal authority exercised by the Algonquins of Barriere Lake.

Understanding settler-Indigenous conflict through the lens of jurisdiction also provides a view into how legal orders meet across epistemological difference and overlap on the ground, producing the interlegal space of settler colonialism. What forms of knowledge legitimate authority on these lands? Canada's assertion of sovereignty over all lands and resources within its borders presumes the forms that law will take despite a multiplicity of Indigenous governance systems each structured within their own unique territories and political cultures. Tension between settler and Indigenous regimes spreads from these overlapping claims and the concept of jurisdiction offers a coherent vocabulary with which to express these spatial encounters where sovereignty discourses fall short. As Lauren Benton observes: "Empires did not cover space evenly but composed a fabric that was full of holes, stitched together out of pieces, a tangle of strings."[20] These "imperfect geographies" have been a fundamental aspect of imperialism. Full (or perfected) territorial control has in fact never been realized as a straight chronological progress toward absolute sovereignty in the colonies at all, as many claim. Rather, new kinds of differentiated legal zones have emerged where Indigenous territorial jurisdiction forms lumps that betray patterns of partial and uneven state sovereignty.

To legal scholars and social scientists, jurisdiction often appears as an object fully formed and conjoined to state power. After all, in the case of conflict, the common law is equipped with doctrinal tools to resolve overlap between authorities, to ensure immunity regarding heads of power, and to establish borders around spheres of governance. These technical remedies in the law disentangle state authority into bundles of governance. But, as Mariana Valverde notes: "Jurisdiction . . . distinguishes more than territories and authorities, more than the where and the who of governance. Jurisdiction also differentiates and organizes the 'what' of governance—and, more importantly because of its relative invisibility, the 'how' of governance."[21] She points to the example of *Re: Eskimo*, where the courts were asked to determine whether Eskimo (Inuit) are Indians. Although the subject of the case was identity, the object of the trial was certainly to determine jurisdiction, which would establish *how* the Inuit should be governed. For Indigenous people, as we will see, jurisdiction has been at the heart of contestation over settler possession since contact precisely because their self-determination has depended on it.

This book examines state strategies to replace the source of Indigenous law with a delegated authority of the Crown through the machinery of state jurisdiction. There are few better guides to state attempts at perfecting settler sovereignty in Canada than the story of the Algonquins of Barriere Lake because few communities have endured the full arsenal of brutal and brazen colonial violence for attempting to define and exercise their self-determination outside of federal policies and legislation. The armory used against them includes a spectrum of weapons, most notably criminalization, financial servitude, and subjection to arcane legislation to abolish the band's customary government. Most of the repression directed at the band was by the federal Department of Indian Affairs. But multiple other agents including private companies and provincial authorities over natural resources were involved and driven by interlaced, yet independent imperatives. In other words, there has not always been a unified logic of jurisdictional imposition that ties up the knot of sovereignty, because it is precisely the *tangle* of authorities that creates the overlays of Indigenous and settler claims to territorial jurisdiction. Assertions of inherent Algonquin jurisdiction block these divergent and interwoven pathways to state control and accumulation.

Cole Harris states in *Making Native Space*: "It may be important not to be too fancy with colonialism."[22] While the machinery of jurisdiction can operate in complex ways, the economic incentives for the state and resource sectors to challenge Barriere Lake's inherent jurisdiction are clear and common features of this conflict, and indeed of conflicts throughout the country. Barriere Lake's assertion of jurisdiction over resource management on their territory through the Trilateral Agreement introduced competing grounds for assessment of land use in the region. By taking into account their own social reproduction as well as other-than-human agency on the land, Barriere Lake challenged regimes of accumulation on their lands and effected powerful controls on the political economy of the territory.[23]

This research is not simply a theoretical inquiry. My focus on jurisdiction in this book turns our attention to practices of settler colonialism in Canada, especially to the role Indigenous law plays in resisting dispossession, but also in shaping the political economy of regions across the nation. Most broadly, my book examines how the Algonquins of Barriere Lake have contested the sociospatial and legal production of state sovereignty claims—vividly expressed in the land claims policy—through the everyday exercise of jurisdiction over their lands. This introduction looks at jurisdiction (1) as a conceptual framework for understanding the specificities of settler colonialism, in particular as a legal-historical concept, distinct from sovereignty, and (2) as a technique or machinery by which authorities may govern across multiple, overlapping scales and issues. These sections are followed by a chapter overview of the book and finally by remarks that situate the book within the broader political context of Indigenous struggles in Canada.

The Work of Jurisdiction

An immediate question one could pose regarding the use of *jurisdiction* is whether or not the language redescribes Indigenous struggle in ways that center Western conceptions of the world. Is this another case of "white-splaining" Indigenous forms of belonging to the land? There is no doubt room for disagreement here, but there does appear to be a remarkable degree of consensus among Indigenous peoples on the centrality of jurisdiction to Indigenous land rights in Canada. Michael Asch documented addresses made by First Nation, Métis, and Inuit leaders at the First Ministers Conferences that followed the historic inclusion of Aboriginal rights in the Constitution Act of 1982. He notes how these conferences showcased the compelling accord of terms that Indigenous peoples understood these rights to signify. Taken from statements of leaders of national organizations, Asch concludes that

Indigenous nations understand Aboriginal rights to mean *political juris-diction that includes a land base*.[24] Perhaps jurisdiction, despite being an English word, can describe both Indigenous and settler ontologies be-cause it marks the inauguration of a legal order, whereupon authorities of various kinds govern the ways in which these laws will be ordered and organized in space, and define its subjects and scope. Emile Beneviste's etymology of jurisdiction links the Latin noun *ius* (law) with the verb *dictio* (the saying or speech of law).[25] First and foremost, jurisdiction is the power to speak the law. As Shaunnagh Dorsett and Shaun McVeigh explain, "In some formulations jurisdiction inaugurates law itself. Thus to exercise jurisdiction is to bring law into existence," and in so doing, to draw law's boundaries, its subjects, and agents.[26]

The concept of jurisdiction also does not rely on an overly deter-mined understanding of law. Lauren Benton and Richard Ross argue for pursuing studies of empire through the concept of jurisdiction pre-cisely because it does not depend on such rigid definitions; for them jurisdiction describes "the exercise by sometimes vaguely defined legal authorities of the power to regulate and administer sanctions over par-ticular actions or people, including groups defined by personal status, territorial boundaries, and corporate membership."[27] It comes into view most clearly in conflict, therefore avoiding any normative or nonrela-tional definitions. It also clears the ahistorical and homogenizing debris of the field of legal pluralism—which often projects the inevitable rise of state power to eclipse "nonstate" or "customary" law—by revealing how jurisdictional conflicts create ongoing structural change in colonial legal orders.[28]

If jurisdiction is so central, though, how did territorial sovereignty come to define legal political authority in the Anglophone settler colo-nies? As Quentin Skinner notes, sovereignty is bound up with the emer-gence of the modern nation state. His genealogy of sovereignty traces the idea's meanings through invocations of the state that begin to appear in the late sixteenth and early seventeenth century.[29] The state began to signify a "specific type of union or civil association, that of a *universi-tas* or community of people living subject to the sovereign authority of a recognized monarch or ruling group."[30] Architects of modern sover-eignty formulated their ideas partly to oppose what they understood to be Indigenous ownership and jurisdiction in the "New World." As James Tully notes, "One of the leading problems of political theory from Hugo

Grotius and Thomas Hobbes to Adam Smith and Immanuel Kant was to justify the establishment of European systems of property in North America in the face of the presence of 'Indian Nations.'"[31] Hobbes, for example, "used savages in America to illustrate the universal negative standards of primal chaos and the natural state of war."[32] Therefore, only through a covenant of the multitude can individuals form a unified body, authorizing a sovereign to represent the commonwealth or *state*.[33] Because no unity can exist between individuals prior to the formation of the social contract, people living in the "New World" have been characterized in Canadian jurisprudence as living in a Hobbesian state of nature. Not only is sovereignty impossible in the state of nature, but the accumulation and transmittance of knowledge down generations is inconceivable.[34]

The Hobbesian concept of the state was famously articulated by Chief Justice McEachern in the Supreme Court of British Columbia in 1991 to justify the denial of Gitskan and Wet'su'wet'en's jurisdiction and ownership over their lands. His judgment stated that "it would not be accurate to assume that even pre-contact experience in the territory was in the least bit idyllic . . . there is no doubt, to quote Hobbes, that aboriginal life in the territory was, at best, 'nasty, brutish and short.'"[35] Canadian sovereignty here is presumed to follow from a state of nature that is "prepolitical": sovereignty is a process that ushers in political authority "as necessary and natural rather than contingent and violent."[36] In fact, it is incumbent on the courts to shield the details of colonial acquisition in order to persist in their reasoning against Indigenous assertions of jurisdiction over their lands. Challenges to state sovereignty are considered *beyond the jurisdiction* of the court, eliding the crucial period of inauguration. McEachern states in *Delgamuukw*: "No court has authority to make grants of constitutional jurisdiction in the face of such clear and comprehensive statutory and constitutional provisions. The very fact that the plaintiffs recognize the underlying title of the Crown precludes them from denying the sovereignty that created such title." This statement is a patronizing rebuke to Indigenous nations for submitting to the authority of the court—among the only presumable democratic channels to obtain their rights—to challenge the taken-for-granted, nonjusticiable (i.e., incapable of being determined by a court of justice) presumptions of state sovereignty.[37]

Colonial sovereignty, according to Achille Mbembe, exists through three forms of violence, including the rights-based form of violence that can help to convert the founding violence of colonization into *authorizing authority.*[38] This originary violence must be recognized as authority, or else the colonized suffer the consequence of being outlaw to the national order. Localizing this insight, Sunera Thobani writes that even if every single Aboriginal rights and title case that came before the courts was determined in favor of Indigenous peoples, "this cannot erase the reality that it is Canadian law, European law, that remains the authorizing authority deciding on the fate of Aboriginal nations."[39] I read this concept of *authorizing authority* as the work of jurisdiction, a component of sovereignty that nonetheless cannot be automatically absorbed into its meaning.

Although I did not realize it during the time I was doing my research at Barriere Lake, recent historical scholarship by Lauren Benton, Lisa Ford, Shannaugh Dorsett, and others richly details the distinct relationship between jurisdiction and sovereignty in the colonies. From the settler-colonial perspective, this distinction collapsed throughout the nineteenth century as sovereignty "perfected" itself by extinguishing recognition for Indigenous jurisdiction over their nations and territories, forming a "legal trinity" between sovereignty, jurisdiction, and territory. Ford describes the "litmus test" of settler sovereignty as that moment of legal obliteration of Indigenous customary law. Multiple international pressures shaped this imperative, but a central force was the "contagion of sovereignty" spread by the American Revolution that recast settler sovereignty in the mold of territorial statehood.[40]

Although this mode of perfection marked a global pattern of shifting power, as Ford notes, "the real content of these claims . . . was local, territorial control over the process of indigenous dispossession."[41] She shows through criminal law cases in Virginia and New South Wales how, despite assertions of imperial European sovereignty, colonial powers exercised almost no territorial jurisdiction until the 1830s; that is, their laws *by mutual agreement* did not apply to Indigenous peoples, who continued to practice legal orders entrenched in their governance systems. Whereas jurisdiction was understood for centuries to claim authority over people in particular places or over those engaged in particular activities, through its settler-colonial articulation it eventually came to claim authority over a bounded, state territorial space. Ford recounts the appeal trial of George Tassel (1830) where the man was convicted of killing another Cherokee man on Cherokee land within the borders of Georgia. The defense argued that this incident took place on the self-governing lands of the Cherokee and was outside of state jurisdiction. The judge responded by asking how anyone who knows what a sovereign state is could call the Cherokee sovereign or independent.[42] The authority of the Cherokee to exercise laws over their lands was deemed impossible within the exclusive jurisdictional space of territorial state sovereignty.

Ford's research shows that the emergence of territorial state sovereignty was introduced in the colonial courts of the United States and Australia through a generalization of the common law as the singular national law.[43] Likewise, Dorsett notes how intolerant Australia's High Court became toward parallel law-making systems, regarding "any attempt to argue multiple jurisdictions" as "an attack on singular sovereignty."[44] Citing case law from America and Australia, Ford traces the transition from a settler legality that claimed jurisdiction over Indigenous bodies only in the case of personal violence toward non-Indigenous people to the period where territorial jurisdiction became a necessary exercise of sovereignty at the turn of the nineteenth century. Indigenous practices of *inter se* justice that had been formerly accepted by colonial authorities as local forms of restitution were reinscribed as violent crime under the jurisdiction of colonial courts.[45] Discourses of "criminality" marked Indigenous justice as "lawlessness" as the stakes of territorial control began to override the values and necessity of legal multiplicity.[46]

The importance of this political, spatial, and legal shift can best be seen in contrast to what preceded it. Until this later period, an uneasy legal pluralism existed between overlapping Indigenous and settler social orders. In the Americas, the world of settler–Indigenous encounters was rife with conflict, but settler authority depended on political currency accrued through favor with Indigenous networks of kinship and trade. Therefore, they accepted distinct legal orders as inevitable. Michael Witgen's *An Infinity of Nations* offers a forceful account of the discrepancy between assertions of settler sovereignty and the exercise of territorial jurisdiction by European powers.[47] These gaps remained explicitly unsettled for decades following the American Revolution and even after the treaty-making period of the early nineteenth century. Witgen deals specifically with *anishnabewaki*—the Anishnabe lands of

the Great Lakes and southern and eastern reaches of its networks—
documenting how Indigenous peoples controlled most of the American
continent save for the eastern seaboard until the mid-nineteenth century.[48] As late as 1832, Witgen shows through the expedition of Indian
Agent Henry Schoolcraft how the young state of America continued to
attempt to establish its authority over a territory it claimed on a map,
but where it exercised no effective sovereignty.[49] The Anishnabe controlled vast intercontinental trade networks that the whites were dependent upon. Whatever limited powers settlers possessed were connected to the fur trade, which Witgen notes was largely disconnected
from the colonial ambitions of the American nation-state.[50] In light of
this awesome Anishnabe power, Witgen laments that too few narratives
recount how throughout the seventeenth and eighteenth centuries no
European empire managed to do much more than set up isolated outposts in the Great Lakes region.[51]

The importance of this kind of research to contemporary legal claims
is that it discredits an influential and persistent fiction regarding settler-
colonial relations. The Supreme Court of Canada in *R. v Sparrow* (1990)
stated: "there was from the outset *never any doubt* that sovereignty and
legislative power and indeed the underlying title, to such [Aboriginal]
lands vested in the Crown."[52] In fact, as Hamar Foster notes, from the
outset there seemed to be little else but doubt as to the sovereignty of
the Crown and its territorial authority on Indigenous lands. From coast
to coast, officials were well apprised of this reality. In the northern interior of British Columbia in 1887 (sixteen years after the province joined
Confederation), Foster cites a Nisga'a chief describing the difference between hanging a British flag—out of respect—and surrendering tribal
sovereignty, which bore no relationship in Nisga'a mind. Foster explains
how "[s]oldiers and colonial officials who had any experience at all with
Indian nations were well aware of these attitudes, and of how theoretical British declarations of sovereignty really were," especially during
the period of early contact, which differed temporally throughout the
country.[53] He cites Sir William Johnson in 1765 stating to the attorney
general of New York that "our rights of soil Extend no farther than they
are actually purchased by Consent of the natives" and General Thomas
Gage making similar admissions a few years later about the lack of actual British authority and sovereignty over the Six Nations.[54]

The perfection of settler sovereignty—that is, the fusing of sovereignty claims with the effective exercise of territorial jurisdiction over Indigenous lands—remains unfinished today. Discourses that erase the authority of Indigenous jurisdiction in the past, as in the *Sparrow* decision, function to deny Indigenous peoples authority over their lands in the present, and it is partly the concept of state sovereignty that creates the "epistemic web" through which this historical revisionism may find traction.[55] The picture that holds us captive is that sovereignty is a singular, exclusive, absolute authority. But sovereignty is claimed through a multiplicity of forces. If we cut off the king's head, as Foucault implored, what kinds of authority flourish in place of this false figurehead of power?[56] For one, Indigenous forms of legal authority; Indigenous jurisdiction demonstrates enduring forms of governance that preexisted and codeveloped for centuries in relation to a plurality of imperial and colonial legalities. Within Western discourses of sovereignty, Indigenous jurisdiction has been largely relegated to a barbaric premodern form of Hobbesian sovereignty.[57] There is no historical merit to this political theory, however, which acts as a rhetorical tool. Instead, settler–Indigenous conflicts over jurisdiction bring to light a proliferation of political agency enacted by a diversity of institutions, individuals, and other-than-human agents that comprise the dynamics of modern sovereignty.

By disentangling jurisdiction from sovereignty, I do not mean to argue that sovereignty is an illusion: it is the dominant political-territorial ideal of the nation-state, which has had an incalculable effect on Indigenous legal orders.[58] What has been done in its name to protect containerized borders and exclusive claims to authority highlights the violent history of white settlement on these lands.[59] Sovereignty is not simply an assumption made by settler nation-states like Canada that can be dismissed by virtue of competing discourses and assertions of power. But the *legitimacy* and *legality* of sovereignty can be called into question in the register of jurisdiction.[60]

As noted, forming national law is another way in which this legitimacy is sought. Although the common law came to take the shape of the state—through the generalization of criminal law, for example—the fit has never been total or complete, for the common law has no mystical or transcendental authority that connects it to territory in the "New World."[61] When the common law of England became the national law in the colonies, its reception by settlers and authority over

Indigenous peoples were deliberately confused: the common law's universalist pretensions were then, and have since been, intentionally articulated against the local and particular formations of Indigenous legalities.[62] Peter Fitzpatrick comments on Justice Brennan's reasoning in the High Court of Australia in *Mabo,* where the justice rejects the common law doctrine of *terra nullius* only to rehabilitate the common law to "recognize" native title: "In such a miasma, not to say vacuity, is the settler's law accorded the impenetrable solidity that would secure its completeness and exclusiveness and utterly subordinate any competing indigenous legality."[63] In the Canadian context, Kerry Wilkins makes a similar point: "Every time someone has sought to challenge in a Canadian court the Crown's or domestic legislation's authority, or the court's jurisdiction, over an Aboriginal person or group, the court has dismissed the challenge as non-justiciable." He concludes that the game is "fixed."[64] The common law works in conjunction with legislative and executive powers to claim and define state territory. It holds the power of enforcement.

In the Canadian parliamentary system, the executive, legislative, and judicial forms of jurisdiction each mark out their spheres of authority. But authority is not pre-given to the Crown. Crown sovereignty, we must appreciate, "is not simply a matter of physically controlling territory . . . sovereignty depends on authority, and authority is something more than physical control over territory."[65] It must be matched with conviction that the exercise of sovereignty is legitimate.[66] Where land was never treated and no effective state control has been exercised, we could rightly ask: have these lands been colonized? Where sovereignty has been asserted but Indigenous jurisdiction persists, what is the status of settler authority?

Jurisdiction and Space: A Thickening Heap of Lines

Jurisdiction is a legal technology that has immense power to organize society. But to see this remarkable power, we have to shake off dominant spatial representations of jurisdiction that have obscured its highly political work. Jurisdiction has been predominantly understood through scale and hierarchy.[67] The standard representation of jurisdiction is a tiered structure that ranks power from the highest to the lowest authority, or in which certain issues are under the *exclusive* domain of particular authorities. In popular television crime shows, for example, local police authorities are pushed aside when the FBI takes over sensitive cases. This shift in jurisdiction reflects a power hierarchy and links jurisdiction to exclusive domains of power. Valverde writes that scale is not simply implicated in governance: *it is governance.*[68] It is the machinery that determines *how* law will be recognized, and therefore has tremendous power in the organization of political governance.

But scale is an aspirational order of settler jurisdiction—it implies a functioning chain of command. If we look instead to jurisdictional divisions of power between the federal and provincial governments, for example, we see the functioning of settler-colonial power manifesting through the complex techniques of governance aimed at erasing Indigenous law.

One legal decision in particular illustrates this point, providing a blueprint for this kind of technical power.[69] In 1997, a landmark Supreme Court of Canada decision came down that adjudicated on whether the Gitskan and Wet'su'wet'en peoples of northwestern British Columbia possessed "Aboriginal title" and "self-government": concepts derived from state policy. Of critical importance here was that the Indigenous nations had initially brought the province to court arguing for *jurisdiction* and *ownership* of their lands, but these issues had been deemed nonjusticiable and were changed to reflect state frames of recognition.[70] While the issue of establishing Aboriginal title may have seemed like the "main event" in *Delgamuukw,* though, the land question in court proceedings was rendered legally knowable and tangible through the presumption of state jurisdiction and ownership.[71]

Further, in this case, the Supreme Court drew on the "Sparrow test" to determine whether the provinces were justified in their infringement of Aboriginal title. As McNeil concludes from his analysis of divisions of power in *Delgamuukw,* "jurisdiction of powers analysis *precedes* consideration of the issue of whether infringement of Aboriginal title can be justified."[72] Provincial authority to infringe rests on the same burden of proof as exists for federal undertakings. But a crucial difference is that the activities defined that constitute "valid legislative objectives" to infringe fall under provincial jurisdiction. When provincial authorities invoke the need to infringe Aboriginal rights and title, in the first place it will always be to champion an intrusion on their head of power, and therefore, in the second place, it will pit Aboriginal rights and title against the revenue stream derived from the provincial authority to tax, permit, lease, license, and regulate natural resource extraction within provincial borders. So, while the federal government, which has authority on a national scale, may have limited powers of paramountcy over provincial governments, jurisdictional divisions of power appear far more determinative than those intrinsic to scale.[73]

As can be seen here, scale has been a limitation in understanding jurisdiction because jurisdiction *exceeds* scale.[74] Valverde finds that jurisdiction can be multiple, overlapping, and simultaneous; a variety of legal systems may converge in a single place, at different scales, and mean concurrent operations of "different, even contradictory, rationalities of legal governance."[75] In contrast to Canada's boundaries of scale, for example, the legal orders of the Anishnabe nation span beyond provincial boundaries or international borders, through the Great Lakes region and the eastern prairies to the edge of the northern boreal forest line. Mapping jurisdiction as scale filters out the details of interlegality.

To visualize the dense jurisdictional overlap of legal pluralities, we can map the thickening heap of lines that construct barriers against Algonquin exercises of jurisiction and thus self-determination on their lands. However arduous these expositions may be to undertake, mapping the boundaries of administrative authority is an exercise instrumental to understanding the production of space under settler colonialism. In this way we can see that the effect on the Algonquins' ability to exercise their self-determination as Algonquin peoples is the result not merely of Canada's assertions of sovereignty, but also of this jurisdictional commotion on their land. A dense patchwork of institutional bodies crowds the region, which govern largely in isolation from each other despite overlaps and contradictions in mandate, jurisdiction, and geographic oversight. For example, although the Grand Lac Victoria reserve was created to protect wildlife and Indigenous livelihood, it is superimposed by provincial park legislation that allows for relatively uninhibited resource exploitation, despite the park's creation under the legislative auspices of the Wildlife Conservation Act.[76]

To complicate things further, although the federal government has exclusive jurisdiction over "Indians and Lands reserved for the Indians," and the provincial government has exclusive jurisdiction over natural resources,[77] governance practices are not easily disaggregated into these divisions of jurisdictional power. Provincial planning processes and land-management plans on Barriere Lake's territory plainly affect "Indians and Lands reserved for the Indians," violating the jurisdiction of the federal head of power.[78] While justiciable, the burden of proof to show that these processes constitute an infringement of Aboriginal land rights falls to the Algonquins and it would be a tremendous and costly undertaking to chronicle these daily violations. The dispersal of land management into multiple kinds of governance reflects a variety of ideological and technocratic arrangements of power. These arrangements offer a glimpse of affective land alienation only when taken together as a whole.

Land governance on Barriere Lake's territory is a study of simultaneously politicized and bureaucratized divisions of power on Indigenous lands. Counties, townships, and parishes were surveyed by the British after 1763, but in the 1980s the historic counties of Upper and Lower Ottawa that were superimposed on Barriere Lake's territory became modern-day administrative regions. Three key sets of administrative boundaries for land and resource-use planning and management were introduced. The first were Quebec's ten administrative regions—the most relevant ones to Barriere Lake being Outoauais and Abitibi-Temiscamingue—which set the boundaries for the regional offices of the various Quebec ministries. As Aird describes: "Although they are meant to be the administrative arm for policies, plans and programs developed at the provincial level, each regional office invariably exercises its own brand of influence over planning and the interpretation of 'headquarters' directives."[79] Further, because there are two such administrative regions on their territory, for Barriere Lake this means that provincial ministries have double the number of regional offices delegated to manage natural resources, fisheries, environmental protection, tourism, and other pertinent issues such as transportation planning and hydro management. Adding to the burden of Barriere Lake's attempts to clarify management of their lands, a bewildering number of regional offices within these administrative regions are necessary to ascertain the status of land use, including Quebec City, Maniwaki, Hull, Senneterre, Rouyn Noranda, La Vérendrye Wildlife Reserve, and the local Quebec corporation responsible for parks and other public outdoor recreation facilities office located in Le Domain (SÉPAQ, Société des établissements de plein air du Québec). In terms of divisions of power within the administrative regions, much of Barriere Lake lands lies within territory Quebec considers to be unoccupied provincial Crown land. Legally and administratively, the Ministère de l'Énergie et des Ressources (Ministry of Energy and Resources) (MER) is the most powerful force on the territory in terms of the allocation and control of land use on public lands. MER can grant resource rights and ownership and access to forestry companies, hydraulics, and mineral and energy companies. It has sweeping resource and land-use planning authority.[80]

The second set of administrative boundaries, introduced in 1986 (and retired by 2013), was connected specifically to logging. Under the general authority of the MFFP, (the Ministère des Forêts, de la Faune et des Parcs, or Ministry of Forests, Wildlife, and Parks) each administrative region is divided into two or more forest management units (UG, Unités de gestion), each with its own manager responsible for planning management of forestry operations. The Trilateral Territory spreads over part of seven different management units and close to a dozen "designated common areas" of public land. The UGs are critical because they form the administrative basis for the negotiation of Timber Supply and Forest Management Agreements (or CAAFs, for Contrats d'approvisionnement et d'aménagement forestier), the lease system for alienating Algonquin land to logging interests.

Quebec is also divided into a hundred regional county municipalities—municipalités régionales de comté (MRCs)—divisions in which municipalities come together, plan, and coordinate municipal-type zoning, infrastructure, and services on "unorganized lands." Internal MRC planning groups prepare maps of the MRC so that all land can be incorporated into land-use development plans. Barriere Lake's territory was divided into two MRCs: La Vallée de la Gatineau (the largest MRC in Quebec) and La Vallée-de-l'Or. MRCs ensure "optimal" natural resource use by "optimizing" for economic benefit to the municipalities. Such planning decisions are relevant to Barriere Lake's interests, but their interests are not taken into account. Although MRCs were developed almost exclusively by local mayors of municipalities, the vast majority of land in both MRCs is nonmunicipal or "unorganized territory" ("territoire non-organisé"). The MRCs have some jurisdiction over unorganized territory, without being required to ensure representation from residents who do not live in municipalities. MRCs are required to send plans to all mailing addresses within their boundaries, but Barriere Lake receives no such information from these institutions.[81]

In addition to these three administrative regions, there are many other kinds of administrative boundaries that map onto Barriere Lake's traditional territory. In 1985, SÉPAQ took over management of recreational activities at La Vérendrye Wildlife Reserve, managing lands subdivided into fishing zones and hunting zones. In addition to SÉPAQ, the registered trapline system is still in place and the territory is also subdivided under the jurisdictional powers of interprovincial borders, private outfitter lodges, provincial security forces, and other issue-based authorities that would take too long here to describe. The singularity of each regulatory and disciplinary body, empowered by a wide range of political processes, hides the total effect of accretion and layering of authority that governs the land. These micropowers, enacted under federal and provincial jurisdictions, have carved out spatial patterns of land use and population control that defy easy mapping. This is because jurisdiction is not just an abstract or descriptive concept, but a practice that "actively works to produce something."[82] Jurisdiction as a "technology" speaks to technique, but it also signifies the Greek *technē* or "craft." It works, as Dorsett and McVeigh explain, by "institut[ing] a relation to life, place, and event through processes of codification or marking."[83] While the microgoverning authorities named above may not hang their power on the mantle of sovereignty, they mark and codify relationships on the ground by virtue of delegated authority from the Crown. For example, they make visible conflicts over land and resources between Indigenous and settler groups, while in their singularity as regulatory bodies, they hide the total effect of accretion and layering that governs place.

In Canada, sovereign territorial space is projected as a discrete, non-overlapping, absolute domain of space, despite how interpenetrated by capital and by competing jurisdictional claims its boundaries may be.[84] The discourse of Canadian and Australian colonials, for example, was "awash" in the urgent desire to systematize abstract space into a new spatial order of governance.[85] As Isin describes, "The entire period of colonization . . . incessantly problematized the question of proper relationship between scales of jurisdiction and their appropriate powers as created corporations."[86] The development of administrative authority in the colonies centered on towns and villages that spiraled "outward" to counties, provinces, and interprovincial systems: the deterritorialization of Indigenous space and reterritorization of settler space "instituted

scalar systems of settlement, which continued relentlessly."[87] An uneven landscape of law was instituted through spatial reorganization.

The landscape was refitted to a new proprietary regime; but it derived its authority through a developing system of delegated authority.
For instance, in Ontario (by virtue of the Upper Canada treaties), every
Crown Patent allocated to settlers signified an expanding grid of spatial order. As Gilbert Paterson writes, "surveyors were instructed to lay
out the townships to be granted as nearly contiguous to each other as
the nature of the country permitted, exercising due care in the running
of boundary lines."[88] A chain of command was instituted to formalize
land settlement and authorize its governance powers along the unseen
scaffolding of jurisdictional divisions of power. But, as we will see in
the case of Barriere Lake, even despite the strong path dependence of
settler jurisdiction (where governance unfolds through the machinery
of chain reaction), a much messier picture develops when we examine
Indigenous law in relation to settler authority on the ground.[89]

What Is in the Book?

My aim here is to bring to light the overlooked machinery that organizes settler colonialism in Canada. Jurisdiction has been enacted by
the state as a form of power to usurp the inherent laws of Indigenous
peoples and replace their authority with the delegated authority of federal and provincial governments. To understand this phenomenon, I
argue that we must understand the ways in which laws exist in place.
Therefore, this work is situated within the rich field of study on the production of legal space, including legal geography and sociolegal studies
that specifically concern the production of colonial space. Reading this
literature in tandem with critical Indigenous studies centers relationships between place, law, authority, and agency within the specificity of
Indigenous lands and histories.

My goal was to create a conceptual map that represents spatially how
settler states claim authority through *taking up* Indigenous space. I pic-
tured a topographic map of Barriere Lake's territory with representations of competing authority contouring the page: lines representing the
geographic scope of particular authorities, colors and symbols representing issues and subjects of governance. Just by superimposing the
forestry, moose hunting, fishing, and recreational camping zones with

the symbols of hydro flows and dams, outfitter lodges, and long streaks of highways, logging roads, and portages, I thought that the nature of jurisdiction within the settler state could be revealed. But how would Indigenous jurisdiction be represented? Perhaps through traplines and hunting territories and common areas and watershed borders and myriad other forms that were indeed adopted and mapped in the land use and occupancy planning undertaken by Barriere Lake in preparation for the Trilateral Agreement. These territorial maps are also filled in with thickening lines and symbols representing sacred areas, fish spawning sites, moose dens, medicinal plants, and so on. How could I represent these overlapping settler and Indigenous spatial claims conceptually as a political, legal, and socioeconomic project of mapping jurisdiction?

Further, in terms of the socioeconomic question, how would I link colonial and capitalist theories of the production of space? Although some thinkers—notably Rosa Luxemburg—address this question directly, oftentimes the harder labor is to determine material geographic forms that cannot be derived from the abstract laws of capitalism.[90] What about social processes that are not coterminous or reducible to the other? Which aspects of colonial policy and praxis are purely economic and which dimensions are ideological, political, and ethical, or congenital to competing social theories of Indigenous authority? Part of the project here is to figure out how to connect the social relations of space in terms of the colonial problem of overlapping jurisdiction between settler and Indigenous government to the production of space under capitalism.[91]

In simplest terms, I construct these conceptual maps through legal, archival, and policy research that demonstrates the means by which the state encroached upon and alienated Barriere Lake lands. I read through extensive logs of correspondence between Barriere Lake and the federal and provincial governments covering twenty-five years of history, documenting the technical, discursive, and political arrangements by which the governments coercively attempted to eliminate Barriere Lake's legal order. I showcase through extensive Access to Information and Privacy (ATIP) documents the security infrastructure that links the state and private capital to a common objective of securing Barriere Lake lands for the circulation of capital and effective exercise of sovereign control over Algonquin lands. I bring to bear the ethnographic, socioeconomic, and environmental knowledge studies commissioned by the community to catalog the band's extensive land-use and occupancy patterns on their traditional territory. I also undertook five years of field research at the reserve of Rapid Lake and surrounding bush camps, where I was taught how to fish, hunt, gather medicines, and speak *anishnabemowin*. In order to understand what Barriere Lake's struggle was about, the elders and community leaders insisted that I spend as much time as possible on the land. The theoretical work that arose from this research is cataloged as the narrative of my book unfolds.

The story of how I came to start working with the Algonquins of Barriere Lake is fundamental to the writing of this book. I came to know the community through the stepfather of my closest friend, whose family I have grown up with for almost twenty-five years. Russell Diabo has worked with the community for decades and he has mentored me throughout this process. He introduced me to the community and garnered me trust before I had even earned it. But when the time came to strike out on my own and negotiate my interests as a researcher, it still meant undertaking deliberate and careful work of setting up a relationship between the community and myself so that Barriere Lake was protected from breaches of trust and legal vulnerabilities. I cover these protocols in chapter 1, where I describe my methodology partly through the story of how Canada's interference in the community's governance system affected my formal university research ethics process. This interference gave me an opportunity to navigate questions of academic accountability beyond the narrow ethics protocols set by academic institutions. This question of accountability and academic integrity fleshed out what I consider to be four pillars of ethical research: centering decolonization, building alliance, honoring treaty, and respecting the role of non-Indigenous peoples within Indigenous cosmologies. Through these pillars, I consider Indigenous peoples' authority over the production and use of knowledge.

One of the questions that I get asked the most about my work is how I reconcile being an activist and an academic, particularly, because I founded a solidarity group for Barriere Lake in Toronto during the period of my research. At the time, I felt that I could not simply write critically about the way my government was treating the Algonquins without using my work and resources to help support Barriere Lake's defense of their lands. But upon even more reflection later, I realize that through this organizing work I was witnessing Barriere Lake's laws in action, as well as documenting firsthand the government's treatment of the community. These kinds of embodied practices informed and deeply enriched my understanding of the story I was trying to tell. There is extensive literature on community-based participatory research that seeks to problematize the objectivity paradigm of academic knowledge and to interrogate the underpinning purpose of an external, intellectual inquiry into people's lives and experiences. Although I value this work, this literature did not speak to my particular circumstances, until I read Sarah de Leeuw, Emilie Cameron, and Margot Greenwood's article critically engaging with the participatory research methodology in relation to Indigenous communities. The authors take seriously the importance of relationships, noting how they tend to be discounted in academic accounts if they fall outside of the formal researcher and research subject dynamic. The networks of relationships through which the researcher herself is constituted is deemed here as determinant of how research is "experienced, known, evaluated, and critically interrogated."[92] To decolonize geographic thought, these forms of relational accountability must be considered as the context in which the conditions for meaningful, mutual reciprocity in research can be undertaken and successfully fulfilled. For myself, my relationship with the community as a researcher, but also my ongoing relationship with the community as a friend and supporter, exists within the web of kinship and alliance that I entered into through my own long-term relationships and commitments.

It is also through these relationships that a researcher can come to better understand the meaning, purpose, and impacts of colonization on Indigenous peoples. In chapter 2, I provide a history of settler accumulation on Barriere Lake lands and argue that there is a continuum between Indigenous peoples' capacity to exercise their jurisdiction relatively undisturbed, the steady accretion of restrictions and regulations that control the use and access of Indigenous peoples to their lands, and the perfection of state sovereignty in the form of absolute dispossession and obliteration of Indigenous law. This history of land *alienation* that I describe does not necessarily mean that Barriere Lake community members were dispossessed from their lands in the form of removal; I thus contemplate a way of thinking about colonialism without dispossession. I raise questions about how to understand the perpetuation of a set of exhaustive administrative regimes that undermine, erase, and choke out the exercise of Indigenous jurisdiction, rendering the people immaterial to any effective participation in land management, even as they continue to reside upon and assert responsibility for their lands. In response, I define dispossession in two related ways. The first way links dispossession to social reproduction and the diminishing capacity of communities to reproduce their social, economic, and legal orders. This "slow violence" is then contrasted to the specifically sited dynamics of accumulation on Barriere Lake lands.

Focusing on the second definition, I find it difficult to understand the nature of jurisdictional overlap without taking into account the economics of colonization in Canada—in particular, state-based and private claims to ownership over Barriere Lake lands. As David Harvey asks: "how can the territorial logics of power, which tend to be awkwardly fixed in space, respond to the open spatial dynamics of endless capital accumulation? And what does endless capital accumulation imply for the territorial logics of power?"[93] Specifically, what kinds of claims to authority are being made on Barriere Lake lands, and how do these occasionally contradictory logics and strategies of possession conflict with Indigenous authority? How do these dynamics produce the current conditions shaping legal authority on the land? In Marx's theorization of the origins of capitalism, he attributes no particular mode of production to the vicious cycle of capitalist accumulation in the colonies. He also provides no nuanced ethnography of its social organization, just the diagnostic of "force."[94] This is no accident: "It enables Marx's writing to fold heterogeneous overseas developments into the history of the West,"[95] a force that acts upon and shapes the world, wrenching it into place within capitalist history. This history presents a specific spatiotemporal understanding of modernity, emanating out from the motherlands of empire in its blunt and brutal violence. But far less often told are how forces of accumulation and state formation that seek to integrate Indigenous lands into the capitalist economy have in turn been shaped by Indigenous assertions of jurisdiction over their lands. Here, and throughout the book, I bring to light relationships between assertions of Indigenous jurisdiction and the political economy of settler colonialism.

Following my account of the steady encroachment on Algonquin jurisdiction throughout the late nineteenth and twentieth centuries, chapters 3 and 4 look at how relations of settler and Indigenous law came to spatially intertwine and overlap. Here I also examine how the

Algonquins bear the load of the thickening controls of settler authority on their territory. In chapter 3, the history of settler accumulation outlined in chapter 2 is matched with a history of accumulated Indigenous knowledge that provides a glimpse of the source of strength behind the community's resistance against settler assertions of jurisdiction. The Algonquins of Barriere Lake's concept of jurisdiction involves an ontology of care; that is, their legal order flows from relations of respect and love for the land that are witnessed here through everyday practices, stories from the bush, formalized through wampum belts, and strings, and told by the fire. This ontology of care not only directs the external organization of authority: it also orders the community internally, within bodies, families, and the nation. It orders relations between the human and other-than-human worlds, too—for example, in the way that Algonquins gather intelligence from the animal and plant worlds. As I explain, the Algonquins have perceived that beaver uses yellow pond lily (*cikitebak, akidimô*) for its lungs and the moose uses balsam fir (*aninâdik*) for wounds and sickness and black spruce (*sesegâdik*) to help females before giving birth. This kind of careful attention to the gifts of the Creator speaks to the sacred responsibility of jurisdiction on their lands. Here I begin to link the relationship between governance, law, and the land in the Mitchikanibikok Anishnabe Onakinakewin.

Among the strategies of perfecting settler sovereignty, the imposition of Western property rights onto Indigenous forms of landholding has been pivotal. Much has been written about this relationship between colonialism and property.[96] But something scholars have struggled with and stumbled over is language to describe what the Indigenous forms of belonging are that resist the private-property paradigm.[97] I argue here that this register is jurisdiction. Chapter 4 illustrates the order-, knowledge-, and space-making practices of jurisdiction on Barriere Lake territory by the allocation of land use through Barriere Lake's tenure system. The Algonquin tenure system differentiates the landscape into spaces of kinship-based care to ensure self-preservation and to protect the land base for future generations. This tenure system, based in the Mitchikanibikok Anishnabe Onakinakewin, is a regime of jurisdiction, rather than one based on the individuated, exclusionary notion of property that defines Western relations. Comparing this land-tenure system to the spatial demarcations of a provincial beaver preserve and the introduction of two government-regulated trapline regimes on the territory reveals how provincial and Algonquin tenure systems overlapped to produce a complex interlegal space. These state *proprietary* systems cannot be separated from questions of *rule,* opening up further questions into law's relations on the territory.

Chapter 4 examines how Indigenous subjects are produced and marked as capable of belonging to Western property law through the apparatus of settler-state jurisdiction. I examine two property systems in particular in the context of Barriere Lake lands: the provincial leasehold system that permits resource extraction on Barriere Lake lands and the conservation regime that legislates restrictions on extraction and exploitation, as well as hunting and trapping. Both the leasehold property right and the conservation regime express a technique of provincial jurisdiction whereby Barriere Lake lands are managed as *supply.* I argue that jurisdiction at Barriere Lake is exercised by the provincial state and the band toward these different respective ends of comportment: *supply* and *care.* I look in particular at the ways in which other-than-human actors have agency within Algonquin systems of jurisdiction and how this fact fundamentally alters Barriere Lake members' understanding of their own authority toward the land.

Chapter 5 brings these discussions of settler-state and Indigenous jurisdiction to bear on the contemporary period, beginning in the 1980s, when the Algonquins were faced with a vast scale of clear-cut logging on their lands. With no recourse, they began blockading the logging trucks, resigning to put their bodies between the machinery and their beloved homelands in order to enact their legal responsibility to their territory. From their perspective, Barriere Lakers were not disrupting the forestry industry through their campaign of blockades, but rather saving it. But they also sought permanent solutions to a crisis over their lands that had persisted for decades from white exploitation. When the United Nations Brundtland Report came out in 1987, commissioned to promote unity among nations toward the goal of "sustainable development," the Algonquins conceived of an idea for a sustainable resource comanagement agreement on their own lands. The idea was for an agreement that would give them a decisive say over land management on their territory, protect their traditional ways of life, and also offer them a modest share of resource revenues so that they could develop their own cultural and economic programs in the territory and gradually untether themselves from the kinds of federal programming that dictated colonial governance over them.

What is critical to understand about what came to be known as the "Trilateral Agreement" is that it was an alternative to the Comprehensive Land Claims Policy (CLCP). The policy was introduced in 1973 on the heels of a Supreme Court decision that took decades of energy for the Nisga'a Nation to pursue to the highest court. The *Calder* court dealt with whether the Nisga'a held underlying title to the land or whether the province was right in claiming that their title was extinguished with the creation of British Columbia in 1871.[98] When the split decision came down, the country was agape that there was a possibility of underlying Aboriginal title on unceded lands, challenging the authority of provincial and federal proprietary regimes. The land claims settlement policy was hastily introduced as a political process to resolve these uncertainties once and for all. But the terms of settlement under the policy can be best described as "termination."[99] I provide a succinct overview of one specific aspect of the policy that directly violates Indigenous jurisdiction: the extinguishment requirement, which requires a land-selection process that effectively surrenders around 95 percent of a community's land base to the Crown. Barriere Lake did not want to cede any of their responsibility for the land through this policy. Their refusal is at the heart of the battle that follows.

Canada and Quebec signed the Trilateral Agreement in August 1991. In chapter 6, I discuss the visions of the Trilateral Agreement and the design of the resource comanagement pilot project. The research and design of the Trilateral Agreement consist of three phases, starting with the study and analysis of data about renewable energy (phase 1), and the preparation of a draft Integrated Resource Management Plan (phase 2). Phase 3—which, as we will see, was only ever partially completed—would have involved the formulation of recommendations for carrying out the draft of phase 2, including a plan for resource revenue sharing. A United Nations report hailed the agreement as a "trailblazer," and the Royal Commission on Aboriginal People (RCAP) report called the Trilateral Agreement a model for coexistence. But soon after the ink had dried on the plan, the governments started to derail the agreement. Just when the Algonquins thought that their struggle was over, they came to understand it was just the beginning. As they told provincial

ministers, who hoped to undermine Algonquin authority by dishonor-
ing the agreement: "Our authority derives from the Creator."

One way to understand the relationship of jurisdiction to the production of settler-colonial space is to reverse the diagnostic applied
to chapters 3 and 4, which deal with Indigenous law and governance.
Whereas in those chapters, after Abu-Lughod,[100] I examined Algonquin
law to understand the meaning and impacts of settler-state incursions
onto the territory, in chapter 7 I reverse this lens to examine settler legislation as a means to understand the power of Indigenous jurisdiction.
As the Trilateral Agreement wobbled forward in the late 1990s through
much struggle and constant effort by the Algonquins, the Department
of Indian Affairs eventually sought to replace Barriere Lake's customary
government altogether. This exercise of power would be enacted first
through an ostensibly *internal* leadership dispute based on the community's customary selection process. Only by picking apart the government's decision to recognize a small, dissident faction of the community
as the legitimate government (one that, not coincidentally, opposed the
Trilateral Agreement) can we see the cunning divide-and-conquer tactics of the settler state to derail and discredit the community's demands.
In this chapter, I bring to light a diversity of agents and institutions that
helped produce a major governance crisis on Barriere Lake lands—for
example, provincial police, child-protection agencies, opposition members of the House of Commons, and lumber companies. However, it was
the powerful economic and political objectives of the state that drove
Canada to ultimately reject the Trilateral Agreement and execute a coup
d'état of Barriere Lake's customary government. In so doing, the federal
government pushed all parties—the Algonquins, forestry companies,
and the province—to the brink of despair and collapse. The customary government is eventually restored, but the Department of Indian
Affairs did not rest until a more permanent solution to the problem of
traditional leadership could be found.

Chapters 8 and 9 address perhaps the most extreme exercises of
power by the state to eradicate the inherent jurisdiction of the Barriere
Lake Algonquins. Following the story chronologically, these chapters
characterize the escalation of the crisis. Chapter 8 describes how the
state used an arcane clause in the Indian Act that had not been exercised for almost a century in order to officially replace Barriere Lake's
customary government system. Canada forced the community to adopt

a municipal, elective system of governance in place of their traditional system by claiming that the community's governance system was the source of leadership conflict in the community. This coercive act that exchanged Barriere Lake's inherent order of self-government for a delegated system of authority was engineered in order to pacify the community and to eradicate further opportunities for the Trilateral Agreement to be implemented. I examine the way insinuations of political and financial corruption rationalized Indian Affairs' actions to absorb Barriere Lake within the internal limits of the state and to neutralize the threat of their inherent jurisdiction.

The strategies the government used to impose the elective system on Barriere Lake's customary government provide a casebook of deceptive and crooked conduct. Department officials ran interference throughout the entire process, including irregularities in voting procedures and polling stations set up in random and isolated parts of the territory, for which no notice was given. This led to a band council voted in by acclamation based on five mail-in votes and from which the appointed chief resigned in protest. During the process, the government remained loyal to a script about the need for transparency and accountability at Barriere Lake, while refusing to respond to invitations from Barriere Lake to witness the strides they had made to reconcile divisions in the community that the government had itself fostered and inflamed. As confidential documents reveal, Barriere Lake was too independent of state jurisdiction to be tolerated. Authorities attributed the band's expectations for recognition of their jurisdiction to the fact that the state did not control the Algonquin governance system, and to the fact that its leaders and laws were not under state authority.

But this project of elimination could not have been accomplished without a surveillance program that tracked the political organizing of the community and extended Indian Affairs' authority into a complex, multijurisdictional architecture of security logics and extralegal controls. Chapter 9 examines the use of force to coerce Barriere Lake into compliance with the new customary council. I argue that this force is part of a larger pattern of coercion, surveillance, and criminalization that has been used against Barriere Lake and communities across the country to manage Indigenous assertions of jurisdiction.[101] Jeffrey Monaghan uses the term "settler governmentality" to describe the construction of Indigenous assertions of sovereignty *as threat* to settler colonialism's primary focus: the acquisition of territory through the elimination of the native.[102] Of running concern in this book are the spatial strategies deployed by the state to contain Indigenous assertions of jurisdiction on the ground. In this chapter, I examine and spatialize rationalities of settler governmentality and tie them to broader patterns of political economy in Canada today.

The pattern that concerns me in particular here is the infrastructure that connects the natural resource sector to global supply chains. In Canadian government and intelligence departments' terms, Indigenous lands are located in geographic proximity to *critical infrastructure*—a vague designation that nonetheless forms the object of intense transnational collaboration. The goal of this collaboration is to ensure the unimpeded flow of commodities through critical infrastructure such as highways and pipelines. Indigenous peoples, such as the band of Barriere Lake Algonquins, form chokeholds in these flows through their disruption both to the extractive industries themselves and to the transportation corridors that deliver these commodities to their markets when they blockade logging roads and highways. Chapter 9 links the political economy of capitalism to the tactics of monitoring, surveillance, and criminalization that contain Indigenous assertions of jurisdiction over their lands to the confines of their reserves. For example, I look specifically at tactics of incarceration, kangaroo courts of criminal justice, sentencing, and bail conditions that stipulate "no protests" and red-zone community members on or off reserves, depending on political circumstance. The ongoing, structural nature of criminalization at Barriere Lake, as well as the kinds of daily harassment documented there, bring to light blurred lines between state, police, and corporate agency and the circuitries of Indigenous containment. To understand these material geographic forms of circuitry, I situate reserves within a particular architecture of security that has emerged in the past few decades.[103]

After surveying a proliferation of regulatory, representational, sociospatial, and security impositions on Algonquin land, people, and resources that have all attempted to smother Indigenous jurisdiction, I close this book by completing a circle that began with Barriere Lake's rejection of the CLCP and that led them to develop the Trilateral Agreement in response. The Conclusion returns to an examination of the role of the land claims policy as a means to remove the uncertainty posed to state territorial jurisdiction and to the natural resource economy by overlapping jurisdiction between settler and Indigenous legal orders. In this way, I end the story of the Algonquins of Barriere Lake by marking the broader struggle in which they are embedded and the hope their vision strikes in the dark.

Situating the Question

I aim to situate this story of the Algonquins of Barriere Lake within the broader political space created by those who assert Indigenous law on a daily basis and create the "problem" of perfecting settler sovereignty for the state. This work is most inspired by land defenders across these lands, from whom I have genuinely learned the most. Only by appreciating the broader political context of Barriere Lake's struggle did I feel capable of putting forward a theory of Indigenous jurisdiction in relation to the colonial violence of the Canadian nation-state.

Let me provide just four examples of these struggles, though there are countless others from which to draw. The first incident unfolded at the Sacred Headwaters of Tahltan territory in 2013, where an encounter was captured on video between a Royal Canadian Mounted Police (RCMP) officer and Tahltan land defenders, whose territory spans the farthest northern coastal reaches of the province of British Columbia.[104] On camera we see a number of Indigenous peoples lying in a green field with low blue mountains in the background, surrounded by police. In this exchange, an RCMP officer tries to convince the Tahltan people blockading mining drills that it is Indigenous peoples who are illegally occupying the site. "So, who gave [Fortune Minerals] a right to be here?" a Tahltan man, Oscar Dennis, asks. "The province of British Columbia," the RCMP officer replies. "The province of British Columbia has this territory occupied. It's no different than the Gaza Strip in Israel. This land has never been treatied." When the RCMP officer tries to deny that the system is privileging the mining company's rights over the Tahltans' rights, Dennis insists: "I'm the colonial subject of your government. We have no rights according to your colonial laws. The problem is the government got too lazy to treaty this land, so therefore that gives us the rights. We've been here ten thousand years." Another Tahltan man, Peter Jakesta, pipes up: "If I was to disrupt a resident hunter, I would be charged. These guys [Fortune Minerals] are disrupting our hunting: nothing happens." It is something a child could understand, they tell the RCMP officer. When you apply one set of rights to one group of people and deny rights to another, you insult people by pretending not to see the difference: "I mean, why aren't you harassing [Fortune Minerals] when they're here drilling and disturbing us? But if we come out to resist—we're *resisting,* we're not *protesting,* we're resisting the colonial situation—and then we get confronted, while those colonizers from Ontario could sit on that drill and destroy our land, and they get no confrontation." Dennis reminds the RCMP officer, who repeatedly frames the Tahltan resistance as "disruption," that it is *their* lives that are being disrupted. The video is amazing to watch because the conflict defining the confrontation over land is laid out both as a problem within settler law and as a violation of Indigenous law.

Second, the Wet'suwet'en Nation is located just south and slightly east of Tahltan territory in northern British Columbia. There one can witness the incredible power of Freda Huson, a leader of the Unist'ot'en land defenders camp. A video shows her evict a security contractor from Coastal GasLink, who was attempting to undertake preliminary prospecting work for a 670-kilometer hydraulically fractured gas pipeline on her people's lands.[105] She describes to him the boundary of the Wet'suwet'en Nation and warns the prospectors: "If you guys don't want to be charged for trespassing, I suggest you guys leave right now." When the prospectors ask if it is "safe" for them to be there, Huson patiently explains to them where it is they have found themselves: "You don't live here, so you don't know. We have berry patches here, we have medicine here. The bears live here, the moose live here. We live here. This is my food back here. That's what they're trying to destroy. And they don't have our authority to do that." Huson asserts jurisdiction here by enacting trespass law to practice her responsibilities to the animals, medicines, and people of her traditional lands.

Third, in 2008, the entire Chief and Council of the Kitchenuhmaykoosib Inninuwug (KI), an Ojicree community in northern Ontario, were thrown into jail for blocking Platinex Inc. from landing a floatplane on their territory to do exploratory drilling for uranium. In court, when KI members defended themselves by asserting their inherent legal right to protect the land, Justice G. P. Smith ruled that two systems of law could not coexist or else "the rule of law will disappear and be replaced by chaos." He was concerned that "[t]he public will lose respect for, and confidence in, our courts and judicial system."[106] This admission underscores the fragility of settler sovereignty, where the coexistence of Indigenous and settler law is seen to potentially discredit the authority of the entire justice system. But it also shows the inherent racism and bias that underlie the pretense of a legal vacuum if settler law is effaced. If the Canadian rule of law disappeared, Indigenous law would govern, as it always has, long before the arrival of white faces on this land.

KI was ultimately successful at evicting Platinex Inc. from their territory. Following a second eviction of a mining company from their territory, the community issued a Water Declaration that iterates the Kanawayandan D'aaki, KI's sacred duty to look after their land: "No outside law can remove us due to our deep intimacy to our lake and territory that has evolved over thousands of years . . . Through our ecological compact we have accumulated intimate Indigenous ecological knowledge and laws that are very deep; they are within us, we live them." David Peerla observes: "The Kitchenuhmaykoosib Inninuwug are turning away from the idea of First Nations as communities with legal rights, defined under the constitution of a colonial state and in non-Aboriginal courts, towards a struggle to bring a different and independent Indigenous world into existence."[107] KI's authority, in other words, is not tied to colonial legalities and imagined sovereignty but to the source of their own legal responsibilities: their relation to the land.

Countless other communities and struggles could be named here. Many have been connected to the national grassroots Defenders of the Land network through meetings and communications. Terry Sappier, of the Maliseet Nation of Tobique First Nation, attended the inaugural Defenders meeting, held in Winnipeg, Manitoba, in November 2009. Isuma TV interviewed her there about the issues the Maliseet were facing in their community. She said the settler governments were trying to convince the community to take its twenty-seven-year land grievance to court, but that its members were refusing. She stated: "Provincial and federal courts have no jurisdiction on our territory, we have a Peace and Friendship Treaty . . . we've never agreed to live under Canadian rule or British rule. It's always been Maliseet law. We told NB Power that if they wanted to come to court, they could come and sit with our elders and plead their case. They've refused to do that, of course, so we are denying them access into our community."[108] Sappier states clearly that the Maliseet do not recognize the authority of the Crown and they are governed by their legal order.

This book is my contribution to these self-determination struggles by Indigenous peoples. By tracking one story closely over the course of a contemporary period of land-based struggle in Canada, I hope to show how the war over jurisdiction is being fought today: through the sheer resilience of a band such as Barriere Lake, and the utter dishonor of settler governments. "All we want is that you honor your word," shouted Maggie Wawatie at the line of riot cops, sent to break up a peaceful demonstration. This book, at the very least, can honor theirs.

1

Flipping the Terms of Recognition
A Methodology

I was born on lands belonging to the Huron-Wendat and the related Petun (Tionnontati), to the Seneca Nation of the Haudenosaunee, and most recently, to the Anishnabe peoples.[1] Although not commonly understood as such, cities are Indigenous space.[2] They play a key role in maintaining settler colonial mythologies and hierarchies. As Victoria Freeman observes, "Cities, no less than nations, articulate founding moments in their efforts to define themselves."[3] Take, for example, the incorporation of Toronto in 1834. Toronto celebrated this milestone by reversing its name from York back to the original Indigenous place-name of Toronto. A common interpretation of the name Toronto derives from Tkaronto, a Mohawk or Kanien'kehá:ka word that means "the place where trees stand in water." This name change signified the city as a uniquely North American place, despite the city's actual displacement of local Indigenous inhabitants. The reversal of "York" back to "Toronto" illustrates an organizing principle of settler colonialism that Patrick Wolfe calls *replacement*.[4] Indigenous societies are destroyed in order to be replaced by settler society, but this replacement, paradoxically, must reference what is destroyed. That is because, to express its difference and independence from the mother country, Toronto must "recuperate" its indigeneity.[5] Metropolitan, but named for its Indigenous "past," the city's modernity is tempered by nostalgia: in the windows of a flagship Hudson's Bay department store in the heart of the city, the iconic black, yellow, red and green-striped blankets that once symbolized the fur trade are displayed as posh accessories. But unlike prairie and West Coast cities, Indigenous peoples themselves are a less visible presence. Many Torontonians will never meet an Indigenous person in their lives.

I myself barely knew a single person who was not Jewish until I went to high school. The sidewalks that lined the curbs where I grew up in Toronto's north end are thronged on Saturdays with families on their way to and from synagogue. Until the age of twelve, I was among those families, but after my bat mitzvah, when the morality of my decisions accrued to me and no longer to my parents, I was given the option and chose to stay home. When I was fourteen, I met Tamara, a Jewish-Salteaux actress, singer, and dancer, who quickly became my closest friend. We lived eight doors apart and crossed back and forth between our houses a thousand times during our teenage years. When Tamara's maternal uncle died, we put down tobacco. When her mother phoned from Ottawa, where she had moved to fight for native rights, we sat afterward in silence and watched movies. Tamara's paternal grandfather had numbers burned into his arm from a death camp in Poland. We shared the history of the Holocaust and its painful secrets of violence and survival. Tamara came over for Shabbat dinners and often for dinner throughout the week. Our younger sisters became best friends.

Over the years, I got to know Tamara's mother Joanna Anaquod, from the Muscowpetung reserve in Saskatchewan, and through her Tamara's stepfather, Russell Diabo, a Mohawk from the reserve of Kahnawá:ke in Quebec. Russell is a big man, with long silver hair and a sparse silver mustache, and he has a dark sense of humor and a caustic, direct way of speaking. He mostly grew up in Erie, Pennsylvania, with his mother, but he also lived in Brooklyn, New York, for a number of years where his Mohawk father worked as a steelworker, as so many men did from his home community. It is difficult to think of another person more knowledgeable on Aboriginal policy or who has been as consistently outspoken about and ostracized for outlining what he calls Canada's war against First Nations. We struck up an unlikely friendship. I first spent time with him when I joined Tamara and her sisters for Christmas in Salmon Arm, British Columbia. Russell was working for the Neskonlith Indian Band and I was stranded in Vancouver after the "Battle of Seattle" protests against the World Trade Organization meeting of 1999. Tamara invited me to join them until I could get money for a flight back to Montreal, where I was living at the time. Over our first dinner, Russell explained to the table that the reason educational provisions in the treaties were included was "to learn the cunning of the white man." As he said it, he made deliberate eye contact with me. But he later warmed up and showed me a map of a plan to crystallize the unceded Secwepemc territory into an independent, self-governing land base. With that map, he began to show me the work that was being done by Indigenous people to reclaim alienated lands and to institute governance regimes that would put Indigenous peoples back into effective control of their territories. In this way, he showed me how opposing capitalism and the state—two moving targets of the antiglobalization movement—did not free up land for settlers to govern themselves, but rather held them accountable to Indigenous peoples, whose anticolonial struggle linked capitalism and the state in pivotal ways. On New Year's Eve when the women went out dancing, Russell and I stayed home and watched television, waiting up to see if Y2K would remake the world.

Over the ensuing years, Russell often talked about a community of Algonquins living in northern Quebec that had suffered unspeakable treatment by the Canadian government. One time in 2006 when I was visiting Russell and Joanna in Ottawa, an emergency Elders Council meeting was held at their place. A boisterous group of men arrived late, having driven three and a half hours straight from the bush that morning. They listened quietly to the advisers and laughed uproariously whenever someone made a joke. They also ordered an implausible amount of meat on their pizza. I had never met hunters before and felt intimidated by their knowledge and their experience and the battle they had undertaken to defend their lands. But most of all, I remember the presence of Jean Maurice Matchewan, who was the customary chief at the time and whom everyone called Pancho. He was larger than life, tall with a deep gravelly voice, and held a sharp focus on the Algonquins' land rights in every point he made. I remember Toby Decoursay, who would become an important contact for me in the community, and his quiet and self-effacing presence, how his laughter came a bit later than that of the others.

Russell told me once that you could learn everything there was to know about colonialism in Canada by working with the Algonquins of Barriere Lake. That is how I found myself in October 2008 catching a ride from Ottawa with some activists up to the Rapid Lake Reserve. It was already very cold in the region and I woke up in Harry Wawatie's dark, warm basement at five the next morning, dreading the freezing blast of air that awaited us. We rode out to the highway on the back of a pickup truck and other trucks were there already, being hitched with sawed-down trees that were dragged onto Highway 117 and piled into a thickening heap to form a barricade against oncoming traffic. Further up the highway in either direction, community members with flashlights and bright vests were stopping traffic, letting trucks and cars know that there was a blockade up ahead. At the access road where the reserve road met the highway, more and more vehicles arrived from the community as the sky lightened behind a fringe of black trees. A fire was made in the center of the highway and soon breakfast was prepared and served to a growing crowd of men, women, and children. At that point, I knew only a few individuals in the community (a handful of community members who had come to Toronto, where I organized a dismally attended speaking event), but people were friendly and I watched from the sideline as assemblies were held in Algonquin periodically to assess the intensifying situation and decide collectively how to go forward.

The blockade was organized by the women in the community to protest the imposition of a band council that many claimed had not been selected according to custom. The community claimed that Canada's recognition of this council represented the same old tricks the government had been up to for years, intervening in their governance system in order to sever their connection to the land and ensure that the Trilateral Agreement was never implemented. Barriere Lake's demand was simple that day: send in a negotiator. The government refused. Instead, vans of riot cops arrived from Montreal. They cleared the road with tear gas, police brutality, and arrests.

I worked as an activist with the community for a year before approaching them to ask if I could write a book about their struggle. I asked how to go about obtaining permission to undertake this sort of thing and I was told to come up to the community and a community assembly would be held to discuss the matter. The meeting was informal—about two dozen people showed up, and I explained my intentions: the struggle for the Trilateral Agreement was important but had never been documented, and I wanted to write a book about what my government had done to them. The customary chief, some councilors and members of the Elders Council were in attendance. They agreed their story should be told. But they insisted that if I were going to write about the resource comanagement agreement, I would have to come up and spend as much time on the land as possible or I would not understand what they were fighting for.

We began to organize the steps necessary to undertake the research project. Through Barriere Lake's tribal council, the Algonquin Nation Secretariat (ANS), we set up an informal advisory committee with a team of experts who had been working with the community for many years, along with members of the Algonquins of Barriere Lake (ABL).

The advisory committee comprised Peter Di Gangi, who was the research director of ANS; David Nahwegahbow, a leading Aboriginal rights lawyer who worked for ANS; James Morrison, an independent historian who contracted for ANS and is likely the world's leading non-Indigenous expert on Algonquin history;[6] Sue Roark-Calnek, who was trained as an anthropologist and had been working for years with the community on various genealogical and ethnographic studies; Russell Diabo, the tribal council's policy adviser; Jean Maurice Matchewan, Barriere Lake's customary chief at the time; and the Barriere Lake Elders Council. The terms of reference for this contract with the advisory committee involved meeting at least once a year, circulating work for approval, presenting ongoing work to the community, and on a case-by-case basis seeking out individual advisory members for feedback, advice, and editorial assistance on specific issues and drafts. I submitted a Proposed Work Schedule and Plan, detailing my long-term research goals and estimated date of completion, as well as ongoing short-term tasks I would undertake that were related to my research (e.g., data transfer of personal interview recordings to the ANS). I also provided a detailed month-by-month overview of what my first year of research would look like. In addition, I agreed to contribute labor (e.g., an annotated bibliography of all ABL-related reports) to the ANS in a work exchange to compensate the organization for the time Peter Di Gangi spent introducing me to the documents, computer database, and broader historical and political context of Barriere Lake's struggle.

I also signed a memorandum of agreement with Barriere Lake, and one with the ANS, each approving access to all relevant research materials, as well as defining proprietary rights, terms by which my research may be used, terms of arbitration in the case of conflict, and outlining a confidentiality agreement and code of ethics for the duration of the agreement. I obtained a Band Council Resolution of the Customary Council (No. 2009–07–15) that authorized me to undertake "academic research in relation to ABL history and customs, and in particular, the Trilateral Agreement," and authorizing the ANS to give me access to all ABL-related materials. I signed two additional contracts specific to confidentiality with the ANS and ABL, ensuring that access to all information I am privy to in the course of my research will not be disclosed, except under the agreed-upon conditions.

I soon found, however, that even the best-laid plans could go terribly awry in the context of a bitter colonial struggle over land. As my book describes, a leadership conflict in the community was causing considerable distress at Barriere Lake at the time of my initial involvement. There was a grassroots effort to resolve this conflict, but in the meantime, the Elders Council at Barriere Lake had also taken the minister of Indian Affairs to court, requesting a judicial review of the minister's decision to recognize one customary council over the other. In effect, Jean Maurice Matchewan's council had been replaced with one led by a man named Casey Ratt who was claiming to be customary chief. On February 17, 2010, the Mainville Decision came down.[7] Despite an earlier favorable reading of the Elders Council case,[8] Justice Robert Mainville decided that neither of the two factions claiming to the be legitimate customary council at Barriere Lake could be recognized as fit to govern under the community's own customary code.

The political implications of the decision were devastating; they form a central discussion in my book. From an academic perspective, the impacts to my research were also troublingly deep. Every last document I was working with had to be returned to legal counsel to be sealed and stored until a time when the leadership issue could be resolved. Otherwise, the tribal council could be held liable for disclosing confidential information to me without permission from the proper authorities, whoever they turned out to be. That meant the return of dozens of boxes filled with land claims research, Trilateral Agreement documentation, years of correspondence between Barriere Lake and the provincial and federal documents, traditional land-use and occupancy studies, interviews with elders, anthropological and ethnographic research on Algonquin society, old photos and maps. Peter Di Gangi encouraged me to work with another Algonquin band in the tribal council. It seemed I had no recourse but to rethink my entire book.

There was one other major problem. I undertook this research initially as a doctoral student. The Matchewan council had signed my university-mandated research ethics protocol, which was approved by the Research Ethics Board long after the Mainville Decision came down.[9] At this point, the university also initiated a new contract between the Governing Council of the University and the Algonquins of Barriere Lake, as per university policy that authorizes only certain persons to sign agreements on behalf of the university. Up until that point, all the contracts I had signed with the tribal council and band council had been between the community and myself. To the university, these contracts were considered null and void. I delayed obtaining Algonquin authorization of the new contract, explaining to the university that it would take time to organize travel to Barriere Lake to acquire the signatures. Based on the contingency that I would finalize these signatures in the coming months, my application was given approval by the Research Ethics Board in April 2011. But the question was, who would re-sign the documents? As of February 2010, according to Canada and the federal court, a cloud of uncertainty shrouded the question of who was legally in power at Barriere Lake with the authority to govern.

I reflected on the situation for months. My graduate committee advised me to lie low and maintain contact with the community, trusting the process and staying open to opportunity. In the meantime, I took fast and careful notes, scanning maps and key reports, before sealing up and sending off the boxes of ABL documents to be sequestered at the law office of David Nahwegahbow in Rama, Ontario. By this point, I had begun to travel up to Barriere Lake frequently from Toronto to meet people, set up interviews, and get to know the territory. Over this early period, the landscape of Algonquin territory began to change for me from indistinguishable trees and lakes to jack pines with roots for sewing, boggy frog water for eczema, and long, narrow, and winding boating paths from one gathering point in the territory to another. I attended funerals and feasts and spent days fishing. Toby was right that these visits shifted my understanding of the conflict. The Algonquins were less "against" the state than they were driven by a responsibility to the land, to all the living things and waterways, and impacted watersheds. Their relationship to the land was structured by their knowledge of the territory and this knowledge secured their authority to protect the lands of the Mitchikanibikok Inik. Gradually, I discerned that in order to resolve my research ethics dilemma I had to answer the following question: what governs my own ethical responsibilities to undertake research with the Algonquins of Barriere Lake?

Cree scholar Shawn Wilson writes that Indigenous methodologies— which he and others distinguish from just doing research in an Indigenous context[10]—must fulfill one's relationship to the world around them. Indigenous methodology must pose different problems than conventional research: "rather than asking about validity or reliability, you are asking how am I fulfilling my role in this relationship?"[11]

Methodology and research ethics blur into one concern: accountability to oneself and to one's relationships. Moreover, as Deborah McGregor, Walter Bayha, and Deborah Simmons write, researchers must respect customary governance processes as a prerequisite for doing credible research that supports the self-determination of Indigenous communities.[12] In the case of Barriere Lake, the majority of the community still considered Jean Maurice Matchewan to be their customary leader. That is not to say that there was unanimous agreement about his role in the conflict or that there was no dissent in the community over his leadership. But by popular support he represented the will of the community, and even the government and forestry companies continued to approach him for consent on resource extraction in the region, implicitly acknowledging his leadership in the community. If the community still considered Matchewan to be the customary chief and to represent the community's responsibility to the land, then I would respect the band's self-determination and consider him to be so, too. Therefore, despite the federal court's refusal to recognize him as chief, Matchewan signed my new application for the University of Toronto Research Ethics Board. He agreed to continue to support my work. I think that at that time, perhaps more than ever, he wanted the story to be told. True to my agreement in earlier signed contracts, I have sought out and ensured that the final draft of my manuscript has been read and approved for publication by my advisory committee and by key community members at Barriere Lake. As far as I have been made aware, there is nothing in this book deemed unsuitable for publication.

In terms of an ethics of accountability, however, many questions still remain unanswered. Outside of personal and academic relationships, how can a researcher be accountable for ongoing abuses of power perpetrated by the government against Indigenous communities? What is the nature and source of this accountability according to the community at Barriere Lake, and to Anishnabe and Indigenous legal and political systems more generally? Here I want to introduce four planks of responsibility on which I believe that my broader legal and political responsibilities to the community are based, and that motivate the writing of this book: a commitment to center decolonization as the object of research, a commitment to honor treaty relations, a commitment to build alliances between settler and Indigenous societies, and a commitment to respect Indigenous law and prophesy. We could also describe this commitment as a methodology of *living in relation to Anishnabe law*. By honoring this approach, I hope to model coexistence in ways that flip the terms of recognition from state-based, asymmetrical, and nonreciprocal forms to relations that rather begin with settlers seeking recognition from Indigenous peoples for our right to be here within their jurisdiction.[13]

The Colonizer Who Refuses

The challenges of living in a society where colonial policies and mindsets persist are demonstrably clear. The national broadcaster, Canadian Broadcasting Corporation (CBC), announced its decision in November 2015 to close down the comment section of stories published about Aboriginal people because of the high incidence of hate speech and racist attack. How to address these social challenges in our approach to academic work is less clear. Albert Memmi writes: "Colonial relations do not stem from individual good will or actions; they exist before his arrival or his birth, and whether he accepts or rejects them matters little."[14] According to Memmi, colonizers who recognize the injustice and despicability of their position may leave the country or else live their lives under the sign of contradiction, where they will never be accepted in either the colonizer or colonized worlds, regarded with suspicion in both.

Refusal to participate in colonization is only the first step on an impossible journey. Memmi warns that the colonizer's racism will be unshakable when confronted with the colonized's ambitions for self-government and liberation, unable to ultimately imagine their freedom. She will come to their assistance, but will not be able to restrain herself from judging their civilization and society. Her prior politics and ideological convictions will be put to the ultimate test, particularly the left-wing sympathizer who must put away her communism, anarchism, liberalism, and democracy when confronted with a national or religious struggle for self-determination. Uneasiness will persist. She will not find the aims of her left-wing tendency reflected in that struggle, and in addition, she will have to live in the midst of it as a colonial. For the sympathetic colonizer who decides to abandon her political principles and accept the position of the colonized wholeheartedly, she will also discover, crushingly, that she cannot and will not adapt to their customs and language, that she cannot share the destiny of the colonized, but rather only the destiny of the colonizer.

Memmi's fatalistic rendering of the settler complex can be read as part fantasy, part warning. It is fantastic because he projects rejection and homelessness into the future of the colonizer who refuses. The fear of rejection nearly exceeds the deplorability of colonialism, as anti-colonial rejection of the sympathetic colonizer is imagined as the tragic, inevitable end of liberation struggle. Memmi's cautions, though, harken to the kinds of ongoing and vigilant work involved in getting out of the colonizers' bind and building a meaningful anticolonial solidarity movement. In particular, settlers must negotiate their relationship to Indigenous communities in a political context where liberation is not defined by newcomers, not primarily about them, and that will not always benefit them, but, on the contrary, will mean sacrifice and compromise. But these anxieties belie the colonizer's work that can be done to address the paradox. Settler awakening is tied to Indigenous jurisdiction and resurgence; though newcomers cannot *join* Indigenous societies, their role is to build strong movements to ensure the transformation of their own communities, which constitutes its own kind of liberation and forms the basis for new relationships. Leanne Simpson describes the Seventh Fire prophesy as "a time when, after a long period of colonialism and cultural loss, a new period, the Oshkimaadiziig, emerge."[15] She states that "[i]n order for the Eighth Fire to be lit, settler society must also choose to change their ways, to decolonize their relationships with the land and Indigenous Nations, and to join with us in building a sustainable future based on mutual recognition, justice, and respect."[16] Decolonization is not a process to be left to the state to helm, nor to Indigenous peoples to endeavor alone, but a reorientation of the people, who must right relations with Indigenous peoples toward a sustainable and just world.

Centering critical Indigenous methodologies and studies in academic work is one immediate rapprochement to colonial absenting and distortion that absolves non-Indigenous peoples of responsibility on these lands. This does not necessarily exclude the use of Western theory or hold it as an irreconcilable or contradictory body of knowledge, but rather repositions Indigenous thought within critical social theory. Although the discipline of geography does not have the same reputation as anthropology for ascribing Western ontological meanings and purposes to Indigenous societies through observation and study, the nature–culture binary of the field has consistently placed Indigenous peoples either outside of "nature," mapping them out of conservation sites and other landscapes, or else outside of "culture," where they are depicted as living in a state of nature.[17] This is both a liability of geography and a main focus of critique within the discipline.[18] As Jay Johnson and Brian Murton explain, decolonization depends on overcoming the construction of nature that fixes Indigenous people both spatially and temporally: "In the process, we have the opportunity also to begin healing the dichotomies inherent within the meta-narrative which has created this displacement."[19]

Unfortunately, one dominant tendency has been to compound the colonialism of the nature–culture split by seeking reconciliation in Western traditions, rather than overcome these dichotomies through reference to other-than-Western ontologies. Juanita Sundberg describes the way scholarship "continuously refers to a foundational ontological split between nature and culture *as if it is universal*." She indicts her own scholarship for reflexively turning to Western authors and not to Indigenous thinkers to heal this rift: "Indigenous authors in the Americas, for instance, outline complex knowledge systems wherein animals, plants, and spirits are understood as beings who participate in the everyday practices that bring worlds into being. These epistemic traditions are not organized in and through dualist ontologies of nature/culture. Does it not seem obvious to consult such work in order to think through methodological difficulties that stem from trying to understand and depict co-production from within a body of thought that tends to purification and segmentation?"[20] Zoe Todd, fed up with an ostensible "Ontological Turn" in the social sciences, names this so-called ontological shift "colonial" in that it continues to elevate non-Indigenous peoples for "discovering" the intermeshing of human–nonhuman orders that have intrinsically ordered law in Indigenous societies for millennia.[21]

Even within a discipline ostensibly geared to foreground Indigenous experience, settler-colonial studies has been subject to similar critiques as academics take up the study of settler colonialism without centering Indigenous people, political struggle, and thought.[22] Supplanting the privilege of expertise requires a shift in the field of power associated with expert knowledge. One challenge for "outsiders" of centering Indigenous people's lives is that

> [f]or Indigenous communities, their oral histories, narratives, and spiritual practices and rituals are important avenues for

knowledge transmission. They contain numerous nuances that only certain community members are privileged to understand. Attempting to decipher this rich code and to represent it adequately requires that the researcher becomes an advocate of the Indigenous knowledge system and at the very least incorporates the "Indigenous voice" in their work.[23]

In other words, to understand settler colonialism, one must engage with Indigenous knowledge systems, and the communities within which they are embedded must be recognized and respected. These are *meanings in context,* which oblige the careful interpretation and analysis of the listener. Everyday conversation, jokes, and practices, as well as ceremonies and feasts, are pertinent background pictures for cultural and legal meaning on these lands.

Another plank of responsibility for academics is the act of treaty. For citizens and residents of Canada or the United States, we are all treaty people. Sharon Venne argues that every non-Indigenous person must know his or her treaty rights and she regrets that most discussions fail to even mention the rights and obligations of non-Indigenous parties: "Everyone who has come to live on Great Turtle Island since contact is living here as a result of a treaty. To discount the treaty or deny the treaty rights of non-indigenous people is to make illegitimate foreign people's occupancy of Great Turtle Island."[24] Treaties establish what James (Sakej) Youngblood Henderson calls the "hidden constitution of Canada," producing "a distinctive federalism" that is meant to protect the autonomy of Indigenous nations from newcomers. Honoring the treaties is also what legitimizes the authority of the Crown to exercise political governance in Canada.[25] To move onto lands without permission and without honoring the terms of permission is simply theft.

Michael Asch also sees treaties as "the basis for the legitimacy of our settlement here," as opposed to Aboriginal rights, which are delegated by the state through the judiciary.[26] "Treaty rights," rather, flow from agreements between settlers and Indigenous peoples, which demand reciprocal obligations. Asch says that we must ask ourselves, "What are the treaty rights we guaranteed to them in return for the *treaty rights they guaranteed to us* to legitimize our permanent settlement on these lands?"[27] In chapter 2, I describe the treaties, wampums, and agreements entered into by Barriere Lake as forms of alliance made between

Indigenous and non-Indigenous peoples on Turtle Island.[28] Even these are not land treaties; according to customary law they are nation-to-nation agreements that must be renewed periodically so that they do not tarnish.

Renewing these agreements can take the form of solidarity alliances. Long before we learned about specific treaties, wampum belts, or the Onakinakewin, a group of people (mostly non-Indigenous) took action to support Barriere Lake's struggle based on the political principle of respect for Indigenous peoples' inherent right to self-determination. In March 2008, when the federal government was taking steps to intervene in the community's customary governance process, activists from Montreal traveled to Algonquin territory and presented themselves at a community assembly to request consent to do community-led solidarity work with the band. The customary government, the people, and the elders agreed and Barriere Lake Solidarity (BLS) was formed. I helped to form a support group in Toronto, and in Ottawa the Indigenous Peoples Solidarity Movement Organization also took on Barriere Lake solidarity work. The solidarity groups have worked together to support the community in a range of ways. They have organized demonstrations in Ottawa, Toronto, and Montreal; coordinated speaking tours for community spokespeople in major urban areas and at conferences across the country; planned a sit-in at the Barriere Lake local MP's office as well as actions in front of the deputy minister of Indian Affairs' office in the capital; and spearheaded two human-rights delegations to the territory. They have also participated in two blockades of Highway 117. The solidarity groups fund-raise to cover legal fees and pay for mining monitoring programs, and have supported travel to New York City to attend a United Nations Permanent Forum on Indigenous Issues meeting. BLS also runs a website and does extensive communication and media work. All of this effort is undertaken with a direct and explicit mandate from community spokespeople, who in turn take direction from their own people, as expressed at community assemblies and in conversations with family and elders. For the solidarity group, Indigenous self-determination is not only the end goal of the process, it is also the basis on which non-Indigenous peoples must build the relationship and renew alliances.

The political struggle at Barriere Lake, and those in communities across Turtle Island, are not simply struggles for recognition from the state, but assertions of jurisdiction over their lands. Communities defend their right to self-determination not only through blockades, but through daily practices such as going to the bush, hunting and fishing without permits, tending traplines, harvesting syrup at family sugar bushes, maintaining their language, and by living in their traditional territory. Non-Indigenous people can enact solidarity, in turn, through political organizing in defense of these Indigenous rights and through material support for Indigenous practices of everyday life. More specifically, in the case of Barriere Lake, their struggle is a fight for rightful jurisdiction over their lands exercised under the authority of their Onakinakewin. The Onakinakewin is a system of natural laws that governs all that which grows on the earth. To break this chain of learning and teaching would disrupt centuries of mutual safekeeping between the land and the people. These laws are passed along through practice and experience. Simply put, solidarity also means working to ensure that people can get out onto the land. A key way to do this is by supporting bush schools and language camps and related gatherings.

There is also a spiritual aspect to the interlegal relationship between treaty partners. A prophesy at Barriere Lake predicts *ka-dish-pog-washni,* "In the future, we will jump high." Barriere Lake's world has been carved out by prophecy. They have knowledge of a time to come on earth when the storms will rage, tornados will violently stir, floods will drench, and the wind will shake the world to its foundations. When that time comes, people from other nations will come to the Anishnabek and seek their knowledge. Barriere Lake holds this prophecy through their seven-diamond belt. In many people's minds, that time has come. The appearance of researchers in the community seeking knowledge from Barriere Lake has been interpreted as prophetic in this light. In all the literature available on methodology, prophecy could be the most marginal. Yet, of all the Indigenous research methodologies covered here, it honors most profoundly and illustrates most eloquently the inadequacies of conventional assumptions about power relations between researchers and Indigenous peoples. Prophecy can reverse expectations about the role of outsiders in a community as primarily exploitative of Indigenous knowledge. For it was based on this prophecy of the coming storms that Toby agreed to share knowledge with me. In other words, I was confirming and performing a role within Algonquin cosmology through my research that allowed the Algonquins to do their work. It is useful to be reminded that Indigenous peoples have their own reasons for sharing their knowledge; it is up to the researcher to take only what is necessary and to make this work available for others who might need it.

Other prophecies, it must be said, are more ambivalent about outsiders. A story I heard often in the community is the Sturgeon River Prophesy. A long time ago, a Mitchikanibikok Anishnabe was walking along the river and came across one silver snake and one gold snake washed up onto the shore. He took them home and fed them. At first, he fed them small things, fish and mice. Then, little by little, he fed them bigger and bigger things, until one day the snakes began to eat people. The man decided that he must feed the snakes back to the Ottawa River from where they came (called Nemeozibi, or Sturgeon River, where it crosses Barriere Lake territory). That is why the Ottawa River snakes around so much, in many winding directions. This prophecy ends with one snake's mouth gaping open, unknown what it will swallow next. That version comes from Toby Decoursay. Harry Wawatie, another elder in the community, also shared this story with his nephew Tony Wawatie, a community leader and spokesperson for the community. One day, Tony mentioned to me that his uncle used to describe two snakes—one made of silver, one of gold—and that Harry told him that the gold snake symbolized the greed, the money that had come into their communities to destroy them, and the silver snake represented technology, which had come to do the same. Harry often warned Tony, "The monster is coming."

Finally, the conditions necessary to protect Indigenous law, in support of Indigenous people, and to protect the knowledge on which we all may someday come to depend, hang on how one understands the logics of settler colonialism in Canada today. Diabo calls Canadian colonialism a low-intensity war against First Nations, fought with legislative policies, public-relations spin, and the full disposal of police and military forces.[29] To honor treaty agreements of peace, friendship, respect, and principles of noninterference in a contemporary context requires taking significant steps against the federal and provincial governments that perpetuate Indigenous land dispossession and assimilation policies. As Frantz Fanon asserts. "Every citizen of a nation is responsible for the acts perpetrated in the name of that nation."[30] In Canada, in a nation of 35 million non-Indigenous peoples and almost 1.5 million Indigenous peoples, the numbers alone speak to a crucial need for strong alliances. To force the Canadian government to honor their treaties and respect Indigenous jurisdiction, non-Indigenous Canada will have to bring its power, privilege, and resources to bear. From the perspective of land, there is a political economy to colonialism that is also critical to understand and that forms a crucial intersection of oppression that will be a central focus in this book. Demands for land restitution go hand in hand with Indigenous jurisdiction because without land, there is no meaningful governance to speak of.

Defending Indigenous law is less about non-Indigenous people recognizing Aboriginal title than about defending the terms Indigenous peoples set by which they themselves agree to recognize Crown title. Here the onus is on non-Indigenous peoples to cast aside the racist anthropology on which Canada was founded by conducting ourselves with respect to the jurisdiction of Indigenous nations. The "we" here is a problem, of course. As a naturalized, white Canadian citizen with full citizenship status and a professional life, my responsibilities to hold my own government accountable may differ significantly from non-Indigenous people who are racialized, criminalized, hold precarious citizenship status, and do not benefit in the same way from their relationship to the state. Nor have the economic benefits of colonialism been distributed evenly among settlers.[31]

But critical scholars have also debunked "natural ally" theories that presume sameness among people of color, which reproduces oppression by erasing differences in the operations of power. As Andrea Smith observes, communities of color can be both victims and complicit in white supremacy. This complicity arises from a stay of discrimination awarded to people of color when they participate in the exploitation of other oppressed groups. Instead, the focus for all kinds of allies should be on solidarity across different forms of oppression.[32]

Ultimately, as Albert Memmi warns, no individual can end colonialism because it is systemic and must be fought on structural grounds.[33] Academics can draw important attention to colonial conditions, but as they build their own careers, secure incomes, and experience personal fulfillment through working with Indigenous law, the political survival of the communities they "study" can be at stake. Many scholars have taken up this task respectfully, supporting Indigenous struggles materially, intellectually, and through advocacy work. For myself, the test of this strength is the ability to keep everything that lives and grows within our horizon of accountability. The Algonquins call this Anishnabe way of thinking *m'dinen'jigen*—our connected sacredness. This is what I understand to be living in relation to Anishnabe law.

A Final Note on Accountability

Barriere Lake is not a homogeneous community. The community members with whom I worked had a base on the Rapid Lake Reserve, where I often stayed to meet with people. All of the people with whom I worked in Rapid Lake also spent time in the bush, at their summer or winter cabins, where I often visited. But there are other village sites on Barriere Lake territory that are not geographically connected to the reserve and operate remotely from reserve life. These are family settlements where people live year-round in their bush homes or in nearby towns and settlements. One of these sites is called Nanotinik and was led by matriarch Lena Nottaway until she passed. When Lena passed away, people in that settlement slowly displaced to other sites. One of those sites was Maigan Agik, near Le Domaine at the northern entrance into La Vérendrye Wildlife Reserve on Highway 117. Members of the Nottaway family are based at Maigan Agik, led by matriarch Elizabeth Nottaway. Another family settlement is at Mattawa, near Roland Lake, and it is led by matriach Pauline Ratt and comprises members of the Wawatie family. Members of the Wawatie family also have an encampment at a site dubbed "Airport" because of its proximity to an old landing strip. This site is often associated with Jacob Wawatie, the nephew of Harry Wawatie, the late customary chief. It was also associated with the late matriarch Louise Wawatie. There are also a number of other year-round settlements scattered throughout Barriere Lake's territory. Algonquins are a decentralized society and they traditionally lived year-round at their bush camps, gathering together for feasts each spring. Some families resisted settling on the reserve from the start, while others moved off for religious or political reasons.

These geographic dispersements are reflected in my research. I did not work with family groups at the village sites just mentioned, though some of the knowledge held in these communities is reflected in my work. Anthropologist Sue Roark-Calnek undertook substantial research with Lena Nottaway at Nanotinik, and I draw heavily on Roark-Calnek's work, particularly in chapters 3 and 4. My work also draws on the knowledge of elders from these communities, many of whom have now passed, but who participated in the early Trilateral land-use and occupancy studies undertaken for harmonization measures with forestry companies.

But in terms of interviews conducted over the course of my research, field site visits, or through regular contact on the territory, my work proceeded quite separately from these groups. There are a number of reasons for this, but I will go into the central reason here. Over the course of Barriere Lake's struggle to see the Trilateral Agreement implemented, divisions arose in the community over the plausibility of Canada or Quebec honoring the agreement. The government's hand in sowing these doubts will be made clear in this book. But disagreements between community members and family groups made access to these aforementioned village sites difficult. This issue proved as much an academic issue as a solidarity problem. Political disagreement in the community also caused a rift between solidarity activists and those community members who resented non-Indigenous involvement by outsiders who adopted demands on the government (for example, honoring the Trilateral Agreement) that they themselves opposed. As a visible member of the solidarity network, this conflict of interest restricted my freedom to move about the community as an "objective" participant or observer. It also drew considerable contention to me from community members, other solidarity networks, and individuals from other Indigenous nations who work politically with these families. These contentions form vibrant internal activist discussions on the ethics of accountability in doing solidarity work within heterogeneous communities.

Thus, the account presented here about the Algonquins of Barriere Lake is not meant to represent the views of all Mitchikanibikok Inik. However, what cannot be contested are the actions of the Quebec and Canadian governments, which is where my attention is largely focused in this book. Too much attention in recent years has been focused on community accountability to colonial governments. Division in communities is seen as a sign of malfunction, but only the most virulent racism in our society can account for holding Indigenous communities to standards of unanimity unexpected in white communities, especially given hundreds of years of colonial oppression of Indigenous social and governance systems and on their economic bases. This book is a story about Canadian illegitimacy, above all, and the ways in which the state attempts to absolve past and ongoing appropriation through the attempted perfection of territorial jurisdiction.

2

How Did Colonialism Fail to Dispossess?

In Cole Harris's excellent article "How Did Colonialism Dispossess?" he outlines with remarkable brevity key technologies of Indigenous dispossession in British Columbia.[1] In so doing, he introduces critical methodologies for appraising the impacts of colonialism on Indigenous peoples' territorial belonging to the land. Harris divides his account into earlier techniques of dispossession (involving direct violence, the imperial state, cultural narratives, and settler self-interest) and later techniques of dispossession (constituted by disciplinary power through the use of maps, demographics, and a reserve geography of resettlement). Although Harris delineates these strategies temporally, a mixture of nearly all these techniques has been deployed at Barriere Lake. These techniques contribute to the dynamic of forces that have shaped jurisdictional struggles over the land.

A caveat to Harris's analysis, though, is to specify what it means for colonialism to dispossess. The early history of settler incursions on Barriere Lake's land did not result in the removal of the community from their lands because people were not actually displaced. Rather, their lands were alienated and reterritorialized through competing use and jurisdictional claims. Impositions of state and private authority grossly undermine, yet do not necessarily succeed in extinguishing, Indigenous governance over their lands through literal expulsion. What do we call a process of colonization where the effect of dispossession is not removal but the perpetuation of a set of exhaustive administrative regimes that undermine, erase, and choke out the exercise of Indigenous jurisdiction, rendering Indigenous people peripheral to effective participation in land governance?

This chapter examines the steady accretion of encroachments and restrictions on Barriere Lake's lands that produce a complex space of overlapping jurisdiction. The brief history of settler accumulation presented here foregrounds two meanings of dispossession that can bring perspicuity to the term and therefore draw into relief the nature of the land struggle at Barriere Lake today. The first meaning of dispossession

defines the term by its relation to practices of social reproduction, indicating the possibility of "displacement without moving."² This kind
of dispossession constitutes what Rob Nixon calls a *slow violence* that
"entails being simultaneously immobilized and moved out of one's
living knowledge as one's place loses its life-sustaining features."³ If
that which was entrusted to Barriere Lake's care is eliminated, this
impacts the terrain of their jurisdiction, and the knowledge that has
been accumulated that is connected to that care is vulnerable to loss,
too. Clear-cut forests, mining, undergrowth poison, overhunting, and
development—these encroachments slowly eradicate that which the Algonquins depend upon to survive, physically and culturally.

The second, related sense of dispossession is connected to the specifically sited dynamics of accumulation on Barriere Lake's lands. While
their assertions of jurisdiction continued to spatialize law on the land—
for example, in accordance with their tenure systems, hunting grounds,
and land-management techniques—the Algonquins increasingly competed against the interests of state and private authorities. Moreover,
these interests were themselves periodically at cross-purposes. Territorial logics of power incentivizing the state toward the perfection of
settler sovereignty clashed with open spatial dynamics of capitalist accumulation, seen where the state's denial of Indigenous jurisdiction led
to blockades that shut down the forestry sector.⁴ To be dispossessed of
governing authority means to be subject to the governing logics of other
forces. Algonquins have used the term "alienation" to describe how the
community's land and resources have been "planned, managed, used
and impacted by non-Native peoples and their institutions and industries," without signifying physical or legal dispossession.⁵

Nicholas Brown articulates this dynamic as *settler accumulation* or
accumulation by possession, shifting the economic emphasis of capitalism onto the often silent processes of acquisition—the racial and legal
frameworks of settler colonialism—that shape and define the development of capitalism on Indigenous lands. Settler accumulation responds
"to the specific forms of anti-colonial resistance it encounters," which
are "dialectically intertwined."⁶ But it is not a matter simply of resistance to colonialism that has shaped the development of capitalism on
Barriere Lake lands. It is the structure of Indigenous governance and
the binding social center of law that creates the barriers to penetration
by capitalism. The last section of this chapter more closely examines

how the boundaries of the settler state are shaped by such assertions of Indigenous jurisdiction.

The Most Dangerous Band in Canada: Mitchikanibikok Inik

It all began with a footprint, at a point on the shore across from the original Barriere Lake settlement. That footprint belonged to a young boy. He walked around the island and saw the plants and animals and everything that grew there. He saw everything that was in the world and made it ready for the Anishnabe people. He found gifts for them— fire, water, and medicine—everything they would need. The sun would be their father, and the earth would be their mother. Because the young boy began here where he found the knowledge, this would be the center of the world.[7] This is where the Onakinakewin came from, the sacred constitution of the Anishnabe people.

From a watershed perspective, the Barriere Lake traditional land-use area really is located in the center of the Algonquin world, with two major rivers forming what almost looks like a heart around the traditional settlement area of the band. At the top of the heart where the two semispheres meet, the northern Gatineau River crosses southwest across the present Cabonga Reservoir and Coulonge River to meet the headwaters of the Ottawa River, which the Algonquins call Kichi Sipi, the great river. The Ottawa River flows westward, then southward, then southeastward for around 1,200 kilometers before joining the St. Lawrence River near Montreal.

Where the Anishnabe lived at their original gathering place, the river was ten feet across from one shore to the other. They put rocks across the river creating a stone weir over which they could easily scoop fish. For this technique, they became known as "the people of the stone weir": Mitchikanibikok Inik. Mitcikinabikong is the "place of the stone fence or weir," and inik is people; the name (pronounced Mi-jibin-ahb-kwi In-ik) marks their presence on the great river. The French translated their name literally into "Lac Barrière." Since time immemorial, the Mitchikanibikok Inik have occupied more than forty-four thousand square kilometers of forested land in what are now the Outouais, Abitibi-Temiscaming, and Laurentide administrative regions of Quebec. Confirming oral history, the archaeological record shows human habitation of the area at least as far back as eight thousand to ten thousand

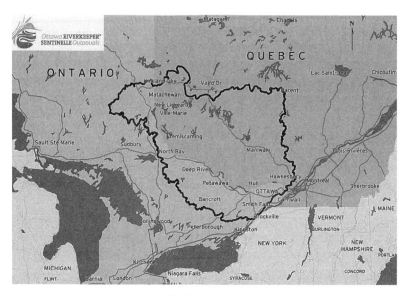

Ottawa River Watershed. First published in the River Report of Ottawa Riverkeeper, *issue 1,* Ecology and Impacts, *May 2006. Courtesy of* Ottawa Riverkeeper.

years ago. The Anishnabe on the territory tell stories of the giant beaver, which would have been part of the ecosystem at this time.[8]

Community members at Barriere Lake rarely refer to themselves as "Algonquin." In their own language, people mostly call themselves Anishnabe people, which generally means "human being," and more specifically carries the meaning of "from whence (Creator) lowered the human."[9] Barriere Lake people can understand Ojicree, Cree, and other Algonquian-based languages, but theirs is the most divergent dialect of the Ojibwe language in the "Middle Tier" of the Algonquian language family.[10] Their language is *mitcikanâpikowinîmôwin,* which is a distinct local subdialect of Algonquin and of *anishnabemowin* more generally.

While language and local dialect convey a distinct social group, the category of "Algonquin" people is an imprecise ethnic category that emerged as a French application ("Algommquin") designated to describe bands and sub-bands in the region of central and eastern Canada who spoke similar languages.[11] Later, the term was applied to a smaller subgroup of Indigenous peoples living in the Ottawa Valley, of whom Barriere Lake was included.[12] But it can be difficult at times to interpret the historical record kept by colonials because of the shifting terms applied to the Mitchikanibikok Inik by a range of early explorers confused by the relationships between various societies. In early French records of contact, Barriere Lake Algonquins (as well as other Algonquin-speaking Upper Ottawa peoples) were called *kichi sipi* Anishnabe and the *nopiming daje inini* or *gens de terres*, literally, inland people or men of the woods, reflecting the location of their territory in the boreal forest. They were also referred to phrenologically as *machakandiby* or *têtes de boule*, which means round heads, but which refers—along with *gens de terres*—to a backwoods, culturally tenacious people.[13]

The Barriere Lake Algonquins are one of ten present-day Algonquin communities in the Ottawa River watershed that straddles the Quebec–Ontario border. As their name and surrounding band names suggest, Algonquin territorial organization and land management are based on these watersheds and waterways that serve as boundaries for family, band, and national territories. The Algonquins once traveled extensively along these watery highways, spending their winters in the bush in extended families, hunting large game like moose and deer, and trapping fur-bearing animals, particularly beaver, which were of critical socioeconomic and cultural significance. The community lived relatively well by hunting, fishing, trapping, gathering plant foods and harvesting traditional medicines, with occasional subsistence gardening, as encouraged later by missionaries. The Barriere Lake Algonquins were also part of an extensive trade network with the Huron and Odawa to the south and southwest of their own territory, from whom they could obtain trade objects, such as wampum beads, and agricultural and fishing products in exchange for furs and dried fish.[14]

Dams have flooded many river waterways in the region today, though elders can still recall the direction of the currents that flow beneath the wide, deep lakes and reservoirs. Families maintain their summer and winter cabins, sugar bushes, medicinal harvesting sites, and traplines. Community members still build their homes and hunt without provincial permits on their territory. But most families now divide their time between the bush and the Rapid Lake Reserve. Norman Matchewan, son of longtime former customary chief Jean Maurice Matchewan, remembers his grandmother returning to the reserve, head bloodied from blows inflicted by game wardens.[15] She had been accosted for hunting and resisted their attempts to confiscate her moose. Game warden

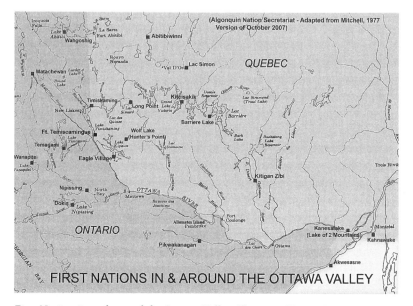

First Nations in and around the Ottawa Valley. Algonquin Nation Secretariat, 2007.

repression is not nearly so bad today with the recognition of Aboriginal hunting and fishing rights,[16] though Norman explained to me that several years ago when he was out hunting, a game warden blocked him in with his jeep and upon Matchewan's return from the bush, the warden informed him that he could not hunt without a permit. Norman in turn informed him, "This is my land, I can hunt when I want." The warden checked Norman's gun for bullets and let him go because the gun was not loaded, but he told Norman he would have to keep his gun in the trunk. Norman refused: "What if I see an animal and need to shoot it?" But he was not particularly angry about the stop and search. "I just explained to him that this was my land, so that he could understand."[17] Nothing the government had ever said or done had persuaded him to the contrary.

In the early history of contact, the fur trade governed relations between the Algonquins, the French, and other settlers. The Algonquins of the Ottawa Valley were trading with the French as early as the second half of the 1500s through Montagnais middlemen along the Saguenay River.[18] The Algonquin nation formally entered into alliance with the

French in the first decade of the 1600s, along with the Montagnais, Odawa, and Huron.[19] The elders at Barriere Lake contend that when the French approached them to become military allies, they made an agreement that the Anishnabe nation would always "be in front" when it came to the land because the Algonquins had their own laws to follow. But the government "has not remembered this agreement," according to Toby Decoursay, and instead has gone about destroying the land.[20]

Barriere Lake's alliance with the French was eventually overturned by the fall of Quebec in 1760, marking a new era of diplomacy between the British and formerly French-allied nations. Known as the Seven Nations, or Seven Council Fires, these former French allies included Christianized Hurons, Iroquois, Abenakis, Algonquins, and Nippisings, and their "allies and dependents," which included non-Christianized bands such as Barriere Lake.[21] Barriere Lake has created a copy of the seven-diamond wampum belt symbolizing this alliance. The Algonquin nation, as part of the Seven Council Fires, signed a series of treaties with the British Crown. The Treaty of Swegatchy (1760) (now Ogdensburg, New York) ensured that the Seven Nations would remain neutral and the parties agreed to the principles of peace, protection of land rights, and freedom of religion. The Kahnewake Treaty (1760) promised peace, alliance, mutual support, free and open trade, antitrespass, protection of land rights, freedom of religion, and economic assistance.[22] These treaties fully incorporated the Seven Nations and allies into the long-standing Covenant Chain Treaty Alliance between the British and the Iroquois, and would have applied to Anishnabe of the Upper Ottawa Valley, including the Algonquins of Barriere Lake, whether or not members were at the 1760 treaty councils.[23]

The Algonquins were also included when the Covenant Chain was polished in 1764 at the Treaty of Niagara, which ensured that no Indian lands could be sold before first being ceded to the Crown.[24] Implicit in these assurances was that Indians owned their lands and that their British allies would protect them from exploitation. The Royal Proclamation of 1763, issued by King George III, ensured these provisions of cession and surrender a year earlier and remain enshrined in section 35 of the Constitution Act of 1982, and in section 25 of the Charter of Rights and Freedoms. However, two central differences between the Treaty of Niagara and the Royal Proclamation speak to the importance of the Niagara treaty as a founding constitutional moment of the settler colony. While the Royal Proclamation unilaterally stated these provisions of land transfer, the Niagara treaty was a mutual agreement, made between more than two thousand chiefs from twenty-four nations and the British Crown, that followed the legal protocols of Indigenous diplomacy on these lands.[25] The wampum at Niagara represents the mutually affirmed relationship of peace, friendship, and noninterference set out in the two-row wampum presented there.[26]

The Algonquins never ceded their lands under the provisions of the Treaty of Niagara. Their lands continue to be governed under the Mitchikanibikok Anishnabe Onakinakewin. Although Barriere Lake signed treaties, none were land treaties. What Barriere Lake does have, however, is a wampum belt dating back to the 1760s that provides evidence of an agreement between the band and the French and British Crowns ensuring the Anishnabe control over their lands. Advisers to the community believe that the wampum was exchanged concurrently with the Articles of Capitulation—in particular Article 40, which affirmed the autonomy of Indians and Indian lands—because the content of the belt makes sense of the transition from French to British rule.[27] The belt was originally constructed from wampum shells, which are beads manufactured from the lining of conch and quahog clamshells, and provides a mnemonic device to record alliances.[28] It depicts three figures in white against a purple background: the Anishnabe in the middle, with French and British representatives on either side, and a white Christian cross to the left of the figures. No mere forgotten relic, Chief Solomon Matchewan read the belt at the 1982 First Ministers Conference to remind the governments of the sacred covenant that had been recorded through customary law. Maurice Wawatie simultaneously translated the reading:

> What our Chief has mentioned is this historic agreement between the French-speaking nations, and the English-speaking nations and all the Indian nations. According to the reading of this wampum belt we have seen to today, is that there had been a negotiation dealing with this land. That the representative of the French speaking nation on one side and the representative of the English-speaking nation on the other side, and on the centre is the Indian nations. And it was agreed at this time that the Indian nations would always be leaders in their homelands. And anything

that was supposed to be negotiated upon, that they would have to negotiate with the Indian people, regarding jurisdictions and how to deal with each other, respecting equality of each nation. That the Indian people will always be the leaders of this continent. And upon finishing this agreement a representative from the Vatican, the priest, was there to bless this agreement, this historical agreement that had taken place at this time. And he pointed toward heaven when he blessed it, this agreement.[29]

The belt depicts an understanding, under the sign of the cross, but through an Indigenous protocol of diplomacy, that no interference would be made into the local Anishnabe ways of life. Woven into hairpins and stamped onto their letterhead, the three-figure wampum has endured to this day as a symbol of the pact between nations. The belt would also provide the interpretive framework for the Trilateral Agreement.

The three-figure wampum embroidered into Elder Toby Decoursay's jacket below the words Mitchikanibikok Inik. Photograph by author.

A Steady Accretion of Restrictions to Self-Determination

If Barriere Lake never signed land treaties and never ceded their territory according to the constitutional provisions, then on what legal
and moral grounds were Barriere Lakers denied the authority to govern
their lands?[30] Colonialism in Canada seems to present a continuum between the uncontested exercise of Indigenous jurisdiction, the steady
accretion of restrictions and regulations that control the use and access of Indigenous peoples to their lands, and the perfection of state
sovereignty in the form of absolute dispossession and obliteration of
Indigenous law.

Advisers to the Barriere Lake Algonquins have used the term "alienation" to describe the ways in which the community's land and resources
have been "planned, managed, used and impacted by non-Native peoples
and their institutions and industries," without signifying physical or
legal dispossession.[31] "Alienation" is also legal term applied to define the
process by which Indigenous peoples can transfer their sui generis title
to the land to the Crown. But formal sale or surrender was not required
to introduce the severe constraints endured by Indigenous peoples
on their lands by a staggering number of Crown and private authorities.
Alienation can also advance through extralegal processes that remove
the responsibility for the land from Indigenous governments and redis-
tribute authority to a wide range of agents and institutions.

A complete history of alienation at Barriere Lake is beyond the scope
of this work, but a survey of human-made impacts on Barriere Lake's
land over the past century is key to contextualize Barriere Lake's demand for a resource comanagement agreement on the territory. The
Trilateral Agreement was designed to mitigate the destructive effects
of commercial lumber extraction, hydro generation, and other physical
incursions that were facilitated by a dense web of federal and provincial
regulatory regimes. Although Barriere Lakers continue to hunt, fish,
trap, travel, settle, and gather medicines on their land, infringements
on their jurisdiction have taken place through a proliferation of incursions and other microprocesses fueled by new bodies of authority popu-
lating their lands.

Settlement on Barriere Lake lands occurred relatively late, unfolding simultaneously to some of the first years of contact between the
British and Salish nations on the western coast of Canada. Although

Barriere Lake had been active in the fur trade, they followed a pattern established in the north, with most of their contact with newcomers happening between handfuls of individuals at established trader forts throughout the territory. In the 1860s, as the fur trade in Barriere Lake's region waned and a period of war came to a close, logging moved to the upper reaches of the Ottawa River, along with permanent European settlement. Logging replaced the fur trade as the main economic activity in the territory, and with logging came incursions by white settlers who hunted and trapped indiscriminately, decimating wildlife populations, and ushering in waves of epidemics of smallpox, diphtheria, measles, whooping cough, and influenza.[32] By the 1870s, the government of Quebec had leased out much of Barriere Lake's traditional territory to timber companies—611 timber limits were licensed in the region north of the Ottawa covering an area of 15,794 square feet of cut timber.[33] From 1870 to 1913, an incredible 59 percent of Quebec's timber revenue came from the two regions that make up the Algonquins of Barriere Lake's traditional territory.[34] The province's fortunes were built on the pillage of Algonquin lands.

A log flotation dam was constructed at the outlet of Cabonga Lake in 1871, backing water up to Barriere Lake settlements and disrupting the natural currents, and therefore the transportation routes and habitats for the people, fish, and animals. Demand for squared timber was already on the decline, but was soon replaced by the sawn lumber industry, and then the infinitely more destructive pulpwood industry, a forest devourer that ushered in an era of mills and larger dams at the turn of the twentieth century.[35] Short-term gains had devastating effects on the long-term occupants of the territory; in Barriere Lake, the people began to starve and die. The Department of Indian Affairs reports from 1875 to 1878 show a rise in relief costs across northern Quebec owing to scarcity of game.[36] The adverse effects from logging were exacerbated by health epidemics brought on by increased contact with the northward migration of settlers. Meanwhile, Quebec plundered the forests for a song, exporting mostly raw materials to the United States and Britain, and engaging in only minor primary processing domestically.[37] The industry was badly mismanaged owing to meager attempts at reforestation, extensive foreign ownership, and volatile commodity prices.[38] For the Algonquins, this ambivalence meant the disappearance of a natural pharmacy, losses of home and wildlife habitat, and diminishing heritage and social peace.

While the federal government did attempt to intervene on Barriere Lake's behalf, Quebec refused to even acknowledge the presence of the Algonquin people in the region. In 1929, no one bothered to inform the community that the Gatineau Paper Company, a subsidiary of the Canadian International Paper Company (CIP), was constructing dams to form a reservoir one hundred square miles wide on their territory with a holding capacity of 43 billion cubic feet.[39] The community was forced to relocate their settlement, leaving behind two cemeteries that were badly damaged and twenty-three destroyed homes.[40] Compensation of thirty dollars was offered to the heads of each affected family for this massive relocation and cultural damage.[41] A few years later and further to the south, CIP constructed more dams to provide power to their mills, this time flooding an additional 150 square miles of land in the heart of the Algonquins' traditional territory to create the Baskatong reservoir.[42]

Early records show that the Algonquins did what they could to stop the flooding of their territory. One incredible record describes Hugh Ray's encounter with the Algonquins of Barriere Lake—or the *gens de terre,* as he called them—as he traveled up the Ottawa River in 1932 to take charge of the Kakabonga Hudson's Bay Company post. He describes a point in the rapids where whitefish and trout tried to come up from Lac Barriere Du Nord to spawn, and "the Indians placed stones at the head of the rapids to turn the fish into the bay above the rapids when they could scoop them out with scoop nets."[43] To Ray's astonishment, the Indians had cut half the dam away, likely with their bare hands or wooden instruments, in order to release the waters from the foot of Lac Barriere Du Sud. The Mitchikanibikok Inik were resolute in the persistence of their traditional harvesting techniques despite the invasive infrastructure on their lands.

Even bigger changes were to come in 1938 with construction for the Mont-Laurier–Senneterre highway (now Highway 117), which opened the region for tourism and sport hunting. Fiercely independent, the Barriere Lake Algonquins pushed deeper into the forest to escape the intrusion. Authorities did their part to encourage their disappearance: Quebec banned the community from hunting and trapping along the ten-mile corridor created on either side of the highway for tourist recreation.[44] The logic of prohibition was to recoup the costs of highway construction through tourism, but the unspoken assumption was that, if sighted, the Algonquins might scare away the whites.[45] The racist scheme failed regardless, as the Algonquins refused to avoid the corridor, and enforcement, proving futile, was abandoned.

The highway also ran directly through the Grand Lac Victoria (GLV) Beaver Preserve, a conservation area created following a joint federal-provincial conference on Wildlife and Fisheries, where the concept of Indian-only preserves was raised. Two game preserves were created as a result: the Grand Lac Victoria Beaver Preserve (6,300 square miles) and the Abitibi Beaver Preserve (4,000 square miles), which were established in 1928 by a Quebec Order-in-Council and covered much of the hunting and trapping territory in the Algonquin communities of Grand Lac, Lac Simon, some lands from Winneway and Wolf Lake, and some lands of Barriere Lake.[46] The beaver preserves were conceived as the solution to the extreme exploitation by settlers that had led the province to simply "close" beaver season to everyone, including Indigenous peoples, who first suffered the privations of settler incursions and then the state's punitive measures against settler greed. At the insistence of fur supervisor Hugh Conn, traditional Algonquin adaptive management strategies regulated the preserves. Conn identified two major Algonquin conservation methods for beaver—rotation of trapping areas and managed culling of beavers in their houses—and also cautioned about the placement of the reserve on Algonquin lands, because "every square mile in the forested portion of Eastern Canada, was owned and occupied buy [sic] tribes, bands, families of Indians even as we divide into provinces, counties, townships and lots."[47] Conn also pointed out to state authorities that the boundaries of the preserve were disruptive. But even given his sensitivity to Algonquin laws and their tenure system, the community remained skeptical. The imposed management regime angered them, especially the arbitrary boundaries drawn onto the territory that disrupted their decentralized kinship landholding system.[48] While the other Algonquin bands gradually eased their suspicions of Conn's efforts, Barriere Lake remained intransigent.[49] Then, in the 1920s and 1940s, the province set up trapline systems to regulate access to small fur-bearing animals outside the preserves, which further broke up the traditional land base and undermined the authority of the customary government. Lands were lost, despite another well-intentioned, though ultimately ineffective, conservation effort.

In 1950, the ten-mile hunting corridor along the highway was expanded to become the La Vérendrye Wildlife Reserve. It created new
jurisdictional conflicts between the Algonquins and provincial authorities. As an Algonquin sense of embattlement grew, so did their resistance to the loss of their lands. Throughout the late 1940s and for the
next couple of decades, the Algonquins refused to abide by restrictive
laws mandating permits for hunting and trapping. They further refused
to be searched for "illegal" beaver pelts by police authorities after trapping had been banned; as a result, they were blackballed and refused
trapping licenses.[50] They further resisted drawing maps of their hunting
territory or to provide demographic information for government collection.[51] In a constant state of adaptation, the Algonquins came to rely
in this period on a mixed economy to supplement their traditional livelihood, engaging in waged labor employment that included trapping,
seasonal work at fur farms in the United States, cutting trees for CIP,
and guiding moose hunters.[52]

Ten years after a substantial swath of their territory was turned into
a park, Quebec finally transferred some land to the federal government
to establish a reserve for the Barriere Lake Algonquins. The community
had been petitioning for land since 1876 and the reserve was finally created in 1961.[53] But the reserve introduced a new slate of problems. They
were given a measly fifty-nine-acre plot of eroded and sandy land totally
insufficient for a few hundred people. In addition, no core infrastructure
was built and no community development plan was established.[54] There
was a lack of firewood nearby; dwellings were not numerous enough; no
groceries were sold on-site; hunting was restricted nearby because of
the overuse of strychnine by provincial authorities to kill wolves, and
the poison was also fatal to beavers and small game; and mechanized
forestry decimated the landscape.[55] The government believed that the
reserve land at Rapid Lake would silence complaints and satisfy the Algonquin band's land claims: it was an accommodation of needs, rather
than a recognition of rights.[56] However, the Algonquins of Barriere Lake
never considered the reserve to be a settlement of their land claims, but
simply as lands set aside from settler incursion. The reserve was sited
on land called Kitiganik, which translated roughly to mean "place to be
planted" or "plantation." The land was once literally a plantation, cultivated as a tree farm of *okik* (jack pines) after a natural forest fire spread
across the lake and burned through the bush. But it came to have a sec-

ond meaning, according to some—that the Algonquins saw themselves as *planted* there by the government, and did not intend to stay there permanently.

That Barriere Lake did not get a reserve until 1961 meant that the community had not had reliable access to schools, medical provisions, housing, or other assistance until after this point. But it also meant a transition to a crowded life of year-round habitation as opposed to the traditional, decentralized form of socialization to which the community was accustomed. As a result, the reserve was mostly deserted for the first couple of decades after its creation. The generation born in the early 1980s, such as Norman Matchewan, still spent most of their early days in the bush. Although Barriere Lakers supported the idea of having lands set aside exclusively for their use, the shock of a measly fifty-nine acres must have been great. To get the reserve, the federal government (eager to resolve the persistent petitioning, but unable to grant provincial lands), the Hudson's Bay Company, and a Catholic order of Oblates petitioned on Barriere Lake's behalf, at first requesting four hundred acres, then, by 1946, for six hundred and fifty acres to be set aside. They were rebuffed by Quebec because the Land and Forests Act does not provide for the transfer of land to the federal government, except in the case of long-term leases, meaning that the Indian band would not get title to the land as requested.[57] Finally, in May 1961, the deputy minister of Lands and Forests approved the lease of fifty-nine acres and a few months later a Quebec Order-in-Council was passed.[58] The community was split over the decision to "plant" at this tiny Rapid Lake site—many people remained at the traditional Barriere Lake settlement and others remained permanently settled in village sites around the traditional territory, excluded even from the minimal resources offered on the reserve.

Barriere Lake was considered a priority for being allocated a reserve by the federal government because their land was so adversely affected by timber development. But conditions in the forest did not improve. In the 1970s, a meeting was held with government officials at Rapid Lake. Paul Matchewan complained about the continuing impacts of settlers on the Barriere Lake people: "The moose, the birds and the fish, things by which his people lived, were being slaughter [*sic*] by licensed hunters from outside. The government derives the benefit."[59] Continuing efforts were made to gain back control over resources on their territory. Several Algonquin bands passed a joint resolution in 1979, including the Algonquin leadership of Maniwaki, Lac Simon, Grand Lac Victoria, Abitibiwinni, and Barriere Lake, "[r]esolving that the area known as Grand Lake Victoria Indian Hunting Preserve, situated within the boundaries of La Vérendrye Wildlife Reserve, be henceforth reserved for hunting, fishing and trapping exclusively by the Algonquin people."[60] Their resolution was ignored.

The toll of residential schooling also wore on the community. Toby Decoursay explains that people had become afraid of what God might do to them and individuals were also dealing with deep internal scars of sexual and physical abuse, as well as from being separated from their parents who had trustingly sent them away. The children attended the French Roman Catholic boarding school—Pensionat Indien de St. Marc-de-Figuery—north of the reserve in Amos, Quebec, and the English-speaking Spanish Boys' and Girls' School in Spanish, Ontario. Most of the children were sent to Amos, where the Oblates ran the school. When the children tried to tell their parents what was done to them, their families thought that they were making up stories in order to stay home. They simply could not believe the stories might be true. Other parents resisted the pressure to send their children to be educated in the white man's world and kept them in the bush hidden away from the missionaries. Jean Maurice Matchewan, Maggie Wawatie, Rose Nottaway, and others lived with their grandparents in village sites and cabins deep in the forest where they could not be found.

The sway of the church affected the community's incentive to fight back. The priests persuaded the people of a punitive cosmology that frightened the community from protecting the land and their children. Decoursay explained: "That's why the people got so weak, you know. 'You don't hurt nobody, you don't fight, love each other, even the white man . . .' So when the people first saw the white man cutting the trees there, they didn't do anything. [The priests said]: 'Let the God do something, they're going to take care of it sooner or later.' So no Indian was going to fight back, because he was afraid of their God, of making a mistake, he has to be good all the way, just to go to heaven, or somewhere. That's what the people are being told. So every night before they go to bed, they say thanks, even in the morning because you didn't die there in the night."[61] That is the reason, he explained, that people did not fight for their rights for a long time.

A number of events transpired to shift the political winds at Barriere Lake. A quasi-religious movement—fervently anti-Christian, based in the town of Maniwaki—convinced community members to take down the cross from the church and the cemetery.[62] Elders in the community were also beginning to stir on their own accord. Decoursay's grandfather, Paul Matchewan, stood up for his rights because he saw that the children did not have enough food to eat, and he saw that the white men in the territory had overhunted the marten, the lynx, and, for a long time, the beaver.[63] Then, around the 1980s, Decoursay took up his grandfather's cause and started talking to the people, telling them that Catholicism and Christianity were not for them. When his grandfather passed away, he inherited a drum. And in a sense, he began to beat it, and things began to change.

Dispossession and the Boundaries of the State

This chapter surveyed some effects of state power on Barriere Lake's lands and has afforded us an early opportunity to reflect on the meeting of settler-state law in relation to Indigenous jurisdiction. The processes of dispossession that unfolded at Barriere Lake—what I identified as (1) the slow violence of losing the capacity to exercise care and (2) alienation—were crucial conditions for the constitution of the settler state. These techniques drew the boundaries of the state at the limit of its capacity to exploit Algonquin lands for its natural resources. Each time the Algonquins refused and fought back, the state attempted to redraw its lines of authority and power.

Timothy Mitchell argues that the boundary of the state "*never marks a real exterior*" because the borders between state and society are not intrinsic entities.[64] Social and political order is maintained rather through an internal network of institutional mechanisms. To analyze these internal methods of order that comprise the modern state, Mitchell offers a number of diagnostics, including addressing the state as "an effect of detailed processes of spatial organization, temporal arrangement, functional specification, and supervision and surveillance, which create the appearance of a world fundamentally divided into state and society."[65] State authority is produced and reproduced by drawing this line of difference around its shifting spheres of influence. In this light, settler-state logic is not a hegemonic logic "out there" but a specific and active construction of authority through the limit-making practices of jurisdiction we can observe being exercised on Barriere Lake lands.

The boundaries of the state are set by the limits of Indigenous juris-diction, but international processes of accumulation also define them, and in turn bear significant agency in processes of Indigenous dispos-session. A key frame through which the international dynamic of state formation has been examined in Canada is through staple theory. Can-ada is what some economists refer to as a "staple state" because of a bias toward its natural resource economy.[66] The "staple theory" of Canadian development is a model designed to account for the unique economic development of a peripheral state within the global system. Staples are minimally processed resources and they set the pace for economic growth because their underdevelopment can deprive regions of invest-ment in complementary industrial and commercial businesses and em-ployment. According to Harold Innis, growth is continually frustrated in Canada because the staples economy is always ensnared in a staples trap: diversification through domestic processing is blocked by produc-ers, often foreign-owned multinational corporations, which do not in-vest in value-added domestic processes prior to export, thus stifling eco-nomic expansion.[67] This theorization of the state presents a local model of economic dynamics. Innis, the author of the staple state theory, did not present a crude core–periphery model, but rather theorized both specific forms of internal differentiation and international cycles of ac-cumulation as crucial to understanding the domestic economy.[68]

Staples theory has a long history of interpretation within chang-ing currents of intellectual thought in Canada.[69] Paul Kellogg's *Escape from the Staple State* convincingly debunks the status of Canada as a staple state, arguing that as an advanced capitalist state—signaled by the organic composition of capital and other key indicators, such as membership in the G8—it is hardly a dependent, underdeveloped hinterland.[70] Although Canada may no longer qualify as a staple state, it is still a land-based economy. As Michael Howlett, M. Ramesh, and Anthony Perl write: "Much of Canada's manufacturing base consists of processing resource-based commodities such as lumber, pulp and paper, and various mineral and oil-based products . . . In all, resource and resource-based activities generate as much as fifty cents out of every dollar produced in this country."[71] Much of this production is destined for export.[72] International trade, as well as foreign direct investment in the natural resource sector, influences state regulation, and is likewise affected by Indigenous assertions of jurisdiction against the state regulation of their lands.[73]

Kellogg readily concedes the centrality of settler colonialism in making sense of the Canadian economy. As he states in an interview: "The [Truth and Reconciliation Commission] report highlights the way in which the acquisition of land and the establishment of capitalist sovereignty were accomplished through racism and violence."[74] But Kellogg still refers to the acquisition of Indigenous lands in the past tense. When he describes the need to go beyond a class analysis to understand the pockets of poverty and uneven development in Canada, he indexes the reserve of Akwesasne as a reminder in his youth of the violent dynamics of dispossession that underpinned industrialization in Canada, again situating dispossession as a prior stage of national economic development.[75] These admissions are important, as they mark a paradigmatic approach to Canadian political economy that tends to sideline the question of land, even while centering its commodification in the resource sector.[76] This point is one that I will develop throughout the book, especially in chapters 5 and 9, but I want to signal its significance here.

I also want to mark two further issues regarding the boundaries of the settler state in light of Indigenous assertions of jurisdiction, particularly as they pertain to the resource sector. The first regards the general absence of Indigenous jurisdiction as a key feature in theories of the Canadian political economy. The second, building on the first, considers how we can interpret Marx's theory of primitive accumulation as an important analytic for reincorporating Indigenous lands into theories of the settler-colonial state, therefore developing a deeper sense of the meaning of "dispossession" in Canada.

The general absence of Indigenous land, sovereignty, and jurisdiction in theories of Canadian political economy is surprising, given the challenge to Canada's underlying title to the land through Indigenous opposition to development, pipelines, mines, clear-cut logging, and oil and gas production.[77] One of the obstacles to addressing Indigenous jurisdiction within the field of political economy is that Indigenous peoples' resistance to colonization has been almost completely written out of Canadian economic historiography. For example, eminent scholars such as Harold Innis and Stanley Ryerson offered a view of Indigenous peoples with diminishing returns: as beaver were depleted, Indigenous societies were destroyed and the sun set on native life.[78]

Frances Abele and Daiva Stasiulis document the "white settler colony" thesis that predominates in Canadian historiography and figures into the new political economy studies of Canadian capitalist development, where scholars continued to mostly ignore Indigenous land interests and economies.[79] An example of such exclusion that Abele and Stasiulis provide is Marxist scholar Leo Panitch's exclusion of the entire treaty process and Métis uprisings in his account of capitalist development in Canada throughout the nineteenth century. Although Panitch foregrounds a crucial link between the staple economy and industrialization, he never explicitly mentions Indigenous land. The irony is that he describes the importance of transportation infrastructure in linking these economic forms but fails to notice the political processes that were opening this land for development. He writes that the railway created a class of petit-bourgeois farmers on the western end of the line and an industrial proletariat on the other, in southern Ontario.[80] The conditions that supplied the land for small farmers to become petty capitalists would be the numbered treaties, one through seven, which dragged a shovel through the west, across the provinces. Between 1871 and 1877, these treaties were negotiated to secure a valuable circuit for industrial production, ensuring access to the fertile southern lands of the prairies and paving the way for the railroad.[81] Despite the eulogies, Indigenous peoples have participated and continue to play a critical role in the nation's political economy post-fur trade and military alliance, and their lands form the literal bedrock to the nation's fortunes.[82]

Theories of primitive accumulation, on the other hand, suffer from a problem of overexposure in relation to colonization. Rather than leaving Indigenous peoples out of the picture, the issue here is that colonization has been so tightly intertwined with capitalism—historically and structurally—that it becomes difficult to disentangle particular forms of settler-state dispossession from the totality of capitalism's ostensible reach.

To take a step back, the process whereby noncapitalist societies are drawn into the market economy is what Marx called "primitive accumulation," where he identified (and politicized) the process that separates workers from their means of production as also what enslaves them to wage labor: dispossession from land invokes people's need to seek paid work to survive.[83] This violent process of dispossession, then, is a primary, necessary feature of capitalism.[84] The site-specific meaning of primitive accumulation in a settler colony complicates its place as a historical stage of capitalism, where Marx locates it temporally. It also complicates primitive accumulation's creation of a "rightless proletariat" that produces the class conflict at the heart of the capitalist system.[85] Marx himself saw that primitive accumulation does not usher in an immediate transformation from serf to wage laborer, but rather involves a gradual transfer of forms of entitlement from ownership based on labor to ownership based on capital.[86] But as Glen Coulthard notes, "when related back to the primitive accumulation thesis it appears that the history and experience of *dispossession,* not proletarianization, has been the dominant background structure shaping the character of the historical relationship between Indigenous peoples and the Canadian state."[87] Further, the kind of dispossession that aims to dismantle Indigenous forms of governance and social reproduction is *ongoing* and not simply a stage in the history of capitalism.

Robert Nichols suggests that disaggregating the concept of primitive accumulation into its constitutive parts can bring clarity to the concept of dispossession.[88] Although the persistence of colonialism today is a convincing premise that primitive accumulation is not simply a historical stage of capitalism, given the ongoing violent attempts at Indigenous dispossession, the structure of primitive accumulation is still in question. Nichols suggests that the strain is too great on primitive accumulation to account for all capitalist expansion and reproduction. Once capitalism has been established in the colonies, he suggests that what follows is "a succession of qualitatively unique spatio-temporal waves, simultaneously linking core-periphery."[89] Although these cycles of growth are not technically processes of primitive accumulation, they nonetheless establish a spatially specific movement that appropriates future forms of social reproduction, much as we have defined dispossession.

These spatial dynamics of accumulation have also provoked specific strategies of resistance and can help us to see the limit-making practices that shape the settler-colonial state through Indigenous assertions of jurisdiction. While Marx painstakingly outlines the social processes of primitive accumulation in the context of England, for example, through his attention to the New English Poor Laws (1834) that captured the dispossessed in workhouses, the colonies were simply taken by the *force* of this necessary violence.[90] What are the specifics of this force? What does it matter? It matters because Indigenous resistance to the colonial state emerges not in the space between subsistence and proletarianization, but from the social and legal orders maintained through Indigenous peoples' connection to the land and to their cultures. Indigenous assertions of jurisdiction over their lands and bodies have been foundational in anticolonial struggles, which compromise the capacity of governments to sell resources on lands that were never ceded or surrendered. It matters, because the natural resource economy is pivotal to the national economy of Canada, and it is time this fact was given more serious notice.

In the Algonquin world, ecological integrity is inextricable from economic principles. George Manuel, the Secwepmec leader, summarizes the principles central to all Indigenous economies: "Our economy carried on because it was being held together by a substance much stronger than the simple list of raw materials with which we worked. The roots and berries, fish and meat, bark and moss, are a list of ingredients that cannot by themselves make a whole cloth. There is only organizing when those raw materials are brought together on the loom of social values toward which people choose to work."[91] What does a political economy look like that is based on Indigenous law? How does the Algonquin loom of social values weave the limits of the national economy? These are questions we need to ask to see where and how Indigenous jurisdiction confronts settler law and accumulation.

3

Jurisdiction from the Ground Up
A Legal Order of Care

The authority of the province of Quebec to govern Barriere Lake lands has been largely driven by logics of accumulation and transaction. In the context of Barriere Lake's lands, permanent settlement never engulfed the territory because the creation of La Vérendrye Wildlife Reserve covered most of their lands. Incursions have been largely restricted to short-term, highly exploitative, profit-driven property relations that are specific to resource-extraction-based economies. With almost no private ownership on their lands, save for scattered outfitter establishments that predated the transition of the region into a provincial park, the primary property relation is the leasehold. The owner of this right has access to fish, hunt, log, camp, or mine within the regulatory constraints. The leasehold to mine or log is governed under the jurisdiction of the province, where the Ministry of Natural Resources has operated, in Jean Maurice Matchewan's blunt terms, in the service of "raping a wildlife reserve." In the next chapter, I describe the legal and regulatory system that drives provincial relations of jurisdiction as managed to ensure *supply*. In this chapter, in contrast, I draw from a number of sources to show that a key feature of the legal order of the Mitchikanibikok Inik is to ensure a relation of *care* over their lands and people.

This chapter is not an ethnography of Algonquin law. An elder, Eddy Nottaway, once bristled when I asked him about a story I had heard about the Onakinakewin. "Stories," he said, "sound like fairy tales or children's books. It is history that we are teaching you." So, perhaps it is most accurate to describe this chapter as tributaries of history that were shared with me and with other trusted researchers. These narratives and concepts provide thin but robust streams through thousands of years of experience in a cherished country. Toby Decoursay explained, "We know this land—we have a language for everything that happens here. That's what the Trilateral is about—that is why Barriere Lake has this and no other nation."[1] The Trilateral Agreement is an expression of what it means to be Mitchikanibikok Inik. It reflects the extensive knowledge and deep interrelationships the Anishnabe have with their territory. The Mitchikanibikok Anishnabe Onakinakewin is Barriere Lake's sacred constitution that contains the law for everything that grows on earth. It is not a set of ideas that can be written down, but rather embodies all of the living relationships in their world, which are governed by the principle of respect. The Trilateral Agreement was meant to ensure that the land was protected so that these relationships would not be lost. It grows directly out of the belts, wampums, and prophecies of the Barriere Lake Algonquins. To understand the conflict over jurisdiction on their territory, it is crucial to recognize the principles of Indigenous governance that are rooted in their legal order.

The time I spent in Barriere Lake between 2008 and 2012 was a period of incredible upheaval and turmoil and research trips were frequently disrupted when political organizing had to take priority. So, the time I spent on the land with community members was as often defined by the work I did as a researcher as the work I did as an organizer, working with the solidarity collective to contribute material resources to the community's political struggle. What I valued most about the time I spent on the land, in the midst of tireless travel and confrontation, was witnessing the deep love families have for their territory and the joy it brings them to spend time in the bush. This love gave people strength: it allowed community members to overcome intense fears of public speaking, to leave young children behind for days at a stretch, to suffer the deprivations of hunger and cold on the blockades, and to endure arrests, brutality, and criminal charges for protecting their responsibilities as Anishnabe people. These two chapters (3 and 4) represent the labor of Anishnabe people on the land, living their law, and take a closer look at the meaning of Algonquin jurisdiction that is at stake.

The Fire Begins the Teaching

Marylynn Poucachiche drove me out to sit with Toby Decoursay on one of my first trips to the territory. Toby told me, *This is where everything starts*: the three-string wampum. It represents the teachings of the Onakinakewin. Unlike the other wampums of Barriere Lake, the three-string is about spirituality, about "how the Anishnabe ruled," he explained.[2] The original three-string was made with a rock: a hole bored through the middle and three strips of hide laced and knotted through.

Toby said it could be buried somewhere on the territory, but no one is truly certain. He considered the newer wampum in his hand and said, "You can look at it this way—this is the earth, the sun, mother nature—everything that grows . . . Even animals—male bear, female bear, and a cub—and birds are like that, too."[3] As he spoke, he separated each of the three strips of hide along his hand, to show its components, and then gathered them together at the end of each count.

The kid who made the wampum was the kid everyone was waiting for. He left the footprint on the rock that is underwater now. He gave the Algonquins the feast and the drum. The little boy then traveled in all directions. There are many stories about his message and where he took it. How he meets with the other messengers, one from each direction, and eventually how he travels across the ocean until he finds the people with the invisible creator, the only ones with the creator that cannot be seen, and he argues with them, but they twist up everything, making a bible that hides many truths, like the power of the sun and the moon.

We were on Toby's land at Barriere Lake, near where the traditional settlement village was once located before it was flooded by dams. Toby wore a band around his forehead and a worn leather jacket. We had spent most of the afternoon with replicas of Barriere Lake's wampum belts, sitting on logs by the still water or on the screened-in porch when it rained. A large freezer stood nearby streaked with blood. Philomene sat by her husband's side each time we spoke and he consulted with her regularly. Toby was chosen at a young age to carry the customs of the Mitchikanibikok Inik. He is a quiet man in his mid-fifties, good-humored and patient, healed after many years of addiction stemming from his painful residential school experience where he was beaten and starved before finally running away for good. He first learned about the Trilateral when he was seventeen. The elders relayed to him a vision that the forests would disappear around them and the Onakinakewin would rise again.

The three-string wampum starts the teaching, Toby emphasized, of "what role to play, how to lead." The three-string wampum is the beginning of the teachings and usually appears when the fire is made. The first time Toby spoke to me of the Onakinakewin was by the fire, where community members had assembled on his land to hear the teachings. He told us then, "What we feed the fire is what comes from the land." He explained that the firekeeper starts the fire and each individual holds something—tobacco or something from the land—and then one by one they burn what they are holding as they speak what is in their heads and in their hearts. This is what creates the fire and this communion is what keeps the fire burning.[4]

A few months later, in his tiny wooden cabin on the Rapid Lake Reserve, Toby counted out the hide straps again. Philomene made tea and then took her place by his side. "The long string is the grandfather, next is the grandmother, then the young generation."[5] These separate components form a crucial whole. He told me about a cultural camp he ran for the kids many years ago. The community as a rehabilitation effort initiated it after sexual abuse charges were investigated on the reserve. The community had insisted that they had their own methods to deal with social issues that arose, and rejected federal programs run by outsiders. At the camp, the kids learned about their territory. They learned toponymy (Algonquin place-names) and a highly specific language of navigation, such as the word for the flow of the current when it splits around a small, mid-lake island. They learned about the medicines and how to harvest medicinal plants. Toby showed me a thick crust of black fungus the Algonquins harvest from pine trees. The *sikinagan* contains a crucial survival trick for winter camping: the black mold can hold an ember for an entire day, allowing hunters to spark a fire in the moist snow to keep them warm through the night. The fire will keep the campers warm, but it will also allow for the stories to be told.

Seasonal Openings Are the Doors to Respect

The Onakinakewin is an oral tradition embodied in the Mitchikanibikok Inik way of life, located primarily in the bush.[6] In Barriere Lake, nearly all stories about the Onakinakewin lead back to hunting. One night, Eddy Nottaway explained to me: "To understand the Anishnabe Onakinakewin, you have to know about hunting and you have come out trapping."[7] He reiterated what Toby had explained: "It's best to tell stories around the fire; that's when they all come back." Then he talked for a long time about trapping beaver. He said, "You have to wait days, weeks sometimes, for beaver." Beavers are clever, he warned. They want to outsmart you, but you have to wait them out. They can stay under for a long time, burrowed down, or escape through multiple exists, outwitting human observation. Others had cautioned me, as well, that if you abandon your hunt for the beaver midway through, you will be cursed with bad luck for the rest of the season. Stories abound of beavers anchoring unfortunate people for weeks to a den.

Understanding how to trap beaver is not simply learning a technique for killing the animal. Trapping is contingent upon understanding the seasons and connects to the ultimate goal of land management to ensure ecosystem protection. When I first met Barriere Lake member Michel Thusky and we were hanging out in my apartment in Toronto, the subject of beaver trapping came up. "You have to make sure you don't get the female beaver in the wrong season," he said. I asked how you could tell if it was male or female and he laughed as if I had made a great joke. "By how it swims!" he said, taken aback by the question. This was an unexpected flash of education for me about the meaning of care. City dwellers can claim, abstractly, to be concerned about the environment and the need to preserve watersheds and ecosystems for the benefit of human and nonhuman life, but we do not possess the ability to do the actual labor of care. When Michel described how one could recognize a beaver's sex by how it swim, he was indexing the crucial knowledge necessary to know which animals to take in order to fulfill conservation values. If too many of either sex are killed, a den will suffer, especially when there are babies that need caring for by their mothers. If beavers are taken in the wrong season, the young can suffer and affect the population's regeneration. When Eddy Nottaway described to me the beaver hunt, he lamented that the government did not understand that nobody owned the land, but that the Mitchikanibikok Inik had the knowledge to take care of it. This knowledge is the repository of hundreds of generations of Algonquins who have lived on the territory; it reflects a certain right mind and right intent in relation to the land. It reflects a certain kind of belonging to the land that is based, in a word, on *care*.[8]

Under Algonquin governing authority, land management is not governed by an instrumental attitude to the territory but is a reflection of the ways in which the bush is a sacred place. Sue Roark-Calnek, an anthropologist who worked with the community and lived on the territory for many years, has documented the "religious" nature of hunting in Algonquin life. She writes that "Hunting is a particular sacred occupation, requiring a moral and spiritual as well as a technical relationship with the game that are stalked (and the spiritual beings and forces that provide them or serve as their guardians)."[9] She lists the rituals that act out this belief: "divination for game; summoning the animals by their respective names and songs; elaborate precautions taken with animal remains, in particular bones and fetuses found in pregnant females inadvertently killed; 'talking to animals' in the bush; feasting; and offerings."[10] Taking an animal's life is itself part of the sacred regenerative laws of the living world. "If hunters comply with the above," she explains, "animals will offer themselves to be hunted when 'it's their time', and they will be reborn or regenerated for future hunts."[11] As an example of this ritualized practice, Toby talked about the old ways of moose hunting, how they used to put the animal to sleep by using a certain pine needle. They would sneak up on the animal at night wearing snowshoes, so they could determine whether it was male or female. If it was female, they determined whether or not she was carrying a baby and should be left alone. If not, they waited for her to sleep, then penetrated the needle slightly under her skin; the moose would jump up once pierced and run quickly for about two hundred feet before settling down to a deep sleep, in which case they would thank the animal and take its life to feed the community.

This kind of genius requires deep and loving care for the land and living relations. Hunting stories perpetually instruct in how to see the world from this Anishnabe perspective. As Michi Saagiig Nishnaabe writer Leanne Simpson writes: "If you do not know what it means to be intelligent within Nishnaabeg realities, then you can't see the epistemology, the pedagogy, the conceptual meaning, or the metaphor. You can't see how this story has references to other parts of our oral tradition, or how this story is fundamentally, like all of our stories, communicating different interpretations and realizations of a Nishnaabeg worldview."[12] Persistent sensitivities to an animal's sex—observed by the beaver's swim or the moose's gait—uncover more than just hunting tips for clinching a kill. There is also knowledge here embedded concerning temporal and seasonal cycles that are considered to be fundamental to understanding ecological relationships on the land—the growth of plants, movement of animals, and their reproduction cycles—and the role of the humans within these cycles. When Eddy's son, Clayton Nottaway, described knowing when to hunt, he talked in terms of temporal windows to explain their customs and reciprocal relationship with the natural world: "Let's say for a moose there, there's female, there's males, there's young calves. And you have to know when to collect their meat, when to shoot them. You have to recognize the body. You have to know what season, you have to know where they live, how they survive. 'Cause you're not just going to kill the first moose you see and not knowing what it is. There's certain times . . ." Clayton turned to his wife Mary-lynn Poucachiche and spoke to her in Algonquin, asking her to translate. "He's just saying, the bear, too. There's a certain time you kill a bear . . . In the fall there when you kill, it's like it opens the door, your door, for you to be a good hunter. If you kill it in the fall, it's the same. You don't kill it anytime and you don't just kill any bear. And then it opens a tunnel for you to become a good hunter."[13] Humans are part of the temporal ordering of the world and must respect the seasons to place the Algonquins in a harmonious relation with the other living beings with which they share the world.

The seasonal openings that Clayton discusses are reflected and expanded upon in the Indigenous Knowledge report, undertaken by Scott Nickels in anticipation of the Trilateral Agreement.[14] The report provides an incredible ethnobotanical and ethnohistorical record, and, as Roark-Calnek notes, taken together with her report on social organization and Terry Tobias's harvest study, it "actualizes the principles of the Onakinakewin in empirical social formations," by documenting the kinds of knowledge and social organization that define and protect Algonquin law.[15] In the Indigenous Knowledge report, Nickels brings to bear hundreds of hours of research interviews with Algonquin community members, cross-checked with customary knowledge holders, and painstakingly translated from Algonquin.[16] He details the four winds described by elders as "beings" who possess power to influence a range of conditions on the land, such as animal movements and hunters' fortunes. He notes that not everyone these days conceptualizes the winds as beings, but the winds are still always considered as instrumental to understanding weather patterns and seasons, and the conditions of success for hunting. To spiritual elders, the winds also explain how spirits "give" the animals to hunters. Kîwedinok, the north wind, is the Father who blows from the northwest and can be either beneficial or dangerous, bringing in cold air, snow, and ice, but also warm weather and game. Câwanok, the south wind, is the Mother who commonly blows in the summer months, and provides sustenance and growth for humans and animals. Wâbanok, the east wind, is the guardian of the animals, bringing the worst weather—freezing rain, humidity—perhaps to the benefit

of hunted animals. Finally, Nigabîyanok, the west wind, is the prevailing wind and is referred to as the boss or the leader. The winds connect
temporal and spatial categories because they transform the surface of
the earth through the seasons. Clayton killing a bear at the right time
in the season signals a balance between âkî (earth), âweysîsik (animals),
and ânicinâbe (human beings), as governed by the winds.

An elaborate classification system exists for the seasons as well, with
eight categories allotted to describe the changing earth cycles. As one
Barriere Lake elder eloquently described the complexity of the cycles:
you must think of the seasons collectively, the way you would observe
how the light and land gradually change over the course of a day.[17] The
seasons are Sîgon, Minokimin, Nîbon, Aptanîbin, Tigwâgan, Bidjîbibôn,
Pibôn, and Aptabibôn; they name the period from the first sign of spring,
when the snow melts slightly and develops a crunchy crust during the
day and the ice on lakes and rivers begins to thaw, to the last phase of
winter. In this final phase, there is extreme cold, the thickest crust of
ice and snow, and the daylight hours linger longer, and the sun rises
further north on the horizon and rises higher in the sky.[18] Each season
brings its own particular regimes of care and reciprocal obligations and
connects the small community to broader ecological and social changes
in the world.

Toby says the Onakinakewin teachings begin in May. "The reason they
say that," he explained, "is because that is when everything that grows
in nature, even the kids, the birds, the plants—that is when they start.
This period of life goes until November. A different set of teachings—
the winter teachings—begins in November. That is when the Algonquins
return to their winter cabins." In the bush the children learn respect for
the animals. "We used to teach why there's a beaver, why there's a moose.
Just like in that thing there," he motioned, referring to the three-string
wampum. "The kids, when they grow up, they're going to know . . . what
to respect, that's what Mitchikanibikok Anishnabe Onakinakewin is all
about."[19] In May, when the teachings begin and they make a feast, they
take the children to see the babies in their nests. "You say: 'Look she's
got a baby, just like you. But if you hurt the bird, the mom is going to get
angry, and if you kill the baby, the mother is going to be lonely, then.' But
when it is really time to work with the children, you have to bring them
to a place where there is no disturbance, like to a small mountain." Toby
described how to teach a child to meditate and to travel in time back hun-

dreds of years using something like the wind, because the winds have
been here since the birth of the world, or to use the call of the loon. That
is when you see something that you may or may not want to see or you
hear a voice. This is how people used to communicate without traveling,
with their minds, Toby says.

The children begin to learn at a very young age how to live with the
land. When Norman Matchewan was asked what the land means for
him, he answered: "It's where everything starts. It is our home. I grew up
connected to the land. I did my harvest with my family and I know how
important the land is to us—to Anishnabek people. Harvesting from
the land is our means of survival—we hunt, fish, and trap for food to
feed ourselves. We share food with families who do not have it. And it
is how our identity survives, as Mitchikinabikok Inik." Language is a
crucial part of the survival, he explains:

> Our language survives through our continued connection to the
> land. Much of our Indigenous language comes from the land—
> naming trees, medicinal plants, water areas, animals and differ-
> ent places. Each area of traditional territory has a specific name
> based on the landscape and the animals that frequent the area, for
> example *Waboos Washak* (Rabbit Bay), *Mitchikinabik* (Stone Weir),
> and *Enegoshik* (Ant hill). Gaining knowledge of our traditional
> lifestyle strengthened my identity as Anishnabe.

He continued: "I've always understood the land was there for us to protect, and understood our role as caretaker. As I grew up, I learned that,
in the face of clear-cut logging, tourism and sport hunting, we had to
continue to protect it, and that the blockades and visit to Parliament
Hill were the only ways the government would listen and work with us
to conserve the land."[20] Norman's role as caretaker is central to his identity as Anishnabe, but so too is the assertion of that jurisdiction against
the incursion of harmful agents.

Laxatives for Bears and Black Spruce for Pregnant Moose

Respect is easily the most important principle in the teachings of the
Onakinakewin and this principle is recited each time the law is invoked.
In *anishnabemowin*, the word is *mana'aji* or *sagi'dwin*, which translates as

harmony, or love for the other. Marylynn Poucachiche, a mother of five, and an active youth spokesperson for Barriere Lake, is often relied upon to travel and speak publicly on behalf of her community. This means that she often has to fill the gaps between worlds by describing for city dwellers what it means to live off the land. At an event during Indigenous Sovereignty Week in Toronto in 2010, she explained to an audience of more than a hundred people her understanding of Indigenous law:

> The people in the community they still use the land, go hunting, fishing, collect traditional medicine plants, and everything that we do for that, there's a teaching, there's knowledge. I guess it's safe to say there are laws in these teachings. Say, for example, one of the things that we've been taught, or that's been passed down, is *respect*—that's the biggest thing. Because we have to live together. We have to live in harmony together with nature and with the animals, with each other, with the settlers.[21]

The overriding principle of respect in Anishnabe culture is reflected not only in hunting, but also in education, family relations, and the gathering of medicines from plants and animals. The medicines, for example, are accompanied by their own teachings and language. Marylynn explains: "There's like, for example, if my child has a fever, there's a certain flower that I would go pick, I wouldn't just pick any flower, unless I know what it's used for. And you don't take that much, you only take what you need. How much you're going to use."[22] Embedded in the teachings of respect for medicines are the composite teachings of gratitude and trust. Marylynn illustrates this when she describes the practice of taking medicine: "And you know people sometimes don't like the smell of things or they think it's nasty. But it's medicine and that's where they teach us: con-winen-jig-wikin, which means, 'not to be disgusted.' This is what's going to make you feel better . . . And you get medicines from the beaver, from the skunk. I know everybody hates the skunk, but it's medicine in there."[23] During the discussion, Benjamin Nottaway, Clayton's brother, communicated to Marylynn in Algonquin and she continued: "That's the other thing, he just said, when you use the medicine, you don't just go pick it and use it. You have to believe in it. So you have to have digwitmween, belief. Bagwa-baga-giwin-tun, you got to use it."[24] The trust in one's ancestors that they have learned and cared for future generations with life-giving and healing knowledge conveys the original trust in the Creator, that the Algonquins have been placed in a territory where everything they could ever need to thrive has been provided for them.

Flipping through the pages of the Indigenous Knowledge report prepared for the Trilateral Agreement, one finds extensive, pages-long charts of Algonquin forest uses, covering food, beverage, medicine, utility, craftwork, ritual and ceremony and commercial uses, that involve the use of mammals, birds, insects, inanimate objects, fish, flora, and fauna. For example, the study shows which trees are good for snowshoes and baskets, which fish make the best glue, which insects indicate the best time to hunt sturgeon along the lakeshore. It details which bird feathers make the best down for pillows, blankets, and comforters and where to find dozens of berries, gums, teas, and saps for consumption and preservation. At least 104 plants have been used by the Algonquins for medicine that treats everything from kidney and urinary ailments, including medicines specifically for women to deal with menstruation and childbirth, as well as for treating cancer and diabetes. This knowledge is so comprehensively understood and researched that it involves preparations that detail, in one case, the addition of the ash of a particular flower to a tincture. One also learns in this report about the use of moose, beaver, and bears, especially for medicinal purposes—an area that is vastly underresearched and poorly understood in the scientific community but is suspected to be of extreme importance to the long-term health of wildlife populations, and represents only a fraction of Algonquin knowledge on the subject. For example, the Algonquins have observed that the beaver uses yellow pond lily *(cikitebak, akidimô)* for its lungs, the moose uses balsam fir *(aninâdik)* for wounds and sickness and black spruce *(sesegâdik)* to help females before giving birth, bears use trembling aspen *(azâdi)* for a spring tonic, laxative, and dewormer, and the black bear uses multiple kinds of bark (such as the white spruce, the mountain ash, and eastern white cedar) to help with hibernation.

Surveying an incredible wealth of knowledge, the author of the study, Nickels concludes: "The multiplicity of plant uses demonstrates the ingenuity of the Algonquin people and their intimate familiarity with the plant world. Few 'Western' Canadians would be able to recognize even a fraction of the plants listed, yet it is the ordinary Algonquin who makes use of such plants within their environment, qualities learned about through generations of observations and experimentation."[25] It is this knowledge, the Algonquins maintain, and their protection of it, that is the source of their jurisdiction.

This legal order of care that gives rise to Algonquin jurisdiction organizes land management according to principles of respect. But it does not only direct the external organization of authority: it also orders the community internally, within bodies, families, and the nation. Marylynn once described to me the culture of care that connects hunting to kinship networks on the reserve. She said that two weeks earlier six men went hunting and killed two moose. The wives of all those men skinned the moose, but Marylynn was not one of the women cleaning the meat because her husband had been excluded from the party owing to charges stemming from a blockade. "When they killed it," she said, "my brother was one of them. My husband can't go anywhere because he is under house arrest so he couldn't participate in the hunt. I asked my brother if he could share it with our family. He took his share and he shared it again between me and my father. That's how it gets divided; it's between the people that go hunting and their families." The two moose fed at least ten families as the meat was subdivided among the extended families of the hunters.

Respect also extends beyond what one knows to respect for what one does not know. *Mime-gwa-shike* is a tiny butterfly woman and *pana-bikwe* has been spotted sitting on the rocks by the river in a deep fog with her beautiful body, long black hair, and fins. Marylynn's grandmother saw a tinkerbell-like apparition flying around one morning in the deep fog. The creature immediately turned her face, so Marylynn's *kokum* (her grandmother) said to her, "Don't be shy. The Creator gave us each different faces and appearances, but we are all created by God." The creature turned her face back to her—*mime-gwa-shike*: it was butterfly woman. Few have caught glimpses of beings: they are reminders, though, of an oft-repeated maxim: one does not know what is out there. Coming from a community whose ancestors have occupied the same lands for thousands of years, the humility in that statement is profound. Many spiritual creatures and mind-bending powers have disappeared from Barriere Lake for the time being. But there are prophecies for when these forces of nature will return.

Governance, Animals, and the Feast

Up until 2010, Barriere Lake was one of only a handful of communities across the country that had never been subject to the election provisions of the Indian Act. Until then, they governed themselves by a custom of leadership selection that goes back hundreds, if not thousands, of years. Under Indigenous law, the customary government is not just about governance between people but involves coexistence with the nonhuman world. The feast *(nimokichanan)* best evidences this reciprocal relationship. In the past, songs were sung for the animals that gave their lives to the hunters and trappers. A handheld drum accompanied these songs and the animals were appeased by this music of gratitude from the Anishnabe.[26] Recently, Toby brought the practice of drumming back and recites a prayer over the food before they eat. Roark-Calnek explains that "[t]hese offerings both thank and propitiate the spiritual forces (now variously understood) who are responsible for the supply of food and for the change of the seasons."[27] Feasts have also played a crucial role in distributing information about the quality and quantity of food on the land and the commitment of families and individuals to participate in collective resource management.[28] These natural and social indicators embodied in ritual obligation contribute critical information to band members, essential in a decentralized society like that of the Algonquins.

The feast has always played a central role in Barriere Lake's governance system and it still does today. Feasts are held seasonally, as an offering to respected guests and to gather people preceding important community assemblies. Traditional foods are served, such as moose, partridge, beaver, and walleye, and the drum is beat, tobacco is put down, and prayers are offered. At a spring feast I attended in 2010, community leaders Maggie Wawatie and Rose Nottaway coordinated the food that was laid out on a sheet of plastic several meters long on the ground, while Toby walked around it pounding his drum in a heartbeat rhythm while everyone gathered. A joyous occasion had delayed the feast for hours: Eddy Nottaway had shot a moose by the lake and it had to be carved up and divided among families. I joined the women in their traditional role of cutting and distributing the meat. They teased me about my shaggy slices, but did not intervene with lessons, forcing me to watch and learn, as they do with their children. Before we ate,

Toby reminded people of the traditional Algonquin values of respect for the land and for one another. Norman Matchewan came around during the feast with a birch basket to which everyone contributed a bit of food from his or her plates as an offering of thanks to the Creator. That evening a community meeting was held in an adjoining clearing in the forest to discuss Canada's worrying attempts to impose a band council election system on Barriere Lake and the urgent matter of lumber companies trying to make their way back onto the land. The meeting was held in Algonquin, around a fire, with tea brewing in the center and distributed to members by Benjamin Nottaway, a former councillor and chief, who otherwise sat next to customary chief Jean Maurice Matchewan and listened attentively. As they strategized about how to resist these interventions, men and women of all ages stood to speak for long periods of time and their words were greeted with short exclamations of agreement or concern.

Toby says: "Every time we make a meeting with someone, we're going to offer people a feast. Like if we make a meeting, it's for the thanks, you come and share what's our knowledge. That's the reason why we use the feast. That's the way of saying 'thank you,' thanks that you have come."[29] In April 2011, a delegation of Indigenous land defenders from the Defenders of the Land network traveled to Barriere Lake along with some of their non-Indigenous allies to show support for the community's political struggle and build stronger working ties. To honor their guests and to welcome them to their territory in a customary way, the community hosted an elaborate feast on the Rapid Lake Reserve. Long tables were set with traditional foods and the guests were seated, joined by almost a hundred Barriere Lake community members. After the feast, a fire was lit, and people encircled it and solidified relationships. An elder from an Algonquin community just north of the Rapid Lake Reserve, Lac Simon, had been invited to the feast and was very moved by the community's traditional foods and the primary use of the Algonquin language, both of which had been largely lost in his community. He spoke of wanting to develop closer ties to Barriere Lake and to participate in language camps with Lac Simon youth. He cried as he remembered his own grandparents and all that they had labored to teach him. Eugennie Mercredi from Pimicikamak in Manitoba, who was leading a fight against flooding by Manitoba Hydro onto their lands, gifted Marylynn Poucachiche with a blanket for her leadership in community matters. This opportunity for the guests to recognize and honor the generosity of their hosts who had hunted for days to welcome them to the territory embodied the same powerful reciprocity that built an economy based on gratitude and shared sustenance with the nonhuman world.

The feast also reveals the way leadership roles at Barriere Lake are understood to be reflections of the animal world. For example, as Toby explains, the Bear *(Mako)* is like the chief. Therefore, at community feasts, respect is shown to the Bear:

> Mako is the head of that feast, and somebody's going to stand up and talk about *mookoo*. They usually have the feast on the ground, so they talk about Mako in that feast, how he represents the Indian people . . .
>
> Like a bear, it's almost like a traditional chief, you could say . . . the bear is the leader of the animals, so in the fall, when the bear's going to go sleep, you're going to ask him to open his door, that's how they explain this, the old people, 'cause the bear is going to go to sleep . . . it's like someone who wants [consumes] everything, like the bear, you ask him for everything, like partridge, moose, in the wintertime, to have something to eat in the wintertime. That's why they have a feast, and they ask for the bear's spirit, for the winter, to have a good winter, to have food, that's why they ask the bear. Because the bear is the leader of the animals, and the birds is for eagle, and the leaders of trees is the white pine. For the fish [it] is sturgeon. That's the one, *neozibi*. Every time you eat fish, you say thanks to sturgeon, but not to god.[30]

In her research, Roark-Calnek also recorded elders recounting the important role of the bear in the feast. As one elder told her: "Like in a feast like when we use a bear in that feast, this is like it represents our great grandfather, and when you talk about great grandfather he represents all the animals."[31] Songs are also used to honor the animals. As Toby Decoursay and Genevieve Matchewan Decoursay explain, all the animals have songs: "When the animals hear their song, they come spiritually to join in the feast." These same songs could be used to heal people through the animal spirit. Different songs are given for different purposes by the animals. On feast day, people would begin singing early in the morning and sing all day, taking turns, depending on what songs they had been given.[32] Much of this song was sadly lost through the residential school system.

Toby explained to me that the councillors represent figures from the animal world. But "councillors" is likely a new description for what were understood in the past as "helpers" to the chief, who had specific roles, such as convening the feast and minding the children. Roark-Calnek's interviews with dozens of elders show that the runner who gathers everyone to the meeting, for example, is the deer *(wâwâckecî)* and the spokesperson that kept the meeting in order was the figure of the wolf *(mahigan).*[33] Toby told me that the wolf works beside the chief, conforming to Roark-Calnek's description, and described the deer councillor's role as follows: "And here he's something like a messenger. When you have a meeting, this one is going to go around and . . . when you hear a drum . . . and as soon as you hear the drum, people are going to come. And the drum carrier is going to start at the end [of the community] and start drumming."[34] As we will see later, Barriere Lake was forced to codify its customary government to protect it from gross misinterpretation by Indian Affairs. The codified customs describe the role of the councillors as representatives of the four directions, rather than by their animal forms. But these representations may be connected. Practically, councillors were likely designated to oversee distinct sections of the entire territory, although they could still have played critical governing roles as represented by their animal form.

The "chief for life" is said to have *okima m(i)skew,* "leadership blood" or "chiefly bloodline."[35] Bloodlines are important at Barriere Lake and people in the hereditary line are preferred as leaders, though community members caution that this tendency should not be overstressed.[36] If a son were considered weak or incompetent—as was the case with David Makokos's son, whose father, grandfather, and great-grandfather governed for three generations, up until 1964—another capable individual in the community would be selected to lead who had "mixed blood"—an ancestral relationship to a hereditary line.[37] Interviews with community members consistently show that leadership qualifications are valued over heredity.[38] Doug Elias concludes that the reasoning for this flexibility is straightforward: "Survival for hunting peoples depended first and foremost on successfully harvesting the resources needed for food,

heat, clothing, shelter, protection, and so on."³⁹ Therefore, a chief's "connection to the land and knowledge of the lands and resources was far
more important that [sic] blood amongst most northern peoples."⁴⁰ The
territory was maintained through the selection of male leaders most
suitable to protecting Algonquin lands.

    While astute Indian Affairs bureaucrats recognized this relationship
(and therefore targeted customary governments for elimination), the
chief of Barriere Lake was usually dismissed as irrelevant in missionary
journals. As Peter Di Gangi learned, their skepticism about the chief was
based on how they interpreted his jurisdiction: "It is him who decides
when the band will leave their encampment, and who decides where the
next encampment will be. That is about the extent of his powers."⁴¹ From
Barriere Lake's perspective, the responsibility of moving people throughout the territory requires an incredible store of knowledge about a vast
territory and the resources it contains. It means understanding the migration of large game, the preferential access points for fishing and plant
harvesting, the history of family occupation throughout the territory.
Furthermore, this leadership in land allocation was done in service of a
profound and critical task of protecting the lands for future generations.
Elias elaborates: "The exact year-to-year deployment of the people on the
land is a consequence of a great many environmental variables, including
the distribution, quantity and quality of food resources; weather; presence and distribution of enemies and competing resource users; and so
on. Movement is also dictated by ceremonial and ritual conditions; social
obligations; the state of knowledge and information available; and the
health of the community population."⁴² Jurisdiction from an Algonquin
perspective deals fundamentally with these concerns about responsible
management and fostering attachments to the land.

    Leadership in Barriere Lake is selected so as to ensure that the On-
akinakewin will be protected. The customary leadership selection process begins with *Wasakwigan*, the "blaze marking" of the future chief
and councillors. The Elders Council leads a process of *Okinamowan*, for
"choosing who will be there," and who will be marked. Once again, the
value of adaptability is crucial. The elders look for certain qualities in
a leader, in particular, as elder Harry Wawatie emphasized, who was
a much-respected former customary chief, the quality of a "flexibly
minded person"⁴³—someone who could look at a problem from multiple

sides and arrive at a judicious solution. This quality is important because a chief generally holds his position for life; in Harry's beautiful phrase, the end of a chief's reign "tied a knot" in a long line of hereditary chiefs.[44]

It can take years to "blaze" a new leader. Once a suitable candidate or candidates have been identified, the elders convene a Leadership Assembly of the People. The purpose of this assembly is for the community to have a say. As Harry Wawatie explained: "All the people have to be the judge and decide if they want him for a leader, does everyone accept him . . . [it's] known if they found fault they would have to ask why they don't want him or what they think and if there's nothing or no faults, [if] there's nothing, he's recognized."[45] In this sense, culpability rests with everyone in this consensus-based system of governance. Reflecting this communally driven process, according to the Onakinakewin, the chief is at the bottom of the decision-making process, while the highest authority is the Anishnabek, "the people." The hierarchy descends from the people to *Ode* (family, or extended families), *Ketizijik* (the elders), *Nikanikabwijik* (the council), and *Oshibikewini* (the administrator).[46] As laid out in the codified Mitchikanibikok Anishnabe Onakinakewin, each institution carries its own responsibilities.

Whereas a chief must always be chosen, councillors can run for their positions.[47] In the days before contact and land alienation through the trapline system, there were traditionally four councillors, reflecting and representing the four cardinal directions and the corresponding areas of the territory. These councillors, sometimes called "subchiefs," were to look after the people and lands in their area. Sometimes the role of councillors overlapped with the chief's role. But Roark-Calnek notes that this is not unusual in a "segmentary social and political order" where "smaller local groups resemble larger regional groups in the way they work."[48] She also speculates that these four councillors "probably represent an old pattern of familistic authority in kin-based local bands, joined together in a larger regional band."[49] So, the kinds of entitlement that root leadership choices at Barriere Lake are based on a combination of kinship relations, hereditary lines, spiritual consciousness, and connection to the land. These are not rigid roles, but rather are advisory, in the context of a consensus-based community that empowers everyone to participate and influence decision making.[50]

It is difficult to capture women's roles in the leadership process based on the formal ceremony. The woman's role is considered inextricable from the man's position and therefore the woman is included in her husband's nomination process. But the women in the community are leaders in their own right, and they guide the organization of blockades, feasts, and community assemblies, and act as spokespeople for the community at rallies, public talks, and for media interviews. Their consensus-building role in the community was formalized in the past into a regular meeting structure, but today these exercises in leadership tend to be much less formal.[51] Women today are part of the blazing process and sit on the Elders Council where they play an instrumental role in selecting future leaders and advising the chief on how to conduct himself and directions he should take on behalf of members.

Algonquin-Speaking Animals and Identity and the Land

The Onakinakewin exposes the background picture of jurisdiction, the "legal expression of power,"[52] which is comported in the daily practices of hunting, gathering, speaking Algonquin, and living on Barriere Lake territory. Jurisdiction is vested in the band, kinship nexus, and external agreements with other First Nations and governments, but retains its integrity through quotidian land use and stewardship. Algonquin-speaking animals connect how knowledge of the territory relates to broader understandings of jurisdiction. Marylynn illustrates an ethics of reciprocal care in the following story about waiting out a moose at her bush cabin:

> Let's say, when you have a dinner out there in the bush, that's where my cabin is. And we've been trying to get a moose for quite some time, and we had a supper with the whole family in my cabin. And we started talking, my father-in-law started talking, trying to communicate, you know, through the mind. And we had supper, we had some traditional foods there, and I made a basket, a birch-bark basket. And we told all the kids there (in Algonquin): "Put a little piece of your food in that basket, it's like giving back to the Creator, so they will give back." And I told them, "Put some little bit in there so we can kill this moose that we want so we can get some meat." So we did that, and I made my daughter go in the bush and to put that basket over there and to say something, you know. And she came back, she said she made a prayer,

(*a-kiden-sa-sha-di-mos*), that's how I said it, "We're going to kill a moose." Sure enough, two days later, the moose came across our lake on Clayton's birthday, my husband's birthday. He shot it down. We had tons of moose meat, we were able to feed seven families . . . And that's one of the teachings that's being passed on from our generation.[53]

Community members say that the animals, for their part, well understand their relationship to the Anishnabe whose land they share. According to the Algonquins, the animals on Barriere Lake's territory understand Algonquin because it is the language of the land. Marylynn told me a story once about the time wolves gathered near her cabin in the bush one winter, watchful of her cabin. She and her family stayed indoors, but her father-in-law Eddy Nottaway went out and spoke to them in Algonquin. Go back home now, he ordered them, you are not welcome here now. The wolves eyed him for a moment, then turned around and went back into the bush.

Marylynn's *kokum,* her grandmother, also taught her at a very young age about this special relationship between the Mitchikanibikok Inik and the animals on their territory. Marylynn grew up at Ottawa Lake and Barriere Lake, and also spent some time in Nanotinik (also referred to as Kukomville). Like all the children of her generation, she was kept in the bush until she knew her language and the Algonquin way of life. She remembers one story her grandmother, Lena Nottaway, told her about a moose. Marylynn said, "I guess she was trying to teach me something." Her *kokum* walked by a moose on her way out hunting. They came across each other and they sort of communicated. "Not by talking there, but through the mind. And she was telling the moose (in Algonquin), 'I'm not going to bother you and you don't bother me.' 'Cause they're just coming across each other. And my grandmother said the moose just walked by and I walked by. That's how they communicated. And I guess that's how they've been communicating, and still communicate today, because sometimes I see them talking, even if they're not talking with their mouths. Like his dad will do that," she says, pointing at her husband, Clayton, and referring again to Eddy: "*A shim-shim mos, a shim-shi-man.*"[54] *Here moose, come here.* When you are in the bush, Marylynn explains, the bush talks to you in Algonquin. That is where the *pook-gin-ninee* live—the spirits who are always present on their land.

In his research with the community, Elias discovered a particular formulation of language acquisition that is profoundly based on one's relationship with the land:

> One community member, who contributed both toponyms and translations to the research, recently said that to use the land one needs to know "the language of the land, of the place." He meant by "language of the land" the toponymy for the area and other ways of describing and talking about it. When asked to elaborate on this, he gave an example about how he would talk about his area to guide someone to and through it. One learned "the language of the land" in the first instance from traveling through one's family customary use areas with older family members. But, he says also that one can learn "the language of the land" for other areas, when invited to hunt with the persons who know that "language" and are willing to share it.[55]

Or, as Norman Matchewan simply put it to me one day: "The land is my identity. Without my language, I lose that connection to the land."[56]

The laws of the Anishnabe embodied in the customary government are as much about protecting these sacred relationships as they are about governing relations between people. This sacred relationship is also embodied in the language. Michel Thusky is married to Maggie Wawatie and is an uncle to Norman Matchewan. Once, when discussing a language camp being held for the youth on their territory, Michel explained to me his reservations about this kind of formalized activity: "You cannot teach a language to your children, you have to *share* with your children. You can teach non-Indian people. But not your own children."[57]

For Marylynn, being Anishnabe is not an abstract identity but a deeply connected way of life. "There's endless work when you go to the bush," she says. "You never get bored there. You go out, practicing every day just by being out there. You don't have to go and pretend this and that, you know to be a good Indian, you just have to do your everyday stuff."[58] In "doing your everyday stuff" you maintain the language of the land, and the language of the flora and fauna. I was staying at Marylynn's cabin, learning Algonquin. On the first morning I was there, we went fishing. What does it mean to be part of the territory? I think it means to find your place in the world. Marylynn tells me proudly that her fourteen-year-old daughter Katie can set out the nets by herself. She boasted, "She'll survive."

I woke up on another morning at Marylynn and Clayton's bush cabin to a bright, hot day. The first thing Marylynn said to me was, "It's a beautiful day for birch bark." After lunch we went out, stopping at some jack pines to harvest their long, stringy roots for crafts. Everyone helped— Clayton dug a small trench around the tree with the back of his ax, looking for roots, and his youngest child, Brennan, followed, imitating his father's movements. Shane, a few years older than Brennan, helped Marylynn pull up the roots from the sandy soil. Along the way to the birch-bark spot, Marylynn shot two partridges and Shane, seven years old, without being told, ran quickly into the woods to retrieve them. Then we headed to Marylynn's sugar-bush trail to harvest birch. The bark was too wet—the lines too spread out and wide—and Brennan was traipsing through the forest again trying to help his dad, disappearing in the thick underbrush.

The morning we went out for the birch-bark harvest, I learned a very important phrase. We were talking generally about feelings and Marylynn tried to translate how you would refer to a thought. There are many different ways of thinking that relate to the past, present, and future. You can think deeply, reflecting on the past or on what someone told you, but you can also think in a way that reveals what Marylynn called "broader" thought. It is the old language, the old way of speaking. *Ki'gi'mam-m'den'dun wishkish* is what an elder might ask you after a story. This translates as "Did you understand the concept of what happened a long time ago, the whole story?" The concept of what happened a long time ago means a certain way of understanding the world: it is a picture of unity between all living things.

4

Property as a Technique of Jurisdiction
Traplines and Tenure

Anishnabe legal scholar Dawnis Kennedy reflects on how when settlers came to these lands they brought with them their own distant memories of tradition that they wished to find space for. "However," she writes, "since Indigenous peoples already governed these lands, settlers could not create such a space except by way of their relations with Indigenous peoples."[1] Insofar as they pursued peaceful means, settlers needed to establish meaningful relations with Indigenous people. One form of these dealings was the relation between legal orders of settler societies and Indigenous societies. Kennedy recognizes that there was a time of mutual legal respect between settler societies and many Indigenous nations, but this shifted over time, evident in gradual interpretations of treaties as a "burden" on the Crown. She notes the disrespect in the jurisprudence that, for example, sources Indigenous law in the Constitution Act, or considers it to have been displaced by Canadian law, or where it is denied altogether. But she writes that even where Canadian authorities reject or deny Indigenous legal orders, they must define themselves and their law through this rejection. After all, colonial laws were developed to colonize Indigenous peoples and their lands. Therefore, the role of colonial law in affirming Indigenous orders is still only affirming colonial law. But, as Kennedy explains, this incorporation acknowledges that "the development of the Canadian state and its legal orders *within Indigenous territories* is at issue" in that it seeks to transform Indigenous law into "forms of relation based on Euro-derived statist models."[2] Nowhere is this enmeshing more clear than in the Western property system.

The meaning of the property right in a settler society, as Kennedy conceives it, is always already in relation to the Indigenous territories on which it is applied. In this chapter, I examine how Indigenous subjects are produced and marked as capable of belonging to property law through the apparatus of jurisdiction. I survey some of the ways the machinery of jurisdiction operates through property relations, property law, and discourses of proprietary ownership, unfolding through a range of instantiations and by a variety of institutions, in response to the ongoing valiance of Indigenous tenure, jurisdiction, and proprietary interest.

Among the strategies of perfecting settler sovereignty, the imposition of Western property rights onto Indigenous forms of landholding has been pivotal to colonization and has produced a rich field of scholarly attention. When I first began writing about colonialism in Canada, property rights seemed to offer the most cogent explanatory power for how the social relations of land were transformed in the "New World" by settlers. Certainly, there is compelling evidence to support this framework.[3] But through my work at Barriere Lake, I found that property rights already presume the state's authority to govern, whereas it is the apparatus of jurisdiction that determines which laws will apply in a given context. In other words, the problem is not just the leasehold, the fee simple estate, or the government trapline system that institute new social relations on the land. The problem is the machinery of jurisdiction that authorizes these proprietary regimes. The confusion in the literature around how to define Indigenous peoples' basis of ownership in contrast to Western property rights partly stems from this conflation between property and jurisdiction. The issue is not whether property did or did not exist in Indigenous societies, but rather that in either case Indigenous jurisdiction governs the social relations of land on the territory, just as settler jurisdiction authorizes Western property regimes.

This chapter illustrates the order-, knowledge-, and space-making practices of jurisdiction on Barriere Lake territory by conflicting land-use patterns produced by provincial regulation and through Barriere Lake's tenure system. The Algonquin tenure system differentiates the landscape into spaces of care to ensure self-preservation and to protect the land base for future generations. Comparing this land-tenure system to a provincial beaver preserve system and the introduction of two government-regulated trapline regimes on the territory shows how provincial and Algonquin proprietary systems overlapped to produce a complex interlegal space. These layers, like shifting tectonic plates, eventually crashed into each other in real time, materializing in conflict between Algonquins, park authorities, logging companies, and other visitors. I argue that at stake in these conflicts is the way in which jurisdiction is exercised by the provincial state and the band toward different respective ends of comportment: *supply* and *care*. I examine how the production of social-scientific knowledge around Indigenous "property" has radically circumscribed, in a range of ways, the Algonquin legal order that governs land allocation and responsibility on Barriere Lake's territory, including the agency of other-than-human beings.

What Is Indigenous Territory?

One evening, Clayton told stories late into the night about the incredible hunting skills of his grandfather, Joe Ratt. One story involved Joe and his hunting partners who saw a moose stumbling along, its belly big against the snow, falling a bit, from side to side. One hunting partner thought it was a pregnant moose, but Joe knew it was a healthy moose that was not pregnant and he shot her. He turned out to be right and the families feasted. Another time, Joe saw six moose walking together and one was walking over on the side. This sixth moose was eating different plants than the rest and Clayton's grandfather knew it must be sick because the leaves he ate were medicine. Joe killed the moose and piled up the meat and bones to leave on the trail as a signal to let others know of the sickness.

These stories that have been passed on to Clayton convey important information for survival in the bush. They also signal the importance of kinship relations in land-use management of the territory. Algonquin tenure is vested in the political community of the band and actualized by the consensual deployment of families and trapping partnerships on the land. Clayton will pass along these stories to his children and their partners and to his grandchildren and extended family. Algonquin kinship is defined by bilateral (blood) kinship; postmarital residence in flexibly constituted extended families; and affinal (in-law) alliance that binds the community together through a network of reciprocal relationships.[4] These networks represent points at which accumulated knowledge is passed along: knowledge passes directly down from grandparents to children to grandchildren, but also across families to cousins, brothers-in-law, or through a woman's new family ties soldered through marriage (4).

Key characteristics of Algonquin kinship include respect for elders (Algonquin *ketizidjek*), who have authority as tradition bearers. There is also an expectation of sibling solidarity and generational complementarity, where the youth repay the care of their elders through their own contributions of labor and material support. Gender complementarity is a defining characteristic of Algonquin kinship, too. Women and men have different roles, as they are raised to provide specific household and political and ritual roles, or to play key roles in community decision making. Relations through marriage are also key, because this is the main form of expansion to the kinship nexus—through marriage Algonquins learn family territories, matrilineal and patrilineal and gain affinal access to resources, ecological knowledge, and skills (ibid.). These extended family alliances persisted after Barriere Lakers settled at the reserve, but there were changes to the kinship nexus: arranged marriages came to an end, there was a greater expansion of kinship through migration to nearby towns, and dense kinship networks were affirmed through housing shortages, where it was not unusual to have twelve extended family members sharing a two-bedroom house. New challenges were also ushered in by changes on the territory, such as the contracting land base, making it more difficult to maintain relations between families, gender, and generations (ibid.).

These kinship principles apply to three major components of the Algonquin social regime: household, task group, and territory (5). While these social regimes are interlocking, territory is jurisdiction's most visible currency. The family territorial system codeveloped with a highly adaptive land-management and conservation system. The Algonquin word for hunting territory or ground is *ânokî(w)akî*. In its prepositional forms, *-akî* is generally understood by Algonquins to mean "an area used by one or *more* persons for one or *more* harvesting purposes, an area that he/they know particularly and for which he/they have particular responsibility" (34). Access to areas of the territory are structured through the kinship and friendship nexus: because large game are migratory, hunting parties may ensure individuals access to moose and bears that will not travel through their own family hunting territories that season. But for smaller game, such as marten, rabbit, or fox, that do not tend to migrate far distances, individuals hold and share traplines where they know the land well and where their families may have been trapping for generations. These landholding practices balance the need for responsibility without requiring exclusive forms of ownership. As Roark-Calnek puts it, the advantages are "social as well as economic/ecological, over *either* a wholly unpartitioned 'commons' *or* the 'unsociable extreme' of rigidly privatized territories" (38). Located somewhere

between these extremes, a unique system developed over time to accommodate the ecological conditions and the values of Barriere Lake
society. It is a system that continues to evolve to this day.

This tenure system also has an external dimension: treaties, agreements, assertions, and mobilizations have secured this tenure across
a range of time and against a variety of encroachments. Trespass laws
represent what is often the key marker of territoriality from an outsider's perspective, because they conform to Western understandings of
property as an exclusive right. An account from trader Alexander Henry
from 1760 describes the system of land tenure as he heard it from the
southern Algonquins who traded at Oka in Southwestern Quebec:

> I learned that the Algonquins, of the lake Des Deux Montagnes . . .
> claim all the lands on the Outouais, as far as Lake Nipisingue;
> and that these lands are subdivided, between their several fami-
> lies, upon whom they have devolved by inheritance. I was also
> informed that, they are exceedingly strict, as to the rights of prop-
> erty, in this regard, accounting an invasion of them as an offence,
> sufficiently great to warrant the death of the invader.[5]

Trespass was historically met with a variety of sanctions if interference
was detected, such as confiscation of prey or amicable negotiation.[6] Stories also emerged periodically from my informants at Barriere Lake, in
hushed tones, about the conjuring powers exercised against trespassers,
mental arrows shot into the bloodstream of enemies hundreds of kilometers away.

But Barriere Lake's laws of trespass were also subject to the adaptive
technologies of their tenure system. Following the impact on land shortages stemming from the registered trapline system, one hedge against
the emergence of a strict ownership regime for the remaining traplines
was "free areas" introduced to mitigate against excessively privatized
landholdings.[7] Today, the highways are considered an open-access area
where anyone can hunt. Marylynn Poucachiche and Clayton Nottaway
told me that a lot of people are afraid to shoot moose on the highway,
though, because they are afraid tourists or locals will call the cops. They
are still afraid of being charged under the old ten-mile no-hunting corridor rule, designed to wipe the Algonquins from public visibility when
the highway was first built. Apparently, game wardens sometimes do

charge people. For example, Marylynn reported that Jackie Keyes got lured with a decoy only to have a game warden pull a gun on him and his children and give him a big fine. Jackie fought the charges in court without a lawyer, arguing that hunting is his traditional way of life and that he hunts to survive. He won the case, but Marylynn tells me that everyone wins these cases. Clayton chimed in to explain: "We used to hunt moose when we traveled, that's the Algonquin way, now we take the highway instead of the lakes, so that's where we're going to meet the moose. Our travels have changed since they dammed the rivers and built all the roads." Later, they tell me stories about shooting moose in front of tourists, who are invariably shocked, and how the Algonquins try to politely wait until the photos are taken before lifting their rifles and aiming.

Ultimately, family hunting territories ensure conservation and social cohesion; there are social, economic, and ecological advantages to structuring access to territory in this way. This system of territoriality "locates and regulates economic behavior within a moral universe in which adults are supposed to be responsibly interdependent, neither dependent on nor competing with each other. They are thus more willing to share costs as well as benefits."[8] The collective survival of the community is also ensured through this system, as a knowledge pool of regional experience is passed lineally and laterally throughout the community. A web of intricate relations secures an expansive reach of jurisdictional oversight and responsibility.

Traplines and Map Lines

One approach to understanding the differences between Indigenous and Canadian expressions of jurisdiction is through Bradley Bryan's work, which offers insightful reflection on *property as ontology*. His work stands out in the property literature on colonization because he comes closest to describing the respective social relations of jurisdiction I witnessed at Barriere Lake. He theorizes that English ontologies of property are based on a conception of the world as "standing reserve."[9] As Bryan explains: "Technology . . . makes a demand of nature, and that demand is one of supply."[10] This Heideggerian concept that describes a world of instrumental modern comportment can be contrasted to an Indigenous comportment that I have been calling an ontology of care. To specify for this context, I mean for "standing reserve" to pertain to two interrelated proprietary systems: the provincial leasehold system that permits resource extraction on Barriere Lake lands and the conservation regime that legislates restrictions on extraction and exploitation. Both the leasehold property right and the conservation regime express a technique of provincial jurisdiction whereby Barriere Lake lands are managed as *supply*. Jurisdiction at Barriere Lake is exercised by the provincial state and the band toward these different respective ends of comportment: *supply* and *care.*

Jurisdiction inaugurates property, and through its actualization as care at Barriere Lake, expressed in a proprietary form through land tenure, we can see how jurisdiction embeds the community in particular relations of mutual reciprocity on the land. In contrast to Indigenous jurisdiction, the commodity form of land in liberal capitalist society aims to erase value other than that which can be expressed in market terms.[11] As David Harvey notes, "The exchange process is ... perpetually abstracting from the specifics of location through price formation. This paves the way for conceptualizing values in place-free terms."[12] Of course, despite the premise of abstraction, value can never actually be disembedded from land. That is what led Karl Polanyi to label land as a *fictitious* commodity at the heart of capitalist crisis: the market seeks to treat it as supply, despite its unpredictable nature.[13] Brett Christophers underscores this point, arguing that perhaps it is time to reevaluate the meaning of "fictitious" in the context of contemporary capitalism, where land is more valuable than ever to the political economy of nations, for example, concerning resource extraction.[14] Land is *real* as a commodity and it literally *supplies* the geographic context for the political economy of the settler state. Even as a principle of conservation, *supply* is a key goal of maintaining wildlife populations, for the purposes of human consumption, survival of the species, and recreational hunting.

What is the ontological basis of life that property expresses at Barriere Lake? I spent a summer learning *anishnabemowin* in the bush at Barriere Lake. Curious about the language of property and jurisdiction in Algonquin society, I asked Toby Decoursay one day if there was a word for ownership in their language. *Kadthaben-duck* or *debendan,* he answered. What about a word for belonging or "to belong"? I asked. "Same thing almost," he said. "*Debendaygayzik* or *debendan.*" Martha Steigman, a filmmaker who was also in the community at the time, asked to clarify:

"To own and to belong are almost the same?" Toby answered affirmatively: "Yep, ours is *tibenindiziwin,* or *debdendan,* or *benjigaywaynan. Nin-diki-bendan. Debendeegayzik.*"[15] The land is *ni(n)daki*—it means my responsibility/autonomy/belonging while referring to everything there: the moose, the sun, the stars, the trees, the eagle, the beaver, moon, the earth, and even the planet. Literally, *aki* is "ground" while *nin* would mean "my."

I did not know exactly what a trapline was when I first started working with the Algonquins of Barriere Lake. I thought it was literally a line in the snow, made of rope or something, maybe a long snare. A trapline is a route or circuit along which a series of animal traps is set. There is no word for trapline in *anishnabemowin,* though nearly every adult in the Barriere Lake community has a designated place to catch mink, rabbit, marten, muskrat, fox, and beaver. One can say, "I am going to set my traps": *inglendo onige* or *on-donige,* and one can even specify what kind of trap one is setting—*wapsheshu onige* if one is going to check a marten trap, or *ameku onige* for checking beaver. There is a verb for "trap" *(onige),* but there is no noun to describe the place one traps specifically. It is part of one's hunting grounds and these hunting grounds are distributed by a system of aboriginal tenure embedded in the Mitchikanibikok Anishnabe Onakinakewin.

The fact that the Algonquins have no word for trapline in their language is indicative of their orientation toward land distribution. A trapline is made up of the places where you trap on your hunting grounds, but it was never something that could be calcified in maps because people cycled through various areas and then areas were left to rest through various seasons. I have already noted that the Algonquins of Barriere Lake's relationship to the land is embodied in the community's constitution, the Onakinakewin, and further along in this chapter we will see how the traditional roles of chief and council for allocating traplines form part of the oral law. The customary government is in turn bound by the laws and customs of the Onakinakewin, embedding the trapping life in the regulatory and moral codes of the customary system.

In the 1920s, the word *trapline* entered into the Algonquins' vocabulary. A trapline system was introduced by the provincial government at the insistence of the federal Department of Indian Affairs because of the massive shortage in game and subsequent starvation on the territory. Following a joint federal–provincial conference on wildlife and fisheries, two Indian-only game preserves were established on Barriere Lake's territory.[16] A Quebec Order-in-Council created the Grand Lac Victoria (GLV) Beaver Preserve (6,300 square miles) and the Abitibi Beaver Preserve (4,000 square miles) in 1928. These preserves covered much of the hunting and trapping territory in the Algonquin communities of Grand Lac, Lac Simon, some lands from Winneway and Wolf Lake, and some lands of Barriere Lake.[17]

The beaver preserves seemed at first to be a positive step toward returning exclusive rights to the Algonquins over their hunting grounds, but the initiative turned out to fall short on meaningful implementation. Quebec had apparently no interest in enforcing these boundaries from settler encroachment.[18] The federal government eventually recommended to Quebec in 1931 the appointment of Royal Canadian Mounted Police officers and Indian wardens to secure the boundaries of the preserves.[19] Quebec agreed, but conditions did not improve. In fact, they worsened with the construction of the Mont Laurier-Senneterre Highway beginning in 1938, which cut through the GLV Beaver Preserve. The new transport corridor was not only ecologically disruptive to the wildlife; it also facilitated increased recreational use of the area. In 1939, the province created the Mont Laurier–Senneterre Highway Fish and Game Reserve along a ten-mile corridor of the new highway, running straight through the GLV Beaver Preserve, and banned hunting and trapping within its boundaries.[20] Soon after, the Cabonga and Baskatong reservoirs were built by the Gatineau Power Company to supply power to Canadian International Paper's Gatineau Mill and for export to Ontario.[21] Hundreds of square miles of Barriere Lake territory were flooded and families lost cabins, hunting grounds, and fishing spots. Two cemeteries were also destroyed.[22] Whereas the beaver preserve was meant to prohibit settlers from hunting all fur-bearing animals, Quebec saw an opportunity for a lucrative grab at permit revenues. The Indian-only preserve perversely became a magnet for non-Indigenous hunting and trapping. Provincial authorities claimed that "fur-bearers" only meant animals one trapped, not big-game animals one hunted, and that non-Indians were free to fish and hunt game inside the preserve—a position that completely contradicted what they had told the Algonquins.[23]

Until 1941, only two game wardens patrolled more than ten thousand square kilometers of land and so, predictably, the poaching continued unabated.[24] That year, a provincial game warden, René Lévesque, was hired to oversee the management of game.[25] He introduced the tallyman system into the beaver preserve, requiring every Indigenous trapper to map his or her trapline territory along with the numbers and locations of beaver lodges. In return, the residents would receive a license (and later tags) validating their right to trap beaver on the territory within the beaver preserve. Trappers would also receive a nominal yearly payment from the department in exchange. The tallyman system was designed as an elaboration of a form of Indigenous land tenure, based loosely on the decentralized system of family hunting grounds. But it was based on Cree land tenure, where *Ndoho Ouchimau*—male leaders—were responsible for the land in different areas of their territory.[26] Barriere Lake land tenure was similar, but decision making was community-based and chief and council governed land allocation under the laws of the Onaki-nakewin; therefore, the tallyman system conflicted with Barriere Lake customary governance.

The tallyman system had originally been established in 1927 in Rupert's House (now the Waskaganish First Nation) Cree territory, about a fifteen-hour drive north of Barriere Lake's territory. A parallel set of responses to beaver depletion in Cree territory had been suggested by the Hudson's Bay Company (HBC) trader James Watt and the Rupert's House Cree.[27] What the Cree wanted was full control of their lands, but they were not to get it. Instead, James Watt's wife, Maud Watts, indicated to them that rather than have their rights recognized by the state, a legal arrangement could be worked out for a state-mandated program of beaver conservation. She convinced the Department of Lands to give the Rupert's House Cree an 18,500-square-kilometer beaver preserve. In short, the tallyman system was implemented and the program was a success, beaver populations were restored, and the government boasted internationally about its management control of the north. But by the 1940s to 1950s, the tallyman system had developed into a state-tenure and governance system instituted through a new bureaucracy that claimed control over the Cree and James Bay region.[28]

The gradual government oversight of Cree territory, where previously there had been little, meant that the occasional visits to the territory by doctors and RCMP officers were expanded in the 1940s to include a professional staff of Indian Affairs agents and officers to take charge of the federal and Quebec beaver preserves.[29] Harvey Feit concludes that the impacts of what he identifies as these new jurisdictional claims had

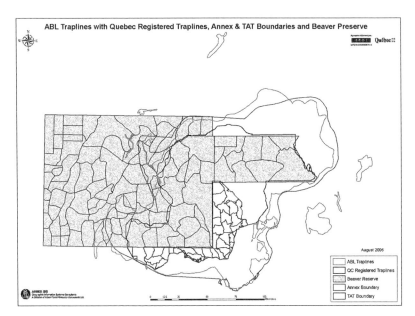

The overlapping borders of Barriere Lake traplines, the provincial system of regis-tered traplines, the Trilateral Agreement boundaries, the park boundaries, and the boundaries of the beaver preserve illustrate the places where different kinds of legal encounters between settler and Indigenous orders define each set of borders.

major outcomes regarding Cree territorial control and tenure: "The bea-ver reserves were exercises in governance that reduced Cree control of the land and of their hunting, asserted the competing claims of govern-ments and fur trade companies for authority, jurisdiction and control of the region and enhanced the legitimacy of their claims of northern rule more generally."[30] He further notes that the more knowledge the government collected about the Cree and their lands, the better it could claim management authority over these lands. Jurisdiction, he shows, need not be established by dispossession, overt flag planting, or legal decisions. The induction of the Waskaganish band into Canadian juris-diction took only the map lines of a new system of management through which the land could be managed and the people could be surveyed and, ideally, controlled as a population.

Sensing this danger, between the early 1940s and 1950s the Algon-quins of Barriere Lake adopted an attitude of noncooperation with and resistance to the Department of Indian Affairs. Instead of complying

with the tallyman system, the Barriere Lake men took out hunting licenses, yet refused to make the maps for trapping permits, knowing that
this information would cede the remaining control they had over their
land base.[31] Resisting the logic of mapmaking, Barriere Lake community members found outside buyers for furs and other ways to circumvent the system that penalized them for refusing to map their territory
for the government. They trusted only their own resource-management
system, and so they ignored designated "seasons" of harvest and they did
not cooperate with game wardens who carried out patrols.[32] No cooperation meant no beaver tags and so community members were persecuted
for hunting and trapping on their own lands; Barriere Lake members
were searched and their spoils of subsistence seized. Despite the consequences, the community fought back with noncompliance and physical
resistance. One game warden report documents the fierce resistance of
Algonquin women who hit back with paddles and whatever else they had
when attempts were made to search and confiscate their hunting and
trapping spoils. Lévesque reported, "I was lucky to see one squaw who
was getting ready to hit Cont [Constable] Christe [Christie] with an axe
and stopped her." He goes on to write: "As the squaws start to hit us with
paddles and whatever they could find I pulled out my revolver which
kind of scared them a little. I have been in some mix-up with Indians but
never seen the like of this trouble we had."[33] The resistance seemed to
be effective, even against the threat of RCMP violence. Lévesque found
that the RCMP demurred from arresting and charging the Algonquins,
concluding that "in the future, we may as well leave those Indians do
whatever they want because if a Mountie *has not got any authority with
them* it is not safe for a game warden to mix up in their business."[34] The
lack of enforcement the RCMP and game wardens could exercise with
the Algonquins demonstrates how settler laws lacked authority at Barriere Lake and set the limits of state sovereignty.

For a time, the game warden considered blacklisting the Algonquins
from obtaining any hunting or trapping licenses at all in an ill-conceived
attempt to pressure the Indians through regulatory exclusion. The game
warden reported that the Algonquins were getting increasingly "unco-
operative" each year. He wrote: "I think that your Department should
call a meeting at Rapid Lake sometime in the spring and after making
a last try to get their cooperation, if it does not work, put them on the
black list . . . I am afraid that the Mounties won't be able to do very

much in the future and if they cannot, it won't be safe for any white man to bother the Indians."[35] Exasperated, Lévesque lamented to the Fur Supervisor at Indian Affairs that "we don't seem to be able to control that Barriere tribe" whereas "all the other Indians seem to try to cooperate with us for the protection of their Reserve."[36]

The trouble continued. Another trapline system was established in 1945 for lands just outside of the GLV Beaver Preserve, but that still fell inside the border of what is now La Vérendrye Wildlife Reserve.[37] Although this attempt to regulate non-Indigenous land use was an overt money grab by Quebec to permit hunting and trapping in the region, attempts at regulation were generally welcomed by the community.[38] Unfortunately, once again, this effort was undermined by the province's autocracy, ignorance, and disinterest toward the prior and operational Algonquin land-tenure system of the region and its boundaries, despite one official's best efforts. By this time, Quebec had staffed the preserve with a "fur supervisor" and hired Hugh Conn to manage the preserve. Conn had intimate knowledge of Algonquin society because he was formerly the HBC post manager at Barriere Lake. He had also previously worked with the James Bay Cree in the north, where he oversaw the management of the beaver preserves.[39] He warned the province that the boundaries of the GLV preserve were "arbitrary and unnatural"—that "portions of some Bands' and/or families trapping territories were left out, and therefore treated differently" within the registered trapline area, for example, Barriere Lake lands east of the preserve.[40] Conn recognized the alienating effects of shifting Barriere Lake's jurisdictional boundaries and recommended changing the borders of the preserve so that it more accurately reflected the traditional territorial boundaries of the band's lands, "which themselves normally conformed to watersheds"; however, this advice was not heeded.[41]

The traplines arbitrarily divided Barriere Lake's traditional territory that fell outside of the GLV preserve into fixed territories of no more than fifty square miles. Lands within these registered trapline areas required payment for annual renewed leases in return for exclusive trapping rights."[42] If the trapper did not trap each year, failed to follow regulations, or defaulted on payments, the license could be lost.[43] In all cases, the GLV preserve was excluded from the registered trapline system, but some Barriere Lake lands outside the preserve were subject to this new registered trapline regime and many of these lands were eventually lost, leased out to white trappers or to Algonquins who lost leases, thus family lands, because of defaults in payment. In some cases, these lands were lost to surrounding bands. In a traditional land-use study dating back to 1993, Harry Wawatie described the process of losing these traplines to a nearby band. Punished for their reticence to participate in the system, others beat them to the all-important and decisive mapmaking exercise:

> You see what happened at the beginning when they first come up with this kind of, when they started making traplines, maps, they started, with the other places first, like Grand Lake, they were coaxed to make these kinds of maps, they were the first ones, took . . . I don't know what . . . advantage, I guess . . . and a little later on they were coaxed to take some of our parts too.[44]

Disruptions to the tenure system created competition not just internally to the band, but with neighboring First Nations.

Hugh Conn's efforts to accommodate Algonquin tenure introduce an interesting opportunity to reflect on how authority is established when laws meet across regulatory and governance divides. Conn did advocate strongly on Barriere Lake's behalf and issued prescient warning about the impacts the registered traplines would have on their tenure. The tallyman system at Barriere Lake did seem to benefit from Conn's willingness to engage with the Algonquins. More lands were lost in the registered trapline system that ignored Algonquin territorial boundaries than in the tallyman system, which attempted to account for traditional land allocation.[45] Conn notes that while people at Barriere Lake were resentful of white interference, they gradually came around in 1942 and agreed to participate in conservation efforts by estimating the number of beaver colonies in the preserve and promising to count beaver lodges in the spring.[46] These compromises, or interlegalities, over trapline jurisdiction meant that authority was being shared between parties, however tentatively.

But even Conn's support for Barriere Lake's tenure system suffered from the uneasy "pluriverse" of two systems of governance—in Walter Mignolo's terms, "a world entangled through and by the colonial matrix of power."[47] First of all, Conn was influenced by anthropologist Frank Speck's fairly rigid account of family hunting territories, stating that "each family head is appointed as guardian on his own hunting grounds" and largely ignoring the broader kinship nexus I have described.[48] This outside expertise displaced the Algonquins from being the regulators of their own tenure system. Second, as a representative of the state, Conn did not act as an honest broker but manipulated and selectively reconstructed the traditional system in the interests of the Fur Conservation Regime.

The anthropological knowledge Conn brought to bear on designing the Algonquin tenure regime played a significant determining role on the organization of space on Barriere Lake's territory. This institutional knowledge, accessible through publication, contributed to the "material and discursive assemblages" in the construction of land-use authority.[49] As Audra Simpson writes in relation to the anthropological disciplining of her own community of Kahnawá:ke, this knowledge is what forms the attention of anthropologists around "culture," rather than "the scene of object formation—ongoing land dispossession."[50] The complicity of anthropologists is a key social process that has had significant agency in shaping the means and matter of colonization in the territory.

Here Come the Anthropologists

Whether Algonquin land tenure is a system that reflects nomadic, proprietary, or jurisdictional interests is a question (for outsiders) that has been around for a long time. Placing the discussion of Algonquian land tenure into a disciplinary context, we can see long threads of controversy in the profession of anthropology for almost a century. Frank Speck was an early observer of what he called the Algonquin "family hunting territory" system (nok'i-'wak'v'), comprised of fixed tracts of land with natural boundaries to accommodate extended social units of kinship.[51] These social units, he observed, were composed of patronymic families, with a system of land allocation distributed across kinship lines.[52] Speck reports that family territories were pretty rigid, though he goes on to show many examples that break with the strict enforcement of paternal family territories, such as sharing territory in bad years, visiting the wife's territory during poor seasons, and hunting on common lands during the spring gatherings. It is notable in his work that little explicit connection is made between governance and land tenure. For example, the chief's responsibilities are not laid out at all in relation to resource and land allocation. There is also a virtual silence on jurisdiction, though implications of a relationship between tenure and jurisdiction exist, for example, through reference to trespass regulations.

Underscoring his interpretation of Algonquian land tenure, Speck's work in the first quarter of the twentieth century challenged the accuracy of Marxist anthropology and argued for a more nuanced understanding of "primitive" societies. Where Marx argued that hunter-gatherer societies held their land and resources communally, Speck and Robert Lowie described "family hunting territories" in Algonquin communities as a direct challenge to this thesis, owing to their quasi-private form. Indigenous societies, Speck pointed out, were comprised of decentralized social units of discrete landholding areas for the purpose of hunting: "The whole territory claimed by each tribe was subdivided into tracts owned from time immemorial by the same families and handed down from generation to generation. The exact bounds of these territories were known and recognized, and trespass, which indeed was of rare occurrence, was summarily punishable."[53] In 1920, Lowie concurred and strongly advised against the "blunt alternative" between communism and individualism, dismissing as "evolutionary dogma" the teleology of property from collective to private.[54]

Speck's work was influential, particularly on D. S. Davidson, John Cooper, and Robert Lowie, but it was by no means universally accepted.[55] As Adrian Tanner notes, many anthropologists were convinced that these territorial allocations resulted from the fur trade, rather than long-standing Algonquin social norms of organization. He explains that Europeans were believed to have infected the Indians with an idea of property that soon took root in their society: "It was the Indians who then supposedly applied the property idea to the animals, and finally to the land which the animals occupied."[56] By far the most influential of these countertheorists was Eleanor Leacock, who first cast doubt on Speck's conclusions in her monograph *The Montagnais Hunting Territory and the Fur Trade*.[57] Leacock dislodged the influence of Speck in the 1950s with her thesis that the fur trade gave rise to individualized and privatized forms of territoriality on the land. Her work supported anthropologist Diamond Jenness's earlier 1925 criticism of Speck and furthered ideas of Indigenous peoples' tenure system as a sign of assimilation into European modes of production, rather than as an Indigenous social form of organization.[58]

Debates continued to wage into the 1970s and 1980s between Leacock and Speck supporter Edward S. Rogers, and the discussion continues with Harvey Feit suggesting that precontact hunting territories were a distinctly plausible historical theory.[59] The controversy also has ideological traction in nonanthropological political spheres. Right-wing pundit and Conservative Party adviser Tom Flanagan used Leacock's work to deny any collective nature to Indigenous society, therefore any basis for sovereignty or self-determination on cultural grounds.[60]

Scholars have struggled to defend—ideologically, ethnographically, and historically—cases for *either* a private or a communal system of property in Algonquin tenure systems. Perhaps this is because an ambiguity in the definition of property cuts across both Speck's and Leacock's camps. After all, do "private" hunting territories mean the same thing as "private" property in Canadian society? Are there any commonalities between fee simple ownership of residential homes in urban centers and the allocation of hunting territories among kinship units on native territory? A major hook for Speck's anthropological work hinges on a faulty brace of ethnocentricity, where property is transformed into ideal types, rather than understood in social context. As Tanner explains: "In the cases I am aware of, Algonquian territories are never 'owned' by anyone other than those who work on them; they cannot be sold, accumulated, or used by the owner to accumulate surplus production. Labeling them private property in 'our' sense of the term thus tells us very little and is actually misleading."[61] Although Leacock and her followers move toward an acceptance that hunting territories are a response to external material conditions—ecological, economies of fur trade, coercive influence of traders and missionaries—their methodology is focused more on the "function and operation" of hunting territories postcontact, rather than their relation to Indigenous social structures and cultural values.[62]

This anthropological knowledge informed conservation regimes on Barriere Lake's territory and continues to inform discussion today on whether Indigenous peoples can actually claim land if they do not possess systems and ideations of "property." This assumption—that Algonquin landholding systems should be transparent to social scientists—has repeatedly failed to take into account the governance systems that have been relentlessly attacked by colonial authorities precisely because of the strong, territorial jurisdiction Indigenous peoples exercised over their lands since white Europeans first migrated across the ocean. Linking Indigenous governance systems to tenure regimes, or more loosely to a band's socioeconomic organization, is a crucial step toward understanding how Canadian proprietary regimes can operate as a technology of colonial jurisdiction.

Property as a Technique of Jurisdiction

Akin to anthropology, a prevalent tendency in liberal theory has been to subordinate the legal orders of Indigenous societies through a series of typologies concerning property rights, constructed to formulize Indigenous demands into the sovereign claims of the state.[63] In brief, liberal theorists conflate *imperium* and *dominion* in social contract theory, which assumes that Indigenous people make demands on society in the register of property rights and ownership, rather than in the register of governance and jurisdiction.[64] The danger of the social contract theory is the way it can elide questions of legitimacy around its proprietary regime. In Robert Nichols's incisive critique of what he calls "settler contract theory," he exposes the fictional product of the alleged contract between founding members of society when it is invoked to "displace the question of that society's actual formation in acts of conquest, genocide and land appropriation."[65] In the Rousseauian formulation, the contract is the deliberative procedure that distinguishes modern life from the *state of nature* that preceded agreement and was brought into being the state.

However, as we can see in the case of Barriere Lake, Indigenous people often primarily make demands on the state by calling into question the state's *imperium*. That is, claims *about* property differ from claims *to* property. The conflation between *dominion* and *imperium* presents the question of Indigenous property rights "as though they may be adjudicated *within* the already assumed prevalence of European legal and philosophical *imperium*."[66] This kind of reasoning and argumentation invokes the civilizing discourses of Hobbesian sovereignty that did not acknowledge that Indigenous people could have exercised leadership over their people prior to state formation, but it also echoes assumptions of more recent anthropological work that denies a relationship between governance and tenure, as I have tried to show.

What a closer look at Indigenous tenure arrangements shows clearly is precisely how *proprietary* systems cannot be separated from questions of *rule*. Before the "white man made the counties," or began to subdivide the land into various jurisdictions, it was the customary council that determined the distribution of band lands. In 1991 at Chestnut Lake, community members discussed this practice of allocation: "The Chief looked at how the land was to be used. Before registered traplines, everyone had a territory. People would rotate use of their territories in partnership with other community members: A would trap his area one season, and then partner with B on B's territory to allow his own to regenerate. Then, the following Season, A and B would go to A's territory . . . Set during the meeting [the feast] the people would decide who to go with, decide who to ask, [say to one another] who are you trapping with?"[67] Feasts took place in the fall and spring and it was there that the chief would deal with issues of overcrowding or shortage of game on the land and move people around accordingly.

Toby Decoursay remembers David Makokos, the life chief who governed for most of the twentieth century, ensuring that there was not excessive overlap of families on the land. For instance, if two families were already heading toward La Bouchette (an area in the park), Makokos would tell the third family to find another place. There were no property lines, but the territory was clearly delineated by Algonquin place-names that contained in their language the geological boundaries and toponymies of a particular area. Toby recalled that people were generally less strict or more respectful of each other's territories in the past. "That's what they say, me I'm going to *kamashgono-gamak* or *gasazibi*; they just say the name of the territory and the chief is going to take care of that. And they know what direction to go and where is the name of the place. And that's it."[68] The traplines at Barriere Lake reflected this governance system, a piece of the tenure regime of land management.

The subchiefs or councillors also played a role in land management. In 1990, at the Romance Lake bush camp, Patrick Maranda described the role of the chief and subchiefs in the time before the beaver preserve: "People used to have meetings before they went trapping. There were four sections, four Councilors responsible for the people . . . The Chief would listen to the Councilors, and the Councilors did the work of visiting around, looking after things."[69] This oral history is confirmed by other community members who remembered how each subchief was chosen to keep one of the four directions, named for winds that reflect a four-pole classification system of the world.[70]

While traplines always existed in practice, their regulation by provincial authorities dug them up from an embedded system of tenure and governance and laid them neatly on the land like two-dimensional lines on a map. In an interview in June 1994 with Toby Decoursay and Maggie Wawatie, they discussed the marginalization of the chief by outside agencies in the establishment of registered traplines: "It was up to the Chief to decide [where people would go]. Everyone would come together in a big feast, make basket[s]. That's where they were told [where] to trap. That's why the Indians didn't fight long time ago among themselves about the trapline. Since the white man made the counties—how big the trapline going to be—that's when the trouble started."[71] The government trapline systems mapped over the existing system of aboriginal land tenure and political governance. Dorsett and McVeigh cite maps as one of the easiest technologies of jurisdiction, because one gets an instant picture of the spatial extent of law.[72] The disciplinary strategy of mapping has long been studied as systems of territorial surveillance that assimilate space into Cartesian grids. But the ways these representations overwrite Indigenous ways of knowing and recording space create specific parallaxes of language, place, and law.[73]

Trapline systems formed a new technique of colonial power that scarred the land with such disjuncture. They constituted a complex set of regulations and jurisdictional claims that impacted the Mitchikanibikok Anishnabe Onakinakewin and inculcated novel ideas of propertization into the governance system. As a result, the new tenure system of traplines wrought unprecedented changes in social relations in the territory. Former customary chief Jean Maurice Matchewan described the impact of the traplines system on the community's communal ethics:

Well, long time ago when the government started putting laws on our land, like, for instance, the registered traplines, that's a government-imposed trapline. People didn't get along good, 'cause as their land got smaller, they started having problems, 'cause they couldn't fit everyone on their trapline. So, it was the government that introduced this trapline idea to get rid of this problem. Families were pretty much fighting over their territory, and with their neighbors and neighboring communities as well. So, that's how the trapline came to be. Before that, they didn't really have a trapline. They just had a territory that they occupied, but it wasn't really specifically given to them, [just] to manage.[74]

What had begun as a conservation effort in fact worked to undermine the jurisdiction Algonquins exercised over their lands. Whereas Barriere Lake traplines could be shared across a number of kinship relations, the government trapline system forced individuals to take ownership of individual traplines in order to secure tenure and avoid confiscation and redistribution of lands to settlers by the government. Essentially, the registered traplines solved a problem of dispossession that the provincial government itself created by creating another mode of dispossession. Feit reports that the trapline system in Cree territory also "led to a more formal and rigid application of leadership, authority and inheritance ideas."[75] Ethnographic research conducted years later on post-beaver preserve life in Rupert's House revealed that the property relations of the Cree could not have been as easily emulated as even the most generous fur-trader managers at first assumed. Feit writes that "hunting territories are not forms of private property, nor results of commodification or assimilation as had been assumed by some mid-century analysts and commentators. Hunting territories are both expressions and means of reproduction of Algonquian [reference to language group, not national affiliation] social relations, symbolic meanings and relations to the land and wildlife, i.e., they are integral to social reproduction broadly construed."[76] By asserting jurisdiction over Cree lands, the governments disrupted Cree self-determination and self-government.

At Barriere Lake, much as people did not own individuated plots of property, aboriginal tenure secured some of the advantages of proprietary regimes. As I have shown, customary or traditional users of the range would have spent many years on that land, and therefore they would have built up an extensive fund of knowledge about the area, making them more successful hunters and gatherers and building families' historical attachments to particular areas. These attachments then led to some measure of responsibility *(tibenindiziwin)* for the areas, ideally managing their resources for other users and future generations, requiring recurrent (not necessarily continuous) occupancy and use. This jurisdiction of care could not be replicated through bureaucratic regimes of ownership.

Partly what outsiders could not perceive was the flexibility in Algonquin social relations of belonging. As Jean Maurice Matchewan illustrates, "if there's one family, if at their trapline there's no animals there, pretty much, another family will take them into their area when their animals are growing. So, those are the kinds of thing they would do to accommodate other families. 'Cause I remember when I was young my grandfather was a great trapper, he used to go out to somebody else's territories, with permission, and there was no problem that way."[77] The Barriere Lake trapline system represents a set of social relationships between community members that respects boundaries between ecological areas but also corresponds to the dynamics of a hunting and trapping economy and the overarching value of ensuring sustenance for all. This flexibility has invoked what often seems like the central question for settlers studying the land interests of Indigenous peoples: is it property? Bryan contends, however, that the main issue should not be whether Indigenous peoples "have conceptions of property and what those are, but rather how an analysis of other cultures' ways of life, using our own terms, serves to rationalize that other way of conceiving of the human's relationship the world-at-large in our own terms."[78] The beaver preserves and trapline systems served to reorder Algonquin society along the lines of Western understandings of ownership, even in the best-intentioned efforts. To remake Algonquin land as individual property was to deny or distort the ways of life that embodied and enacted the community's legal and political order.

Paul Nadasdy similarly chronicles the failure of Indigenous knowledge to be integrated into the comanagement of Ruby Range sheep in the Yukon Territories. Crosscut by a range of administrative and political boundaries, and subject to intensive resource extraction, the Kluane First Nation involved in the project had to navigate myriad jurisdictional barriers to participate in comanagement, ultimately failing to make an impact with their contributions. Nadasdy observes that "arbitrary geographical divisions directly affect people's experience of the land and so structure their knowledge of it; yet they overlap and otherwise fail to correspond to one another."[79] In the context of conservation, Nadasdy argues that while trust may be placed between Indigenous and settler parties, whether or not action will actually be taken on the say of Indigenous partners is another question altogether. He warns that comanagement agreements can take for granted existing Indigenous–state relationships and perpetuate, rather than transform, unequal power relations.[80] In this sense, the registered trapline system would prefigure the problems of the Trilateral Agreement to come.

The trapline system reveals how the alienation of Barriere Lake lands through multiple regulatory plans and authorities impacted the community's jurisdiction. Unevenly applied and enforced, legislation meant to protect wildlife and habitat for Indigenous use ended up carving up the territory into restrictive zones, eventually facilitating recreational sport, and running up constantly against other planning authorities for the region that built transportation corridors and flooded reservoirs throughout the preserve in pursuit of commercial enterprise and energy generation. Foreign systems of land allocation—even the tallyman system that was based on Algonquin tenure—undermined the traditional roles of the chief and council through these new differentiations of space, and, perhaps more important, through disruption to the expansive kinship nexus that facilitated land use on the territory. It is on this point that I would like to focus my final argument on Indigenous jurisdiction.

Reproducing Life

Land-use clashes are inevitable and widespread throughout the country precisely because Indigenous landholding systems are subject to imposition, incursion, and outright denial, violating Indigenous laws and trampling on invisibilized turfs of Indigenous responsibility and belonging. As Peter Usher, Robert Galois, and Frank Tough put it: "The state system of resource tenure and management exists as an *overlay on,* not a *replacement of,* aboriginal systems—hence the frequency of land and resource conflicts."[81] These overlays are not mere lines on a map. They produce the materiality of the region, partially generated through the technologies of settler property rights that attempt to render Indigenous land tenure obsolete.

This act of overlay affects not only human beings, but also the "other-than-human" beings on the land. Here we uncover another insight into the failure of Conn's good intentions to replicate Indigenous principles of land management that caused the profound loss experienced by the Algonquins. As Kim Tallbear observes, "Indigenous peoples have never forgotten that nonhumans are agential beings engaged in social relations that profoundly shape human lives."[82] "Objects" and "forces" such as stones and thunder form part of this "ecology of intimacy" between all living things on the land.[83] Where Indigenous peoples assert jurisdiction through protection of their tenure system, they are also extending this care to other-than-human "tenures" or ecosystems. For example, Jean Maurice Matchewan describes the impact on animals from dams and logging, invoking the problems the animals are having as the community's own:

> When I was growing up and first started realizing what was happening, and hearing my grandfather talk about what was happening . . . this Cabonga reservoir used to be full of logs, people had a hard time going through with their canoes; even in the little creeks, logs were cutting across the river, blocking the river, ; made it pretty hard for people to travel, 'cause, you know, they didn't care if they were near a creek or river, they would just chop down a tree and block a river or a creek. So, it really affected the way people used to travel. Even in their portages to go to other areas, it would be just impossible.
>
> The moose are having the same problem now—they've been using the same route for I don't know how many years and years— all of a sudden it's all chopped down and blocked in there, they get lost too, they need to find new routes, just like we had to. That's why we use the road nowadays. But everything that happened, like for all the sport hunting, we got less and less animals, and all that, and the flooding is very hard to travel on it and the beavers freeze in the wintertime when they lower down the water, and down below where they release it, too, they drown all the beavers 'cause the water raises up so fast, so it affects, in a way, how we travel, and the food that we eat has also been affected.
>
> And we have to go further and further into the bush to go for beaver, for instance. There's no beaver once they lower down the water. They lowered down the water ten feet—that means the beaver has to walk ten feet to get to the water and it's under ice. And they have no food—the food they store in front of their cabins—

it's in the ground, it's supposed to be in the water, that's why
they put it in the water, and a lot of time, they're on the ground,
especially on the reservoir here. And the moose sometimes will
just go through the ice. Those are some of the problems we have
with everything they're doing.[84]

The Algonquins' preoccupation with the impacts of colonization on the
animals is a critical intervention into studies of property and jurisdiction. Human–animal interactions are not just objects of colonization:
these relations are colonial subjects that enable colonial expansion.[85]
A case in point, the dogged efforts pursued by provincial authorities to
collect data on beaver habitat and populations not only enacted a loss
of land and subsistence for the Algonquins but radically changed the
world of the beaver, whose living conditions were increasingly produced
by way of the empirical and scientific knowledge used to manage their
homelands.

Scott Lauria Morgensen addresses the way settler colonialism is in
fact "exemplary" of biopower.[86] Drawing on Patrick Wolfe's seminal
work on the ways in which settler colonialism is a structure of elimination rather than an event, Morgensen writes: "Wolfe emphasises that
elimination may follow efforts not to destroy but to produce life, as in
methods to amalgamate Indigenous peoples, cultures and lands into the
body of the settler nation."[87] But the production of Indigenous life is
not alone sufficient to incorporate First Nations into the settler body;
the work to produce all life on the territory as *supply* is what ensures a
structure of elimination. As Toby Decoursay put it, the land "is from
where our customs are built. When the government opens the hunting
season, taking bears, moose, and beaver without regard to their families
or their role in the order, this is where they start to destroy my beliefs."[88]
To understand this complex biopower, we need to take seriously what
Indigenous people mean when they warn that without their land they
will lose their identity.

As Vanessa Watts explains, this warning issued by Indigenous
communities is not just about dispossession or displacement from
their lands, but the theft of the "ability to act and govern" when their
homelands are damaged and their epistemic frames are subject to ig-
norant misinterpretation.[89] From an Indigenous point of view, governance is intimately tied to how agency is circulated through human and

other-than-human worlds in the creation and maintenance of society. Watts describes Haudenosaunee and Anishnabe creation stories to illustrate this theoretical understanding of the world through physical embodiment. From the Anishnabe perspective, for example, the Fifth Fire and Sixth Fire of the Seven Fires of Creation are crucial here. In the time of the Fifth Fire, Gizhe-Manidoo, the Creator, places his/her thoughts in seeds; in the time of the Sixth Fire, Gizhe-Manidoo created First Woman, a place where the seeds could root and grow. The place where thoughts root and grow can never be separated from the seeds where they were planted, so Watts calls this Place-Thought: "Place-thought is based on the premise that land is alive and thinking and that humans and non-humans derive agency through the extensions of these thoughts."[90] It is these connections with the living land that form the societies in which Indigenous peoples thrive. These other-than-human lifeworlds "have ethical structures, inter-species treaties and agreements . . . Not only are they active, they also directly influence how humans organize themselves into that society."[91] Human thought, in turn, expresses the thinking of particular places, drawing obligations to maintain this balance and remain in communication with its desires, will, intent, and labors. When the Algonquins' jurisdiction is undermined, these lifeworlds become "compromised because this relationship is continuously corrupted with foreign impositions of how agency is organized. Colonization has disrupted our ability to communicate with place and has endangered agency amongst Indigenous peoples."[92] Colonization corrupts Indigenous peoples' capacity to exercise care, but this form of dispossession also affects the other-than-human world in the exercise of its own reciprocal agency.

The kinship system at Barrier Lake has changed a lot over time. Norman Matchewan said it used to be that there were no family territories—people would move around from place to place. I asked when that changed, and he said maybe with the traplines.[93] Then he showed me his grandfather's trapline on a map where he and his cousin Benjamin Keyes trap together. His uncle gave the trapline to him and showed him all the best places to catch marten when Norman was broke and could not afford to pay his bills. Fortunately, while the rigidity of the government trapline system reified these family territories owing to sudden "shortages" of land, trapping has been a flexible system to begin with, with room for adaptation to changing circumstances, to which the families, chief, and subchiefs would attend. Today, the trapline system calls less upon the customary government for adjudication and allocation, but it is still entrenched in the territory of Barriere Lake's ecological boundaries and within the purview of the customary government's jurisdiction. It is attuned specifically to the movement of animals and the needs of families. One thing for certain is that control of "populations"—human and other-than-human—is always subject to forces of resistance on the ground. A trapline is only as colonized as the map lines in which its jurisdiction falls.

5

"They're Clear-Cutting Our Way of Life"

Throughout the early history of settler accumulation, Barriere Lake's resistance to the state's assertions of jurisdiction on their lands was mostly a nonconfrontational mix of noncompliance and evasion. As the thickening heap of lines continued to carve up their territory and authority into dozens of agencies and departments, Barriere Lake found ways to subvert these new forms of spatial and legal differentiation and to carry on as best they could in their traditional ways of life. They adapted to the cash economy by working on mink farms and acting as guides for private outfitters, but their economy and social orientation were still based primarily in the bush. There came a point, however, when the tension between their legal order and the state's regulatory system boiled over, and this encounter set their lives on a new path toward coexistence that would be firmly based on Algonquin jurisdiction over their lands and resources.

By the 1980s, more than thirty-eight logging companies had leases in Barriere Lake's territory. The provincial government had begun to issue twenty-five-year, nonrevocable logging concessions to companies such as Canadian Pacific Forestry Products (now Domtar) to clear-cut large areas of La Vérendrye Wildlife Reserve. New logging roads cut fresh pathways through the territory, along which timber was extracted and sport hunting flourished. Despite these incursions, the Algonquins continued to practice their traditional ways of life, but under tremendous threat—not only was the natural habitat being destroyed by logging, but pesticides and herbicides were sprayed, killing vegetation and poisoning animals. Soon the people got sick from eating the animals.[1]

One day, a couple of community members came to see Jean-Maurice Matchewan, who was customary chief at the time. They had in hand letters from the Ministry of Natural Resources that had been left at their bush cabins on Pomponne Road (otherwise known as Moose Lake Road), notifying them of spraying taking place in the area.[2] They were told they would have to move out of their cabins for three weeks. Matchewan real-

126

ized with a shock that the authorities were planning to spray herbicides right around their homes. He said the band's next move was resolute, knowing then that it was only a matter of time before the whole community would be poisoned and the woods around their cabins were all torn down. They could see what was coming by what they observed in the bush; the effects of the herbicide were already clear: "Sometimes you would see a moose that was only five hundred pounds; you know they get sick from that."[3] The first blockade the Algonquins mounted was a traffic slowdown on the highway at Lake Roland, where Pomponne Road began, interfering with the logging operation and raising awareness about what was being done to the land.[4] Quebec eventually sent a letter stating that it would not be spraying anymore, claiming it was because it was getting too late in the season. The government never acknowledged Algonquin opposition, and this total lack of recognition made the community angry, but their success nonetheless encouraged them.

The spraying had been the last straw for the beleaguered community, though it was only one of a number of grave concerns. Spawning areas were being ruined because of fluctuations from the dam, and, worst of all, the community witnessed the devastating landscape of the clear-cuts.[5] The Algonquins have prophecies that warn precisely of the dangers of this scale of ecological destruction. The prophecies envision this destruction manifesting on a global scale, with especially disastrous effects on weather patterns and water bodies. On their own lands, they observed changes to animal migration patterns, precipitation, and plant life, but this knowledge was not valued outside of their society. So, in the late 1980s, Barriere Lake commissioned a report on the impacts of forestry on their lands that would speak in the voice of modern science. The Quebec Forestry Act of 1986 had set forth a new forestry regime for the public domain that accelerated the forestry industry's path of destruction. Quebec required that all existing timber allocations be abolished, replaced by timber-supply management agreements: CAAFs (Contrats d'approvisionnement et d'aménagement forestier) are twenty-five-year agreements with five-year extensions every five years if the holder complies with obligations. Rebecca Aird, an environmental consultant who worked on Barriere Lake's commissioned report, confirmed that CAAFs were simply oriented to secure an adequate supply of wood for the mills. They made no reference to wildlife, plants, or any other forest uses, least of all Indigenous habitation and use.[6] Aird concluded that industry's interest in forest management was limited to the timber harvest, putting all other forest values at risk, including support for Indigenous life.

Condemning the total invisibility of Algonquin land rights to Quebec, she wrote that "many aboriginal communities such as Barriere Lake, whose livelihood and culture are integrally dependent on conditions in the forest, were not consulted on the policy, the Act, or the regulation, nor on the land use designation applied in their area. Neither are they to be party to the development of the CAAFs" (6). In fact, CAAFs arose from closed-door negotiations between the provincial government—represented by senior bureaucrats in the Ministry of Energy and Resources and the director of the forest-management unit in question—and the forestry companies. No attention was ever paid to those who would have to live with the consequences of the new forestry regime.

Remarkably, no wildlife area within the La Vérendrye Wildlife Reserve was set aside for conservation, save for one heronry. Aird reports that "[t]he land-use designations of [La Vérendrye] reflect not only the continuation of a historic 'fiefdom' for the logging industry within the reserve, but also reflect the fact that MLCP [Ministère de Loisir, de la Chasse et de la Pêche, Department of Recreation, Hunting, and Fishing] wildlife managers do not have the necessary research and information to clearly delineate critical wildlife habitat" (13–14). The wildlife reserve was being clear-cut, yet no wildlife studies had ever been done of moose, beaver, waterfowl, and other wildlife habitat and use. Although the Algonquins of Barriere Lake have extensive knowledge on wildlife habitat, plants, and sacred areas thanks to millennia of land use and occupation, no attempt was ever made to draw upon this knowledge in the development of land-use management plans for the area. As a result, Aird warned that "[i]f the CAAFs are negotiated on the basis of the current land use designations, there is little hope for adequate protection of the wildlife, asthetic [sic] and recreational values of the La Vérendrye Wildlife Reserve, nor for the future of the land-based economy of the Algonquins of Barriere Lake" (14). Aird supported Barriere Lake in advocating for an eight-month moratorium on industrial and recreational harvesting in the park and for a moratorium on the negotiation of CAAFs to allow for a more sustainable regime of habitat-management strategies to guide forestry practices (ibid.). These demands fell on deaf ears.

The early traffic slowdowns against spraying had shown the Algonquins that such tactics could work. In the late 1980s, the Algonquins erected roadblocks on the access roads through the forest to prevent logging equipment from reaching the trees. But they soon found that they were fighting a wide range of development encroaching on their lands. In July 1988, they blockaded Highway 117 to protest the hydro-electrification of their reserve, and handed out two thousand pamphlets to alert the public that power lines would disrupt their traditional hunting grounds and asking for support.[7] They also learned at this time that Quebec was proposing that 40 percent of La Vérendrye Wildlife Reserve be privatized, a move they also opposed.[8]

An underlying issue for the Barriere Lakers was the question of jurisdiction that was driving development and keeping decisions out of their reach and control. As their lawyer, David Nahwegahbow, explained to the *Ottawa Citizen,* the Algonquins had been severely affected by clear-cut logging in their forests and saw electrification "as promoting further outside development without having their title resolved."[9] Not one to mince words, Chief Matchewan made clear, however, that it was not title itself that was at stake, but rather the survival of his people.[10] Title would never prove to be the post Barriere Lake tied itself to in negotiations. Instead, they fought for governance powers, rooted in the jurisdiction over the lands that defined them as a people and obligated them to act for its protection.

The community had put their lives on hold to stand out on the highway in an attempt to get the government's ear. Finally, after months of federal inaction, the Algonquins took to the nation's capital. In September, they occupied Victoria Island for several days, a traditional Algonquin meeting place behind Parliament Hill, but they still could not get the government's serious attention, despite good media coverage of their protest. More than one hundred community members eventually left Victoria Island, promising to return until the issues were resolved.[11] The next week, the Algonquins made good on this promise, this time taking over Parliament Hill. Their demands were clear and consistent: no hydro lines through their hunting territory; an eight-month moratorium on logging; no privatization of the park; and, most important, they had a vision for a conservation plan that would cover their traditional territory, governed by the principle of sustainable development. Once again, they were rebuffed. In an incident still widely remembered and discussed in Barriere Lake today, the Royal Canadian Mounted Police

(RCMP) were brought in to do the government's business. In September 1988, Lena Nottaway, a seventy-five-year-old grandmother, was one of about twenty people arrested on Parliament Hill for "trespass." She is quoted in the press chiding cops not to drop her as they carried her to an awaiting vehicle.[12] Nottaway, along with the others arrested, was issued a summons to appear in court the following month for illegally camping on public land. The case was stayed when the Crown decided that the Algonquins' claim to Parliament Hill as unceded land would cast a bright and potentially embarrassing light on the true identity of trespassers in this case.[13]

Although only a fraction of the protesters were arrested, the RCMP confiscated all of the Algonquins' belongings and refused to return to them their sleeping bags and tents.[14] It was a mean and spiteful refusal, given the community's poverty and cause, and their need for this camping equipment in the bush. Chief Matchewan insisted to the media that they would not have needed to travel all that distance and risk arrest if the government had simply responded to urgent requests that the community had been making for months. He pointed out the irony that Prime Minister Brian Mulroney was away at the United Nations discussing human rights and the environment while Barriere Lake's land was being clear-cut—mere hours away from Ottawa—and the government could not be bothered to respond.[15]

Quebec finally stepped away from its insistence on the privatization of the park and the hydro line through Barriere Lake's territory. But the logging went ahead unabated. The community persisted with their demands and moved their protest camps to block six new logging roads. In the meantime, Barriere Lake also made a desperate bid to win in the courts with an injunction against Quebec over lands in forestry management units (FMUs) 73 and 74, large parts of which were in the La Vérendrye Wildlife Reserve and the Grand Lac Victoria Beaver Preserve. The injunction was an attempt to abort the distribution of CAAFs to companies in their traditional territory.

They lost badly. Barriere Lake's lawyer on the case, Gerard Guay, immediately pointed out the sheer prejudice evidenced by Superior Court Judge Orville Frenette's decision to refuse the injunction. Multiple errors in judgment included a willful misinterpretation of Barriere Lake's demands, which the judge mischaracterized as stipulating a permanent halt to all logging in the territory; the assertion that Barriere Lake failed to establish that they have any rights to the land, despite such evidence as the Grand Lac Victoria Beaver Preserve, where the ABL have exclusive hunting and trapping rights; and the fact that Judge Frenette completely ignored a series of legal violations Quebec had committed in the distribution of CAAFs that should have forced the province to re-evaluate their applications.[16] Most glaring was the blatant discrepancy in the standards of evaluation regarding the evidence: Barriere Lake submitted to the court six lengthy affidavits by community members and environmental and forestry experts, yet, as Gerard Guay wrote, "the Judge gave more weight to a flimsy, contradictory one and a half page affidavit by the Regional Director of Forestry."[17] The courts were clearly not the avenue for justice that the Algonquins sought.

Fortunately, in the 1980s, the social conscience of North American nongovernment organizations (NGOs) was trained on forests. NGOs in the developed world created campaigns to "save the rainforests" in the south, raising money to buy up lands, lobby governments and industry, and promote consumer habits that did not rely on rainforest destruc-tion. Barriere Lake realized that they would have to wake Canadians up to the fact that devastating clear-cuts were destroying Indigenous lands in their own country. The Algonquins had already begun a campaign of blockades to protect the forest when the United Nations report of the Brundtland Commission, "Our Common Future" (1987), commonly known as the Brundtland Report, was released. The report reflected serious concern about the impact of human development on the envi-ronment. It suggested that Indigenous people should play a significant role in the sustainable management of natural resources, given their unique and particular knowledge of their homelands. Sections of the re-port were translated into Algonquin and discussed between elders and community members with their political advisers. The Barriere Lake Algonquins were attracted by the concept of sustainable development, which explicitly recognized the needs of future generations within the framework of resource extraction. Barriere Lake, under customary chief Matchewan, formulated a strategy to demand that the Canadian gov-ernment act on the report's recommendations by allowing them to im-plement a conservation strategy on their territory.

The government continued to ignore their concerns, so the Algon-quins took matters into their own hands. Barriere Lake had only one card in their pocket and they continued to play it powerfully and relentlessly. This time, blockades occurred during the 1989 provincial election and began to attract politicians' attention: all it took was a visit from a Parti Québécois candidate for the Liberal provincial minister of Indian Affairs to swoop in for a quick chat. Clifford Lincoln, former special representative to Barriere Lake during the Trilateral negotiations, believes that the Trilateral Agreement was signed to solve a problem of electoral politics. He told me, "My sense of it in the interim is that the provincial election was the catalyst. There was an election in the fall of 1989, and the government was anxious to put looming problems to bed, those of the Algonquins of Barriere Lake versus forestry companies being a persistent one. This I think was the great motivator in looking for a way out, which became the Trilateral Agreement eventually signed in 1991."[18] Other external pressures the following year, though, would seal the deal.

In 1990, Barriere Lake was back to blockading Highway 117. Lumber baron Claude Bérard was seeking permanent injunctions against the community and the Quebec ministry of forests was supporting these injunctions.[19] Barriere Lake did not have the money to intervene in court, nor could they otherwise get Quebec's attention—instead, they took over the highway.[20] In July 1990, acting to protect a sacred grove of pines, a group of Mohawks in Kanehsatà:ke were inspired by Barriere Lake to erect their own blockades to protect Haudenasaunee traditional lands.[21] Now Quebec had two major crises on its hands and fear of an incendiary summer of Indian insurrection was palpable.[22] It is not hard to imagine what happened next. The Liberals were in power in the province and Quebec Native Affairs Minister John Ciaccia had replaced Raymond Savoie in the recent provincial election. He flew in a helicopter from Oka to Barriere Lake to finally discuss an agreement.[23] In the shadow of Oka, a tentative deal was struck.

The Thorn of Jurisdiction

From an Indigenous perspective, the Barriere Lake Algonquins were not disrupting the forestry industry through their campaign of blockades. They were saving it. Most people in the community had never been against logging in the territory. Rather, they were against the destructive clear-cuts and the sheer neglect of forest life that was being endangered by provincial land-use management. Their determination to blockade through harsh winter conditions, with their families and young children on the front lines, created economic conditions that would ultimately challenge the forestry regime over a substantial area of land in the province. Barriere Lake's challenge to clear-cut logging pitted the jurisdiction of the federal and provincial governments against a small Indian band to determine how the territory should be governed.

In early September 1990, after Barriere Lake succeeded in getting Quebec to the table, the province immediately tried to short-circuit negotiations. It attempted to change the language of the proposed comprehensive conservation strategy from "sustainable development" to "sustainable yield"—language that lacked any clear definition even in the Quebec Forestry Act.[24] The Algonquins rejected this bait-and-switch tactic, interpreting the language as a means to continue tree farming on their territory.[25] The community also rejected Quebec's assertion of "exclusive jurisdiction" over resource management in the wildlife reserve.[26] In response, Chief Matchewan hit back, asking: "So does that mean when we go outside (the reserve) we're squatters? We don't have the right to say anything about what happens outside these 59 acres?" Barriere Lake's position was uncompromising: "This is Algonquin jurisdiction, too. We never gave up this land."[27] Despite the fact that the Quebec cabinet agreed in principle to an Algonquin conservation proposal, the government refused to take seriously the idea of coexistence and comanagement that the Algonquins envisioned.[28]

In the meantime, logging continued unabated. Following another series of blockades, Barriere Lake allowed the Gatineau lumber company to get back to work until October 1, 1990, as gesture of good faith. But they warned that if Quebec made little progress in signing a conservation deal, the Algonquins would be back on the blockades.[29] A year later, the governments and Barriere Lake were still negotiating. John Ciaccia had convinced Barriere Lake to dismantle their blockade of Highway 117 on the assurance that he would bring their conservation strategy to the Quebec government for approval. He agreed with the conservation strategy in principle, but he had to convince the province to go along with an agreement. The longer the province stalled, the more tense relations grew with the logging companies that endured costly delays and constant uncertainty. Ciaccia also agreed to contact Gatineau lumber company operator Claude Bérard and ask that he withdraw his injunction against Barriere Lake. Bérard insisted to the press, though, that he would go ahead with the injunction, demanding his right to fulfill the logging contract.[30] He stated that "if the band won't respect the law," the police or army should be brought in to remove the blockade.[31] The Algonquins responded by stating that they would not fight the injunction in the Quebec Superior Court because they recognized neither the injunction nor the authority of the court's jurisdiction over their lands.[32] Two could play the game of withholding recognition, especially in the context where Barriere Lake's resilience had created substantial political leverage.

Relations softened after this last volley of threats, though. Quebec brought Bérard to the negotiating table, where he was included in discussions regarding conservation measures in the park. Bérard also sought some authority in negotiations: "The Algonquins have rights but I have rights too," he told the media, referring to his twenty-five-year forestry contract with the government.[33] A leasehold is technically a property relation enacted through provincial authority to legislate and regulate natural resources.[34] Bérard's leasehold rights did not actually have equal standing to Aboriginal rights, because property rights are not constitutionally protected in Canada, whereas Section 35(1) of the Constitution Act of 1982 recognizes and affirms "the existing aboriginal and treaty rights of the aboriginal peoples of Canada." However, the courts and government have proven reluctant to violate private property rights when they are challenged by Indigenous claims. Instead, de facto property rights have been protected, despite their lack of constitutional protection and in spite of the special status of Aboriginal lands in Canada. The relationship between these leasehold rights, Aboriginal rights governed under federal jurisdiction, provincial jurisdiction over natural resources, and Indigenous inherent laws of jurisdiction became the central tussle to resolving the logging conflict, as well as the machinery that would determine how governance would be led on the territory.

The federal Department of Indian Affairs was at first much more supportive of Algonquin demands for a conservation strategy over their territory than the province. This might seem surprising because the federal government would have to reconcile some authority in agreeing to share power with Indigenous peoples. However, from an economic perspective, it was the province of Quebec that was financially liable to the forestry companies, because natural resources are governed under provincial jurisdiction. The federal government at first must have assumed it had little material wealth to lose. In the early days, Quebec was the recalcitrant partner in negotiations, but eventually civil servants and elected officials within the federal government would conclude that they had as much to lose from recognizing Algonquin jurisdiction as the province did. The institutionalization of shared powers through the Trilateral Agreement undermined Canada's deeply flawed national land claims policy, which is described later in this chapter. As Nahwegahbow describes, at a meeting with Deputy Minister of Indian Affairs Scott Serson, the official blatantly accused Nahwegahbow and the band of "back-dooring" the Comprehensive Land Claims Policy.

Despite the federal government's initial support, the Department of Indians Affairs could not do much beyond petition the province for support because most of Barriere Lake's territory is classified as provincial Crown land. Although Quebec certainly prefers to create the impression that the province holds exclusive ownership rights to the territory, these ownership claims should be legally subject to confirmation and recognition by Indigenous peoples, according to both Canadian and Indigenous law. Forestry Canada reports that "[a]pproximately 170,000 hectares of Quebec's productive and accessible forests are currently located on Indian lands."[35] That amounts to about 90 percent of the province's productive forest lands.[36] But, as the Assembly of First Nations of Quebec and Labrador (AFNQL) notes, Quebec provincial jurisdiction on "public lands" is not absolute. Rather, it is defined in Article 109 of the Constitutional Act of 1867, which allocates underlying title to the province "subject to . . . any Interest other than that of the Province in the same." The AFNQL states:

> The limits to the ownership right of article 109 define the field of application of section 92(5) *[The Management and Sale of the Public Lands belonging to the Province and of the Timber and Wood thereon]* and, therefore, of all provincial laws which stem from it. Among these provincial laws, we find the Act respecting the lands in the domain of the State, the Forest Act, the Mining Act and the Hydro-Québec Act. *The field of application of all these Quebec laws is subordinate to the First Nations title and to other ancestral rights, since it is clearly established by the jurisprudence* (particularly in the *Delgamuukw* judgment) *that the provincial laws cannot extinguish these rights.*[37]

The AFNQL makes clear here that the limits to provincial ownership are Indigenous title and rights to the land. Long before the *Delgamuukw* decision was reached by the courts, Barriere Lake was asserting that their jurisdiction had not been extinguished by Quebec. To wit, Quebec had been having difficulties granting access to lands it did not own for decades, most dramatically showcased in the 1970s by the successful lawsuit by Cree and Inuit hunters that brought a massive hydro development project screeching to a halt.[38]

Quebec Sovereignty, Quebec Colonialism

To complicate matters, during this period the province of Quebec was not only in conflict with the federal government over the Algonquins, but locked in a constitutional battle with Canada over the very future of confederation. A national separatist movement was in full bloom during this period in Quebec and Indigenous peoples' land rights became entangled in the aspirations for both federal and provincial territorial sovereignty.[39] Barriere Lake's demands were perceived by Quebec as a direct threat to their short-term profit strategy for the forests, but also as a problem that should be only theirs to solve, and not under the purview of the federal government. The tension between federal and provincial sovereignty claims raised the outstanding question of the status of Indigenous peoples in a future, potentially sovereign, Quebec.

Once again, Barriere Lake would serve as a reminder to both governments of their lack of jurisdiction over Algonquin land, but also of the special relationship Indigenous nations have with the federal Crown. In 1992, as grand chief of Barriere Lake's tribal council, Jean Maurice Matchewan vocalized the Algonquin position on Quebec secession from the Canadian state:

> Quebec claims a right of self-determination. But self-determination belongs to peoples. It does not belong to territories. If Quebecois and Quebecoises claim the right to determine their own future, then the Algonquins have a prior right to self-determination.
>
> We take the position that Quebec cannot secede with Algonquin land without our consent. And we have put Canada on notice that, until we advise otherwise, we intend to hold Canada to its

fiduciary duty with respect to our traditional lands in the Province of Quebec.[40]

Quebec's political success and legitimacy as an independent state rested on Aboriginal people. The Mohawks, Inuit, Naskapi, Miqmaq, Maliseet, Montagnais, Abenaki, Atikawekw, Algonquin, and Huron are all peoples whose lands have been demarcated and circumscribed as belonging to "Quebec." During the period of constitutional uncertainty, Mary Ellen Turpel expressed doubt regarding the real commitment of Quebec to Indigenous self-determination because of incidents like the military standoff at Oka,[41] but also because of the province's attitude that Indigenous rights could be dealt with later and do not need to be resolved up front: "It is not a perfunctory matter, or an administrative decision considering how best to transfer a head of jurisdiction (Indians and lands reserved for Indians) from the federal authority to a newly independent Québec state."[42] Rather, "[t]he claim by Québécois for full sovereignty . . . appears to rest on the erasure of the political status of aboriginal peoples and the denial of their most fundamental rights to self-determination."[43]

An explosive atmosphere toward Indigenous peoples was also revealed when the National Chief of the Assembly of First Nations Ovide Mercredi appeared in 1992 before the Quebec National Assembly's Committee to Examine Matters Relating to Accession of Quebec to Sovereignty. He appeared with chiefs and elders from First Nation communities from across the country and said:

> There can be no legitimate secession by any people in Quebec if the right to self-determination of First Nations are denied, suppressed or ignored in order to achieve independence. Our rights do not take a back seat to yours . . . Only through openness, of the mind and of the heart, can questions of such vital importance to your people and ours be reconciled. The alternative, which we do not favour, is confrontation.[44]

The speech was met with outrage in Quebec, even though Mercredi was considered a moderate in Indian country. Indigenous peoples were called "warriors and criminals" and depicted as holding the province hostage to their petty demands and holding back provincial aspirations for independence to do so. Turpel expressed no sympathy for this intolerant and discriminatory attitude: "The era of disciplining aboriginal peoples for being different is over. Political support for the aspirations of Québécois will not be won in Canada or around the world with this type of denigration."[45] "Maîtres chez nous" (masters of the house)—a slogan of Quebec separatism—after all, could easily apply to Indigenous demands for self-government and self-determination. Indigenous peoples are not simply an item under a head of jurisdiction, as seems to have been presumed by many Québécois and others outside the province, Turpel sternly rebuked. The first peoples in Canada are political entities—"peoples" in the international sense—which means rights to self-determination.[46]

Selling the Forests for a Nationalist Song

The province's bid for secession failed. Near the end of 1995, the second of two referendums was held to ask voters whether Quebec should proclaim national sovereignty and become an independent country. The economic risk of secession had been a persistent, underlying uncertainty in the movement for Quebec statehood.[47] But when the dust of defeat settled, the same old economic problems in the forestry sector persisted, and Quebec's financial liability to the logging companies finally pushed the province to consider Indigenous land rights; the costs of ignoring Algonquin demands had become unfeasible. Prior to his invitation to the negotiating table, lumber baron Claude Bérard had threatened: "I might just close the plant and sue the God-damned government," likely articulating a growing fear in provincial government corridors: a rush of lawsuits that could cost the province millions of dollars, and worse, create a chilly investment climate at a difficult time for the forestry sector.[48] Barriere Lake's capacity for economic disruption, exercised through the instability they caused in the forestry sector, was documented in a report commissioned by the Trilateral Secretariat in 1996. The consulting firm found that the rough total estimate of economic value generated in the Trilateral zone was around $56.5 million annually.[49] Hydro Quebec's revenues were estimated to be a further $50 million, calculated by another consultant and added to arrive at the conservative sum of $100 million.[50]

In 1994 alone, forestry accounted for 59 percent of economic value in the region, which is more than $33 million in annual revenue.[51]

The economic value of logging to industry and the province, however, was impossible to sustain given the province's poor management policies. Geographically, Barriere Lake's territory in the Outaoais region of Quebec is highly desirable for logging: it is widely accessible by road and only 320 kilometers north of Ottawa, minimizing transportation costs. At the time of the early 1980s blockades at Barriere Lake, Quebec boasted the most productive forestland in Canada.[52] But from an Algonquin perspective, Quebec was mismanaging the land in ways that would have catastrophic and long-lasting effects. The tragedy of Quebec's forest-management regime was that even from a profitability perspective, the forestry sector was making little economic or ecological sense. Quebec's forest management was by some standards the worst in the country: between 1980 and 1988, Quebec claimed to have only reforested 39 percent of clear-cut forests. In terms of managing harvested areas, from 1985 to 1990, a mere 7 percent on average was weeded, thinned, or fertilized compared with a national average of 25 percent.[53]

The industry was also seriously suffering from underdevelopment. The pulp and paper industry in Quebec had been largely resting on its laurels since earlier in the century. The industry was in desperate need of modernization; the machinery was hopelessly out of date, constraining growth. Among other issues eroding Quebec's competitiveness, key was the loss of markets for its forestry products. From the beginning, Quebec's softwood pulp industry was dependent on foreign consumers, especially the United States and Britain. Changing markets positioned Quebec in a cycle of continental and global trade at a time when Europe and the United States were producing specialized products for export. IKEA, for example, was exporting cheap softwood furniture to Canada, where a glut of raw wood was selling for a song on global markets. At the time, lumber prices had risen twice as slowly as the consumer price index of the previous two decades.[54] Exporting these products during this disastrous period was a "source of impoverishment" for Quebec, contributing to the crisis in the forestry industry.[55] Rather than increase the value of lumber through the development of high-value manufacturing capacity, Quebec let others produce the value: by exporting high-quality wood fiber abroad, the province contributed to extreme underdevelopment in the industry that would continue to have consequences later on.[56]

In the wake of this ecological and economic mismanagement, the province offered no incentive for companies to assume any responsibility for the future of the forests. Barriere Lake, on the other hand, had a real vision for how to sustain the forest for future generations, allowing a mix of economic systems to coexist. Their vision was for a tripartite system with the provincial and federal Crowns to form a partnership allowing the Algonquins to have a decisive say over the resource management on their lands. They were proposing a comanagement arrangement unlike any other agreement signed in Canada at the time. It was not based on property notions of settler exclusion but on principles of coexistence, based on Indigenous knowledge. To Barriere Lake community leaders, coexistence was a meaningless term unless it translated into a real transfer of responsibility, rights, and economic wealth. In terms of the forests, Barriere Lake's assertions of jurisdiction were not merely a political or environmental claim, but also an economic assertion based on legal jurisdiction over traditional lands. In its radical reimagining of interlegal coexistence between settler and Indigenous governments, Barriere Lake sought a path outside of the colonial trenches of power. But in its alterity, the promise of hope competed with the government's fear of change, bringing to light both the limits and the expansionist strategies of state power.

Rejecting the Land Claims Policy

To fully appreciate the context of the Trilateral vision, the tripartite vision for coexistence that Barriere Lake proposed must be set against the proposed policy solution that they were rejecting. There is much to analyze and critique about the Comprehensive Land Claims Policy (CLCP) and the conclusion to this book expands these concerns. Here I want to focus on the principal controversy of the land claims policy as it relates to jurisdictional conflict: the extinguishment requirement. My aim is to show how the Trilateral Agreement process, described in the next chapter, sought to resolve this controversial core mandate of the CLCP. In the Conclusion, I canvas the policy more widely, setting it into a national context of colonization.

The modern treaty process was ushered in with some excitement in

1973. It emerged entirely in response to the considerable efforts of Indigenous peoples to assert jurisdiction over their traditional territories. The policy was an outcome of the ruling handed down in a case brought by the Nisga'a tribal council, at its own expense, against the government of British Columbia. In 1971, the case made its way from the British Columbia Supreme Court to the Supreme Court of Canada.[57] The lower courts in British Columbia had not been able to grasp Indigenous land ownership. In a starkly racist example of this failure to connect, Chief Justice Herbert William Davey stated that native peoples were far too primitive to have any notion of private property—the sign of civilization—and therefore any right to claim underlying title.[58] But three judges on the Supreme Court bench found otherwise. Emmett Hall was the most outspoken judge who recognized that Nisga'a title had preexisted Confederation and the creation of the province; he argued that it had never been extinguished and that it could still be asserted today.[59] He urged the court to adopt a progressive view of Indigenous peoples and not be bound by the outdated notions of Indians from the past.

When the *Calder* decision came down in 1973 it was a split decision of 3:3:1 (three in favor of the plaintiffs, three against, one dismissal based on a technicality), but it opened up the possibility of Aboriginal title in British Columbia and on unceded lands more generally. The decision shocked then Prime Minister Pierre Elliot Trudeau, who had to confess, "perhaps you had more legal rights than we thought you had" and reversed his denial of special rights for Indians articulated in his Department of Indian Affairs' 1969 White Paper.[60] But, as Johnny Mack notes, while the *Calder* decision marked a space away from the harsh denial of Indigenous rights represented by the White Paper, it was also a movement toward a "soft imperialism," "characterized by a rejection of a colonial apartheid/assimilation mode of operation in favour of one marked instead by integration and selective toleration of indigenous difference."[61] This soft imperialism was signaled by the introduction of a settlement process for outstanding land grievances. Within six months of the *Calder* decision, a new policy was rolled out to deal with all the Indians who had not signed treaties. On August 8, 1973, the federal government issued a "statement of policy" demonstrating a willingness to negotiate for land with Indigenous peoples, and acknowledging its obligations under the Royal Proclamation.[62]

Calder was first heard at the Supreme Court the same year that

Premier Robert Bourassa announced the James Bay hydroelectric project. In 1972, the Cree and Inuit took the government to court, ordering a
halt on the massive construction project that would damage their lands
and ways of life. Quebec denied that the Cree and Inuit had any such
rights of claim to the land. The statement on land claims put out by the
Trudeau government was a political policy and not a legal obligation, but
soon after the *Calder* decision came down, Quebec decided to settle as
quickly as possible with the so-called Quebec Indians so that the hydroelectric project could go through.[63] That deal led to the historic signing
of the James Bay and Northern Quebec Agreement (JBNQA) in 1975—it
was the first land claim settlement signed since 1930. The JBNQA was
not signed under the CLCP but it set a framework in place that has yet
to be dislodged despite repeated attempts at reform. Article 2.1 of the
JBNQA reads:

> In consideration of the rights and benefits herein set forth in
> favour of the James Bay Crees and the Inuit of Quebec, the James
> Bay Crees and Inuit of Quebec hereby *cede, release, surrender, and
> convey* all their Native claims, rights, title, and interest, whatever
> they may be, in and to land in the territory.[64]

All Indigenous parties negotiating modern treaties from that day forth
would be forced to extinguish *(cede, release, surrender, and convey)* title
to their lands.

This requirement became even clearer when the 1981 policy was released. The policy revision, which hardly differed from the 1973 version,
stated that the policy's objective was "to exchange undefined aboriginal
rights for concrete rights and benefits," calling for the *"extinguishment of
all aboriginal rights and title as part of a claim statement."*[65] The requirement
of Indigenous nations to extinguish their land rights upon settlement
was met with controversy from the start, but a pattern would persist of
policy revision without reform for decades to come. To take just one example, in 1985 a federal Indian Affairs–appointed task force, dubbed the
"Coolican Task Force" after its chairman and author, concluded that "the
extinguishment policy was unjust and unnecessary."[66] A coalition of six
groups negotiating with the government over land at this time actively
endorsed the Coolican Report as the necessary spark for change.[67] But
the coalition failed to get traction. Although they worked closely with the

government to develop a series of policy recommendations, they were challenged in this task by the radical nature of Coolican's assessment of policy failure. The Coolican Report identified the need for long-term solutions to overcome the political lack of will by the government to share power and authority with Indigenous peoples. Compressing structural change into policy recommendations proved hard and ineffective. As Fenge and Barnaby explain, reaction to the revised policy proposal was largely met with ambivalence by federal agencies:

> Much of this reaction seems to have been the result of ignorance about the legal and moral bases of land claims. To aboriginal peoples the question of land claims is compelling and consuming, but to senior civil servants in Ottawa it is a peripheral issue of no great importance or urgency. Most decision makers listened politely to the representations of the coalition but carried on as before, unperturbed.[68]

The policy recommendations were laid to rest, and following a cabinet shuffle, Bill McKnight became minister of Indian Affairs. After considerable lobbying by the negotiating groups, he introduced a new policy on land claims released under then Prime Minister Mulroney's 1987 "Blue Book."[69] The revised policy introduced the concept of "alternatives to extinguishment" to deal with the most pressing concern, but featured extremely limited forms of self-government that bore no constitutional protection. Ultimately, the essence of the policy remained unchanged.[70]

Although it was progressive, the Coolican Report should by no means be viewed as an ideal expression of a land claims policy, because the report continued to frame the policy objective as a means to build strong and distinctive societies within confederation, whereas a fundamental issue for Indigenous peoples has been the recognition of distinct legal, political, and social orders.[71] The report in some way then gestured toward the conclusion that the Algonquins of Barriere Lake reached about the CLCP more generally: they would have to look outside of the policy to devise a model and build a relationship with settler authorities that was not already rooted in the presumed jurisdiction of the state over their lands.

The federal government has tinkered with the language in the CLCP but has never changed the underlying extinguishment requirement.

This feat is actually quite ambitious, given the significant judicial, political, and international developments that have unfolded since the CLCP was introduced. In terms of legal discrepancies between the policy and recent judicial decisions, the model perpetuated through the CLCP is not based on recognition of rights, but rather on an *exchange* of Aboriginal rights and title for treaty rights, which is contrary to Section 35(1) of the Constitution and to a string of court cases defining these rights.[72] For example, extinguishment provisions are contrary to *Sparrow*—the first Supreme Court of Canada decision to come down postpatriation of the Constitution to adjudicate on the scope of Section 35(1) rights. *Sparrow* required Canada exercise "as little infringement as possible" as part of its fiduciary duties to Indigenous peoples.[73] Further, whereas according to *Delgamuukw* Aboriginal title encompasses "the right to exclusive use and occupation" and the right to "choose to what uses the land can be put," as well as containing an "inescapable economic component"[74]— albeit with grounds for allowable infringement—the CLCP diminishes the nature of these rights by allowing a broad scope of infringement in favor of third parties.[75]

The discrepancies between the common law and the CLCP are clearly deliberate, as we can see in the case of the Nisga'a Final Agreement (NFA). As Paul Rynard explains, the general provisions of the NFA were "worded to supercede" *Delgamuukw*: "In that decision, the Court stated that Aboriginal title existed in Canadian law as a real common law right to property which encompassed full ownership of lands and natural resources. Any First Nation that can demonstrate that it exclusively occupied territories where British sovereignty was asserted can claim ownership as Aboriginal title to these lands."[76] However, the wording of NFA (2.24) begins: "Notwithstanding the common law," and goes on to forfeit these rights as set out in the agreement. In other words, the obstacle of Aboriginal rights as common law had to be explicitly overcome. Although there are limitations to the jurisprudence on Aboriginal rights, title, and the scope of Section 35(1) rights, it is not an exaggeration to state that new legal precedents have not affected the CLCP in the least.[77]

In the international context, the United Nations (UN) and other human-rights bodies have passed protocols that protect ancestral Indigenous lands from state expropriation. For example, Article 8.2 of the United Nations Declaration on the Rights of Indigenous Peoples (UNDRIP) (2007) declares that states "shall provide effective mechanisms for prevention of, and redress for: (b) Any action which has the aim or effect of dispossessing them of their lands, territories or resources."[78] UN human-rights bodies have further advised Canada that it needs to stop requiring Indigenous peoples to surrender or extinguish their land rights. As early as 1998, the UN Committee on Economic, Social and Cultural Rights relayed concern to Canada regarding "the direct connection between Aboriginal economic marginalization and the ongoing dispossession of Aboriginal people from their lands" that include "the extinguishment, conversion or giving up of Aboriginal rights on title."[79] Canada failed to respond to the recommendations of the committee, but when faced with criticism of the policy mounted by the Indigenous Network on Economies and Trade's "shadow report" on Canada's performance regarding their treatment of Indigenous peoples in 2006, Canada responded that it no longer requires Indigenous groups to extinguish their Aboriginal rights and title upon settlement.[80] Instead, it boasted of new approaches that included the "modified rights model" and the "nonassertion model."[81] However, the special rapporteur of the Commission on Human Rights responded that "the inclusion of clauses in land claims agreements requiring Aboriginal peoples to 'release' certain rights has led to serious concerns that this may be merely another term for extinguishment."[82] The UN committee was wise to Canada's attempts to skirt the issue by merely changing the language of the policy.

The language of "extinguishment" disappeared from the policy when the Nisga'a Final Agreement was negotiated in 2000, but as the UN report noted, the federal government has never changed the underlying extinguishment requirement. A language of "modification" and "exhaustion" was adopted in the Nisga'a Final Agreement in 2000, which was the first treaty signed in British Columbia under the CLCP (more specifically, under the regional form of the CLCP, the British Columbia Treaty Process).[83] The concept behind this new language was that Aboriginal rights were being modified, but not extinguished. What is sometimes called "certainty language" by negotiators substitutes the language of "modification"—to ensure the "nonassertion" of aboriginal rights—for the earlier language of "cede, surrender, and release." But, like extinguishment, these euphemisms still require Indigenous peoples' cession of Aboriginal rights and title in exchange for an emaciated list of treaty rights.

When the Nisga'a treaty was being negotiated, great efforts were made by government negotiators to distance themselves from the language of extinguishment. But the Nisga'a rightly wanted to know the point of spending decades achieving recognition for their unextinguished underlying title only to trade away these rights upon treaty settlement. Negotiators responded that the reason for doing so was that those Aboriginal rights, protected under Section 35(1), were ill defined and vague and that they wanted to replace them with "certainty," that is, spelled-out treaty rights. Nisga'a negotiators replied, why don't we just spell out those constitutional Aboriginal rights, then? But the government said "no."[84] Instead, Canada's negotiators pressured the Nisga'a to agree to the nonassertion of their constitutional rights in exchange for a new set of rights where neither Section 35(1) rights nor Aboriginal title could be listed as treaty rights. So, while there was no formal surrender, the modified rights model amounted to significant forfeiture of Section 35(1) protection, a violation of what Section 35(1) is ostensibly meant to protect.[85]

The most recent "reform" to the land claims policy pays close attention to Section 35(1) rights. In late September 2014, Canada quietly introduced the first major reform to the land claims policy in thirty years.[86] Douglas Eyford was hired to produce the interim policy, which states that opportunities for Aboriginal "long-term success and economic prosperity" cannot be achieved without addressing Section 35(1) rights.[87] Section 35(1) is interpreted to be fundamentally about *reconciliation,* which is seen as best expressed through the land claims and other nontreaty agreements that manage conflict over land by replacing Indigenous jurisdiction with the "certainty" of Crown ownership. In a confusing description provided by INAC, the policy states that a "certainty" or "legal reconciliation" technique will ensure the continuation of Section 35(1) rights posttreaty:

> This legal technique reconciles the coexistence of existing Section 35 Aboriginal rights with treaty rights by enabling the continuation of the group's existing Section 35 Aboriginal rights while ensuring that, to the extent the continuing rights are inconsistent with the treaty, they cannot be used to undermine the agreement of the parties.[88]

If we unscramble this language, it suggests that wherever Section 35(1) rights are "inconsistent with the treaty" they will be voided. Thus, the modern treaty evacuates any meaningful Indigenous jurisdiction that Section 35(1) could be interpreted as protecting.

The *Tsilhqot'in* decision is not mentioned as a motivating factor for the recent evaluation of the policy. However, the interim policy was introduced on the heels of that Supreme Court of Canada decision. In *Tsilhqot'in v British Columbia,* 2014, for the first time in Canadian history the court ruled that an Indigenous nation held underlying Aboriginal title to its territorial lands. As Russell Diabo and I reflected, this opened up new possibilities of comanagement of lands and resources by First Nations and the Crown, as well as affirmed the right of First Nations to benefit from economic activity and refuse development on their title land. We argued that "[t]he court's decision held out the possibility of a true reconciliation, if Canada would seize it. The government [of Prime Minister Stephen Harper] could have embraced this opportunity to engage in good faith discussions with First Nations, recognizing the need to rethink a failed policy approach that has wasted billions of dollars over three decades, added a debilitating legal debt to the balance sheet of First Nations at the negotiating table and produced only a small handful of agreements. Instead, the government opted for a unilateral, backsliding approach, doubling down on the current comprehensive claims policy."[89] Instead, the policy of extinguishment persisted, as evidenced by the stark differences in recognition of Aboriginal title between the Supreme Court and the CLCP.

One such difference between the Tsilhqot'in Nation's title recognition versus the CLCP is apparent in terms of the amount of land settled.[90] The Tsawwassen First Nation (TFN) received 724 hectares of land and the Maa-Nulth First Nations (MFN) (5 bands) received 20,900 hectares through land claims, all of which had to be converted into private property upon settlement. To give a sense of the portion of traditional lands recognized through settlement, the Nisga'a Nation received 8 percent of total lands claimed.[91] Contrast these numbers to the two hundred thousand hectares of Aboriginal title lands recognized for the Tsilhqot'in Nation, which are still held in their collective, customary, sui generis form. Extinguishment is not simply a legal requirement in the process, it is built into what is called the "land selection" process as well, which amounts, on average, to a cession of around 90–95 percent of a negotiating group's land base.[92]

Perhaps the most troubling aspect of current negotiations is that the government refuses to explicitly name the core mandates of the policy. Indignant that Indigenous peoples are expected to enter blindly into high-level discussions regarding their ancestral lands, the Algonquin First Nations have nonetheless had an impossible time getting disclosure on these terms. They describe how "[a] variety of excuses have been provided for this absence of a transparent and explicit policy statement, including the suggestion by officials that it's *like the Common Law* and can be found in all of the existing agreements and Cabinet mandates (the latter of which are not available to First Nations or the public)."[93] The formula, then, must be discerned through combing through signed agreements to calculate average land and cash settlements, final terms of settlement, nonnegotiable items, and other key perimeters for negotiation.

A leaked document, however, gives unprecedented insight into the intended impacts of the policy on Indigenous jurisdiction and governance. Prepared in the wake of a streamlining process by the federal government to take "A Results-Based Approach to Treaty and Self-Government Negotiations," a questionnaire was designed to assess the progress of each negotiating table. The "results-based approach" set out to "focus resources on the most productive negotiating tables so that agreements can be reached sooner," so a thorough checklist of obstacles was produced for negotiators to complete.[94] The document surveys the transition of title land into private property, the loss of tax exemption and winding down of transfer payments, and the incorporation of the band into a business entity under the law. In the section on governance, the text states: "Agreement on law-making over provincial/territorial jurisdictions will require the provincial government to be party to the agreement; provincial or territorial governments will also be required to be a party if the agreement is going to be constitutionally protected." In other words, Indigenous lawmaking authority will be subject to provincial/territorial laws and oversight in the event of jurisdictional conflict. Any decision Indigenous peoples seek to make that overlaps with provincial/territorial jurisdiction will require participation and agreement by those settler authorities. Further, any agreement must contain provisions "setting out detailed descriptions of the Aboriginal government's law-making powers." Any exercise of Indigenous jurisdiction, then, must be subject to the authority of provincial/territorial governments.

To date, twenty-six modern land claims have been concluded under the CLCP and there are currently ninety-nine First Nations at negotiating tables across the country.[95] More than half of the current pending negotiations concern BC First Nations, where almost no treaties were historically signed, meaning that the vast majority of the province is unceded Indigenous territory. Some land claims negotiations are grouped in "regional tables," such as the British Columbia Treaty Process (BCTP) or the Atlantic tables that tend to be grouped by province. While framed by Canada as unique processes designed to suit the particular local needs and context of First Nations, these regional processes all fall under the CLCP.[96] There simply are no other negotiating protocols that exist on the federal level to resolve land claims in Canada. By factoring in all the modern treaties, agreements in principle, and final agreements prepared to date, we can state conclusively that Indigenous peoples must give up their constitutional protections, however undefined, in exchange for ceding most of their lands.[97] For a band the size of Barriere Lake, the onetime payout would be around $1 million in exchange for Aboriginal rights and title forever. Compare that sum to the $100 million of resources extracted from the territory on an annual basis, or to the $1.5 million in annual resource revenue sharing laid out in the Trilateral Agreement. In this light, the CLCP represents a significant discount for governments on Indigenous land value.

The Trilateral Agreement anticipated these failures and shortcomings of the federal policy. It was carefully designed to avoid the pitfalls of state models of recognition for Indigenous lands. Although this strength ultimately became its liability (from the governments' perspectives), the Trilateral Agreement offered a viable alternative to a widely denounced state solution to dealing with unceded Indigenous lands.

6

The Trilateral Agreement Is Born

Struggles for jurisdiction over Barriere Lake lands were being worked out on the ground, but in the early 1990s they also moved to the negotiating table. The governments were finding that the Algonquins of Barriere Lake were neither easily distracted nor placated with vague assurances. To the contrary, the Algonquins insisted that overlapping jurisdictional claims to their lands be resolved through an explicit power-sharing agreement. They further insisted that their own knowledge of the land be respected as a guiding reference in any arrangement over resources on the territory.

The power of the Algonquins to make these demands in part derived from their economic leverage vis-à-vis the forestry industry. But a deeper strength was necessary for Barriere Lake to endure the daily and yearly hardships of leveraging this power. Many Indigenous struggles are derailed by a colonial politics of recognition. As Glen Coulthard explains, "the reproduction of a colonial structure of dominance like Canada's rests on its ability to entice Indigenous peoples to come to *identify,* either implicitly or explicitly, with the profoundly *assymetrical* and *non-reciprocal* forms of recognition either imposed on or granted to them by the colonial-state and society."[1] While the politics of recognition tends to drive state efforts at reconciliation and pacification at the negotiating table, the Algonquins proved relatively immune to these forms of management that operate through colonial forms of subjectivity. An incredibly adaptive society, the Algonquins did not premise their insistence on resource comanagement based on state-dictated forms of recognition or on limited terms of accommodation to development on their lands. Rather, they saw their role as comanagers to remind the state, through their sacred customary constitution and the three-figure wampum, that Canada and Quebec *needed the Algonquins' consent* to authorize extraction and encroachments on their lands. It was by these forms of jurisdictional authority—their belts, their laws, and the commitment to their ancestors and grandchildren—that the Algonquins found strength to carry on their struggle.

For two years following the tentative agreement with Quebec, the Algonquins endured constant negotiation, ongoing blockades, stalling, and debate, until an agreement was finally arrived at on August 22, 1991. The Trilateral Agreement, signed by the Algonquins of Barriere Lake, the government of Quebec, and the government of Canada, would give the Algonquins ultimate decision-making power over resource management on their territory. The Trilateral states that "Quebec and the Algonquins of Barriere Lake wish to ensure, on the territory currently used by the latter . . . the rational management of renewable resources in view of making possible, with a concern for conservation, their versatile utilization, and the pursuit of the traditional activities by the Algonquins of Barriere Lake." Land would explicitly be managed to ensure the pursuance of traditional activities by the community and to ensure sustainable resource use for future generations.

In the years to come, and as awareness of the agreement spread, praise tellingly focused on Barriere Lake's key demands. A United Nations report hailed the agreement as a "trailblazer" and pointed to six important features of the plan: it put the doctrine of sustainable development into practice; it established a real partnership between government and an Indigenous community; it blended Indigenous knowledge with modern development processes; it provided for a working partnership that fostered mutual respect between Canadians and Indigenous peoples; it established an important scientific and technical experiment that would help amend forestry practices; and it created an important educational and operational model, not only for Canada, but for the rest of the world.[2]

The Royal Commission on Aboriginal People (RCAP) report called the Trilateral Agreement a model for coexistence and commended the fact that it upturned the common insufficient conventions of comanagement.[3] Rather than simply institutionalize a joint management arrangement over a particular region and species, the Trilateral laid the groundwork for cooperation between parties to develop an integrated resource-management plan over 1 million hectares of land covering a major portion of Barriere Lake's traditional land base.[4] Moreover, mediating extremely different visions for Barriere Lake's territory, this form of jurisdiction sharing was designed to control access to the land by industry, tourists, and settlers *through the Anishnabe people*. This time, coexistence would be based on Indigenous leadership, forging a new relationship through the ecological and social damage of colonization.[5]

Three Phases toward Peaceful Coexistence

The Trilateral is technically a study and recommendation process agreement, referred to in the agreement text as a "pilot project." Although the agreement clearly states that it is without prejudice to Aboriginal rights and pushes the issue of title aside, the Trilateral is a politically and legally binding agreement, which is repeated several times in the agreement itself. In a mediator report in 1993, Quebec Superior Justice Réjean Paul acknowledged that the agreement would likely be recognized to have "treaty-like" status if challenged in the courts. As he writes, in light of the *Sioui* case (1990), "it is far from certain that the Supreme Court of Canada and, more particularly, the lower courts, would not characterize this Agreement as a 'treaty' with the Algonquins of Barriere Lake."[6] This treaty agreement gives the community a decisive voice in the management of ten thousand square kilometers of their traditional territory, protects Algonquin land uses, and gives them a share in the resource revenue from natural resource development on their land.

But what made all the difference between the Trilateral Agreement and other resource comanagement agreements (and the land claims policy) was the funding the Algonquins secured to undertake traditional land-use and occupancy research and mapping. In general, the lack of financial, administrative, and technical capacity in Indigenous communities erodes their ability to negotiate on even ground with governments and industry. Likewise, without detailed maps of traditional land use, having a say at the table over resource management would be reduced to doing lengthy consultations with elders for each individual proposal to log or engage in other resource extraction, which would have been quickly dismissed as unworkable. With the financial resources to collect, correlate, and map the community's traditional knowledge of their land, the Barriere Lake Algonquins would possess a blueprint for how the territory could be collectively managed, based on a transparent, easily referenced, common base of ecological understanding and knowledge of the territory. In Article 3, Quebec and the Algonquins agreed to share the costs of the study and recommendation phases, with Canada further agreeing to pay all of Barriere Lake's costs. According to the Trilateral, the collection, inventory, study, and analysis of data about renewable resources and their uses would constitute the first phase of the Trilateral Agreement, and the preparation of a draft Integrated

Resource Management Plan (IRMP) would constitute the second. This IRMP would be the outcome of thousands of hours of interviews with land users, in particular, elders whose education derived almost exclusively from the bush.

While I deal with the traditional land-use and occupancy studies in closer detail in the following chapter, it is important to note here the sophistication of this crucial work of these first and second phases. Undertaken chiefly by Terry Tobias, Scott Nickels, and Sue Roark-Calnek, the Indigenous Knowledge agenda of the Trilateral Agreement involved individual and joint interviews with harvesters, elder field trips, and extensive data collation and analysis. For example, elders identified each tree species found on the territory, then described to what ends they were best used, in the construction of which specific implements, in what season to harvest their bark, and how best to undertake this harvest. This work overlapped with sensitive area studies (SAS) mapping for the IRMP phase of the research, which also relied on extensive interviews and field trips, and included Tobias's two-year Harvest Study report, designed with input from Peter Usher and Doug Elias. Scot Nickels, a cultural geographer, produced a two-volume study of Barriere Lake traditional ecological knowledge—comprehensive work that formed the basis for his dissertation research and informed many of the specific reports that followed, such as Doug Elias's "Socio-Economic Profile of the Algonquins of Barriere Lake."[7] Sue Roark-Calnek's three major reports—on family narratives, toponymy, and social custom—formed the major ethnographic synthesis of the data. For example, her social customs report analyzed Tobias's data on household and cabin cluster composition, trapping partnerships, and moose-hunting task groups, and her toponymy report presents a complex geomorphology of historical ecological knowledge, including information on family traplines, territorial boundaries, animal life, and medicines. The collation of this research data was equivalent in this regard to binding an encyclopedia of oral knowledge of the territory.

The third phase of the Trilateral research—which was only ever partially completed, as we will see—would have involved the formulation of recommendations for carrying out the draft plan of phase 2, including a plan for resource revenue sharing. Although the agreement set out for completion of the plan by 1995, because of delays in the agreed-upon process, caused first by Quebec (1991–93) and then by Canada (1996–97), the 1995 goal was not reached. Although Barriere Lake believed that the signing of this agreement, for which they had fought and sacrificed so much, was the end of their struggle, they soon discovered it was only just the beginning.

"Our Authority Derives from the Creator": Governance, Jurisdiction, and the Trilateral

The Trilateral specifies that the agreement be between parties from "within their respective jurisdictions," so, although Indigenous jurisdiction is not prioritized, the fact that the Algonquins are implicitly recognized as being under their own jurisdiction seemed a respectable basis for negotiation.[8] However, the question of jurisdiction was central to Quebec's stall tactics that delayed the implementation of the agreement for nearly two years in the early 1990s. Immediately upon signing the agreement, all parties (as stipulated) appointed special representatives—one each for Quebec, Canada, and Barriere Lake—to form a body that had the authority to meet and oversee the implementation of the scheduled work plan. However, Barriere Lake soon found that Quebec never intended to work cooperatively with Barriere Lake. Rather, it seemed to perceive the Algonquins as simply a group to consult with in the course of upholding rigid interpretations of existing laws and regulations. Despite the fact that the Trilateral Agreement was signed by the Quebec minister for Native Affairs, the minister for Canadian Intergovernmental Affairs, the minister of Forests, and the minister of Recreation, Hunting and Fishing—an impressive array of the highest-ranking officials in the National Assembly—Quebec still refused to accept the very purpose of the agreement, which was the shared management of resources in the wildlife reserve.

The new relationship the Algonquins had hoped would restore ecological integrity to their lands was quickly disintegrating. Algonquin input on Quebec's action plan for Trilateral work was mostly ignored, cut plans went forward in sensitive and sacred forested areas without Algonquin consultation, and funding from the federal government was not forthcoming for the traditional land-use studies, meant to be completed in the first phase of the Trilateral process.[9] Quebec refused to acknowledge what it considered "outside interference" to its ministries by the Algonquins of Barriere Lake and its special representative repeatedly made promises and assurances he did not keep.[10] In February 1992, for instance, Quebec officials showed up to a meeting with a hastily, handwritten one-page document—neither signed nor dated—that they had clearly prepared that morning. The note contained their recommendations to the Trilateral Task Force on harmonizing logging with Algonquin land use. These so-called recommendations were essentially reiterations of provincial policy. Meanwhile, Quebec had rejected the Algonquins field team's initial report on moving forward with the first phase of the Trilateral Agreement.[11] A task force had been specifically set up as a technical team under the authority of the special representatives to develop the terms of reference for what became the measures to harmonize Algonquin–settler land use and to identify "sensitive zones." But Quebec struggled against sharing the jurisdiction and control promised in the Trilateral Agreement.

A particular exchange in 1992 between Chief Jean-Maurice Matchewan and Quebec Minister of Native Affairs Christos Sirros is telling of what the agreement meant to the different parties. Sirros penned a letter to Matchewan regarding the Trilateral process conveying that "there is no question of shared jurisdiction and co-management of resources on the territory covered by the Trilateral which confers no authority or power on the Algonquins of Barriere Lake in this regard."[12] An astonished reply followed from Matchewan, reminding the minister that the last time they met in Quebec, in the presence of other Quebec ministers, at Sirros's insistence Matchewan had agreed to put the matter of jurisdiction aside and leave discussion of the matter off the table.[13] Out of a desire to accommodate the process, Matchewan agreed to this on the condition that they would *all* steer clear of the issue. Now, Sirros's assertion of exclusive jurisdiction betrayed this agreement and laid bare the power struggle that nested beneath the surface of their fretful negotiations. Matchewan wrote to Sirros that he was cognizant of the minister of Natural Resources' responsibilities on public lands under Quebec laws and customs. But he also made clear to what law and customs he was bound by as chief of the Algonquins of Barriere Lake:

It is not our position that the Trilateral Agreement is the source of our authority or jurisdiction. Our authority derives from the Creator who placed us upon our lands many hundreds of years ago, prior to the arrival of European settlement and the creation

of Canada and Quebec. And our authority derives from the
traditional knowledge of our elders which has been passed down
from generation to generation and accumulated over hundreds
of years of occupation of our lands. It derives from our sense of
responsibility to the land and forests and wildlife and our desire
to maintain the integrity of those things so that we may continue
to benefit from them in our traditional pursuits.[14]

The letter urged a mutual respect of views on the matter of jurisdiction
and authority.

The Algonquins knew that their unprecedented agreement would encounter difficulties. Displaying characteristic Algonquin humility and
strength in the face of great insult and dismissal, Matchewan adds to
the letter the following: "It is against our ways to be exclusive and in-
flexible. Thus, our position is tempered by the importance of sharing in
our society as well as the realities that prevail on us today."[15] In many
ways, this comment articulates the vision of the Trilateral Agreement in
its clearest form: the Algonquins recognized the necessity of sharing the
land with the new occupants, and even the need to be flexible in these
accommodations, but they would never violate their own laws to do so.
The chief concludes the letter noting that the parties have reached an
impassable section of the road. He proposes that Quebec and the Algonquins move forward through a mediation process, overseen by a Quebec
superior court judge.

Meanwhile, a jurisdictional tussle was playing out between Quebec
and Canada as well. Canada, for its part, refused to approve budgets to
move forward with the work plans set out in the agreement. Its special
representative constantly tried to shift the responsibility for decision
making on financial matters back onto Quebec, despite the federal government's approval of Article 3 of the agreement, which put the burden of Barriere Lake's financial commitments squarely onto Canada's
shoulders. Instead, Canada tried to insist that Barriere Lake submit
receipts on a monthly basis for reimbursement, operating as such in an
ad hoc manner. This introduced impossible conditions for the Barriere
Lake secretariat—the coordinating body for the Trilateral Agreement—
constraining its ability to pay salaries or make regular rental payments
on its office.[16] Somehow, the Barriere Lake band was meant to front

these costs. At times, Barriere Lake was forced to divert crucial community programs and services dollars toward field research.[17]

Negotiations remained at a standstill with Quebec. Pleading Algonquin disobedience, Quebec officials accused the community of being unreasonable for continuing to assert their right to determine how forestry decisions were made on their territory. Sirros made a point of emphasizing to Chief Matchewan that the "appropriate instance for the recognition of rights *you may feel you have* is the judicial system or preferably a negotiating table that could be created for this purpose *in the framework of existing policies.*"[18] Sirros was likely recommending the Comprehensive Land Claims Policy as the existing and preferred framework for settling conflicts over land. But Barriere Lake would not budge.[19] After a protracted struggle with Quebec, Justice Réjean Paul of the Quebec Superior Court was finally brought in to mediate, forcing the province back to the table. Justice Paul was shocked at the conditions he found under which negotiations were proceeding: "[t]he Algonquins of Barriere Lake have, from their own Band budget and to the detriment of their other programs, unilaterally funded certain anthropological studies and have produced maps of an excellent quality indicating, among other things, their sensitive zones and their sacred territories . . . *It is David and not Goliath who is attempting to sustain the Agreement.*"[20]

Perhaps the most compelling vindication of Barriere Lake's vision and struggle was Justice Paul's plaintive question: "Why . . . are we at a point where we can almost see such a beautiful project collapsing?" Remarkably, Barriere Lake had still managed to undertake sensitive area studies throughout these grinding battles with Canada and Quebec. The community was propelled forward by the urgency to protect these areas, because Quebec had started handing out logging permits again despite assurances to the contrary. As Boyce Richardson explains, "The one glaring weakness of the Agreement was that the provincial government's management deals with logging companies were allowed to stand, guaranteeing the companies continued access to the trees."[21] Barriere Lake believed that, armed with the sensitive area studies maps, they could officially stop logging in those areas of the territory. Justice Paul, in Barriere Lake's defense, found that the logging permits distributed by the province may have been legal but that they in fact respected, as he put it, "neither the spirit, nor the letter of the Agreement."[22] His

recommendations included "the transfer of power to the special representatives, the transfer of control of the technical work from the Quebec ministries, and the protection of sensitive zones within the existing timber agreement."[23] He lamented that an agreement that finally
sought to converge government and First Nations interests so perfectly
could be lost.

In spite of the mediator's report, Quebec unilaterally withdrew support for the agreement again in 1993, and the process nearly collapsed.[24]
Quebec continued to allocate CAAFs and sensitive and sacred areas
continued to be logged with no regard paid to the Algonquins. Against
overwhelming odds, Barriere Lake pursued their fight to force the province to implement the agreement. Relations between the Algonquins,
industry, and the government resumed their hostility. By February
1993, the Trilateral Agreement seemed to be on the brink of collapse.
That month talks collapsed over disputes concerning the dimensions of
sensitive area zones—the Ministry of Forests maintained that a band of
trees twenty meters around water bodies was sufficient for the survival
and reproduction of plants and animals, but the Algonquins maintained
that in certain cases zones should go from twenty to seventy-five to one
hundred meters. This conflict over riparian zones held work up further.

Algonquin authority to log was sought at one point, but not through
the institutionalized task force set up through the Trilateral Agreement.
In April 1993, Quebec minister of Native Affairs Christos Sirros sent a
letter to Chief Matchewan informing him that cutting was scheduled
to start in the territory in a matter of a week. Sirros suggested the formation of an ad hoc task force with representatives from Barriere Lake,
Quebec, and the forestry companies, and suggested a draft IRMP for renewable resources could be produced.[25] This was the last straw. Barriere
Lake angrily rejected Quebec's proposal for the ad hoc committee. Chief
Matchewan said in a statement to the press, "We are still looking for a
negotiated settlement, but Christos is dishonest in forming a committee on the eve of cutting operations starting when he himself broke off
negotiations last February."[26] Clifford Lincoln, the community's special
representative, was furious too. It was Sirros who initially interrupted
the sensitive areas mapping work in the cutting sector. Lincoln fumed:
"Two months later with no notice, he proposes the creation of a committee which would have to do exactly what we were doing last winter. It
takes 45 days to identify the sensitive zones in a cutting plan. Mr. Sirros

calls us only one week before forestry operations are to recommence. It's nonsense."[27] Matchewan insisted that the Algonquins would come back to the table only if the federal government was involved and if the negotiations proceeded under the Trilateral framework.

The Algonquins did not sit back and wait. They invited to the territory the national chief of the Assembly of First Nations and human-rights and religious organizations to tour the logging camps. Media were also invited to attend.[28] And then, just when it seemed that the Trilateral Agreement was on the brink of total collapse, everything flipped back in the Algonquins' favor:

> A combination of factors, including an effective Algonquin public relations campaign, top level political communication, intensified contacts between the Algonquins and industry, and the prospect of rather unpalatable alternatives, prompted the provincial government to consent to the Algonquins' requests. Virtually overnight, a special interim management regime was established for the Agreement territory, belatedly creating a setting in which the Barriere Lake Trilateral Agreement can be successfully implemented.[29]

The administration of the agreement was taken out of the hands of the Quebec Ministry of Forests and placed directly under the premier, easing tensions and creating a warmer climate of negotiations that actually reflected respect for the Algonquin way of life and its place in the modern Canadian economy. Throughout the rest of 1993, the Algonquins of Barriere Lake accompanied logging crews to ensure that sensitive areas were not disturbed by forestry operations. The completed sensitive area studies led to the production of maps reflecting the extensive knowledge of Algonquin elders and knowledgeable hunters. They included sites that the community and the animals in the territory depended upon, such as "moose yards, bear dens, fish spawning sites, beaver streams, sugar (maple) bushes, specialty wood areas, eagle nests, travel routes, and various special sites, such as burial grounds sacred places and old settlements."[30] These sensitive area zones comprised about 12 percent of the total Trilateral Agreement area.

Work began now in earnest on the measures to harmonize forestry operations with Algonquin land use, with the aim of sustainable development on the territory. For one of the first times in Canadian history, Indigenous knowledge was being integrated into land-use management plans and future natural resource operations by non-Indigenous authorities. The potential role that Algonquins could play in land management remained wide open. They could be involved as guides, employed in tourism, silviculture, or fisheries development, or establish small-business operations. With a modest share of revenue from natural resource extraction a central plank of the Trilateral Agreement, the community would finally be able to develop their own programs and services, rather than rely on cookie-cutter government programs. There was a growing sense that the Algonquins' time had come again.

7

Coup d'État in Fourth-World Canada

One way to understand the relationship of jurisdiction to the production of settler-colonial space is to reverse the diagnostic applied to my
earlier ethnographic chapters dealing with Indigenous law and governance. Whereas in those chapters we examined Algonquin resistance
and adaptation to understand the meanings of jurisdictional power
on the territory—shorthanded to relations of *care* and *supply*—in this
chapter, we will examine one of the governments' key targets of interference as a diagnostic of the valence of Indigenous jurisdiction from
the state's perspective. In other words, we read resistance through practices of state power. As I have described, Barriere Lake was alienated
from their territory by means of mounting restrictions and encroachments aimed at replacing their Indigenous system of land tenure and
jurisdiction with the laws and regulations of settler society.[1] But, as the
Trilateral Agreement pushed ahead, power was also nakedly produced
through attempts at replacing their Indigenous government altogether.

Customary governments have long been key targets for colonial interference in Indigenous societies. This interference dates back to the
mid-nineteenth century. One of the earliest attacks on Indigenous
governance was dealt in 1857 by the influential Methodist missionary
and departmental adviser, the Reverend T. Hurlburt.[2] A letter penned
by Hulburt to Superintendent General R. J. Pennefather provides a
solution to the problem of native leadership: a coercive law against the
"petty chieftanships" that should be leveled to abolish and replace them
with colonial administration. The results of this kind of interference,
though, led to "pernicious" results among bands in the State of New
York; therefore, the Report of the Special Commission of the Legislative Assembly of Canada of 1858 at first did not encourage interference,
which had been deemed futile.[3] As one scholar concludes, however, this
directive toward noninterference "appears to have led to the conclusion
that powers of management and control should not be conferred on
the traditional government," in effect choosing to "starve out" Indigenous leadership rather than actively pursue its abolition.[4] This practice

became widespread, yet conferring legal power to Indigenous governments remained unavoidable for some time.

Gradually, a series of statutory maneuvers unfolded, aimed at replacing Indigenous customary governments with an elective system devoid of jurisdiction and governing power: the municipalization of Indian society. The legislative means to accomplish the abolition of customary governments appeared in Article 12 of the Gradual Enfranchisement Act of 1869, which introduced an electoral system designed to undermine traditional and hereditary chiefs.[5] It gave the superintendent general of Indian Affairs the power to direct elections and depose any chief deemed afflicted by "dishonesty, intemperance, or immorality." There would also be no more chiefs for life, and instead a three-year electoral cycle where only "the male members of each Indian Settlement" could vote. These changes were meant to disable hereditary government systems, where leaders were endowed with lifelong responsibilities, and to remove women from their crucial role in maintaining social order. As historian J. S. Milloy sums up, new electoral institutions were aimed at shouldering aside customary governments in exchange for "unchallengeable departmental control."[6] Justification for this internal meddling was explained in the Annual Report of the Indian Branch of the Department of the Secretary of State, 1871:

> The Acts framed in the years 1868–1869, relating to Indian affairs, were designed to lead the Indian people by degrees to mingle with the white race in the ordinary avocations of life. It was intended to afford facilities for electing, for a limited period, members of bands to manage, as a Council, local matters—their intelligent and educated men, recognized as chiefs, should carry out the wishes of the male members of the mature years in each band, who should be fairly represented in the conduct of internal affairs.
>
> Thus, establishing a responsible, for an irresponsible system, by law was designed to pave the way to the establishment of *simple municipal institutions.*[7]

The irony of this ambition was that the elective system introduced only the most limited governing powers, affecting no meaningful form of assimilation into white society as supposedly intended, but rather creating infantilized conditions for state wards. Under the 1884 Indian Ad-

vancement Act that boasted expanded powers for "civilized" bands—
consisting of trivial oversight such as on-reserve taxation—the minister
still exercised control and management over all governance issues and
an Indian agent attended and oversaw all band council meetings.

Indigenous peoples did not submit to these circumscribed conditions
willingly, as previous disastrous results foreshadowed. The St. Regis
band, for example, known today in Canada as the Mohawk community
of Akwesasne, was widely discussed by the Department of Indian Affairs because of its strident opposition and its rejection of the elective
system.[8] But by the time the Indian Act was introduced several years
later, in 1876, much of the damage by earlier acts had already been done
to customary governments.[9] Band councils had begun to replace customary systems. By 1946, it was observed that most bands in Ontario,
Quebec, and the Maritimes were under the elective system and with
increasing white settlement the government expected that bands would
inevitably transition their governments to conform to the model of surrounding communities.[10] Barriere Lake was one of the few communities
in the entire country that managed to hold out.

Colonization is a centralized project insofar as it is driven by federal
legislation and policy, but it is also a dense jostle of competing authorities on the land that can determine the extent and manner in which
formalized policy and lawmaking are applied. In this chapter, I bring
to light a diversity of agents and institutions–provincial police, child
protection agencies, opposition members of the House of Commons,
lumber companies—that helped produce a major governance crisis on
Barriere Lake lands. But it was the powerful economic and political
objectives to perfect settler sovereignty on Algonquin land that drove
Canada to ultimately reject the Trilateral Agreement and to execute a
coup d'état over Barriere Lake's customary government. In so doing, the
federal government pushed all parties—the Algonquins, forestry companies, and provincial authorities—to the brink of despair and collapse.

The Inherent Powers of Customary Indigenous Governance

At Barriere Lake, authorities largely ignored the community and the
customary system persisted, long after the vast majority of bands in
Canada had converted. An oral system of law was transmitted from one
generation to the next through shared experiences on the land and the

community organized itself by way of customs that reflected these laws. But by the turn of the twenty-first century, state authorities could no longer tolerate the persistence of Barriere Lake's customary government because it underpinned their struggle for the Trilateral Agreement. Therefore, the government sought an opportunity to undermine the social order on which the community's jurisdictional claim was based: their customary government system, based in the Mitchikanibikok Anishnabe Onakinakewin. Here we have an opportunity to ask: What was the threat of the customary government to state power? Precisely what obstacle did it put in place to colonization? What does the continuous state directive to implement municipal-style government on reserves tell us about the resistant order of Indigenous jurisdiction?

Practically, the problem of a "life chief" within the customary system is that a hereditary chief is simply in power for too long. A municipal election system promotes assimilation into white government by replacing customary law with settler legislation, but it is the insurance of leadership turnover that provides a key mechanism for the shift in power. Election cycles under the Indian Act fall into two-year terms, which can mean a steady cycle of inexperienced new band councils on which settler governments can prey. At Barriere Lake, leaders are groomed for life from a young age to learn the customary law, as well as skills of diplomacy and negotiation. They do not fight among their peers to lead but are selected by elders who know their character and trust their ability to learn quickly and grow into the role. According to elders at Barriere Lake, a hereditary chief governs for life because it takes a lifetime to learn how to lead. The election cycle gives settler governments opportunities to intervene, for example, with funding incentives for favorable councils, or to mete out punitive measures for disobedient chiefs, and it circumvents the reign of a "life chief" who learns his paces through years of exposure to the governments' tricks and cannot be fooled into compliance. In addition, oral traditions operate beyond the control of settler governments, and this unknown, uncertain element of citizenship, belonging, and legality is an impediment to colonial oversight.[11]

But, most important, a municipality is an ideal form of assimilation because it has no constitutional protection or status, and only narrow, medieval powers; it is a "creature" of the province because its governing powers and decision-making authority are delegated through the legislatures. As it stands, an unceded Indigenous territory such as Barriere

Lake's is not subject to the domain of federal *or* provincial authority where they violate Indigenous rights. Nor is the authority of a customary band such as Barriere Lake determined by the Canadian state. Customary governments are considered under Canadian law to be an *inherent* right. In contrast, band councils formed under the election provisions of the Indian Act are considered to possess *delegated* powers of authority from the federal government. The customary government poses a problem because the federal government has no authority over the governing practices of customary bands, and therefore no control over the social order of the community. At Barriere Lake, the community has consistently exercised their jurisdiction toward protecting the land, and it is the culture of the band that supports this land defense in the face of government leasing and permitting that has been identified as the core scaffold of Algonquin resistance to the land claims policy.

When the state targeted Barriere Lake's customary government, it was under the pretense of bringing the Indigenous government into line with the rest of Canadian society. Framing the customary government as a "premodern" form of social, political, and legal organization produced the knowledge to bring Barriere Lake under state jurisdiction. The *civilizing* discourse, used in the past to discipline Indians into "advanced" forms of municipal governance, was resuscitated in the language of *evolution* to describe necessary reforms to Barriere Lake's customary governance.

Bait and Switch

In Barriere Lake, while David bravely battled Goliath, the young king was also fighting Babylon at home. Dissent brewed in the community. Some perceived a failure of leadership to be responsible for problems in getting the Trilateral Agreement off the ground; others questioned why the community had to allow any measure of logging at all on their traditional lands. Moneys were being spent, but no discernible results could be seen—logging continued unabated. Personal conflicts between community members simmered into political divisions and eventually government and industry saw an opportunity to derail the Trilateral Agreement from the *inside*.

Chief Jean Maurice Matchewan ("Pancho" to those who know him) is an especially polarizing figure. He has a big personality and does not like to be pushed around by anyone, least of all the government. He is an intimidating presence—a large man, keenly intelligent, in full possession of himself, with a shrewd sense of humor and a penchant for devastating understatement. Once, when a bragging Quebec minister went on for more than forty minutes about his deep connection to his family's rural property in the province, Matchewan dryly responded: "Us, we've been here for a few years, too."

As a leader, Matchewan was chosen in 1980 in an usual leadership selection process. As Toby Decoursay explained it to me, with the territory being clear-cut and the wildlife disappearing, the elders knew the community needed a fierce leader who could lead a lifetime of struggle against these external forces. So, they approached the youth and they asked, "Who amongst your peers is fearless and strong?" Jean Maurice Matchewan was already in the hereditary line to be chief, but he was also a young unruly spirit who did not seem to fit the part. His peers, however, knew he was tough and held him up to be chief. After the usual deliberations ("blazing," as it is called in English) the elders chose Matchewan and the community approved the decision at a community assembly, as was their custom. Reflecting on this blazing years later, Matchewan revealed to me the best advice his father and former chief, Solomon Matchewan, ever gave him about dealing with white governments when he passed on the mantle: "They are all thieves."

According to Russell Diabo, policy adviser to Barriere Lake for more than twenty-five years, the Trilateral Agreement might have never gotten off the ground in the first place if it was not for Matchewan. The politicians could see that Matchewan did not mince words or make empty threats; he would lead the community to fight with everything they had. Matchewan was no lone wolf or rogue despot. He spent hours with the elders taking directives based on Algonquin law and taking his punches when they did not approve of his approach or decisions. Yet, regardless of his successes and his great sense of accountability, his confrontational tactics worried some in the community who were not fully apprised of what challenges Barriere Lake faced in the corridors of Canadian and Quebec power. Tactics that effectively worried the government and brought them repeatedly back to the table also made some community members anxious for alternatives.

Luckily for Indian Affairs, the coup d'état at Barriere Lake was first engineered by other outside parties. Gerard Guay, Barriere Lake's former legal counsel, had a vendetta against the community for firing him. They had let him go because he refused to take direction from the band.[12] He sought revenge by exploiting Matchewan's natural enemies. The dissidents at Barriere Lake were led by Joseph Junior Wawatie, who was the grandson of the great matriarch Lena Nottaway. Wawatie was eventually named official spokesperson for the "Kitiganik Anicinabek Provisional Government"—the name the group first chose to replace what they called Matchewan's "Barriere Lake Indian Government." The "Provisional Government" began their campaign to replace Matchewan's council in April 1994 with a series of newsletters denouncing the council and claiming to be the new government. The attacks also focused on band administrator Michel Thusky, adviser Russell Diabo, and legal counsel David Nahwegahbow. The Provisional Government's newsletters contained allegations of fraud, embezzlement of Trilateral funds, and "authoritarian" domination.

Wawatie sent in a petition to the Department of Indian Affairs claiming that a newly elected group had formed a counter-council to Chief Matchewan's council. He submitted a list of five new councillors that he claimed comprised the Provisional Government.[13] Within days, Jérôme Lapierre, associate director general of INAC, replied that "[i]n light of the submitted documentation we cannot come to the conclusion that the custom of the Barriere Lake Band has been followed nor that the provisional council has the majority support of the community." Lapierre informed Wawatie that the department would continue to work with Jean Maurice Matchewan's council.[14] On November 30, 1994, the minister of Indian Affairs, Ronald Irwin, confirmed this position to Wawatie, writing that "[u]nder the Indian Act . . . the Department of Indian Affairs has no authority to intervene in the selection of Chiefs and Councils, which are carried out in accordance with the customs."[15] These would prove to be famous last words.

Over the next year and a half, INAC repeatedly rebuffed the dissidents' attempts to claim legitimacy, consistently asserting that the department does not interfere in the customs of a band. The circumstance of Barriere Lake's customary government made things especially tricky for the department, which could not regulate the leadership selection of custom bands because these inherent rights of governance had never been delegated to Canada.[16] Nor would the department have any basis of knowledge of the band's customary traditions to intervene and adjudicate an election dispute. Department officials instead encouraged Barriere Lake to resolve their internal dispute by codifying their oral customary code in order to make the leadership process more publicly transparent.[17]

In the meantime, Trilateral negotiations staggered along. New stall tactics were deployed to thwart progress on the work plan. While governance issues divided the community, the Sûreté du Québec (SQ), the courts, and provincial government agencies all abruptly found complaint with the community in what looked like a smear campaign. In 1994, two women from the dissident faction at Barriere Lake accused Chief Matchewan of assault. Bail conditions set by the Quebec prosecutor forbade Matchewan from returning to Barriere Lake at a time when Trilateral issues were coming to a head.[18] Soon after Matchewan's arrest, the SQ was invited to a community assembly by band administrator Michel Thusky to be questioned on why it only reacted to complaints by the dissident faction and not to calls by other community members.[19] Weeks later, when attending Matchewan's trial, to his great surprise Thusky was arrested in a spectacular and egregious show of force by *twenty-five* police officers. He was accused of detaining two police officers in the band office and refusing to allow them escape—an inconceivable rendering of the assembly the SQ had attended.[20] Thusky's bail also forbade him from returning to the community, where he played a critical role as political strategist and negotiator alongside the Matchewan council. Both sets of charges were eventually thrown out of court, but the damage was done—the community had been sidetracked into legal issues for the better part of 1994.

In 1995, Quebec once again walked away from the Trilateral process, now citing allegations raised by community members concerning rampant sexual abuse on the reserve.[21] Journalist Charlie Angus recalls that "[w]hat the allegations had to do with completing a forestry agreement remained unclear to Band leadership."[22] The band council agreed immediately to an investigation, but found proceedings slow, increasing the risk of a media circus that could undermine the community's political credibility. There is no evidence to suggest for certain that dissident members alleged this abuse, and furthermore, the law protects the identity of those bringing forth allegations, so their identities may never be known. But anomalies plagued this set of charges, raising the band's suspicions. Bizarrely, the Outaouais assistant director for Direction de la protection de la jeunesse, Luc Cadieux, made public statements to the *Ottawa Citizen* during the investigation claiming that 50 percent of the sexual abuse cases were justified.[23] In fact, *only one person* was ever charged for sexual abuse, and about a half dozen children were treated for substance abuse.[24] But the final report released by the Quebec youth protection office never disclosed these extremely low figures, citing privacy concerns under law.[25] Although the youth protection agency was very open about allegations of abuse to the press, reporters had to struggle to obtain information regarding resolution of the matter. An *Ottawa Citizen* reporter wrote that "Quebec has made getting the truth difficult by withholding critical information on the scope of abuse."[26] The sex abuse allegations appeared to be a manufactured scandal to paint Barriere Lake's public image as a community without the moral integrity to govern itself.[27]

But this was still not to be the end to the mudslinging campaign. The sexual allegations were soon followed up by further allegations of financial misconduct related to the band's deficit, which led to federal threats to freeze Trilateral funding. These allegations were also later disproved.[28] As Justice Réjean Paul's report had clearly found, the result of the federal government's financial hoarding had forced Barriere Lake to pay for Trilateral research from their meager program funding, wreaking havoc in their financial accounts.

Allegations of financial misconduct were then expanded to the band's advisers. Following a visit to the community by Reform Party members, on June 22, 1995, John Duncan, who served as an MP for the Reform Party, raised a question in the House of Commons about allegations of misappropriation amounting to $255,000 in legal fees paid to David Nahwegahbow, Barriere Lake's former legal counsel. Following inquiries, Indian Affairs concluded that there were no grounds for an RCMP investigation because Nahwegahbow was acting as special representative for the Trilateral Agreement and these moneys were owed to him in salary.[29] The large sum in fact represented considerable back pay because Trilateral employees often had to wait months for remuneration. However, Nahwegahbow was not spared the public stain as his name was dragged through the mud.

A final devastating blow: seemingly out of nowhere, fortunes turned for the dissidents at Barriere Lake. What had started out as a letter-writing campaign in 1994 escalated into a coup d'état by 1996. The

Provisional Government, now calling itself the "Interim Band Council" (IBC), presented a petition in November 1995 claiming they had won a recent leadership election. They claimed that 259 people participated in this election and that 156 people had signed a petition in favor of the IBC, compared to only 62 people for Matchewan's council. An unusual mode of leadership selection, the IBC claimed that Barriere Lake's customary code had "evolved" to "election by petition."[30] On January 23, 1996, the IBC was formally recognized by INAC as the legitimate governing body at Barriere Lake.

Coup d'État

The very next day following the IBC's recognition, an internal briefing to the minister cautioned him to avoid any investigation into the Matchewan council's claims of IBC fraud. Instead, INAC staff issued talking points that the department should keep to on the matter of the validity of the IBC. They recommended that INAC insist that the IBC received a strong vote, with more than a hundred signatures on their election petition, and that the new council had a mandate to write up the electoral customs by June 30, 1996, after which another election would be held. Finally, the memo stated that "[o]nce a proper custom selection process is in place, a new Chief and Council will be chosen."[31] There is no direct mention of why the current chief and council—Matchewan's council, to be exact—fell short of the criteria for a properly selected council. Ignoring Matchewan's submissions attesting to his ongoing support by community members,[32] the minister was advised in the memo to continue to emphasize the need for the community to codify their customary code and to resolve their leadership dispute through "an electoral custom"— neither of which conformed to Barriere Lake's leadership traditions or addressed Matchewan's protestations.

Up until December 1995, the Department of Indian Affairs had firmly and publicly rejected any intervention into the community's customary code of governance. But a set of internal briefings shows that by at least the end of 1995, senior officials in the department had undergone a change of disposition toward the customary government at Barriere Lake.[33] In January, just weeks before the federal government's recognition of the IBC, departmental bureaucrats recommended increasing collaboration with SQ forces. Closer to the date of IBC recognition, bureaucrats began to focus on financial matters, now including recommendations for the nomination of a third-party manager to control the band's budget. The briefing assures the minister that if the recommended action to recognize the IBC election is taken, "*in the meantime DIAND will be in control of programs, services, and budgets.*"[34] These tactics listed in the briefs—codification of the customary selection system, coordination with security forces, and complete financial control—would prove pivotal to the department's strategy to sterilize the power of the customary government.

Seeking advice from the Department of Justice (DoJ), INAC was warned unequivocally that "in strict legal terms, there is no such thing as 'recognition' of a band council."[35] The consequences, then, of "recognizing" the IBC would be that "any subsequent actions that the Minister might take with regard to the newly recognized band council would be subject to review by the courts in one way or another." DoJ counsels that "*the most wise course would be to make the determination of who is regarded as the true band council in a procedurally fair matter, in order to help ensure that the correct determination is made.*"[36] As we have already seen, INAC did quite the opposite. Following the initial circulation of a petition by the dissidents in November, Matchewan invited INAC to hold a referendum in the community to verify the support Matchewan still held, but INAC ignored this request.[37] Then Matchewan communicated to the department that there were egregious problems with the petition signatures, including many names of people who did not live in the community or who claimed to have been misled into signing for the IBC.[38] Matchewan even countered with a petition attesting to the community's support of his council—containing 152 signatures—to no avail.[39] Calls to the minister of Indian Affairs for the immediate suspension of the IBC went unanswered.[40] The department, as outlined, had no means to verify the legitimacy of the "newly elected" council because it had no knowledge of Barriere Lake's customary code. So, how could it have felt assured that its arbitrary decision reflected a "procedurally fair" adjudication of Barriere Lake's leadership selection practice? This was precisely the legal predicament DoJ presciently warned INAC to avoid.

It would take years for evidence to surface confirming Barriere Lake's conviction that this coup d'état was in part the product of Canada's change of heart regarding the Trilateral Agreement. In 1999, in relation to a labor dispute at Barriere Lake concerning the IBC, adjudicated by

Madame Justice Danièle Tremblay-Lemar, two findings of particular interest were submitted as matters of fact in her ruling: the first confirmed that the agitation by dissident Barriere Lake members was instigated by Gerard Guay, the disgruntled lawyer the customary council had fired for unprofessional conduct, and the second that Indian Affairs was advising the group of dissidents on how to seize power.[41] In September 1995, the department had written to the dissident group and explained to them how to become officially recognized.[42] It was Indian Affairs that had "evolved" the Mitchikanibikok Anishnabe Onakinakewin into election by petition.

The Interference Archive

I would like to point out that this careful reconstruction of the "coup d'état" is not aimed to single out the "good" guys at Barriere Lake from the "bad guys," but rather to emphasize that this incident cannot be dismissed as simply an "internal dispute," as often is the case when media or governments seek to explain governance conflicts in First Nations communities. Certainly, there was substantial misinformation circulating in the community about individuals and about the Trilateral Agreement and its funding arrangements. There was also a genuine rift in political opinion, much as one would find in any society, or between individuals at any level of government. The conflict described here is not intended to cast stones at any particular faction in the community, especially in the context of a band under considerable external duress, but rather to provide a damning indictment of Canada, Quebec, and the unethical mores demonstrated by individuals and firms in the law industry. In chapter 8 I examine another leadership dispute that focuses more specifically on reconciliation efforts, and I hope it contributes further nuance to the divide-and-conquer tactics exercised by settler governments.

To reiterate, the broader context of this current "internal dispute" is crucial. Recognition of the IBC was convenient for a federal government increasingly anxious about the precedent that the Trilateral Agreement could set for other bands. In 2002, Barriere Lake received a letter from Prime Minister Jean Chrétien's office. The letter was a response to concerns raised by Barriere Lake's special representative at the time, Michel Gratton, questioning the federal government's commitment to the Trilateral process. Chrétien blatantly expresses his preference for the land process as a "solution" to the crisis: "I am . . . confident that a positive long-term solution can be found, specifically through negotiations concerning global territorial claims."[43] Over a decade after the department's recognition of IBC, more definitive evidence of such federal concern surfaced in a protected document released accidentally through court disclosure in another matter. In a briefing to the minister, a high-profile government official acknowledged the threat the Trilateral could pose as an alternative to an unpopular land claims policy. Former diplomat Marc Perron counseled the minister of Indian Affairs at the time, Chuck Strahl, on the terms Barriere Lake continued to set for negotiation and their potential effect:

> The former Chief clearly indicated that the ABL [Algonquins of Barriere Lake] had no interest in comprehensive claims. They hoped to maintain Federal responsibility (and their obligations) and to obtain rights and co-management on the territory (including royalties) . . . A question we could ask: why bother negotiating a land claims agreement when we can obtain benefits (at least partially) through a partial accord like a trilateral agreement? Other First Nations would be justified in questioning this matter. *And it's the current overall comprehensive lands claims and self-government negotiations which could be questioned.*[44]

This alarming admission exposes the real threat senior bureaucrats feared the Trilateral posed as a viable alternative to the Comprehensive Land Claims Policy. We will revisit the full meaning of Perron's extended report in the context of its commission in the following chapter.

Partisan politics also accounts in part for the federal minister of Indian Affairs' sudden unwillingness to implement the Trilateral Agreement. According to Clifford Lincoln, it was the Liberals who started to pull away from the table at the end of 1993 after taking over federal power from the Conservatives. Lincoln had been Barriere Lake's special representative up until this point and when he was elected into the House of Commons Michel Gratton took over. As Lincoln tells it: "After we got elected, the first minister of Indian Affairs . . . he started to get very inimical to the Algonquins. First of all, the cost of it was starting to bother them, and certainly, the Liberal ministers increasingly got 'anti-Trilateral Agreement'—they thought it was a waste of money, a waste of time. And it also coincided with the opposition there, the petition—where they destituted the band—and so all this was one. They didn't want the Trilateral Agreement, they were fed up with . . . Matchewan—and felt that the people there were too demanding, too aggressive. So they welcomed the petition, which caused a huge up-heaval in the community."[45] Lincoln also felt that the push toward the land claims policy was firm as the logical solution to the problem of the Algonquins of Barriere Lake.

The struggle over the Trilateral was getting personal as Matchewan repeatedly came up against the same solid bloc of opposition within the civil service, but the conflict also reflected different party approaches to federalism in Canada. When Brian Mulroney came to power in 1984 on an explicitly cooperative model of federalism—in contrast to Pierre Elliot Trudeau's strong national approach, for example, instituting a National Energy Board—the new Conservative prime minister promised to build collaborative and respectful relations with the provinces. The Trilateral Agreement reflected this governing approach in theory, if not always in practice. When Jean Chrétien's government in 1993 ousted Mulroney, constitutional reform became the "third rail" of Canadian politics and was avoided at all costs by both provinces and the federal government.[46] Matters of overlapping jurisdiction between the two lev-els of government were dealt with in the Chrétien era in a more "ad hoc" and bilateral approach.

As far as Quebec was concerned, the fact that Barriere Lake would keep all of their lands in the Trilateral process had serious economic implications for the forestry companies operating in the territory. The logging industry was nervous about loss of wood volumes and control over cutting sectors. If the governments had incentive to terminate the Trilateral Agreement, so did the logging companies. Barriere Lake had successfully won an injunction against their former lawyer, Gerard Guay, who represented the Provisional Government for a short time, but the community soon learned that the IBC was now legally repre-sented by the sizable Winnipeg law firm of Thompson Dorfman and Sweatman, *the same firm that represented Domtar Inc.*, which had the largest logging concessions of any company in the Trilateral area.[47] The dissidents were receiving counsel from Domtar lawyer Rhada Curpen, girlfriend to Gerard Guay's brother.[48] To the community that supported

Matchewan's council it was as much a government coup as a corporate takeover. The law firm of Thompson Dorfman and Sweatman, on behalf of their Indigenous clients, filed a motion in December 1995 with the federal government requesting the dismissal of the Barriere Lake customary council.[49] They also asked that Matchewan's council turn over all documents pertaining to the Trilateral Agreement, "including, but not limited to . . . all records . . . band records, accounts and books."[50] In his capacity as acting special representative for the Algonquins of Barriere Lake, Nahwegahbow provided an affidavit stating that this conflict of interest "would entitle Domtar, through their legal counsel, to gain access to the confidential records of the Algonquins of Barriere Lake"—a terribly compromising outcome for the Algonquins who still hoped to see the Trilateral implemented.[51]

Domtar's legal gamble failed, however. With INAC's recognition of the IBC as the legitimate government at Barriere Lake, the dissident council attempted to withdraw their application filed in December 1995 with the federal government requesting the dismissal of the Barriere Lake customary council. The judge refused, agreeing with the attorney general of Canada—and in fact, concurring with the advice that DoJ had given INAC—that the basis on which the ministerial decision was made was "purely administrative in nature and was made solely for the purpose of permitting the Minister to discharge his duties to the Band."[52] The trial went ahead and Justice Madame McGillis determined that "the question of the legality of the selection of the Interim Band Council remains to be determined."[53] Suddenly, INAC was in precisely the precarious position it had been warned against by the DoJ when it recognized the IBC—subject to a barrage of legal violations it was now forced to defend. The fact of the matter was that there is no such thing as an "Interim Band Council" under the Indian Act, nor under the Barriere Lake customary code. The question of IBC's legal status as a band was resolved as "uncertain," and the political status of negotiations hung in the balance.

A Puppet Government in Exile

The dissidents had by now set up as a government in exile in the town of Maniwaki, 130 kilometers to the south of the Rapid Lake Reserve. Barriere Lake's lawyers fought to stop the transfer of Trilateral documents.

As far as the Barriere Lake customary government was concerned, "the Trilateral Agreement [would] be effectively dead if something [was] not done soon to reverse the decision of DIA."[54] The community believed that Chief Matchewan was deposed because he was leading the fight against the logging companies and taking a stand against a colonial land claims policy. With Matchewan out of the way, logging could proceed unabated and the Trilateral Agreement could slowly die of neglect, removing a dangerous model for Indigenous self-determination from the slate of options for bands. The federal government had suspended the Trilateral Agreement after the IBC took power. In just two short months from the time the IBC was recognized, the community had been scheduled to renegotiate the Trilateral Agreement—an agreement the IBC had vilified repeatedly in its communications, though ostensibly still claimed to support.[55]

So, now the IBC proved instrumental to the federal and provincial governments on several fronts: the council successfully ground the Trilateral negotiations to a halt and was actively pursuing access to all the research and files connected to the Trilateral, which it hoped to use against the Matchewan council in whatever way it imagined to be possible. Perhaps it thought it could discover financial fraud to discredit the process, or perhaps the land-use and occupancy studies would be used to justify more conducive land-management plans to the forestry companies. But the government also sought to neutralize the band council into the foreseeable future. To get control of a band's finances, INAC flexed a policy called "third party management" that authorizes the outsourcing of financial management and accounting of First Nation band council funds to external consultants.[56] It is therefore an unlikely coincidence that on the very day that the IBC was recognized by INAC, the newly minted council approved the nomination of Anthony Blouin of BDL Management and Consultant Inc. as third party manager of the band.

A final question of timing is raised by the date of federal recognition for the IBC. On the day that Matchewan was deposed, he was scheduled to make a critical announcement regarding a study undertaken on the quality of the federal education program at Rapid Lake. The education report, prepared by Rosalee Tizya and Louis Bouchard, found that the Department of Indian Affairs "totally and absolutely failed to meet" basic provincial standards of education. At a press conference on the day of the IBC's recognition, Tizya expressed her "outrage" to the media "at the lack of services these students have received for the past 18 years and we have to ask ourselves, where on earth was the Department of Indian Affairs when this process was going on?" Wide-range assessment tests that were done the previous fall on children from grades three to seven determined that half of those students were working at a kindergarten level in spelling, math, and reading. Ninety percent of the students of Rapid Lake who traveled to Maniwaki and Hull for high school ended up in remedial programs. Tizya and Bouchard stated: "Nowhere in this country has any school board tolerated a record like this, nowhere."[57] Barriere Lake had endured eighteen years of this impoverished and failed education system.[58] The story, however, was buried in the sudden chaos caused by recognition of the dissident faction.

People close to the community believe this timing was no coincidence.[59] Within a few days of the IBC appointment by the department, the new council dismissed the volunteer education authority that had struck to revive and improve Barriere Lake youth learning outcomes with Algonquin-based knowledge and curriculum at the Rapid Lake Federal School on the reserve (an elementary school program). Over the course of a year, this volunteer work had led to a dramatic uptick in attendance, from twenty students to 110 students, along with a youth center now constantly filled to capacity. The model was hailed as a framework for other First Nation schools across Canada.

The IBC declared its intent to take over band educational services without ever setting foot in the school or meeting with staff or the education authority. In protest, community members pulled their children out of school. Only 15 percent of students remained. Two months later, the IBC terminated an adult training program for thirty-nine Barriere Lake members, among whom were members of the volunteer education authority, receiving certification to be formally employed as educational instructors at their children's school.[60]

The staff immediately jumped to the community's defense.[61] Tireless advocacy by the teachers and principal to get the federal government to intervene led to veiled threats from the department and baffling grounds to abstain from action. Denis Chatain, regional director general of Indian Affairs, Quebec Region, replied sharply to teacher Stephen Pearson: "*For your own benefit,* I would think that, in the future, you should avoid mentioning that the quality of the educational services given by the Federal School in the past was inadequate based on the results of the WRAT test." Chatain goes on to insist that the deplorable test results are invalid owing to the fact that English is not the native language of students and that they live in a rural area where, for reasons unexplained, "the results can be of little value."[62] Denying the broader educational crisis, the government continued to also ignore the current crisis of hundreds of students at Rapid Lake cut off from access to education. Instead, it made preposterous claims that it could not respond directly to concerned staff and parents because it was "inappropriate" and that it could only deal with the IBC because it was the "governing council."[63]

Principal Robinson's pleas are heartbreakingly modest—he asks for just enough money to get the generator going and ten dollars per student to complete the year at an alternate location. He writes that everyone—including the staff, principal, and volunteers—was willing to work for no remuneration until the issue is settled in court. He vows to call twice a day every day until his pleas are answered.[64] But there seemed to be no will at the department to see the children in the community educated. Perhaps officials did not want to be seen as undermining their appointed council. But if they had wanted to rescue the Algonquin education initiative, they had the power, and they chose not exercise it, knowing well the attendant impacts of the educational legacy they bestowed on future generations. In this light, it is both eerie and infuriating to read the recommendations for new Aboriginal education legislation from the Truth and Reconciliation Commission, struck in the aftermath of a legal settlement for survivors of the residential school system in Canada. The new legislation would incorporate principles to develop culturally appropriate curricula, protect Indigenous languages, including instruction in these languages, enable parental and community responsibility, control, and accountability—enabling parental participation in the education system—and improve attainment levels and success rates.[65] Once again, the Barriere Lake Algonquins had presented a model for coexistence, decades ahead of their time, which was ignored.

Starve or Submit, or Wait Out the Thieves and Win

The immediate aftermath of the DIA's recognition of the dissident council was devastating. Once again, the Algonquins put their bodies on the line for the land and their customs. Thirty community members occu-

pied the band council office to prevent the IBC from setting up an organizing base there; another two dozen teachers and parents occupied the
federal school on the Rapid Lake Reserve.[66] True to INAC's internally
communicated plans for "collaboration," the SQ patrolled the reserve
daily.[67] The Rapid Lake Federal School was soon shut down by the principal, Jonathan Robinson, to ensure public safety, as the factions grew
increasingly hostile. One hundred and ten kids—aged one to seven—
were left without formal education.[68] The IBC were forced to govern
from Maniwaki because they were not accepted by the community as
legitimate representatives, so the federal government cut off programming dollars and welfare money to the reserve in what Charlie Angus
called a "starve or submit scenario" to force Barriere Lake to surrender
and accept the IBC as their governing council.[69]

Angus's words were not rhetorical. The community's sacrifices literally meant a spell of hunger. For more than a year, the children were not
in school and the community lived without power, electricity, or reserve
medical services, with phone lines partially cut off; they survived on
what they could hunt in the bush. Marylynn Poucachiche remembers
the hardship of those long, dark months:

> So the majority of our community was here for a year and a half
> without electricity, without running water, without medical
> services or any programs and services for that matter. We were
> all on welfare at that time. I remember I had just had my baby
> at that time, my two babies, I was young myself. It was hard for
> me. It was hard for a lot of people. There were people getting sick
> and oftentimes we'd have to do our best that we could to trans-
> port ourselves when it came to surgeries and stuff like that. But
> oftentimes we would use our bush medicine when it came to
> our babies coming up with fevers or colds. That is how we would
> survive using our bush medicines as much as we could, feeding
> off the land, going hunting, setting nets so we could feed a couple
> of families at a time. At that time, when they would kill a moose,
> they would try to get a piece to each person in the community.[70]

Despite the hardship, Barriere Lake showed no sign of surrender. They
mounted new barricades to stop the clear-cutting in 1996 and the blockade remained in place through a second harsh winter without supplies,

food, or school for the kids. Michel Gratton, former provincial cabinet minister and special representative for the Algonquins, reported to the press about living conditions at the time at Rapid Lake: "They have nothing to eat. Almost everyone's on welfare. With the barricades they haven't had a chance to hunt for moose. They are suffering many hardships. People have lost weight. They look despondent. The community's patience is wearing extremely thin."[71] Things got to the point where the community had to request emergency food from Quebec.

Eventually, word got out about Barriere Lake's destitution and the federal government began to feel the heat. Feeding the fire, Gratton issued a strongly worded critique of the federal government in the *Montreal Gazette,* stating that "[t]his unilateral decision to replace the Chief and Council . . . is the imposition and diktat of raw power by the department against a small community without the resources or ability to defend itself."[72] Another *Montreal Gazette* article noted the irony of Domtar's taking the worst economic hit from the crisis because "many Algonquins believe [the company] encouraged Ottawa to remove former Chief Matchewan from office." The most indicting fact reported, however, was that "[a] Domtar lawyer had admitted to advising a dissident faction of pro-forestry Algonquins who campaigned for Matchewan to be removed."[73] In the meantime, the blockades resulting from violations to the Trilateral Agreement were costing Domtar enough money to lay off one hundred forestry workers in the week after the blockade went up. Domtar then moved on to other areas but claimed that ongoing costs of disruption threatened to close down its Grand-Remous sawmill that employed 125 workers.[74]

By now, Quebec was also pressuring the federal government to resolve the leadership dispute. Pressure from the forestry companies was intensifying, affecting the province's bottom line. Guy Chevrette, Quebec minister of Natural Resources and Native Affairs, sent a "stern letter" to federal Minister of Indian Affairs Ronald Irwin demanding action and pointing to the way federal intervention in leadership wreaked havoc on provincial land and resource management.[75] At last taking action on the file, despite being outside its jurisdiction, the director general of the Quebec Region for the DIA responded to an Elders Council request in the community and appointed Michel Gratton and André Maltais as facilitators to assist in resolving the leadership dispute. Through an extensive community consultation, the community reaffirmed Harry Wawatie as the rightful chief of Barriere Lake, with Charles Ratt, Eddy Nottaway, Antoine Decoursay, and Peter Poucachiche as councillors. (A month earlier, Chief Matchewan, councillor Jean Ratt Paul, and administrator Michel Thusky had finally resigned, citing legal harassment from both the federal government and Interim Band Council).[76] Quebec's interventions, despite lacking formal jurisdiction, were successful at overturning recognition of the IBC. On April 17, 1996, the federal Department of Indian Affairs at long last recognized Chief Harry Wawatie's customary council as the legitimate leadership of the band.

Aftermath and Recovery

A lengthy process of restoration of relations between the governments and the band began with the appointment of Quebec Superior Court Justice Réjean Paul on May 7, 1996. Among his key findings, he addressed INAC's recognition of the IBC and issued a formal report to the minister of Indian Affairs that found that elders have a supervisory role and responsibility for leadership customs, contrary to IBC's claims.[77] Historian and researcher Doug Elias's expert historical opinion was solicited by the facilitators; he concluded that the Mitchikanibikok Anishnabe Onakinakewin (MAO) is consistent with Barriere Lake customs, that Barriere Lake does not have a modern tradition of selection by petition, and that according to their customs only members who have knowledge of and connection with their traditional land are entitled to participate in decisions regarding customs and leadership selections.[78]

The customary government system was restored to recognition. Nonetheless, in order to avoid at all costs a repeat of the devastation caused by the department's recognition of the dissident faction, the community felt pressed to submit to a process of codifying their customs on governance, as urged by the federal Department of Indian Affairs and recommended by Justice Paul. Elder Harry Wawatie foretold that the codification would come back to haunt them in the end.[79] These customs were affirmed and proclaimed by declaration and formally produced the MAO written code. Also, in addition to the code, through community consultations, Barriere Lake produced Amendments 1 and 2 to the MAO, which augmented existing customs to reflect changing circumstances, such as the inclusion of an election process for a board of directors to handle the administration of programs and services for the community.

The codification of the ancient oral customs of the Barriere Lake Algonquins is a complex story unto itself because the nature of the sacred constitution defies such flat literal representation. But it is important to emphasize that the core governing mandate for both the IBC and the federal government was to codify the community's customary government system in writing. The IBC's unsuccessful August 30, 1995, petition to Indian Affairs resolves that "Our community revise, update and reduce to writing, as soon as possible, our electoral custom for selecting a Chief and Council, and establish a code of conduct for our Band Council." In an internal document prepared in response to field public queries regarding federal recognition of the IBC, the text states: "[IBC's] main duty is to write custom rules," and this mandate appears repeatedly in the department's rationale for the IBC appointment.[80] As I have suggested, without a written code or an elective system, the federal government could exercise no control over the government of Barriere Lake: the band, and therefore the governance of its lands, remained outside of federal jurisdiction. It is impossible to know whether or not the federal government influenced the IBC to include codification as a core governing mandate. But either way, the convergence of these objectives was fortuitous for the department.

Following the findings of Judge Paul's mediation, the community contemplated litigation against the minister for INAC's 1996 intervention. There were still many grievances and outstanding issues to resolve, not least of which were the deficit and financial complications leftover from the IBC's unauthorized reign of power. Barriere Lake would have a strong case in the courts, given that even the DoJ had informed INAC that its actions were illegal prior to its decisive move. But the facilitators—Michel Gratton and André Maltais—convinced the community to restore relations through negotiation. Hence, the community went forward instead with a Memorandum of Mutual Intent (MOMI) in the hope of restitution after the years of turmoil, hunger, and despair. The Department of Indian Affairs, for its part, promised an era of reconciliation and peaceful relations. In October 1997, with the blessing of Minister Jane Stewart, Deputy Minister Scott Serson signed the MOMI, committing the federal government to building new housing, completing the final phases of the Trilateral work, and electrification of the community. Other community priorities were also identified, such as building a multifunctional community center, growing local capacity through community, social, and educational development moneys and administrative development, and finally, promising restoration and consultation costs for the Trilateral Agreement, which the agreement described as "fundamental to the future of the First Nation." The plan was laid out in an annex titled "Global Proposal for Rebuilding the Community," with estimated costs neatly labeled next to each commitment.

Barriere Lake was also negotiating with Quebec on issues particular to provincial jurisdiction. In 1998, a bilateral agreement was signed with the government of Quebec addressing what was called key "quality of life" issues for the Algonquins such as expansion of the Rapid Lake Reserve, connection of the community to the hydro grid, and access to economic opportunities on the territory, including resource revenues.[81] The joint recommendations introduced in the bilateral agreement were negotiated with John Ciaccia, who had been appointed special representative for Quebec at this time. He also discussed with the community an approach to complete Phases 1 and 2 of the Trilateral Agreement and move forward with the implementation of the integrated resource-management plans.

Collapse

Word had begun to spread about the cutting-edge research, modeling, and land-management planning the Algonquins were undertaking, and they received considerable outside support from forest conservationists, First Nations, and environmentalists who admired the integration of traditional ecological knowledge with non-Native land-use needs.[82] Although disagreements persisted, the Trilateral research inched forward.[83] By May 2000, Gull Lake, the first Integrated Resource Management Plan (IRMP) of seven management areas of the Trilateral area, was under way. The community was heavily involved in reviewing the plan and technical work that incorporated their traditional knowledge into the land-management plans. In June 2001, Barriere Lake announced that they were submitting the Gull Lake IRMP to Quebec planners. This area was the most contentious of seven management zones for which Barriere Lake was preparing "measures to harmonize" plans; it brought to bear sensitive area studies work with harvest studies and the Phase 1 field research with elders and regional harvesters. It was to be the model for all the other areas. Among the protected measures at Gull Lake was the preservation of spawning sites, sugar bushes, wildlife habitat, and medical plant collection areas. The average size of clear-cuts had been reduced to between 20 to 30 hectares and the total area harvested had been reduced from 3,000 hectares to 600 hectares. The resource-management plan was setting the pace as a framework for sustainable land use, guided by the deep Indigenous ecological knowledge of the territory.

In the wake of this tremendous progress, a mere month before the completion of the Gull Lake IRMP, federal officials complained that the Trilateral Agreement was costing too much money, taking too much time, and that there were not enough concrete results to date. Canada had by this point spent $5 million, and the province $2.5 million. Canada walked away from the table again. Sophie Lise Ratt of Indian Affairs, in an act nothing short of cruel mockery, told the community that if they wanted to complete the project, they could use their housing dollars.[84] (Health Canada issued a report less than a year earlier that highlighted the deplorable condition of housing on the Rapid Lake Reserve, including several warnings concerning houses where residents had developed chronic respiratory problems suspected to be linked to mold in the buildings).[85] Ratt then proceeded to stand up the community for a meeting she was confirmed to attend on the urgent issue of logging operations in the wake of the crisis the federal government had invoked.[86]

The deputy minister of Indian Affairs was no more forthcoming in his communications. In response to an eight-page detailed letter from Harry Wawatie that surveyed the department's failure to fulfill its multiple obligations under the MOMI and the Trilateral Agreement, Marc Lefrenière replied in a brief, terse letter that ignored all mentions of agreements that the federal government had signed with the community, expressing his understanding that it was the IRMP that was *most* important to the community and thus advising them to take it up with Quebec and the region to identify a proper approach and resolution.[87] He then complained that the process of Trilateral work had been lengthy and inefficient and that the federal government would regretfully no longer be involved. Clearly appalled, the chief responded by reminding Lefrenière that the MOMI was signed *in the aftermath of his department's illegal deposition of the community's chief and council.* Lefrenière's department and the Algonquin community facilitated the MOMI jointly in order to *rebuild* the relationship between them. As a result of those two years of INAC meddling—and in addition to the early years when the federal government deprived the Algonquins of funding to carry out the plan—the community lost years on IRMP work, yet the department had the audacity to raise the lack of progress on the Trilateral Agreement.[88] On September 26, 2001, INAC went one step further and put out a statement claiming that the MOMI was simply a declaration of intent and goodwill "which did not create legally enforceable rights or obligations."[89]

Why did Canada adopt such an absolute strategy of refusal just as the Algonquins were on the brink of submitting the first and most comprehensive of land-management plans for the territory? The coup d'état had failed. The criminalization of leaders had failed. The attempts to starve the band into subordination had failed. Trumped-up charges of sexual abuse and financial misconduct had failed. Barriere Lake had still not been prepared to give up the Trilateral Agreement. Whatever goodwill had been extended to extract the department from the disaster of the IBC recognition burned up quickly as the community approached completion of the Gull Lake resource-management plan. The fact remained that the government had signed an agreement that was not in sync with the federal land claims policy. Russell Diabo claims this was behind Canada's hardline withdrawal, stating that "Comprehensive Claims is definitely where the federal government is trying to push all the Algonquins."[90] Michel Gratton concurs with Diabo's assessment that Barriere Lake's refusal to enter into the Comprehensive Land Claims framework for land claim settlement was a key part of the incentive to shut the project down: "They hate the idea of the Algonquins negotiating *not* a land claims agreement. But you know the process with the land claims agreements—the lawyers' fees eventually come out of whatever the community gets. And, with the Trilateral, it was a different procedure and they hated it."[91] Canada walked away from the Trilateral Agreement because within sixteen months the whole process would have been complete.

Negotiations with Quebec were only slightly better. The province was demanding that Barriere Lake complete all their Trilateral work in four months, despite an assessment—jointly conducted with their own department—that the work would take a minimum of sixteen months to complete.[92] Again, the hypocrisy was extreme. For example, while it took eight months for Quebec senior officials to draft the terms of reference and an action plan for the Wildlife Working Group—a Trilateral subcommittee—the province now expected the community to complete the entire wildlife management assessment in half that time. The bilateral agreement fell apart.

My Enemy's Enemy

Barriere Lake and the forestry companies were plunged into crisis by the sudden withdrawal of Trilateral funds. The community was forced to suspend all logging in the territory, informing companies that when cutting was complete in areas that had been measured to harmonize with Algonquin land use, they would have to leave the territory. Chief Wawatie sent letters to each of the forestry companies operating on their land: Domtar, Lousiana Pacific, Bowater, Bois Omega, Davidson, and Commonwealth Plywood. He addressed them as allies, rather than as enemies: "As you know, since we signed the Trilateral Agreement . . . our First Nation has endeavored to maintain a stable environment for forestry companies operating within the area. Despite our greatest efforts, the process has been frequently suspended or delayed . . . Of course, the main victims have been those who have the most to lose: the companies and our community."[93] Several of the forestry companies wrote to the federal and provincial governments to support the Trilateral Agreement and emphasizing the real achievements of the land-management plan. Even Domtar rose to the occasion; the company had warmed to the Algonquin perspective on land management since the days of advising the dissident council. Senior Vice President Craig McManus wrote to Minister of Indian Affairs Robert Nault:

> Domtar is concerned that the breakdown of this negotiating process will produce harmful effects. Domtar is striving to achieve genuine harmonization between industrial forest use and traditional aboriginal activities: all on the basis of collaboration and partnership. We felt that the spirit of cooperation encouraged by the Trilateral Agreement process is helping to build a more

trusting relationship between the parties and has yielded more concrete results.[94]

But even industry's demands fell on deaf ears.

The state can be a powerful obstacle to capital when Indigenous jurisdiction is at stake because tensions arise between the state's logic of territorial acquisition and the mobile logic of capital accumulation. As Giovanni Arrighi's theory of the long twentieth century contends, there is a "recurrent contradiction between an 'endless' accumulation of capital and a comparatively stable organization of political space."[95] The common project is to make the world safe for capitalism. But these logics, Arrighi observes, have not historically operated in isolation from each other, "but in relation to one another, within a given spatio-temporal context."[96] The Algonquins' case presents an example of both ambivalence and strategic cooperation between territorial and capitalist logic: throughout negotiations between Barriere Lake and the federal and provincial governments, forestry companies exerted pressure in two directions—toward Indigenous rights and toward infringement and violation of these rights—depending on the economic risks perceived in each type of intervention at particular moments of accumulation.

By the early 2000s, tensions between settler-state logic and the logic of capitalist accumulation were at a historical disjuncture. Barriere Lake territory was the site of intense jurisdictional conflict that the state was determined to resolve through land alienation, and ultimately, extinguishment by the land claims process. In contrast, the logic of capitalist accumulation in the forestry industry had led to the logging companies' adaptation to Algonquin sustainable land use. From industry's perspective, the threshold for tolerance was manageable: Algonquin demands on surplus value were relatively low and the Algonquin landmanagement system was focused on long-term sustainability for nonrenewable resources, not an outright ban. Industry's bottom line would ultimately hurt more if it continued to violate Indigenous jurisdiction; therefore, the best way to protect its proprietary interests in the lumber would be to respect Algonquin jurisdiction.

Industry's assessment of who had jurisdiction over Barriere Lake's lands was ultimately recognized by way of who had the power to regulate economic activity on the territory. The forestry industry's preference was at first primarily for a stable property-rights system, protected and enforced by the state, backed by security forces if necessary. But Algonquin resistance to destructive clear-cut logging practices created ecological and financial incentives for the companies to respect Algonquin stewardship. The *how* of jurisdiction involved a negotiation over different kinds of proprietary interest: the Algonquins had obligations to steward the land for future generations; the foresters had short-term profit-motivated goals. Through a comanagement regime that prioritized Algonquin land use and forms of life—with promised economic benefits to come in the final phase of agreement implementation—industry found a way to secure its property under Indigenous law. In turn, this security ensured recognition of Indigenous law within this period of accommodation.

Deborah Rose Bird writes that, for Indigenous people, *who* you are is *where* you are, thus "to get in the way of settler colonialism, all the native has to do is stay home."[97] On Barriere Lake's territory, proprietary interests were leveraged as a productive technique of jurisdiction in the struggle to defend Algonquin lands. The spacing of Indigenous jurisdiction on ten thousand square kilometers of their lands through the Trilateral Agreement configured authority over Barriere Lake's territory, even when the state's recognition was absent; Indigenous governance became the de facto regime of governance. This spatial assertion of jurisdiction also acted to negate claims by the state to possess a monopoly on modern forms of governance. The perpetration of an "evolved" system of Algonquin governance by the federal Department of Indian Affairs through its appointment of the IBC was a land grab perpetrated through the racist, historical discourse of progress. As Timothy Mitchell observes, "Historical time, the time of the West, is what gives modern geography its order, an order centered upon Europe."[98] To the state, Barriere Lake lands could not possibly exist outside of this European spatial order. But, of course, Indigenous jurisdiction poses precisely this dislocation to state narratives of sovereign power.

In this story, time loops slowly in circles, knotting itself into a long quilt of struggle. In October 2001, the Algonquins arrived on Victoria Island in Ottawa. Victoria Island, near Parliament Hill, is a tourist site with teepees and tents for visitors to learn about Indigenous cultures. Now the tents and teepees teeming with real Algonquin life and struggle took the place of nostalgic representation. A cold rain fell, but families refused to leave until the deputy minister agreed to meet with them. The national chief, Matthew Coon Come, visited the Algonquins on the island to show his support for the Trilateral Agreement, drawing critical national attention. But it was only after marching to an Indian Affairs building in Hull and occupying the lobby that they were they finally granted a short audience with the deputy minister. Canada would still not budge. In a prescient news report, a reporter covering the Victoria Island occupation foreshadowed the worst-case scenario: "It's been fourteen years since the first protest here on Victoria Island. Fourteen years of fighting for a future for these children. The Elders worry they still may be here fourteen years from now: different kids, different faces, but the same old fight for basic needs."[99]

8

The Government Must Fall

The last two chapters preceding my conclusion represent perhaps the most extreme exercises of power by the state to eradicate the inherent jurisdiction of the Barriere Lake Algonquins. Following the story chronologically, these chapters characterize the escalation of the crisis. In this chapter, I describe how the state used an arcane clause in the Indian Act that had not been exercised for almost a century in order to officially replace Barriere Lake's customary government system. Canada forced the community to adopt a municipal, elective system of governance in place of their traditional system by claiming the community's governance system was the source of leadership conflict in the community. This coercive act that exchanged Barriere Lake's inherent order of self-government for a delegated system of authority was engineered in order to pacify the community and to eradicate further opportunities for the Trilateral Agreement to be implemented. But it could not have been accomplished without a surveillance program that tracked the political organizing of the community and extended Indian Affairs' authority into a complex, multijurisdictional architecture of security logic and extralegal control. In chapter 9 I detail these logics and the forms of criminalization, coercion, and repression directed toward the spatial containment of Barriere Lakers to confined expressions of jurisdiction on their territory. Chapter 9 also develops an analysis of the ways Indian Affairs rationalized this kind of intervention through discourses of criminality and deviance.

In this chapter I examine the way insinuations of corruption—political and financial—rationalized Indian Affairs' actions to absorb Barriere Lake within the internal limits of the state and to neutralize the threat of their inherent jurisdiction. The legislative powers at Indian Affairs' disposal to depose Barriere Lake's government was archaic but effective: a "Section 74" order could unilaterally replace the Mitchikanibikok Anishnabe Onakinakewin with an elected band council system. This section of the Indian Act gives the minister of Indian Affairs sweeping powers to abolish customary bands, which are currently accounted for under Section 2(1)(b) of the Indian Act, under the definition of a band.[1] Section 74 states: "Whenever he deems it advisable for the good governance of a band, the Minister may declare by order that after a day to be named therein the council of the band, consisting of a Chief and Councillors, shall be selected by elections to be held in accordance with this Act."[2] Until it was imposed on Barriere Lake, Section 74 had not been exercised coercively on a customary band since 1924, when the RCMP raided the lodge at Six Nations and chain-locked its doors, imposing band council elections on the fiercely independent confederacy.[3] It had been eighty-six years since such a desperate measure had been taken. As I will show, Quebec took advantage of the situation to secure the proprietary interest of resource industries without interference from the powerful hereditary government that had challenged provincial jurisdiction for decades.

Earlier, I recounted how Russell Diabo once stated that everything a person needed to learn about colonialism in Canada today could be learned through the state's treatment of the Algonquins of Barriere Lake. One key aspect of this colonial control is through leverage of financial matters against Indigenous peoples. Fiscal relations have long played a key role in the disciplinary management of Indigenous populations, particularly since the institutionalization of individualized welfare distribution on reserves and formalized "contribution agreements" from the federal government to band councils in the 1960s and early 1970s.[4] Although it remains a relatively unexamined technique of governance, the use of government transfer funds increasingly forms part of a core strategy to consolidate state control over Indigenous peoples in Canada. Therefore, it is telling that financial matters precipitated two further government imbroglios at Barriere Lake before the imposition of Section 74 was announced.

In the first section of this chapter, I look at how fiscal relations played a role in leadership conflicts that eventually led Indian Affairs to impose Section 74 on the community. Barriere Lake's rejection of the imposition of Third Party Management prompted stress and conflict within the community that the government used as premise to accuse the band of financial mismanagement and dysfunction. Script in hand, Section 74 was imposed by the state with the hope that business could finally proceed smoothly on the territory, having vanquished the strong customary leadership and moved it to the sidelines of governance.

The Hand That Feeds Is the Hand That Closes

The governmental interventions that marked the rocky path to Section 74 were primarily set around financial matters. In July 2006, Harry Wawatie resigned as chief of Barriere Lake over INAC's decision to appoint a Third Party Manager to control the band's financial and administrative affairs.[5] Citing ill health and old age, he surrendered the burden of the fight to the next generation. Later that month, Jean Maurice Matchewan was reselected as customary chief by the Council of Elders.[6] A small faction ran a parallel leadership selection; they also claimed to have adhered to the Customary Governance Code codified in 1997 as part of the Mitchikanibikok Anishnabe Onakinakewin Customary Code and they selected William Nottaway as chief.[7] Indian Affairs refused to recognize either the Matchewan council or William Nottaway's council. Instead, sensing a crucial rift that it could rend further apart, for a second time it put the community under Third Party Management, claiming it was justified by Barriere Lake's large deficit and uncertain leadership situation. The Customary Elder's Council led by former Chief Harry Wawatie immediately challenged the minister of Indian Affairs' decision in federal court, arguing that the deficit issues could be cleared up if the money owed to Barriere Lake from the 1996 funding deprivation was repaid as promised. In the yearly funding budget, negotiated by the Third Party Manager (TPM) and Indian Affairs in 2007, the money owed by the government had simply been struck from the record.[8]

Matchewan's council was eventually reinstated as an outcome of mediation. In the spring of 2007, Superior Court Judge Réjean Paul was called in for the third time and he confirmed the legitimacy of Matchewan's council, calling the challengers a "small minority" who "did not respect the Customary Governance Code."[9] He also named the tactic of replacing the legitimate customary council with these small dissident factions a "'guerilla movement' existing on the Reserve and extending as far as Maniwaki and Val d'Or for many members living off the Reserve."[10] In terms of the imposition of Third Party Management, by agreement with the deputy minister of INAC, a special ministerial representative was appointed for the community to resolve the impasse on financial debts. The legal proceedings on Third Party Management were adjourned in exchange.

The intervention failed to achieve results because of the flagrant disrespect the mediator had for the community. Marc Perron was unilaterally appointed as a special ministerial representative assigned to draft a report to "fact-find" and make recommendations regarding the department's imposition of Third Party Management.[11] His mandate was fuzzy in contrast to the demands of Barriere Lake, who claimed that the imposition of Third Party Management was a breach of the Crown's fiduciary obligations and insisted on its repeal. On December 20, 2007, Perron submitted his report to Minister of Indian Affairs Chuck Strahl, concluding that his engagement with Barriere Lake led to a "dead end" owing to the community's "self-destruction mode."[12] Perron attributed the "rift" in relations between Barriere Lake and the department to the result of the band leadership's "confrontational attitude" on the one hand, compared to the "deep commitment of the civil servants" to ensure that services "reach the underprivileged" on reserve, on the other. He accused the leadership of feeding "on a culture of miserabilism" and self-interest because they demanded a share in the benefits from the land and the opportunities for self-sufficiency promised in the signed agreements. Tone deaf to the contradiction in his recommendations, Perron mercilessly attacked the Trilateral Agreement, labeling it a "mythical treaty" while decrying the disaster of poverty on the reserve, which "is a result of dependency, negligence and total irresponsibility." Rather than support the community's desire for economic independence that would come from the modest resource revenue sharing in the agreement, Perron recommended more federal dollars for programs to put Band-Aids on structural problems, including education, which is a case study in how dependency is formed and was clearly shown by an examination of federal action on this issue at Barriere Lake. The report also reflected an ideation toward federal–provincial collaboration, recommending a working group between both levels of government to cut Barriere Lake altogether out of input into governance on their territory.

The Perron process was construed as an "alternative dispute resolution" (ADR) for which the Algonquins of Barriere Lake suspended their court proceedings against the federal government regarding the imposition of Third Party Management on their band. Barriere Lake resumed legal proceedings against the government for Third Party Management soon after the report was released.[13]

But if Canada could abandon the Trilateral Agreement, Quebec was far more entwined in its fortunes. Around this time, the province picked up where the federal government dropped its commitments to the Barriere Lake band, even offering to pay the full costs for sensitive area studies in order to prepare the "Measures to Harmonize" (MTH) for forestry companies to determine acceptable areas to cut in the territory.[14] The Algonquins refused, stating that they would accept the money only on condition that a fund set aside on their behalf was established to complete the IRMPs for the seven Trilateral Management Areas that were the goal of the Trilateral Agreement.[15] The MTH were always meant as interim measures while the more substantial resource comanagement plan was carried out for the entire Trilateral territory. But there was a new aspect to the dynamic of confrontation with the settler governments that the community had not anticipated. While the Barriere Lake Algonquins had once successfully leveraged one level of government against the other to keep the process moving along, now the federal and provincial governments began to close ranks.

Indian Affairs: To Divide-and-Conquer

In the fall of 2009, things went seriously sideways. Jean Maurice Matchewan stepped down as chief as a result of pending charges.[16] He was being closely watched and, when pulled over and searched one day, was found to be in possession of marijuana. The Council of Elders selected Councillor Benjamin Nottaway as acting chief to replace Matchewan until the charges could be cleared. But no sooner had they selected Nottaway as acting chief than another group in the community held their own leadership review process to select a leader to replace Matchewan. On January 30, 2008, a separate Council of Elders from those who selected Nottaway to replace Matchewan nominated Casey Ratt as chief.[17] On February 4, Elder Harry Wawatie sent a letter to Indian Affairs strongly rejecting Casey Ratt's claims to be chief.[18] Nonetheless, on March 10, 2008, INAC recognized the Ratt council as the legitimate chief and council of the Algonquins of Barriere Lake. The minister did not provide an explanation for his department's decision to recognize the Ratt council over Acting Chief Benjamin Nottaway's council or respond to Wawatie's February 4 letter. Even the court worker assigned to observe Ratt's selection process put in writing that he could not confirm the legitimacy of this customary government.[19]

In a secret memo obtained by the *Dominion*, deliberations over the decision to recognize the Ratt council over the Matchewan council are outlined. INAC expresses a preference for the Ratt council, which officials describe as less "dogmatized" than the Nottaway council and which would offer "improved collaboration."[20]

Elder Harry Wawatie hand-delivered a letter to Minister of Indian Affairs Chuck Strahl on March 31, 2008, informing the department that it was "once again wrongly interfering in our internal governance" and that the Ratt council would not be accepted as legitimate leadership in the community.[21] Wawatie further identified the root causes of this ongoing Indian Affairs interference: "We view DIA's decision as no more than a divide-and-conquer tactic to get us to fight amongst ourselves and to avoid obligations in agreements it signed with our First Nation."[22] This time, the Elders Council led by Wawatie (hereafter referred to as the Customary Elders Council), wasted no time appealing to the judiciary to resolve this dispute. It filed a notice of Application for Judicial Review of the minister of Indian Affairs' decision "to register the results of a purported leadership selection and to conduct his relationship according to those results with a purported council."[23] The application was at first struck down by Prothonotary Kevin Aalto on August 25, 2008, but Aalto's ruling was reversed on appeal by Mr. Justice Russell Zinn on January 6, 2009. The minister had tried to claim that he had simply "registered the results" of the Ratt council and therefore bore no culpability for alleged "decisions" taken by the department.[24] But Zinn concluded otherwise: in effect, he accepted the applicants' appeal to *Haida,* which engages the Crown's duty to consult with the band.[25] Zinn also affirmed that in the case of customary bands—as confirmed previously with the legally invalidated IBC—the minister has no authority to determine the legality of customary leadership.[26]

This judicial review into the minister's decision to recognize the Ratt council over the Matchewan council unfortunately would go no further. Legal entanglements in another courtroom would ultimately undermine both parties' standing in the courts.

Before we continue with this story, however, it behooves us to examine the internal dynamics of the leadership dispute between the Matchewan and Ratt councils. Could the matter have been resolved within the context of Barriere Lake's Indigenous jurisdiction, without appeal to the judiciary or to the public more generally? This matter is in fact of great political importance. Media opinion weighed heavily in the government's favor when Canada claimed that this latest conflict was simply the natural outcome of Barriere Lake community dysfunction. Why the community harbored internal, competing claims to government—common in governments across the country but held as exceptional in Indigenous communities—and why Barriere Lake felt they had no recourse but to obtain legal affirmation as to the status of their customary governing council must be examined. What is necessary is a postmortem of what Wawatie called "divide-and-conquer tactics."

The "conquering" objective here appears to tie closely to the Trilateral Agreement. It is not difficult to understand the Ratt council's frustration at the progress of negotiations. Matchewan saw that if the Trilateral Agreement was implemented and the modest revenue sharing was distributed at $1.5 million per annum as agreed, the community could design and manage their own cultural programs and economic development initiatives without being dependent on handouts from the government. But this insistence on tying funding to settling the question of jurisdiction and resource management—outside of the preferred land claims process—challenged the Crown's willingness to negotiate in good faith. The Trilateral Agreement, the MOMI, and bilateral agreement with Quebec all hinged on recognition of Barriere Lake's right to have a say over their territory, and Matchewan, and Wawatie (before and after him), refused to compromise these rights in exchange for short-term infrastructure investment and programs. This meant that so long as negotiations on land management were stalled, so was progress on all fronts that could improve the daily living conditions of the Algonquin community. In a fall 2009 press release, the Ratt council clearly explained its apprehension with the way politics was being played by community leadership: "Several members believe that the previous Council, led by former Chief Jean Maurice Matchewan, focused too much of their attention on the trilateral agreement at the expense of other areas such as education, health, policing, and socio-economic development."[27] Complicating these stalled Trilateral negotiations were rumors of alleged corruption that continued to circulate about Russell Diabo and David Nahwegahbow surrounding Trilateral funding dollars. But ultimately, it was the land issue and agreements that remained poorly understood.

Crystal clear, however, was the crippling poverty on the Rapid Lake Reserve, surrounding family village sites, and among band members.

Casey Ratt believed he could solve these pressing material concerns: "For the first time, steps are being taken to address the issues within our community by developing action plans to bring about structure in all areas of our governance that will focus on community involvement and accountability."[28] The Ratt council did work earnestly to secure what gains it could derive from the programs and services dollars on offer, but ultimately it too failed to make any progress on social and economic development in the community, in part because it did not have the confidence or consent of the majority of the community to govern.[29]

Attempts by the Nottaway council and the Customary Elders Council to resolve the leadership conflict with the Ratt council failed to solicit any cooperation from Ratt's group. The Nottaway council and Customary Elders Council suggested that the Ratt council appoint their own independent co-facilitator to help design and implement a new leadership process that ensured fairness, neutrality, and good faith. The Ratt council refused to participate. Despite this refusal to engage, the Customary Elders Council remained insistent until the end that a new leadership selection process be postponed until the full participation of the Ratt group could be obtained. Finally, it became clear, however, as Keith Penner put it in his independent report on the leadership selection process, that "every exchange on this issue was only used as delaying tactic."[30] Further, the Ratt council's legal counsel, Michael Swinwood, filed injunctions on May 12 and 13, 2008, to stop a new leadership selection process from going forward altogether. The injunctions failed and finally, after considerable delay, the Customary Elders Council attempted to end the leadership impasse by holding another leadership selection process strictly according to the Mitchikanibikok Anishnabe Onakinakewin. They invited independent observers and planned to hold the government accountable to registering and recognizing the results of this renewed process. Jean Maurice Matchewan was reselected as chief.

Keith Penner agreed to serve as independent facilitator for the leadership process in late June 2009. A former public official and author of the "Penner Report" in 1983 on Indigenous self-governance, he concluded of the Barriere Lake leadership selection

that the *Customary Code* has been followed and adhered to in each and every respect. The new Chief and Council are the legitimate and properly constituted leaders of the community of Barriere

Lake. It only remains now for DIAND to appropriately and
correctly recognize and register the results of this Customary
Selection in accord with the terms of the Indian Act set out in
s.2(1), "council."[31]

Six letters were sent to INAC between June 24, 2009, and late October
2009 requesting that the minister make a decision regarding recognition
of the new Matchewan council. On October 30, 2009, the community
finally received a response. Minister Chuck Strahl no longer recognized
either the Matchewan or the Ratt councils and intended to impose Section 74 on Barriere Lake, putting them under the Indian Act elective system if the leadership issue was not internally resolved by April 1, 2010.

The Specter of 74

It was a serious blow. An option never far from the minister's grasp,
the decision to impose Section 74 on Barriere Lake was nonetheless an
extreme strategy designed to give the department control over the community. It seems that despite its opposition to the Trilateral Agreement,
the Ratt council had failed to ensure the department control over the
community owing to its lack of credibility.

   Meanwhile, another judicial proceeding was making its way through
the courts. Back in September 2009, the Ratt council, its Council of Elders, and its supporters responded to the selection of the Matchewan
council by launching a Judicial Review Application challenging its validity under the Mitchikanibikok Anishnabe Onakinakewin.[32] Matchewan's legal counsel, David Nahwegahbow, advised that in light of the
minister's Section 74 order an alternative dispute resolution of leadership would be appropriate in order to resolve differences by the minister's deadline of April 2010.[33] A court-supervised reconciliation process
would have allowed them to hold off the threatening order. But Michael
Swinwood, representing the Ratt council, rejected the proposal, claiming that his clients preferred to litigate.

   This miscalculation by Swinwood and his clients was enormous. On
February 17, 2010, the Honorable Justice Robert Mainville issued his
decision in the lawsuit. He accepted that Matchewan's selection was
valid but was deeply critical of this group's use of the Mitchikanibikok
Anishnabe Onakinakewin, and also of the decision of the Customary

Elders Council to select Benjamin Nottaway as acting chief. Rather than remaining *impartial* to the process, as Justice Mainville believed that the Customary Elders Council was required to be (though there is no such concept or law expressed in the Mitchikanibikok Anishnabe Onakinakewin), he criticized them for siding with the Matchewan–Nottaway council, accusing the elders of unfair bias, for example, when they brought the judicial review against the minister on behalf of the Nottaway council. Justice Mainville also severely criticized the Ratt group for its own misappropriation of the Mitchikanibikok Anishnabe Onakinakewin in its leadership selection process and for refusing to participate altogether in the leadership reselection process.[34] Ultimately, Justice Mainville decided that he could not recognize the validity of *either group's claim* to leadership of the Algonquin band.[35] According to him, neither of these Algonquin councils was fit to govern their society.

The fallout from the Mainville decision led to major changes in the community. When it was recognized by INAC, the Ratt council had immediately withdrawn from the band's tribal council, the Algonquin Nation Secretariat (ANS). But the ANS had continued to support the Nottaway and Matchewan councils, pending judicial hearing. Now, the tribal council could no longer legally represent the Matchewan council of Barriere Lake through its organization. The band lost major institutional support and its research funding dollars were completely cut. Worse, a political vacuum opened in the community—something unaccounted for in the laws of the Mitchikanibikok Anishnabe Onakinakewin. This political vacuum provided Quebec with an alibi to suspend resource comanagement negotiations under the auspices of this "leadership imbroglio." Forestry companies moved in and, unsure how to consult with the local Indian band, now sent letters to both Casey Ratt and Jean Maurice Matchewan for approval of cuts.[36] The community hired Hutchins Legal Inc. to help them to navigate the forestry incursions on their territory and to use this sudden spate of natural resource development as leverage to get the governments back to the negotiating table.[37]

Meanwhile, the specter of Section 74 cast a pallor over the entire community. Despite considerable conflict between the Ratt and Nottaway factions, neither group supported any abrogation of the customary government system.[38] With the unexpected common ground gained through the Ratt and Matchewan councils' shared contempt for the threat of the Section 74 order, a cautious reconciliation began to unfold at Barriere Lake. Youth took the lead in the reconciliation process, meeting repeatedly throughout 2009, extending open invitations to their discussions to all community members, and affirming the unanimous community rejection of the Section 74 order.[39] The wounds were deeper for the older generation in the community, though Casey Ratt's father, Severe Ratt, was one of the first to cross the fault line and rejoin his peers who included Jean Maurice Matchewan, Toby Decoursay, and Michel Thusky.

On December 15, 2009, the elders of the community issued a resolution to reject the minister's plan to impose the Section 74 elective system and a Barriere Lake community resolution quickly followed that day, affirming support for the elders and their resolution.[40] These resolutions were not simply words and signatures but provided the catalyst for travel and communication between family settlement sites on the territory to discuss the future leadership of the community. The band communicated the progress of the reconciliation process back to INAC and the minister of Indian Affairs on a constant basis. For example, in a letter dated May 26, 2010, four youth—including supporters of both the Matchewan and Ratt councils—wrote to Pierre Nepton, regional general director for INAC in Quebec stating: "We hope that your department will not interfere with our community process as it will also address our reconciliation. We advise the department to respect our process and our wishes for reconciliation."[41] Once again, hope was stirring in the community that the next generation of leadership would resolve the differences of the past, and, more important, that the community could join in a common struggle against the governments that they all now agreed were lined up against them.

To repeal the Section 74 order, INAC wanted to see amendments to the customary governance code that would clarify disputes over leadership, the role of elders, and the terms of leadership review for future disputes. The community was ready to take this up through their community-driven reconciliation process. However, the "opportunity" that INAC offered Barriere Lake to repeal the invocation of Section 74 was not to be through an internal Algonquin process. INAC instead mandated strict terms and conditions by which Barriere Lake had to undertake the required amendments through the federal Conversion to Community Election System Policy (CCESP). As Minister Strahl writes in his October 30 letter, in which he initially warns the community of the imminent

Section 74 threat, "Over the next several months, I am offering the community the opportunity to develop and ratify a clear leadership selection process that includes secret ballot voting, and that respects the principles set out in the Department's Conversion to Community Election System Policy."[42] The paradoxical intent of the CCESP is "for the purpose of determining that an order pursuant to Section 74 of the Indian Act be repealed so that a First Nation may conduct its elections under its own community election system (custom)." But the policy cannot do both: in the case of Barriere Lake, these very CCESP provisions undermine the basis of the Algonquin customary system of governance.

That is because the required provisions of the CCESP strip away the connections between land and leadership guaranteed in the Mitchikanibikok Anishnabe Onakinakewin. One constitution is pitted against the other: the CCESP, Section 2(d), states that the policy "is consistent with the *Charter of Rights and Freedoms,* which, among other points, includes: voting rights to off-reserve members; a realistic mechanism by which off-reserve electors can participate in the electoral process (e.g. mail-in ballots); and the opportunity for off-reserve electors to hold positions on the band council." While the Charter may define these criteria as essential Canadian citizen rights, the impact of these stipulations would effectively wipe out Barriere Lake's customary governance code and all structures built in place to protect it. The function of the CCESP is to essentially allow a small degree of flexibility to Indian Act election provisions. The government then calls these minor modifications a "conversion to custom." The impacts on a customary band that has never been governed under the Indian Act, however, are severe.

Being governed under the Indian Act would change the very nature of recognition for Barriere Lake's customary government. As Nahwegahbow explained to the community: "Under custom, the powers are inherent, which is what the Federal Court said in *Bone v Sioux Valley.*[43] On the other hand, the powers exercised under the *Indian Act* are strictly delegated; in other words, they come from the Act and are delegated by the government."[44] Nahwegahbow also warned that the imposition of Indian Act election provisions might have long-term effects on the community's ability to hold, exercise, and prove Aboriginal title and rights. According to the Supreme Court of Canada, a "substantial connection" to the land is required to prove Aboriginal title.[45] Currently, this requirement is embedded in the Mitchikanibikok Anishnabe Onakinakewin. If the Onakinakewin ceases to be recognized as the governance regime at Barriere Lake, the potency of their claim over their traditional territory is also drastically undermined over time. Finally, and perhaps most controversially, the customary governance code requires that participants in the leadership selection process maintain a connection to the land but does not stipulate whether community members live on- or off-reserve. The Indian Act forces a distinction between band members on the basis of where people live, causing a new arbitrary basis for divisions in the community. Under the Indian Act, everyone on the band list is able to participate in selections, shifting the *authority* of the governance structure from jurisdiction over the land to management of band members.

Barriere Lake's customary governance code provisions are Aboriginal rights protected under section 35(1) of the Canadian Constitution Act of 1982. However, the courts have said infringement is allowed if a strong case can be made for intervention.[46] Under the CCESP, a Section 74 action is considered "the antithesis of self-government" and warns that it should only be exercised "where the dispute is so volatile that no other option is viable."[47] Minister of Indian Affairs Chuck Strahl made the case for infringement at Barriere Lake by referencing community embroilment in ongoing leadership disputes. But was the dispute volatile beyond repair? Time and time again, the community informed the department that a reconciliation process was under way. INAC officials had the opportunity to see this for themselves on several site visits to the Rapid Lake Reserve. On April 6, 2010, Pierre Nepton, Quebec regional director general, reports on a meeting held on March 31, 2010, at Rapid Lake with both Jean Maurice Matchewan and Casey Ratt in attendance: both men "gave us an indication that they were willing to work together with the community to bring some modification to the customary code."[48] The joint efforts of formerly disputing chiefs negate suggestions of volatility in the community, yet it appears that the target had been already set.

"The Government Is Breaking the Law, but through Our Actions We Are Protecting It"

Before the ax dramatically fell on Barriere Lake's customary government in August 2010, there were many forewarnings that the customary band's days were numbered. As early as 1995, during the first leadership crisis with the IBC, the Department of Indian Affairs debated imposing Section 74 of the Indian Act onto the community as an exit strategy to the Trilateral Agreement.[49] In March 2008, an internal report summarizing impact scenarios of Ratt council recognition over the Nottaway council also offered the possibility of not recognizing both councils and instead imposing Section 74 on the community.[50] Despite repeated references to Section 74 over the years in regard to Barriere Lake, these discussions remained internal to the department until October 2009. That month, Barriere Lake received notice from Minister of Indian Affairs Chuck Strahl that an order pursuant to Section 74 of the Indian Act to bring Barriere Lake under band council election provisions was being actively considered.[51] The context of the Section 74 ministerial order was presented as the internal leadership dispute, but INAC had continued to interfere with Barriere Lake's internal governance procedures prior to this 2008 conflict, undermining the community's capacity to govern. At least the department made no secret of the severity of the measure. Camil Simard, director of Negotiations, Governance and Individual Affairs for the Quebec Region of INAC, told *Indian Country Today* (after the fact) that "[t]he Section 74 of the Indian Act . . . is an extraordinary measure that is taken very rarely and only under extraordinary circumstances."[52]

Barriere Lake was well aware of the severity of the threat. A series of meetings were held in the community between INAC representatives and Barriere Lake between December 2009 and August 2010. One meeting in particular illustrates the independent character and identity of the Barriere Lake people. On December 15, 2009, Nepton visited the community to consult about the Section 74 order. With Nepton seated at the front of the room, ready as a delegate of the government of Canada to lead the meeting, the community held a community assembly in their own language of *anishnabemowin*, facilitated by Tony Wawatie, a respected community member in the hereditary line. At the end of their ninety-minute meeting, when everyone had had a chance to speak, the community took a vote and the Indian Act election system was resoundingly rejected. The results of the "consultation" were communicated to Nepton.[53]

In a follow-up letter to the department, the chief and council explained what had transpired at the meeting:

What you observed during the meeting of December 15th is that it was attended by supporters of both our Council and supporters

of the Casey Ratt group. What you also observed is that despite
the differences between us, both groups are adamantly opposed to
the Minister either issuing or threatening to issue an order under
section 74 of the Indian Act, to put us under the elective system.
There is a broad consensus in our community in favour of retaining our customs and against a section 74 order.[54]

Nepton had sent a notice expressing his disappointment that Tony
Wawatie was not interested in providing him with an opportunity to
address the community.[55] Barriere Lake chief and council replied, cor-
recting this and other claims: "[Tony] asked the people if they wanted
to hear you and they told him, in no uncertain terms, that they did not
want to hear from you. Their only purpose was to give you a very clear
message that they were opposed to the Minister either issuing or threatening to issue an order under section 74 of the *Indian Act*. Once this message was delivered, many people walked out. As a courtesy, some people
stayed to listen to your presentation."[56] The council then refers the department to the two resolutions passed that day by the Elders Council
and the community rejecting the imposition of Section 74 and reaffirm-
ing the MAO as the customary government system at Barriere Lake.
One exemplary line from the community resolution that soundly rejects
the attack on their customary government reads: "we, the Mitchikinabikok Inik, vow to continue the efforts of our Ancestors to protect our
identity, our Culture, our language, our territory and our Onakinakewin
against assimilation, marginalization and discrimination such as the
Ministers [*sic*] decision of October 30, 2009."[57]
      Meanwhile, the minister of Indian Affairs invoked his power under
Section 74 to impose the elective system on Barriere Lake based on the
"leadership process" as the source that "continues to fuel the difficult
governance situation" at Barriere Lake. He concludes that the community "is lacking the political will and the governance tools to resolve the
matter." As evidence of further governance issues, elections officer Bob
Nepton referred to "several cases . . . involving various parties, [that]
are currently unfolding before the Federal Court." Although this was
the pretense for the imposition of the elective system, this communication strategy defied and denied reason and evidence to the contrary. The
court cases were referred to as proof of endless internal conflict and the
incapacity to resolve issues on their own. There were in fact four cases

before the federal court, but three of them were against the minister.[58] Besides, Barriere Lake asked the department why they should not have recourse to the courts, especially since the minister himself had said that he has no jurisdiction to adjudicate the dispute. As to the accusation of constant leadership disputes, the community had in fact had only one prior leadership dispute in 1996, making it ten years between occurrences. As they point out, "we consider that quite infrequent considering the frequency of leadership disputes within the current minority Parliament in Ottawa."[59] The source of these legal proceedings and leadership conflicts, furthermore, was actions of Nepton's own department—recognition of the IBC, undue process in the imposition of TPM, failure to honor agreements, and politically motivated recognition of councils—all contributed to the chaos and unrest in the community.

There were also a series of exchanges of communications that clearly expressed the community's progress in their internal reconciliation process.[60] Nonetheless, on June 18, 2010, Nepton rejected the community efforts at reconciliation. He informed the community that he had received the elders' resolutions and outline of plans for a reconciliation process toward a new government in Barriere Lake but said that it fell short of requirements INAC had laid out for customary code modification. The nomination meeting for an Indian Act band council would go along as scheduled by Electoral Officer Bob Norton.[61] At the end of July, the community blocked the first nominations meeting from taking place by driving trucks across the entrance to the reserve from Highway 117, preventing the electoral officer from getting into the community.[62] There seemed to be no choice by this point but for the Algonquins to try to physically prevent the band council elections from going forward. As Marylynn Poucachiche put it: "The government is breaking the law, but through our actions we are protecting it."[63]

The second time the electoral officer entered the territory, however, he had learned his lesson. Rather than publicly announce the nominations meeting, Norton arrived early in the morning, hours before the community living at Rapid Lake was told he would arrive, and held a nomination meeting on a site off Highway 117. He had not obtained permission to be there from the family whose territory he was on and, when questioned later, he would not provide any information on how he came to hold the nomination meeting at that time and place. When information finally reached Rapid Lake and around twenty-five community members arrived to find out what had transpired at the nomination meeting, Norton and his colleagues immediately packed up their things and made to leave, claiming that everything was void. Independent journalist Courtney Kirkby, reporting for CKUT radio in Montreal, caught the exchange on camera.[64]

NORMAN MATCHEWAN: Who was nominated?

BOB NORTON: Nobody, 'cause we didn't have a nomination meeting. I'm just checking with a lawyer now and I think the whole thing is dead.

ROSE NOTTAWAY: Dead?

BOB NORTON: I'm just waiting for a legal opinion. Because the law says we have to have a nomination meeting before an election is activated.

NORMAN MATCHEWAN: But there were people who showed up to nominate people and we want to know who that was. I think we have a right to know. I don't think you should be nodding your head "no."

BOB NORTON: I can tell you legally that if those nominations are recognized, they will be posted and you'll know who nominated who.

NORMAN MATCHEWAN: Can we have a copy now to confirm that?

BOB NORTON: No, because they're not valid right now.

NORMAN MATCHEWAN: So this whole thing is not valid?

BOB NORTON: That's my opinion right now. I'm just waiting for a legal opinion. (He holds up his cell phone.)

In the video, Norton continues to fixate on his cell phone before finally leaving the site without word from the lawyers. As he leaves, he says: "They're void. Everything's void. There's no chief and council." Matchewan asks for a written confirmation attesting to that statement, but Norton ignores him. As community members encourage Norton to leave and to never return, Kirkby asks Norton whether or not he has received any mail-in nomination ballots. Norton refuses to respond.

On August 16, 2010, community members saw a notice hung up in the health clinic. It informed them that a new band council had been elected to govern the community. Because two nomination meetings were "disrupted," Norton determined that any attempt to hold a third nomination meeting would fail. Therefore, he declared that the candidates elected through mail-in ballots would be acclaimed as chief and council to form a band council for a two-year term. Only five people had submitted ballots.[65] The acclaimed councillors were Anida Decoursay, Steve Wawatie, Chad Thusky, and Hector Jerome. Casey Ratt was nominated as chief but he immediately resigned in protest of the Indian Act elective system, stating that "We will not surrender our rights nor will we allow the Department of Indian Affairs to do away with our Customary selection process."[66] The new band council sent out a notice a month later, claiming that their council was directed by the community to accept the nomination.[67] Shock and anger set in throughout the community. Another coup d'état had taken place. But this time, an entire system of governance had been replaced.

An INAC Band Council at Barriere Lake

When Barriere Lake blocked Norton from coming onto the reserve to hold the first nomination meeting, there was a palpable sense of defiance in the community, but also of desperation. An unbroken system of law that had been handed down since time immemorial was suddenly under threat of the Indian Act elective system—supposedly, a more "democratic" form of governance that was meant to restore order to the chaos the government had itself caused at Barriere Lake.[68] Tony Wawatie, a community spokesperson and natural leader with great reverence for the teachings of the Onakinakewin, stated to the press that day:

> The Canadian government is trying to forcibly assimilate our customs so they can sever our connection to the land, which is at the heart of our governance system. They don't want to deal with a strong leadership, selected by community members who live on the land, that demand that the federal and Quebec governments implement the outstanding agreements regarding the exploitation of our lands and resources.[69]

Jurisdiction over their lands was under imminent threat of becoming a delegated power of the state rather than recognized as an inherent right based on Indigenous law and custom. The two-year election cycle of the Indian Act system was just one way in which the Canadian system seemed philosophically flawed and shortsighted to the Algonquin elders. What could a leader learn in two years? What could he accomplish?

The Barriere Lake people were not alone in their condemnation of the Section 74 imposition. Thanks to Tony Wawatie's efforts, that summer the AFN General Assembly passed an emergency resolution condemning the minister of Indian Affairs for its invocation and demanding that he rescind the imposition of Indian Act band elections.[70] In the fall of 2010, National Chief Shawn Atleo met with youth leaders from the community and agreed to their proposal for a fact-finding mission to examine the situation in the community that led to the imposition of Section 74—the AFN would appoint one delegate and INAC would appoint the other.[71] The government chose not to respond to this request. On August 25, 2010, Barriere Lake sent the last of four unanswered letters to Minister of Indian Affairs Chuck Strahl, and to Robert Nicholson, minister of Justice and attorney general of Canada, Pierre Corbeil, Quebec minister of Aboriginal Affairs, and Jacques Dupuis, minister of Public Security, demanding the cancellation of Section 74 elections.[72]

In the weeks following the Section 74 imposition, Barriere Lake Solidarity (BLS)—a tri-city collective based in Toronto, Ottawa, and Montreal that had been working with the community since 2008—organized a human-rights delegation to the community that brought together members of major unions such as the Canadian Union of Postal Workers (CUPW) and Public Sector Employees Union with political party delegates from the Green Party and the New Democratic Party (NDP), and representatives from churches, social-justice groups, and environmental NGOs. The delegation saw firsthand the living conditions in the community, heard about the Section 74 order and its implications, and met with Toby Decoursay on Barriere Lake's traditional territory where he shared teachings about the three-figure wampum belt. BLS also organized a major demonstration in Ottawa in December 2010 attended by busloads of supporters from Montreal and Toronto, around one hundred people from Rapid Lake, and dozens of Ottawa activists and supporters who marched in freezing cold from Parliament Hill to Indian Affairs, led by the children of Barriere Lake. Only one year earlier, Prime Minister Stephen Harper had prorogued Parliament, shutting down the House of Commons for two months, avoiding a probing inquiry into the treatment of Afghan detainees, grinding to a halt the progress of numerous government bills, and allowing the Conservatives to take control of the Senate. At the demonstration, there were bright signs everywhere that read "Harper Has Nothing to Teach Us about Democracy." Referencing the extremely low voter turn-out for provincial and federal elections in Aboriginal communities, Norman Matchewan put it to supporters this way: "We stay out of your elections, you stay out of ours."

At the Ottawa demonstration, a number of high-profile supporters spoke out against the imposition of Section 74 on the community, including the national president of CUPW, Denis Lemelin, and NDP leader Jack Layton, who spoke by invitation of longtime advocate MP Charlie Angus. Spirited community members spoke out as well, including Marylynn Poucachiche, Norman Matchewan, Tony Wawatie, and Tillis Keyes. The event was emceed by Clayton Thomas-Mueller, a powerful Cree organizer who worked for the Indigenous Environmental Network (IEN). The morning of the demonstration, Joseph Boyden, Giller Book Prize winner, wrote an op-ed in the country's eminent national newspaper, the *Globe and Mail,* supporting the community, and the AFN put out a press release calling for Canada to rescind the Section 74 order.[73] Following up on this action, BLS launched a call-in and write-in campaign to pressure INAC to rescind Section 74. BLS also drafted information pamphlets, organized a speaking tour for community members, and held fund-raisers to support the campaign.

INAC, for its part, stuck closely to the script. The INAC script, as iterated by Camil Simard, constantly emphasized the "help" that INAC was prepared to give Barriere Lake, specifically through the conversion to custom legislation.[74] She also expressed to *Indian Country Today* INAC's great disappointment that Barriere Lake consistently rejected these offers of support: "The Department (INAC) since 2006 offered help and funding so the community could try to resolve this thing internally."[75] In fact, 2006 was the year in which the department refused to recognize Jean Maurice Matchewan's council until forced to do so through a mediation process. In an effort to discredit the community's traditional governance system, Simard then referenced Justice Mainville's decision in which he suggests that different factions in the community were manipulating the customary code to their own benefit. She neglects to mention that Justice Mainville concluded that Barriere Lake is also one of those "rare bands" that may "select their leadership in accordance with their customs unimpeded by any conditions or requirements which the Minister may deem appropriate to allow reversion to customary election."[76] In line with Justice Mainville's decision and recommendations, the community had initiated their internal reconciliation process, under which the customary code was to be amended through their own governing process.

Although Barriere Lake's leaders felt secure in their constitutional standing against a Section 74 order, they did not have the resources to take a lengthy and costly legal challenge to court. But they were suddenly presented with an opportunity to address the legal status of band council leadership when the "INAC council" (as they came to be called by Barriere Lakers) demanded access to the Trilateral Agreement documents. These documents were in the possession of lawyer David Nahwegahbow. As acting legal counsel for Barriere Lake over the course of more than two decades, Nahwegahbow had the Trilateral records stored at his law office, where the community believed they would be kept most safely.[77] Nahwegahbow recognized immediately that there were significant uncertainties as to whether the INAC council had the legal authority to govern at Barriere Lake (given the earlier legal precedents and the unique constitutional standing of customary bands). He determined that the wisest course of action would be to let the courts identify the rightful owners of the Trilateral documents. This legal determination, he reasoned, would ascertain whose permission was needed to release the records, thus providing a legal assessment of the status of the INAC council without a costly and lengthy court case. He entered an interpleader application to the superior court of Ontario to resolve the matter.[78] Under the supervision of Justice Stephen O'Neill, a series of conference calls were convened between the justice, David Nahwegahbow, Jean Maurice Matchewan, Casey Ratt, and the INAC council. The lawyer who would be representing the INAC council was none other than Michael Swinwood, the lawyer who had represented the Ratt council and now sat across the table from Casey Ratt, representing his opponents.[79]

As opposed to the AFN–INAC fact-finding mission that the customary government supporters at Barriere Lake had recommended, the INAC council proposed that the Trilateral documents be turned over to the fact-finding mission, which would be comprised of two INAC council representatives, one representative from the Matchewan group, and one representative from the Ratt group.[80] Matchewan and Ratt rejected this option after consultation with the community but came up with a counterproposal, again requesting that a representative from outside the community undertake the fact-finding mission. They also advocated a more balanced representation of parties on the fact-finding committee—one INAC council member, one delegate from the Matchewan group, one delegate from the Ratt group—and a broader mandate. Matchewan and Ratt proposed that rather than simply undertake a report "disclosing how and where the Trilateral Agreement funding was distributed," as the INAC council was recommending, instead the fact finder investigate in addition "all financial documents, financial receipts, reports and audits, proposals, Band Council Resolutions, correspondence, maps, study reports, and all equipments to develop a draft report."[81] This way, all the spending could be correlated with the work undertaken to complete Phases 1 and 2 of the Trilateral Agreement. Arguments were heard at the superior court of Ontario in Sudbury on October 25–26, 2011. This mediation was indefinitely suspended, though, when the INAC council's refusal to negotiate ground discussions to a halt.

All the commotion about an audit on the Trilateral documents had no material bearing on the present circumstances and was understood by the community as a way to steer them away from their focus on Section 74. Furthermore, there had already been an INAC-directed audit on financial management and the Trilateral Agreement covering the period of April 1, 1993, to June 30, 1996, under the pretense of allegations mainly from one anonymous source.[82] At the time of this first audit, the customary council at Barriere Lake pointed out the peculiar timing of it, given that the time frame of the audit corresponded with increasing pressure from the forestry sector and federal and provincial governments to destabilize their leadership and derail the Trilateral Agreement.[83] Nevertheless, the customary council had agreed to fully cooperate with the private auditing firm hired by INAC. Four years passed without further notice of the investigation until the community became embroiled again in 2001 with the government of Canada in a renewed political contest to see the Trilateral implemented. Suddenly, Nahwegahbow was contacted by the RCMP, which hinted that it might be reviving this financial investigation again.[84] This time, the customary council put star lawyer Clayton Ruby on retainer, believing that "in light of the foregoing, that the RCMP investigation constitutes continued harassment and likely emanates from political interference from within the federal government."[85] So, it was with relative certainty that the customary government supporters viewed the INAC council's Trilateral witch hunt as another delaying tactic to avoid dealing with the Section 74 issue until the audit was complete.

Fiscal Relations and the Great Resource Grab

If the INAC council had been truly concerned about Barriere Lake's finances, it might have devoted some energy to ridding the community of the Third Party Managers who were leaching hundreds of thousands of dollars out of the community each year at INAC's behest. The year 2011 would mark the fifth anniversary of the community's bondage under Third Party Management. According to Casey Ratt and Jean Maurice Matchewan, Third Party Manager Lemieux Nolet's annual take for its financial administration services was six hundred thousand dollars— paid out of band funds, which total only $5 million annually.[86] No government oversight strategy appears to have been devised to monitor Nolet's operations or to transition the band back to administering its own affairs, despite assurances to the contrary made by INAC. One could ask what the interest would have been to this Quebec City firm in writing itself out of a lucrative job. Nolet's final audit report was due in July 2011. The community never saw it.

To make matters worse, when Nolet lost a bid with INAC to renew the company's contract around the time the INAC council took over, the government hired *two more* Third Party Management firms to take its place. BDO Canada LLP Aboriginal Financial Services Group was hired to deal with all administrative affairs and Atmacita Hartel Financial Management was hired to manage all files related to the health sector. Considerable problems have already arisen with Atmacita Hartel. Community members have complained that access to health services and medical transport has become difficult.[87] Because the community has been unsuccessful, despite numerous unanswered letters to Indian Affairs, to obtain any accounting audits of their financial situation, they have no way of knowing whether or not the community is still facing a deficit, and if so, what the current shortfall might be.[88] The foreign accounting firms handling band finances exercise extraordinary control and discretion over all spending, acting like internally placed austerity comptrollers.[89] Through fiscal policy, Canada effectively controlled what little governing authority Barriere Lake could exercise as an elective council. Little oversight exists over Third Party Managers, and despite being paid by Barriere Lake, they are hired by and accountable to INAC, so accountants can maneuver with almost total discretion.[90] As we will see in the Conclusion, these accountants continue to reign over Barriere Lake to this day.

On the ground, the youth leadership was meeting with the INAC council and requesting that the council step down as a sign of solidarity with the community. Stepping down would also confirm that the band council was against the Section 74 order, as they insisted.[91] Although the INAC council assured the youth that it too valued the Onakinakewin, it maintained its refusal to resign as councillors and attempted to maintain appearances of accountability to the community. The community was kept in the dark for the better part of a year, until eight months after taking office the band council distributed an information package community-wide that contained a detailed overview of its activities, including a list of each meeting it attended and minutes of negotiations, such as those with Hydro-Quebec.[92] After reading over the meeting list, the customary government realized that its former lawyer, Peter Hutchins, was now representing the INAC council.

Although the INAC council updated the community on occasion, no public meetings were ever held at Rapid Lake. The INAC council well understood that the community did not consider the band council their legitimate representatives and would never accept their purported leadership. As well, though the leadership takeover in the community had placed Barriere Lake in a weaker negotiating position with resource-extraction industries, the unintended consequences of internal fragmentation might also have inadvertently worked to the community's advantage. The band council, after all, neither numerically represented the community nor procedurally reflected the governance customs of the community. Its authority did not secure guarantees for logging or mining companies. As one INAC official admitted: "Where there's uncertainty of leadership it's difficult to make advances in social and economic development."[93] Despite the ongoing divestment of settler governments in the Trilateral process, Barriere Lake remained steadfast in asserting their jurisdiction on the ground, with or without sanction from the state.

This was put to the test when the community first learned about mining on their territory in early 2011 through a researcher at the Ottawa-
based NGO Mining Watch. Ramsey Hart warned Barriere Lake that a
stake was being claimed nearby under the project name "Rivière Doré."
Unbeknownst to the community, Quebec had been dropping "torpe-
does" into their lake system from helicopters to root up sediment that
it could test for mineral concentrations. The province then promoted
its findings to industry; as a result, Cartier Resources received a permit
from Quebec to do some minor exploration work north of the Rapid
Lake Reserve. According to its website, the mining company claimed
that its "100% owned" land base of 439 square kilometers boasted rich
copper-nickel deposits. It was working with Copper One Inc., which
earned an interest in the project by funding all the exploration work.[94]

The INAC council met with Phillippe Cloutier, president and CEO of
Cartier Resources Inc. in mid-March. According to the minutes of this
meeting, Cloutier confirmed that the company had done no consultation with Barriere Lake band members, believing that its permit from
the province was sufficient to begin exploration work. According to the
minutes, "The Band Council and the ABL members [from Maigan Agik,
Airport, and the reserve] demanded that Cartier Resources to [sic] suspend their activities until further notice was provided by the Algonquins
of Barriere Lake."[95] The INAC council requested that Cloutier respect its
authority in these matters. Elsewhere on the territory, the customary
government supporters exercised the authority and jurisdiction of the
Mitchikanibikok Anishnabe Onakinakewin to protect the land from the
Cartier mining incursion. In order to ensure that the project did not
proceed without proper consultation and an environmental assessment,
they determined to halt the company's line-cutting activities that would
prepare the ground for exploration by opening paths into the bush to
transport drilling machinery and to identify claim sites. Workers on
site, predominantly Crees from the Mistassini and Oujebougamou First
Nations, agreed to leave when the Algonquins arrived and explained
their opposition to the development.[96]

On April 13, 2011, still in the dark regarding the dealings of the band
council, the Mitchikanibikok Inik Elders Council followed up this direct action with a letter to the Quebec ministers informing them that
unless two demands were met, there would be no natural resource extraction on their territory: they demanded a completion of their lead-

ership selection process—affirming the Mitchikanibikok Anishnabe Onakinakewin and rejecting the Section 74 band council—and they demanded that the government of Quebec negotiate with the duly selected customary chief and council the implementation of the Ciaccia– Lincoln Joint Recommendations.[97] The elders reminded the Quebec ministers that section 7 of the 1991 Trilateral Agreement states that "Both Quebec and the Algonquins of Barriere Lake agree to examine seriously the recommendations . . . that will be submitted to them by the special representatives and to negotiate an agreement on the carrying out of the recommendations retained."[98] A few months earlier, prior to the Section 74 imposition, Quebec had expressed a willingness to implement the bilateral agreement as a way to move forward with logging in the territory, if they dropped the two most important recommendations retained by the special representatives: resource revenue sharing and comanagement.[99] Following a community government meeting, Matchewan rejected Quebec's proposal, stressing the central features of revenue sharing and comanagement in the Trilateral Agreement and killing negotiations from proceeding along these lines.[100]

The community knew it would take more than giving the line-cutters a few days off work to stop the mining exploration on their territory. With the support of Montreal organizer Martin Lukacs, Norman Matchewan attended Cartier Resources' annual general meeting in Montreal on May 20, 2011. Following Cloutier's presentation and a polite round of questions, Matchewan raised his hand and stood to speak. He told the board members where he was from and emphasized that there would be no discussions about mining in the territory until the Trilateral Agreement was honored. He highlighted the community's resistance to past resource development as well as examples in Ontario where First Nations communities stopped mining companies, such as the Ojicree community of Kitchenuhmaykoosib Inninuwug (KI) in northern Ontario who expelled Platinex from their traditional territory. Lukacs also rose to say a few words. Stressing the political obstacles and financial risks of the Rivière Doré project, he explained that the provincial government had clearly misled the company about the security of such a project and of the costs and liabilities if the community chose to challenge Cartier Resources legally. Matchewan and Lukacs distributed copies of the Elders Council letter that reiterated the two demands for moving forward with natural resource extraction on their territory. The message was clear: this was a matter between governments. Two months later, Cartier Resources sent out a press release declaring a two-year moratorium on mining in Barriere Lake's territory, suspending its work on the Rivière Doré project.[101] A source on the board revealed to Lukacs that Matchewan's presentation was persuasive; the company decided to cut its losses before things went too far.[102]

In the meantime, logging was also on the upswing in Barriere Lake's traditional territory, and once again, the elected band council struggled to assert its authority under increasingly difficult conditions. The INAC council sent a letter to the community in mid-June 2011 expressing the challenges it faced in its ability to govern over land and resource management given the widely different perspectives of various families in the community. The letter urged unity around land-management issues.[103] In the case of the Mitchikanibikok Inik Council of Elders, its demands on logging companies were that no extraction take place on the territory that did not conform to the 1991 Trilateral Agreement, the 1998 bilateral agreement, and the 2006 Ciaccia–Lincoln Joint Recommendations.[104] On the other hand, the Traditional Council of Elders of the One Nation—representing the off-reserve community of Maigan Agik, mostly the Wawatie family—suggested that it was the sole legitimate body for negotiation.[105] In a letter to the community, the INAC council attributed this disagreement and conflict over land management to the "confusing management legacy of the Trilateral Agreement."[106] Nonetheless, for the purpose of the 2011–12 year, the band council announced that it would allow for Measures to Harmonize within the traditional territory and the Trilateral Agreement territory, conditional on securing consensus on a number of issues, including guaranteed employment for Barriere Lake members in the logging activities, no mining exploration activities within the traditional Trilateral Agreement territory, and that Quebec and Canada agreed to cover all costs for a fact finder for the Trilateral Agreement fact-finding process.[107]

No consensus was ever reached between groups, nor did the families of Barriere Lake feel any pressing need to build unity with the INAC council, which continued to refuse to step down from its positions. The effort was clearly disingenuous; community members were aware that meetings had been taking place for almost a year between the band council, the Quebec Ministry of Natural Resources and Ministry of

Aboriginal Affairs, and the multinational logging companies Abitibi-Bowater and Louisiana Pacific in Maniwaki, Quebec.[108]

Many skirmishes erupted over resources during the course of the year: logging proceeded in Jacko Thomas's, Hector Jerome's, and Jacob Wawatie's territories. While Thomas and Jerome consented to logging on their family lands, the Wawatie family erected blockades throughout the year to stop the clear-cuts by Abitibi-Bowater from taking place. In December 2011, Louisiana Pacific began logging on Benjamin Keyes's territory without permission from the family. A group of community members from Rapid Lake, led by Norman Matchewan, drove out to the site to find out what they could about the situation. The loggers informed him that the Quebec Ministry of Natural Resources had authorized the logging and claimed that they had secured agreement from the family. Following their visit—where the damage had already been done: a moose stand was clear-cut—Matchewan delivered a letter to the Louisiana Pacific office from the Mitchikanibikok Inik Council of Elders requesting that all logging activities be suspended "until the mandated consultation with TMA [Trilateral Management Area] 2 [and] members of the Algonquins of Barriere Lake" was carried out.[109]

Finally, the lack of control the customary government exercised over resource extraction faced it with the hardest choice many of its members had ever made. They could either watch from the sidelines as their lands were destroyed by mining and forestry or they could form a band council themselves and be elected under Indian Act provisions. When he was running, Norman Matchewan sent friends the following communication: "Well its [sic] official I am an Indian Act Candidate. We nominated Casey Ratt for Chief and 6 Councillors. It still hasn't sunk in, it was a very hard decision but if we didn't do anything our land our people will continue to suffer leaving us with no say."[110] On August 13, 2012, Casey Ratt became the chief of a council that included Norman Matchewan as band councillor. The victory was bittersweet. The INAC council was defeated, but the community's case for challenging the legality of Section 74 was probably irreparably compromised by their participation in the system.

That summer, Resolute Forest Products' (formerly Abitibi-Bowater) rampant logging on Gabriel Wawatie's family hunting territory would test the new council. Community members, led by Norman Matchewan, formed a campsite to block the mining, and were soon joined by Maigan Agik members. The logging protest camp drew media attention and support throughout the summer: more than six hundred people sent letters to stop the logging to the MNR through the Barriere Lake Solidarity website, and at the height of Quebec's "Maple Spring," Barriere Lakers posed in the woods with red squares of cloth to show their solidarity with the students against the Quebec government. The students repaid the solidarity, with CLASSE (Coalition Large de l'ASSÉ) representative Gabriel Nadeau-Dubois speaking at a demonstration outside of Resolute headquarters in Montreal.[111] The antilogging campaign soon came to a close, however, when in September Resolute was granted an injunction against protesters threatening any remaining community members and supporters with arrest if they refused to leave the site. The injunction was challenged separately by Maigan Agik and the new band council, with separate legal counsel and demands. Maigan Agik claimed that the Trilateral was a thing of the past and tried to bring forward a title case, while Michel Thusky, representing the community, asked that Measures to Harmonize be implemented on the logging concessions, at least to protect the sacred areas in the interim. The Quebec court overturned both attempts to reverse the injunction, partially because separate motions had been brought by presumably the same party. As Margaux Kristjansson describes, the injunction sought by Resolute against the Wawatie family was then extended to apply against all Algonquin people, with the court proposing that it was only an injunction against disruption, not one against presence on the land.[112] The potential for disruption was broadly applied to everyone, though. As the justice stated, "the Crown is of the opinion that the order should encompass everyone, especially as Resolute do not know the names of all members of ABL likely to disrupt their work."[113] The criminal intent of the community became generalized as part of a larger pattern of pacification described in the next chapter.

9

Security, Critical Infrastructure, and the Geography of Indigenous Lands

The kids are searching for "blockade" on YouTube and talking about getting teargassed. Later that day, on the way back to the reserve from swimming in a nearby lake, Maria and Shane bring up the blockade again. They ask me if I was there and I say, "Yes." Maria reports that Shane was crying when they got teargassed, but Shane retorts defensively: "Everyone was crying." Maria finally agrees. She tells me that Shakira was playing in a car while all the other kids, around twenty-five of them, were driven back to the reserve (Shakira is four years-old and loves to lock herself in cars). The rest of the kids had bolted in fear two kilometers down the road and had to be gathered in a pickup truck and driven home. Then Maria tells me that a "handicap" got pepper-sprayed. I misunderstand and ask, "Teargassed?" No, Maria says impatiently, sprayed *in the face,* demonstrating with her hands the difference between gases.

In the fall of 2008, a group of more than a hundred community members of the Algonquins of Barriere Lake twice blockaded Highway 117 in an attempt to pressure the government to send in a negotiator. The community demanded that the government restore Trilateral Agreement talks and, even more urgently, that it halt interference into their internal customary affairs. The blockades were precipitated by the decision taken in January by the Department of Indian Affairs to recognize Casey Ratt and his government as the legitimate customary chief and council of Barriere Lake. As Norman Matchewan explained to the media during the blockade: "This is not the first time that they have pushed aside our chief and council and put in place a small minority for their benefit, so they can get out of this [Trilateral] Agreement. They have played divide and rule in our community for too long. The community is standing up and we are not going to give up."[1]

The decision to blockade had not been taken lightly. The people of Barriere Lake had spent years trying to set the Trilateral Agreement on a positive track. Then once again they were faced with a new council to which the majority of the community did not consent. Norman Matchewan defended their tactics to the media on the day of the October 2008 blockade: "We did not want to get to this point, but they've ignored us for two years—we've been chasing them around, protesting in Ottawa for days, we did a sit-in in [MP Lawrence Cannon's] Buckingham office, we've been to Maniwaki, we've organized campaigns, they *still* did not get back to us."[2] In an op-ed piece published in the *Montreal Gazette*, Norman wrote, "We have always preferred co-operation to confrontation. We do not wish to disrupt the lives of Canadians. Unfortunately, it seems their governments otherwise ignore or dismiss us—or worse, treat us with contempt."[3] The specific incident of contempt Norman refers to happened at the sit-in at Transport Minister Lawrence Cannon's office. Cannon was the MP for the riding of Pontiac, where the Rapid Lake Reserve is located. When the Algonquins arrived, planning to stay until their demands for a meeting were met, the minister's assistant told Norman to come back when he was sober. But things went from bad to worse, as Norman explains: "[a]fter the media scandal forced Cannon to hold a meeting we had been requesting for two years, he vilified our community's majority as 'dissidents' in an op-ed in regional papers."[4] One racial stereotype had snowballed into a volley of smear tactics.

Highway 117 is the main arterial road between Val-d'Or and Maniwaki, Quebec, and detour routes can add as many as six hours to a commute. Hoping to alert the media and local citizens to their issues and use this leverage to demand face time with government officials, Barriere Lake community members determined that they had no choice but to blockade. This strategy of last resort further led the state to entrench its position. At the first blockade of Highway 117 on October 6, 2008, riot police were deployed to the region from Montreal. A quiet morning of food and discussion on the highway was followed by a tense confrontation when the riot cops moved in and teargassed the community, including elders and children, and violently shoved them off the highway onto the five-kilometer access road that led back to the Algonquin reserve. Nine people, including an elder, a pregnant woman, and two minors, were roughly arrested and one customary council member was hospitalized after being hit in the chest with a tear-gas canister.[5]

It was an affecting sight. "This is how much the government is willing to pay to keep us in that fifty-nine acres!" Marylynn Poucachiche

SQ Riot Police on the access road from Rapid Lake Reserve to Highway 117, pushing community members back on their reserve, October 2009. Photograph by author.

shouted as the riot line moved in mechanical formation toward the crowd. "Look at how much money they spend on you guys . . . You want to keep us on this reserve? Tiny little reserve? Well, we're not going to stay here. You guys, you can stand here for maybe twelve hours. Us, we can be here another five hundred years."[6] Families held hands and walked together, slowly and defiantly, with the cops literally pressing at their backs. The violent policing efforts they would experience on their territory that year would cost the province nearly as much as if Quebec had allocated the modest revenue-sharing agreement in the Trilateral Agreement that the Algonquins had been demanding for years.[7]

It is difficult to imagine a scenario where white, rural families could be treated so brutally by police with barely a peep from the mainstream media. As a result of outreach by Barriere Lake Solidarity and a viral blockade video made by filmmaker Martha Steigman, hundreds of people spoke out against the violence and were mobilized to learn more and get involved in solidarity efforts. Angus Toulouse, the Ontario regional chief of the Chiefs of Ontario, sent a letter to Prime Minister Stephen Harper and Quebec Premier Jean Charest condemning police actions and calling on Ottawa and Quebec City to follow the Ipperwash Inquiry recommendations.[8]

Nonetheless, at a second blockade at Barriere Lake, on November 19, 2008, neither was the political nature of the protest taken into account, nor were federal representatives involved to intervene, despite being engaged and deeply implicated in the conflict.[9] Instead, community members were constrained from asserting their jurisdiction by way of escalating carceral tactics. Marylynn Poucachiche was one of several community leaders targeted for arrest. Her arrest followed assurances by the SQ that so long as protesters remained peaceful, they would not be charged. Poucachiche was eventually released on condition she not attend public demonstrations or protests until her case was cleared. Rose Nottaway, another outspoken and respected community leader, was also arrested, as was Sonny Papatie, a youth committed to the community's political cause and to the Trilateral Agreement. Acting Chief Benjamin Nottaway was also arrested at the blockade when several riot police broke out of formation and tackled him to the ground. He was charged with three counts of mischief and breach of conditions stemming from March blockades on Barriere Lake's access road, when a spontaneous protest blocked the Ratt council from entering the reserve.[10] Nottaway, a father of five, received the heaviest sentence, imprisoned for sixty days at the Hull Detention Centre in Gatineau, Quebec. The Crown wanted to send him away for an entire year, but the judge Jules Barriere explained that this would be illegal because the maximum sentence for the crime was just six months. He agreed, however, that a stern message needed to be sent to the community and punished Nottaway accordingly.[11]

The use of force to police Barriere Lake into compliance with the new customary council is part of a larger pattern of coercion, surveillance, and criminalization that has been used against Barriere Lake and communities across the country to manage Indigenous assertions of jurisdiction.[12] Jeffrey Monaghan uses the term "settler governmentality" to describe the construction of Indigenous assertions of sovereignty *as a threat* to settler colonialism's primary focus: the acquisition of territory through the elimination of the native.[13] He demonstrates through archival materials that Indigenous communities were under surveillance and infiltrated by Indian Affairs spies since the mid-1880s because assertions of jurisdiction by Indigenous leaders such as Poundmaker and Little Bear were perceived as dangerous and deviant. Monaghan ties the

logic of elimination to the failure of racialized Indigenous communities to integrate into Canadian society, therefore posing a threat to the
identity and security of the white nation: indigeneity itself was seen as
a threat to the prosperity of the colony.[14] Andrew Crosby and Jeffrey
Monaghan develop this idea of settler governmentality further by theorizing Canada's imposition of Section 74 on the Algonquins of Barriere
Lake.[15] They demonstrate how Barriere Lake's calls for implementation
of the Trilateral Agreement were "secured" by the state through targeting characteristics of Barriere Lake's indigeneity (i.e., customary governance) in order to eliminate the threat of Indigenous jurisdiction to the
settler state.

The concept of settler governmentality contributes a radical genealogy to critical security studies by exposing the nature of Indigenous
"risk" that states seek to secure. While the field of security studies
trades in a commonsense and apolitical concept of safekeeping and
peace building, critical security studies rather theorizes "security" as
a political technology of liberal state making.[16] As Adrian Smith puts
it, the logic of security "obfuscates resistance to injustice by recasting
it as an ongoing threat; it is reified and as such obscures unequal social
relations."[17] Where George Rigakos writes that security discourse is a
"fabrication of a social order," the directives of this social order can be
examined through state responses to Indigenous assertions of jurisdiction on their lands.[18]

In this chapter, I examine and spatialize rationalities of settler governmentality and tie them to broader patterns of political economy in
Canada today, with specific case studies focused on the Algonquins of
Barriere Lake. I argue that the geographic dispersion of reserves created
"an archipelago of spatial containment" linked to a circuitry of capital
accumulation and its fixed infrastructures of commodity production.[19]
To understand these material geographic forms of circuitry, I situate
reserves within a particular architecture of security that has emerged
in the past few decades.[20] In Canadian government and intelligence
departments' terms, reserves are located in geographic proximity to
critical infrastructure—a vague designation for fixed capital that forms
the object of international security collaboration between states and
industry to protect global supply chains. The securitization of this critical infrastructure involves a multijurisdictional infrastructure of surveillance and coordination to mitigate the risk of potential disruption

to commodity circulation. Although this topic is too large to examine here comprehensively, I bring to light key aspects linking security logics, Indigenous jurisdiction, geography, and the natural resource economy.

Fomenting Hot Spots of "Civil Unrest"

The logic of security at Barriere Lake forms part of a hidden architecture of surveillance that structures intelligence sharing between departments, security agencies, and the private sector in Canada. Internal documents obtained through Access to Information and Privacy (ATIP) requests from Indian Affairs and the Royal Canadian Mounted Police (RCMP) reveal widespread and systemic surveillance of Indigenous communities who are asserting their land rights and jurisdiction. Shortly after forming a government in 2006, Prime Minister Stephen Harper had the federal government tighten up on gathering and sharing intelligence on First Nations to anticipate and manage potential civil unrest across Canada.[21] INAC was given a lead role in national operations. The stated goal of "monitoring" is to identify the First Nation leaders, participants and outside supporters of occupations and protests, and to closely monitor their actions.[22] To accomplish this task, INAC established a "Hot Spot Reporting System," which falls under the Emergency and Issue Management Directorate (EIMD). These weekly reports highlight all those communities across the country that engage in direct action to protect their lands and communities.[23] Information on protests and occupations is also collected by the RCMP and then shared across a broad range of government, industry, and security stakeholders.[24]

Like the Indian agents once positioned on reserves to control and repress dissent, the rationale for INAC's participation in security monitoring is justified precisely by the need to "mitigate" and "avoid" "impending incidents."[25] Legal and policy strategies are only as effective as the means of discipline and execution with which to enforce them. Thus, managing dissenting groups that step beyond the bounds of INAC's policies appears to be within the department's mandate and collaborating with security forces provides the means to intervene. The discourse of "civil unrest" even provides a kind of spatial license for INAC to intervene beyond its jurisdiction to *off-reserve* lands under the auspices of the department's position "to better understand issues that may have triggered these protests and to mitigate risks to individuals and property."[26]

The department's "understanding" comes largely from its involvement in activating disputes. When the hot spot surveillance project was exposed in the press in late 2011, INAC protested that this monitoring was a simple matter of public safety and claimed that "[t]he government co-ordinates efforts across departments to ensure public safety in Canada."[27] However, it was contradicted by its own analysis of the situation revealed in the documents. In a 2007 presentation to the RCMP, INAC states that "the vast majority of Hot Spots" of so-called Native unrest are "related to lands and resources," with most conflicts "incited by development activities on traditional territories."[28] It seems, in other words, that "Native unrest" is largely a euphemism for bands and other groups that are protecting their lands from development—most likely because of ecological exploitation or lack of consultation and consent—or, in the case of land claim disputes, dispossession. Even the RCMP note that "[t]he law and context of Aboriginal protests is fundamentally different than non-Aboriginal protests, such as labor or political disputes, and as a result require a dedicated and unique police resource, strategies and responses." It adds that the "assertion of rights is a fundamental and defining characteristic of Aboriginal protests" and that a wide range of authorities across jurisdictions tend to be involved that "raise public policy and legal issues beyond the scope and authority of the police."[29] Multijurisdictional participation appears essential to colonial pacification, including between public and private sectors.

The functioning of liberal democracy is contingent upon state–industry collaborations to both undermine Indigenous self-determination and then manage the protest provoked by such destabilization. In the Idle No More protests that were sparked in the winter of 2012–13, the Government Operations Centre (GOC) of Public Safety Canada was monitoring teach-ins, fund-raisers, community gatherings, and the tent at Victoria Island on Parliament Hill where Chief Theresa Spence was fasting in defense of her people's treaty right to housing.[30] Months later, the very impetus for some of the changes to legislation affecting Aboriginal rights was linked to consultation between the oil industry and the Ministries of Natural Resources and the Environment.[31]

Sifting through an extensive stack of EIMD reports, what emerges is a clear picture of INAC's organizational awareness of its role in fomenting "civil unrest." Around the time of INAC's recognition of the Ratt council, a bureaucrat at INAC warns the deputy minister: "Other protests can be expected until the leadership challenges at Barriere Lake are resolved."[32] INAC's interference creates and justifies its own raison d'être for managing conflict in First Nations communities. Rather than understand this role played by INAC as a conflict of interest, we must see how these roles fit together. INAC's position is the instigator, overseer, and negotiator, provoking "civil unrest"—the department monitors and mitigates this unrest through collaboration with law enforcement and other agencies. Thus, the department determines the scope of lawful assertions of Indigenous jurisdiction (or "resistance") by drafting the policy and legislation that will define the exercise of Indigenous rights and title to their land. Operating outside of these federal policies then invokes assertions of Indigenous jurisdiction and starts the cycle all over again.

Here we can return again to Shaunnagh Dorsett and Shaun McVeigh's definition of jurisdiction as a form of legal ordering and *crafting*—a technology that creates legal relations.[33] The inverse logic to this legal carving is to examine those shavings that fall to the floor: what escapes the frame and becomes understood as non-law, lawless, or the negative force of positive law? Nicholas Blomley argues that liberalism always locates violence outside of the law, creating a powerful divide between those who may legitimately dominate and those who may not. Bringing to bear private property as a reflection of colonial social norms, he writes that those claiming recognition to a property right outside of settler-colonial legalities of ownership are deemed to be "property outlaws," such as the "savage" and "uncivilized" Natives or the "wilds" of street-involved and low-income people in urban downtown cores who own no property.[34] If violence is framed as located *outside* of the law, then criminalization and repression of Indigenous peoples is justified by the need to pull them back "into" the law by subsuming their jurisdiction under state control.[35]

Regarding Barriere Lake, one INAC report outlines four demonstrations in which former interim customary chief Benjamin Nottaway supporters were involved following the controversial INAC recognition of the Ratt council in 2008. INAC had engineered this recognition, despite the protests of the majority of community members, and internal communications show that it anticipated these results. INAC was prepared to mitigate this predictable blowback: under the heading "Road Blocks, Violence and Protests," it states that "The current response to protests is to involve the police with appropriate jurisdiction."[36] Above all, a key objective of the surveillance project seems to be that it allows INAC to develop elaborate communications strategies to respond to situations on the ground and to craft spin to counter communities' grievances and demands. This counterspin—of criminality, dysfunction, financial corruption, and so on—allows it to produce distorted public knowledge of "native unrest," necessary to justify its indispensable role managing First Nations' affairs, and therefore to colonize Indigenous lands.

Surveillance networks do not stop with Indigenous peoples but seek also to intervene in the networks between Indigenous and non-Indigenous people. Much information in the EIMD reports is gleaned from the Barriere Lake Solidarity (BLS) website, which is the public platform for Barriere Lake political organizing, and obviously a valuable source of intelligence for INAC and security officers. For example, INAC reported on an upcoming demonstration in Ottawa in 2010 for several months before the event took place, taking notice of planning activities through BLS efforts to promote and mobilize supporters for the action. BLS events also gave security officers an opportunity to infiltrate organizing efforts. In an e-mail exchange between an RCMP corporal and an unknown recipient at INAC, the corporal reports that "a group calling themselves the Barriere Lake Solidarity are having an Emergency meeting on a campus in Montreal and the speaker is one Norman Matchewan (son of the old Chief Maurice Matchewan who leads the other group against Casey Ratt and the new Chief)."[37] A handwritten scrawl on the printed e-mail says "police inside," likely indicating undercover police presence at the Montreal event. This infiltration raises critical questions about the channels solidarity efforts create for law enforcement to intervene.

Non-Indigenous organizers acting in solidarity with Indigenous peoples themselves have become the target of security monitoring. Martin Lukacs, who founded BLS in Montreal, was visited by the Canadian Security Intelligence Service (CSIS), which sent two agents to visit him on April 13, 2010. They wanted to talk to him about Barriere Lake, specifically about what the officers referred to as the "possibilities of violence."[38] Almost exactly a year later, Pei Ju Wang, an organizer with the Indigenous Peoples Solidarity Movement Ottawa (IPSMO) who worked mostly on Barriere Lake support at the time, reported that Ontario Provincial Police (OPP) officers appeared at her front door, dressed in civilian clothes and wanting to come in and talk. The constable detective mentioned Barriere Lake and tried to draw her out, but she refused to let them into her home. Later, Wang learned that the detective constable was from the Hate Crimes/Extremism Unit/Provincial Operations Intelligence Bureau of the OPP.

In 2010, IPSMO also learned of an undercover police operative named François Leclerc who had infiltrated it for two years before being exposed;[39] Leclerc had frequently volunteered to do frontline support work for the Algonquins of Barriere Lake, including helping with transport, food delivery, and the logistics in Ottawa for demonstrations. Leclerc was on the internal organizing Listserv as well, where campaign strategy, sensitive community updates, and actions around Barriere Lake were developed and worked out. How had Leclerc aided authorities in their campaign against Barriere Lake? Because the government had exploited internal disputes, the sensitive information that circulated within the group was likely the most damaging.

The argument that the threat of violence justifies infiltration and surveillance is the rationale given for intervening in Indigenous assertions of jurisdiction. In the recommendations of the Ipperwash Inquiry, Commissioner Sydney Linden maintained that "despite the vast majority of protests by Indigenous peoples having been characterized by little to no violence, there is a persistent perception and representation of such events as risky and threatening based on a perceived *potential* for violence."[40] The response to this constructed risk has been to introduce surveillance regimes, which become a self-fulfilling prophesy in perpetuating mistrust and anger in Indigenous communities. The constructed threat of Indigenous peoples becoming "violent" is also matched by the potential—and possibly greater threat—of Indigenous peoples forming coalitions with environmental groups and "multi-issue extremists." RCMP Intelligence reports mention these concerns, for example, where apprehension about a Defenders of the Land call for groups to hold Indigenous Sovereignty Week events in 2009 was flagged for concern owing to "[t]he inclusive nature of the call out for events," which "increases the likelihood that participants will include a broad spectrum of the Canadian population including members of activist groups."[41]

CSIS has also closely monitored these coalitions, as documents show, marrying the threat of coalition building with property destruction ("violence") or disruption: "Multi-issue extremists [including environmental groups] and Aboriginal extremists may pursue common causes, and both groups have demonstrated the intent and the capability to carry out attacks against critical infrastructure in Canada."[42] As Monaghan and Walby observe, casting a wide net around terrorist entities and ideologically motivated activists deploys the concept of *critical infrastructure* to begin to make common cause in the construction of terror identities, an issue I will address later in this chapter.[43]

In EIMD documents obtained through ATIP requests, Barriere Lake features prominently and repeatedly from 2007 to 2011.[44] This appears to be connected to the fact that of particular concern to governments and industry are bands that reject federal land-settlement policies. INAC's presentation to the RCMP betrays concern about protests "outside of negotiation processes" with elected councils. Although this statement refers to "splinter groups," the presumption is that while band councils ("the elected leadership") are compliant with federal negotiation processes, manageable, grassroots Indigenous groups critical of such federal policies are a problem to be controlled. Barriere Lake poses a particular problem because their customary leadership represented neither a splinter group nor a compliant band council. But in either case, Canada seems clearly agitated by the specter of First Nations asserting land rights beyond the narrow confines of Crown land claims and self-government policies. This in turn explains why Barriere Lake has endured considerable RCMP and INAC attention since the hot spot surveillance reporting was first established.

Kangaroo Court

The reason that the Comprehensive Land Claims Policy (CLCP) is so central to the land-reform agenda is that it forms the front line of risk mitigation against Indigenous jurisdiction in Canada. The government's first line of defense against Indigenous jurisdiction is simply to deny that such Indigenous land rights exist. If that fails, the government supports either litigation through the courts or negotiation under the CLCP. Radical deviations from the CLCP are rarely tolerated, and the negotiating process in itself is a coercive mechanism that forces bands to extinguish their Aboriginal rights and title. The federal and provincial governments are equally invested in this process: the CLCP secures the extinguishment of Aboriginal title, and therefore access to Indigenous lands and resources. But in the case that a First Nation, Métis, or Inuit community will not submit to the CLCP, access to resources must be secured through other means.[45]

In 1996, Barriere Lake's special representative in the Trilateral secretariat commissioned an economic study of land and resources on the Trilateral Agreement area—about ten thousand square kilometers concentrated in the Outaouias region of Quebec. The report set out to evaluate regional economic structures to assess potential development in the region over the long term and to better harmonize the goals of competing users. Specifically, the report would quantify the economic value of forestry, tourism and recreation, other related activities, and noneconomic activities (such as camping and picnicking) in the Trilateral zone. Excluded from its evaluations would be government activities, from which sources of revenue came from outside the zone, such as Hydro Quebec. The consulting firm found that the rough total estimate of economic value generated in the Trilateral zone was around $56.5 million.[46] Hydro Quebec's revenues were estimated to be a further $50 million, calculated by another external consultant and added later to arrive at the conservative sum of $100 million.[47] Of that total revenue, the Algonquins of Barriere Lake received nothing. Quebec refused to set a precedent of revenue sharing with the Algonquins lest other bands should follow suit with similar demands. Barriere Lake, for their part, have refused to let the province off the hook; they continue to resist resource extraction on their lands, rejecting anything outside of the sustainable development plan laid out in the Trilateral Agreement. This resistance has turned out to be a model the province wants to prevent from replication.

One month following Norman Matchewan's eviction of mineworkers on his territory, he received a summons to appear at a court in Val-d'Or for mischief charges stemming from a peaceful blockade that had transpired two years earlier on a small logging road in Barriere Lake's territory.[48] It appeared as though the summons had been tucked into someone's back pocket in anticipation of a moment to put it to some use. Knocking Matchewan out of capacity as a key community organizer against mining might have been classified as such.

The logging itself was in violation of the Trilateral Agreement and had been unlawfully authorized by Quebec's Ministry of Natural Resources. But there were also oddities with the charge. Every criminal

offense can be tried as either an indictable offence or a summary conviction. Indictable offenses are more serious. Because the statute of
limitation had run out after six months on issuing the charges as a
summary conviction, Norman's charges had to be tried as an indictable
offense. But the indictable offense of mischief did not seem to specify
any crime.[49] Norman's lawyer, Jared Will, further explained that the
Crown had no direct evidence for any of the events other than the first
incident. It was also not calling witnesses regarding any of these other
interactions. "I was puzzled," he said. "They didn't seem to have any idea
what their strategy would be."[50]

Among several defenses Will prepared, the most difficult and complicated was a "color of right" defense, mounted when one believes there is
a legal justification for an action that is deemed to be a crime. Norman
believed that the logging was unlawful and Will thought Norman had
a strong case because of the leadership dispute that called Casey Ratt's
authority to consent to logging into question, and because of anomalies
in consultation.[51]

Slightly aside from the charges, one remarkable aspect of the trial
was revealed in the discrepancy between the province and the court's
interpretations of the Trilateral Agreement versus the federal government's spin on Barriere Lake's "utopic" fantasy that the Trilateral still
exists: all the interim measures of provincial consultation were evaluated based on the terms of the Trilateral Agreement.[52] This involved
the forestry company's obtaining a permit from Quebec, submitting a
cutting plan, and getting approval from the MNR about where it could
cut, all of which would be based on "Measures to Harmonize" with
Algonquin land use. When Vincent Larin, regional Aboriginal Affairs
coordinator for the Quebec Ministry of Natural Resources, was cross-
examined about provincial compliance with "Measures to Harmonize"
between community uses and industry cut plans, he responded: "It's a
good neighborly procedure."[53] In this case, however, the MNR issued the
permit without approval from the Ratt council. As Will explains:

There was a protracted negotiation between the Ratt council and
the MNR that seemed to be just stagnant. And then the MNR sent
them a letter on July 15, 2009, saying, look, we need your answer
by July 27; if you don't get back to us, we're just going to issue a
permit. And then they didn't hear back, so they issued a permit

the day after that [July 28]. And then two weeks later they did get a letter from Hector Jerome, apparently, that said, that's fine, you can cut there, as long as you follow the general parameters of the usual precautions.[54]

But Quebec knew it was risking legal exposure by negotiating with the Ratt council because the Matchewan council had been selected according to custom at the end of June. A letter had circulated within the department in mid-July attesting to knowledge about the new leadership selection process. But this selection was ignored because, as Larin states in his testimony: "We come to this point where either we give out a permit or we close down the operation."[55] Will concludes, regarding the Trilateral, that "It seems to me that nobody has figured out how to kill it. So they're just hoping it will die."[56] But the province was finding that it could not simply be ignored.

The trial date had been scheduled relatively quickly following Norman's summons. Set for June 4–6, 2012, it ended first thing on the second morning. On June 5, 2012, Norman was acquitted on what community members alleged all along were politically motivated charges. The forestry company representative for Abitibi-Bowater (now Resolute Forest Products) was caught repeatedly lying on the stand. Yves Paquette claimed that he encountered no police on the site and was not able to enter because the logging road was entirely blocked by the cars of the Barriere Lake community members. However, after seeing video evidence that refuted his claim, he also admitted to speaking to two intelligence officers from the Sûreté du Québec (SQ) who counseled him on the scene. Larin bluntly acknowledged the province's failure to consult and negotiate with the Algonquins and to doctoring the date of the logging permits.[57] In the end, Will did not have a chance to present the color of right defense because the case unraveled itself.

Finally, there is good evidence that the department played a strong hand in Norman Matchewan's mysterious summons to appear on the mischief charges. In an EIMD notification dated September 1, 2009, INAC reported that a group of "Matchewan supporters and others" approached Domtar workers on Barriere Lake's territory to request that they stop harvesting wood.[58] INAC reported that "the situation is currently remaining calm on both sides of the dispute."[59] In a follow-up notification, the protest was identified as a "roadblock" and the terms of this disruption are clearly outlined: "Members of the Matchewan group are setting up a camp at the site in attempt to prevent machinery from being brought out of the worksite. They have been quoted as saying that the camp would stay in place until an agreement is reached."[60] The "Matchewan group" informed Domtar that the tree harvesting was affecting the trapping territories of some Barriere Lake community members; they wanted assurances that no more logging would take place without their consent and that affected families would be consulted prior to the cutting and harvest of trees.[61] What was clearly a political and legal act, devoid of criminal intent and expressly carried out to protect hunting and trapping grounds on his community's unceded territory, eventually became fodder for Matchewan's charges. Given INAC's monitoring of the action, to what extent, if any, was INAC involved in orchestrating Matchewan's ensuing charges? Is it more than coincidence that Matchewan's summons followed so swiftly after his opposition to mining on Barriere Lake's territory, which had also been closely watched and noted?[62] My speculation builds not merely on suspicion but on the record of INAC strategies revealed in confidential, internal briefings that repeatedly stress collaboration and coordination with law enforcement.[63]

Tactics of police repression produce a specific geography of containment at Barriere Lake. At the first blockade, riot police corralled community members off the highway by forcing them onto the narrow, dead-end access road leading to their reserve. When that proved unsuccessful, at the next blockade police targeted community leaders for arrest and Crown prosecutors sought tough sentencing penalties and bail conditions that controlled people's movement through house arrests, no-protest stipulations, and incarceration. Containment does not end there, however: those criminalized for asserting jurisdiction on their lands were forced into the circuitry of the criminal justice system that demobilized community members through house arrest in their homes and on reserve, or through incarceration or conditions that stipulated living off reserve, segregated from the community; in all cases, these tactics of *pacification* subsumed Indigenous law under the criminal jurisdiction of the state.[64]

Pacification is key to security efforts that aim to undermine Indigenous assertions of jurisdiction on their lands. As Mark Neocleous theorizes:

To see security as a constitutive power or a technique deployed and mobilized in the exercise of power is to read it as a police mechanism: a mechanism for the fabrication of a social order organized around a constant revolutionizing of the instruments and relations of production and thus containing the everlasting uncertainty and agitation of all social relations that Marx and Engels define as key to capitalism; a mechanism, I suggest, in which the key task is pacification.[65]

These tactics of pacification are fused within a circuitry that controls the movement of people and capital through territory. There are, of course, legal, policy, and legislative frameworks that spatially differentiate First Nation lands and peoples from non-Indigenous lands and people in Canada.[66] But here I want to focus on the economic geography of settler-colonial space and the logics of security that contain disruption to supply and circulation on the land.

Reserve Incarceration at Barriere Lake

Anna Zalik observes that the tendency toward criminalization of Indigenous peoples defending their lands "emerges from a heavily securitized response to social claims on capital extraction that has repressed and constrained popular protest."[67] Comparing the policing of the Alberta tar sands in Canada to Nigerian oil fields, Zalik notes that while state pacification in Nigeria involves armed struggle, Canadian means by which to repress demands for Indigenous jurisdiction over resources trade on the boundaries of legality and illegality—demarcations produced by the internalization of particular norms of engagement.

Key to this engagement is the exercise of the "duty to consult" precedent set by *Haida* and *Taku River*, which shapes the discursive boundaries of extraction and manages resistance by setting the terms of consent for resource development.[68] With no veto power allotted to Indigenous peoples, the duty of governments to consult with First Nations when their Aboriginal or treaty rights might be affected by development can be dispensed without significantly altering the course of extraction or logging. Noncompliance with this legal technique of pacification exposes the state's monopoly on *legitimate* violence; those who cannot internalize settler law but are physically subject to extraction become object instead to the increasingly militarized armed tactics of the state.[69] For Barriere Lake, who refused to engage in consultation procedures without meaningful respect for their jurisdiction, their lives become acceptable targets of violence and criminalization.

During the period between being issued the summons and going to trial, Matchewan reported that he was pulled over by the SQ on a regular basis and held for questioning whenever he left the reserve.[70] He said clear grounds for the stops were never given but that they seemed meant to serve the purposes of harassment and attempted intimidation. Targeted police harassment both on and off the reserve has become common practice. I witnessed this on several occasions. One night, I watched the SQ pull over a young man and search his truck. It was after midnight, and he was being detained while dropping off garbage at the dump, about three hundred meters from the reserve along the access road.[71] The stops were so extreme in 2010 that Norman Matchewan had to obtain special permission from police for Katherine Keyes's funeral so that no one would be randomly stopped along the road and everyone could attend. The funeral was held in an island cemetery (relocated from flooding) at the traditional gathering lands of Barriere Lake, a thirty-minute drive from the reserve.[72]

SQ patrol cars frequently perch where the access road to Rapid Lake meets Highway 117, which allows for constant observation of the comings and goings of all community members, frequent stops and harassment, and the mounting sensation experienced by the Algonquins that they are being imprisoned at Rapid Lake. Many, like Matchewan, report that they cannot leave the community without being pulled over by the SQ. During a visit to the community in August 2010, I was detained immediately after pulling onto the access road from Highway 117 and questioned about my business on the reserve. The next day I learned that an SQ vehicle had followed Jeannette Wawatie and a friend from the highway into the reserve, where officers sat outside Wawatie's house for hours, refusing to leave. Before Wawatie had entered the house, an SQ officer had rolled down his window and asked the middle-aged women where they were going. When they replied noncommittally that they were tired, the officer asked: "Can I come to bed with you?" Wawatie was afraid to leave her house until the vehicle finally dispersed.[73]

There are five small roads that cross through the clusters of housing on the fifty-nine-acre reserve and it is about a two-minute drive to get from one end of the reserve to the other. Given this compact geography, it is not difficult to imagine how invasive a patrolling SQ vehicle would be, especially when parked immediately outside of a community assembly or a feast. It is particularly unnerving for community members to be constantly observed by SQ officers stationed nearby.

Since March 2008, police harassment escalated in the community, but one would be hard-pressed to discover this information through formal records. According to community members, the SQ consistently refuse to register filed complaints from politically outspoken individuals. Norman Matchewan compiled an unofficial list of such incidents, which provide examples of police brutality and repression. To begin, Matchewan counted twenty-five Barriere Lake community members arrested from March 2008 to March 2013, all in relation to blockades defending their land or to protests against government interference in their customary leadership selection process. Many of the unregistered complaints stem directly from the March 2008 protests over the contested recognition of the Ratt council by supporters of Acting Chief Benjamin Nottaway. Although the formal record presents a one-sided picture of instigated violence and property destruction by Nottaway supporters, the image changes dramatically when the list of unregistered complaints by Nottaway supporters is taken into account. For example, on March 7, 2008, Matchewan reports that two SQ officers assaulted a minor, Angelo Decoursay (a Nottaway supporter), during the arrest of Michel Thusky. Witnesses saw an SQ officer hit Decoursay in the face with his fist, but the assault was never registered. Another incident on that day involved the SQ pepper-spraying two minors—Kyle and Jim Nottaway—also Nottaway supporters. The incident was caught on video but never reported. Sergeant De Prato from the SQ was also recorded on camera shoving Mindy Nottaway, who was four months pregnant and there to protest the Ratt council recognition. This complaint of assault was reported but was not registered. Dissidents allegedly vandalized Juliette Keyes's vehicle but the SQ refused to register her complaint.[74]

From early on, long before the Trilateral Agreement, Barriere Lake's relations with the police played out in a colonial dynamic of oppression. In 1993, a youth at Barriere Lake was the target of a highly militarized raid on Barriere Lake lands conducted by a special unit of the SQ specializing in violent crimes. A least a half dozen officers arrived on the scene with what witnesses described as "military" weapons. An SQ helicopter hovered overhead as two marked cars, three unmarked cars, and one police van arrived on the scene. The SQ did not inform the chief and council that they intended to conduct a military raid on Barriere Lake lands against one of their community members and the SQ on the scene refused to answer questions or speak to any Algonquins. The situation was ripe with opportunity for things to go fatally wrong: in the presence of so much live ammunition, the area was never secured, and young children and elders with their families stood around watching the operation unfold. Ironically, the young man in question had fled the scene of a crime because of his fear of police and because he did not understand his rights and obligations under the circumstances. He turned himself in to the Maniwaki police station one week later.[75] Jean Maurice Matchewan, who was chief at the time, wrote an outraged letter to the force alleging that the SQ had endangered the lives of his community and describing its militarized response as a wildly inappropriate action for what was, in effect, a jurisdictional conflict: "Our young people sometimes act out of frustration when they realized that on our traditional lands, there is a growing presence of ZEC's [zones d'exploitation controlée or "controlled exploitation zones"], outfitters and logging companies."[76] These experiences with security forces only worked to entrench the deep connections between land dispossession and the role of police in the minds of the Algonquins.

Norman Matchewan understands the legacy of struggle that his generation has inherited. "To keep your rights, you have to fight for them," he says.[77] Unlike the earlier days when his grandmother was beaten by game wardens, however, charges and even arrests represent only the initial activation of a lengthy criminal justice process for community members. Matchewan explains: "A lot of people . . . they've been criminalized. Charges for peaceful protect, for highway blockades. A lot of them got house arrest, probation, [conditions] not to be at a protest for like a year. If they breach that, they end up in jail. Like Marylynn, she's under house arrest for a month now" (ibid.).

At the time of the interview with Matchewan, Marylynn Poucachiche was serving a month of house arrest for her participation in the November 2008 Highway 117 blockade. Poucachiche echoes Matchewan's philosophy on the pacification of community members: "It's not even criminal what I did. It's only the right thing to do" (ibid.). At the trial, the Crown aimed for the harshest possible sentence for Poucachiche, but the judge was more sympathetic, pointing out to the Crown that she was the mother of five children with no prior offenses, and obviously a person of considerable personal integrity. Poucachiche said, "Well, they were asking me why I did that, blocking the road and putting the logs on the road. Well, I basically told them we wouldn't have been there if the government would have lived up to their commitments . . . and honor agreements they have signed" (ibid.). Her house arrest sentence was disappointing, but it meant that soon she would finally be free of the "no protest" conditions meant to hamstring her organizing efforts over the previous couple of years while her charges had worked their way through the court. She said, "I guess I was kind of scared of what my sentence was going to be, 'cause I had heard the first time I went to court that I was going to get three months. So I guess that was hanging over my head. I wouldn't have minded if I fought it out and stayed in jail for three months there, but it's just that I didn't want to take it, with my baby there, and my kids. It would have been hard on my kids. After my conditions is over, I'll be involved again with the community. This time I'll be there without worries or hesitation. So I'm on board for another big political battle" (ibid.). This willingness to fight made her a target for pacification; Jean Maurice Matchewan had been listening on the CB radio to the police channel during the November blockade and heard the SQ send out the order to arrest Poucachiche.[78]

In another example of targeted pacification, Jean Maurice Matchewan himself was arrested for appearing on the access road to Rapid Lake during the November 2008 blockade. He was forced back into the court for another lengthy defense against mischief charges. In an astonishing decision, he was denied legal aid on grounds that his lawyer, Jared Will, described as shocking. Matchewan's counsel was using a "color of right" defense, arguing that Matchewan believed he was protecting his lands and that it was therefore "in the interests of justice" that legal aid be granted. The grounds for denial of legal aid were that the case was not presented as being in the personal interest of the applicant, but rather for the general public interest. The courts said that having the land rights of a community recognized may be in the general interest but it is of no particular personal interest to Matchewan. The criminal court, however, has no jurisdiction to recognize land rights in any general sense—it can only make a finding that Matchewan is not guilty if he had a genuine belief that he was entitled to block access to the land. Matchewan's legal counsel reports to have been told informally that the Crown was contesting the legal aid so vociferously precisely because it was someone from Barriere Lake who wanted to invoke color of right. It was concerned about having to fund other such cases.[79]

In the village site of Maigan Agik, reports also abound with stories of police harassment and abuse. In 2000 and 2001, the media reported that Jacob Wawatie, Mary Whiteduck, and others were arrested in blockades against Domtar for protecting their lands against logging.[80] More than a decade later, on June 24, 2011, Solomon Wawatie of the Anishnabe Traditional Council of Elders—the elders group from Maigan Agik—sent out a message on behalf of elder Mary Whiteduck reporting that she was assaulted by the SQ and subsequently hospitalized as the result of forbidding an unspecified logging company from cutting on her traditional family territory: "The SQ told us its [sic] no longer our traditional territory, and now its [sic] Public Territory." An urgent message regarding Whiteduck's arrest was circulated on several message board and social networking sites. It is unclear if charges were ever pressed against the SQ or what is the status of Whiteduck's charges.[81]

The geography of resource extraction on Indigenous lands demarcates the territory along the lines of logging roads and mining line cuts, but it also determines the mobility of community members to move freely across the land according to their laws of jurisdiction. As early as the 1980s, Norman Matchewan remembers living in the bush with his father, who was "red-zoned" from the community as a result of his blockade charges. Red zoning is a term that refers to the deliberate displacement of criminalized and street-involved people in urban areas from downtown cores in order to protect commercial interests and property owners. It is used here to represent a similar spatial strategy that polices Algonquins out of the reserve and their communities, denying them access to these spaces through their bail or sentencing conditions.[82] Red zoning abounds at Barriere Lake. The spectacular targeted arrests of Matchewan and Thusky that were described in chapter 7 (correlated with the crucial time-sensitive Trilateral work that Canada and Quebec seemed intent to disrupt) led to bail conditions that prohibited these leaders from living in the community. Mary Whiteduck was removed from the territory as a result of her stand against Domtar. At a public forum in Toronto, Clayton Nottaway became tearful as he described his own red zoning from the reserve in March 2008 as a result of charges for protesting the recognition of the Ratt council. He could not hunt and therefore could not provide for his wife and five children; he had felt ashamed, helpless, and depressed.[83] From red zoning community

members from the reserve, to holding trials in towns at least 150 kilometers away that are costly and difficult to attend, to house arrests, no
protest conditions, and imprisonment far from home, this geography
of pacification protects crucial access of government and industry to
resources on Indigenous traditional lands.

For Indigenous peoples, "retribution has always been swift" for those
who exercise their self-determination against the policies of the state.[84]
As Arthur Manuel explains: "Many of those who stand fast find their
names dishonoured; those who dare to try to protect their land quickly
face armed assaults and mass arrests."[85] He describes the decades of
the 1990s and 2000s where more than two hundred political arrests
were made of Indigenous peoples who faced charges from criminal contempt to mischief to intimidation and obstruction of a peace officer,
as well as the escalated conflicts at Oka and Gustafsen Lake, which led
to shootouts and death. These incidents are always described as native
occupations and blockades, but, as John Borrows points out, settlers,
whose tenuous land claims and property deeds are rarely depicted as
occupations but who regularly blockade Indigenous peoples from reaching and using their lands, have used these strategies predominantly
throughout Canadian history.[86]

Critical Infrastructure and Colonial Circuitry of Containment

The need to secure physical resource-extraction infrastructure—in the
case of Barriere Lake: forestry, mining, and transportation corridors—
supports Nicholas Blomley's premise that there is an intrinsic geography to the violence of state law regarding property.[87] From 1989 when
Jean Maurice Matchewan was violently arrested at a blockade (subdued
by a half dozen officers), to the targeting of his son Norman on charges
of mischief in 2011 for allegedly interfering with forestry harvesting operations, security forces have played a vital role (both legally and extra-
legally, through police violence) alongside the government to contain
the community's political assertions of jurisdiction within the space of
the reserve.[88]

The colonial strategy behind the geographic dispersion of reserve
lands was to weaken internal Indigenous economies and land defense. It
was also a strategy of spatial containment to isolate Indigenous peoples
to prevent united political action and to remove obstacles to white settlement and commercial interests.[89] Today, the reserve system constitutes

"an archipelago of spatial containment" that physically separates First Nations from Canadians, but also spatially differentiates their respective rights according to their relative access and relationship to resources and supply chain infrastructure.[90] When Indigenous peoples disrupt development or commodity flows, security responses by the state and law enforcement expose the ways a space like the reserve forms a part of the carceral state "by providing a solution to that which exceeds and destabilizes sovereignty via a spatial reorganization of populations and depoliticization of that process."[91] This dynamic of fixing populations in the midst of fluid and deterritorializing economies must be understood in the context of settler colonialism, where technologies of containment are not simply about building walls to keep people out, but more precisely form "a technology of separation and domination" within an internal settler-colonial occupation.[92] The reserve–prison circuitry is primarily about securing territorial jurisdiction where the state claims sovereignty but cannot exercise effective control.

Indigenous feminist scholars, concerned with the high rates of disappearance and murder of Indigenous women and girls in Canada, have for decades made powerful arguments connecting space, violence, and the reserve. As Sarah Hunt argues, like the land, Indigenous women and girls' bodies can be subject with impunity to violence because they are understood as *already possessed* by white settlement through the category of "reserve" with which they are identified. In this way, their bodies exist—and are contained—in states of exception.[93] Indigenous women's and girls' lives are also considered inherently violent because of "risky lifestyles," without consideration for the vulnerabilities to which they are subject through colonization. As Patricia Monture-Angus observes, "The individualizing of risk absolutely fails to take into account the impact of colonial oppression on the lives of Aboriginal men and women."[94] Therefore, the broader economic geography of dispossession is erased and all that is left is the thin wire of "criminality" to circle the spaces they occupy.[95] Increases in sexual violence and exploitation, for example, which have emerged in Indigenous communities as a result of resource-extraction industries on their lands, are simply bracketed.[96]

Despite the deliberate spatial fix of reserves, the dispersal of Indigenous peoples across the vast terrain of Canada has made reserves a formidable force with which to reckon, because—contrary to siting and assimilation efforts—reserves lie on valuable mineral deposits, forests, transportation routes, and hydro corridors, and Indigenous peoples continue to assert jurisdiction over their lands. Reserves in most parts of the country are protected from mineral exploration and extraction.[97] Nonetheless, even where they are not direct sites of production, they are sites of geographically strategic capital extraction and circulation, as well as the organizing base for protecting larger treaty and unceded lands.[98]

Reserves are located today in the relative space of what government and intelligence departments call "critical infrastructure." Indigenous protests, blockades, and assertions of jurisdiction over land and resources disrupt, as the RCMP puts it, "infrastructure, both tangible and intangible, that is essential to the health, safety, security or economic well-being of Canadians and the effective functioning of government."[99] This wide net has been cast as a central concern for the RCMP for policing First Nations' protest, especially as it unfolds through "criminal acts committed," including "the blocking of major critical infrastructure such as railways and major highways." (A footnote next to "major highways" in this report indicates Barriere Lake's blockades on Highway 117 in Quebec).[100] The RCMP National Security Criminal Investigations have prioritized four critical infrastructure sectors: finance, transportation, energy, and cybersecurity.[101] Indigenous resistance threatens transportation and energy sectors most directly.

In terms of transportation, the circulation of goods, resources, and energy through territory is the very essence of capitalism today. This vulnerability is deadly to the logistics industry. Logistics is a business science concerned with the management of goods and information through global supply chains. As the World Bank has declared: "A competitive network of global logistics is the backbone of international trade."[102] For an industry dependent on maintaining open channels for capital circulation, a blockade means massive losses: the trucking industry alone is worth $65 billion and employs more than 260,000 drivers.[103] On January 5, 2013, alone, during the height of the Idle No More movement, its protests included five border-crossing blockades, bridge blockades, and rail-line disruptions spanning the country. Railway blockades included Aamjiwnaang First Nation near Sarnia, Ontario, and the Mi'kmaq from Listuguj First Nation who blocked the railway at Pointe-à-la-Croix in Quebec for several weeks.

As Nicholas Blomley notes: "In the case of blockade activity, a system of colonization has itself become the focus and the weapon in a counter-colonial struggle."[104] A blockade can interrupt international borders such as those between the United States and Canada, but, it also erects border crossings between Indigenous and settler jurisdictions within Canada's state borders. In northern British Columbia, for example, the Big Frog Clan (C'ihlts'ehkhyu) of the Wet'suwet'en people, the Unist'ot'en, are directly in the path of an energy corridor with seven proposed pipelines from the tar sands megaprojects in Alberta and liquefied natural gas from the Horn River Basin Fracturing Projects in the Peace River Region.[105] From their resistance camp at Talbits Kwah at Gosnell Creek along the Morice River, the Unist'ot'en land defenders have already evicted surveyors working for Pacific Trails Pipeline from attempting to construct a pipeline route through their unceded, traditional territory to the Kitimat port. The Government Operations Centre (GOC), which is the central hub for federal situational awareness relating to critical infrastructure, has been assessing this disruption to economic flows.[106] In a classified document, the GOC evaluates the "Critical Infrastructure Impact" of the resistance camp and states that highway blockades, rail-line disruptions, pipeline blockades, and possible property damage present a medium-low risk assessment. However, the "trigger" factor of inspiring other protests is considered high. In addition, the *Tsilhqot'in* decision is said to "have strengthened the *perceived* First Nations control over resource development within their traditional territories. *The Unist'ot'en Blockade Camp is the ideological and physical focal point of Aboriginal resistance to resource extraction projects.*"[107] Once again, a model of resistance and jurisdiction is at risk of being replicated, and the fear of collaboration is pronounced: "[c]onvergence can strengthen the arguments of these other groups, increasing the profile and possible effectiveness of their opposition."[108] The documents convey coordination across departments and ministries, citing Natural Resources Canada, the RCMP, the Public Safety Regional Office (British Columbia), and INAC as "Partners Engaged," though one partner listed in the Appendix is redacted.

Critical infrastructure is 85 percent privately owned and operated and it is instrumental to the free flow of commodities.[109] Therefore, supply-chain security has in fundamental ways become national security with the goal of minimizing disruption. As the "Critical 5" (Canada, the United States, the UK, Australia, and New Zealand) state: "disruptions of critical infrastructure *can affect the timely delivery of goods and services that are imperative to national economies,* which can be measured in the loss of business and tax generated revenue in the affected areas."[110] The international nature of critical infrastructure is highlighted in the report as well. Critical infrastructure is defined as "not geocentric" but able to "transcend national boundaries" with the aid of collaborative regimes of cooperating national governments. It goes on to state that "The global supply chain and global economy are increasingly important considerations for businesses and government entities because of the reliance of critical infrastructure on materials originating from outside their own borders and the impact of these to national economies."[111] In other words, the domestic "problem" of Indians in Canada has become the international problem of supply-chain management.[112] The risk of Indigenous proprietary rights and jurisdiction in today's economy is that they can help protect geographically crucial sites for future development and resource extraction.[113] In essence, the state regulates the terms of rights and access by private capital to "public" resources, while simultaneously struggling to assert and maintain ownership over these resources against Indigenous claims.

The pacifying of Indigenous dissent has intensified alongside the securitization global supply-chain infrastructure. Deborah Cowen states that the network space of circulation produced by the logistics world remakes the world of nation-states and national territory. This has not meant the end to national territory, though. Rather, what is at stake is a transition from "a particular historical and geographic instantiation of territory organized through nation states."[114] The decline of this form of territoriality has led to the rise of new "transversally bordered spaces that not only cut across national borders but also generate new types of formal and informal jurisdictions . . . deep inside the tissue of national sovereign territory."[115] Here is where critical Indigenous theory can contribute to geographic and critical logistics thought: by providing a picture of sovereign territory that is tattered and remade not only by international geoeconomic forces, but by virtue of Indigenous jurisdiction.[116]

Patrick Wolfe wrote that "Territoriality is settler colonialism's specific, irreducible element."[117] But the meaning of territoriality shifts with changes to global systems of extraction and circulation, and the agency of Indigenous peoples in shaping these new forms along the historical and contemporary "enclaves and corridors" of settler sovereignty must be taken into account. Likewise, scholars of critical Indigenous studies might do well, strategically, to pay attention to the shifting nodes of power and connective tissues of the accelerated new mode of just-in-time production and circulation that snag them into increasingly tangled global webs of accumulation.

Conclusion
A Land Claim Is Canada's Claim
Against Extinguishment

Only a small icon symbolizing the Rapid Lake Reserve marks the presence of the Algonquins of Barriere Lake on the tourist maps of the La
Vérendrye Wildlife Reserve. Hundreds of these maps are distributed
each year to mostly Québécois and American visitors. On the very bottom shelves of the permit offices in the park one can also find a stack
of quarter-sheets titled "The Algonquins in La Vérendrye Wildlife Reserve," published by the Quebec Ministry of Recreation, Hunting, and
Fishing. Wishing to bring to the attention of visitors the "particular
context" of the reserve, the pamphlet explains that approximately
four hundred Algonquins make their home there at Rapid Lake and the
nearby Grand Lac Victoria Reserve of the Lac-Simon First Nation. The
pamphlet explains that the Algonquins hunt, fish, and trap in the Grand
Lac Beaver Preserve, a space of about nineteen thousand square kilometers that was once the exclusive domain of the Indians.[1]

Of course, these pamphlets omit word of any conflict between the
Algonquins and settlers, but they do subtly take a stand on the issue.
The pamphlet describes how under Quebec provincial regulation the Algonquins are permitted to practice their traditional activities. A space
is delineated for these activities as well as the authority by which Algonquins can use this space: "On their traplines, in the beaver reserve
which covers three quarters of La Vérendrye Wildlife Reserve, the
Algonquins may . . . hunt and fish for food under the 'Regulation respecting hunting.'" Quebec's authority to "permit" the Algonquins their
hunting and trapping privileges belies sui generis Indigenous rights to
hunt and fish on their unceded traditional territory.[2] In spite of these
rights, the source of Algonquin land occupation is repeatedly alluded
to as discretionary to the province: the title of the pamphlet locates the
Algonquins "in" the park, though the park is situated within Barriere
Lake's traditional territory. The province's presumed exclusive authority over unceded Barriere Lake lands tidies up the messy space of jurisdictional overlap. To put the Algonquin people's authority back in the

frame requires identifying and demystifying these overlapping claims to power on Algonquin territory.

This pamphlet and the accompanying map mark provincial claims to jurisdiction over Barriere Lake lands through the representational and regulatory apparatuses at the province's disposal. But within its jurisdictional ambit, the province can only govern where it can successfully assert authority over the Algonquins. We have surveyed in this book a proliferation of regulatory, representational, sociospatial, and security impositions on Algonquin land, people, and resources that have all attempted to smother Indigenous jurisdiction, foregrounding the polyphonic struggle between Indigenous and settler legal orders. But a blunter instrument exists that seeks the elimination of Indigenous jurisdiction through explicit and legal consent by Indian bands. I want to close this book by completing a circle I have been drawing that began with Barriere Lake's rejection of the CLCP and led them to develop the Trilateral Agreement in response. I want to examine the role of the land claims policy as a means to remove the uncertainty posed to state territorial jurisdiction and to the natural resource economy by overlapping jurisdiction between settler and Indigenous legal orders.

The CLCP aims to achieve this removal through the extinguishment of Aboriginal title. But there are a number of other critical issues regarding the policy that bear in particular upon the question of jurisdiction. First, I will examine the way in which land under the policy must be transformed from unceded Indigenous territory into private property; second, I review some of the ways in which coercion is structured into the policy to trouble the notion of "consent" around the surrender of Indigenous jurisdiction; and finally, I examine how land claims are one of a slate of "termination" policies that turn Indigenous communities against one another, because one band or nation's cession of jurisdiction impacts all other nations' rights and title.[3] In this way, I end the story of the Algonquins of Barriere Lake by marking the broader struggle in which they are embedded and the hope their vision strikes in the dark.

Take It in Fee Simple or Leave It

A land claim is not an accurate description of Indigenous peoples' assertions of jurisdiction over territory in Canada, insists constitutional expert Peter Russell. A land claim implies that Indigenous people are making a claim against Canada, when in fact, according to Indigenous law, the onus is on Canada to enter into treaty with Indigenous nations.[4] The CLCP is firmly rooted in a framework of claim within the institution of confederation. A treaty, on the other hand, depicted movingly in Harold Johnson's *Two Families* in the context of his nation, is an adoption ceremony, where the Nêhiyaw (Cree) incorporated their *Kicimanawak* (cousins) into the family.[5]

What Canadians need to understand is that their property rights are contingent upon recognition by Indigenous peoples. As Arthur Manuel explains:

> Aboriginal title is not a burden on so called Crown title, our ownership is the underlying Title that all subsequent land interests rest on. I know the Canadian courts have been giving their interpretation about our Title as Indigenous Peoples but they do not have the capacity to make us subservient to so-called Crown interests because they as judicial institutions are created by the sovereignty of Canada and are in a conflict of interest with our sovereignty as Indigenous nations.[6]

Rejecting the Canadian hierarchy of jurisdiction that places Indigenous peoples at the bottom of the authority structure, Manuel puts in plain terms what Canadian courts have been finding, but refusing to interpret as within their jurisdiction to name: if the sovereignty of the Canadian state depends on a bounded territorial space, which in turn depends on an exclusive claim to that space through the mechanism of jurisdiction, then unceded Indigenous territories challenge the legitimacy of the state and the legal and political orders contingent upon state claims to govern.[7]

The justification for transitioning unceded Indigenous lands into fee simple property through the CLCP is framed as achieving "economic certainty," but the question is, *for whom?* From a business perspective, modern treaties are favored because they remove undefined rights of Aboriginal title and replace them with a stable and transparent property registry system.[8] However, the fact that Aboriginal title is considered unstable means that all Crown lands and fee simple property—despite being registered—are also uncertain by virtue of their imposition onto unceded Indigenous lands.[9] Extinguishing title in exchange for fee simple property is a key step in the termination of collective Indigenous lands as well as in perfecting settler sovereignty. Fee simple subordinates Indigenous land under provincial jurisdiction, terminating its distinct legal order. This major transformation of Indigenous territorial space is a nonnegotiable aspect of the policy.[10]

To understand the implications of the fee simple requirement in the modern treaty process, I visited Bertha Williams of the Tsawwassen First Nation (TFN) in British Columbia, where she met with Arthur Manuel and me at her home on the former reserve. British Columbia is "ground zero" in the modern treaty process in Canada today because the vast majority of bands in the province have never signed treaties and live on unceded lands. In 1992, the province finally agreed to establish a process (under the British Columbia Treaty Commission) for land claim settlements after resisting since the mid-1970s, when the CLCP was first introduced. In December 2007, the Tsawwassen First Nation became the second "modern treaty" signed in British Columbia after the Nisga'a Nation.[11] Unable to stop her community from voting in favor of the agreement, Williams traveled to Geneva in February 2009 to launch an unsuccessful emergency appeal at the United Nations Committee on the Elimination of Racial Discrimination (CERD) Working Group on Early Warning and Urgent Action in attempt to stop the treaty from coming into force. At that point, the federal government had still not ratified the agreement, so she had some hope. She told the CERD that she feared the outcome of the extinguishment of her band's Aboriginal title: "This is my birthright handed to me by my parents and grandparents and ancestors. This is a legacy that I want to pass to my children and grandchildren. But, it will be severed come April 3, 2009 when the Tsawwassen Agreement comes into force."[12] In April 2009, the Tsawwassen Final Agreement did come into force, in the midst of almost deafening provincial celebration cheering on a badly needed victory for politicians following eighteen years and millions of dollars of failed treaty making in the province.

Williams continues to be a lone voice of opposition in her community against the treaty and a strong supporter of other bands and individuals opposing treaty negotiations.[13] She is one of the few people publicly raising alarm about the realities of the posttreaty world. Now that their lands are held in fee simple ownership, I asked her whether people wanted to sell their homes or mortgage their property on TFN's former reserve, which is now legally held in "the estate in fee simple" (equivalent to how the state holds Crown Land) by the TFN government, which is also no longer legally a "band" under the Indian Act of 1876, but is now a corporation. She said that technically they could now lease their lands for ninety-nine years to someone on the reserve. She said there was a woman who had a "For Sale" sign on her lawn who had hired a real-estate agent to try to sell her house but she was having a hard time. Arthur Manuel interjected to ask a question: "I can't really see what the difference is when it was under the Indian Act. 'Cause under the Indian Act, you only could lease it under ninety-nine years, too . . . A ninety-nine-year lease isn't really the capacity to sell." He asked: "There's no such thing as selling property outright? How come they say it's private land, then?" Williams answered by describing the situation as "fee simple-ish."[14]

"Fee simple-ish," as Williams put it, describes the overlapping property regime resulting from two systems of jurisdiction theoretically sharing power on the former Tsawwassen reserve. In an e-mail exchange, Colin Ward, manager of policy and intergovernmental affairs at TFN, explained to me that the ninety-nine-year leases are not a stipulation of the treaty itself, but were rather the result of a decision taken by TFN that is expressed in the Tsawwassen Land Act.[15] He explained that the nature of all title held by the TFN corporation was fee simple, which is in effect the allodial title to the land with no reservations or conditions held in favor of the Crown. These are called Tsawwassen Public Lands. However, there is also another interest called the Tsawwassen Fee Simple Interest (TFSI), "which is set out in the Treaty, but is further defined by our law, and which is roughly equivalent to fee simple or freehold title held by a private person elsewhere in the province. This TFSI is subject to reservations, conditions, etc. in favor of TFN, as set out in the Final Agreement and our law."[16] TFSI is in effect an iteration of the municipal zoning code laid out in the TFN Land Use and Planning Development Act, which has been incorporated into Metro Vancouver's Regional Growth Strategy. The TFN has been guided by its legal order, but it must also be compliant with certain provisions of regional context statements for changes to land-use plans.[17]

According to Williams, confusion has ensued as an outcome of overlapping jurisdiction. The TFN is charged with the authority to enforce provincial regulations, which it does at its political discretion, and new codified band regulations must comply with provincial regulation, but also with the band's customary law. "It sounds like there's a lot of overlapping jurisdiction," I commented, to which Williams replied, "The band has no oversight and they even have their own judicial council."[18] Indigenous law seems to have become de facto provincial law, despite institutional provisions to empower TFN governing authority. In this sense, it is not difficult to see why Russell Diabo calls these posttreaty settlement lands "ethnic municipalities."[19]

Ninety-nine-year leases may protect the former reserve from wholesale abdication by TFN members, but, according to Williams, many people on the former reserve are feeling increasing pressure to lease their lands before the land taxes kick in under the new property regime. Some of the landowners are intent to have their lands developed, but first they must put their TFSI lands into the TFN public lands and proceed through the Strata Property Act, recollectivizing their private property now in a way Williams calls "insulting."[20] Under the Indian Act, TFN lands were collectivized under federal jurisdiction, but now they must be transferred to provincial forms of collectivization like any other municipality. The difference is that when TFN lands are leased to non-TFN persons, these residents will have no citizenship rights on reserve and cannot participate in TFN governance. The Land Act also prohibits the sale of any property to non-TFN persons in order to ensure that no TFN lands are alienated from the corporation.[21]

But the hospitality extended to nonresidential property holders vying for valuable Tsawwassen lands is much warmer. Almost exactly one year following the signing of the TFN Final Agreement another groundbreaking ceremony took place near TFN treaty lands: the opening of the Tsawwassen Gateway Logistics Park on the shore of the Georgia Strait.[22] As Cowen notes, the Delta port, which forms part of Tsawwassen's settlement lands, is "the single most important facility in the Vancouver Port Authority's portfolio."[23] The container port and coal port facility was expanded by about 44 percent and, despite major environmental concerns, passed the joint British Columbia–federal environmental impact assessment with relative ease.[24] The Tsawwassen land claim settlement played a role in the development of this global supply-chain infrastructure. During the early stages of project planning for the port in 2004, under the headline "Critical Requirements for Deltaport 3 Berth," a presentation slide by the Vancouver Port Authority (VPA)

included as a bullet point the "Tsawwassen First Nation agreement."[25]
A political agreement was secured between the VPA and TFN leadership
in 2004 that ensured that the TFN would support the port expansion
at Roberts Bank, where the port facility is located, which is also "in the
vicinity" of TFN Settlement Lands, as identified in their Agreement in
Principle (the penultimate stage of the treaty process).[26] In exchange,
the band received a payout of $9.25 million.[27] But they also had to for-
feiture key protections of their Aboriginal rights and title: they had
to accept the Memorandum of Agreement (MOA) with the VPA as the
dispensation of the company's legal duty to consult and accommodate
the band on Roberts Bank Port Facility and Expansion and in the Environmental Assessment process, and the band committed that "the TFN
shall not raise any Environmental concerns, issues or objections nor
make any Environmental comments or submissions that could not legally be raised or made by a non-aboriginal Person."[28] Only by securing
the surrender of these Aboriginal rights and title could the port expansion proceed with "certainty." As the vice president of infrastructure
development of the VPA stated: "This agreement allows us to put to bed
a longstanding concern with an important port stakeholder and to create greater certainty in terms of future development at Roberts Bank."[29]

At TFN, benefiting most from treaty are businesses moving in to take
advantage of a newly cash-strapped population that owns a scarce commodity in the real-estate frenzy of the British Columbia lower mainland: undeveloped land. In the coming years, TFN members will need to
rely on their own source revenue to pay taxes and other expenses associated with peri-urban life. Located adjacent to Port Metro Vancouver's
Deltaport container terminal, the Logistics Centre stands in proximity
to three freeways, the Vancouver International Airport, and the South
Fraser Perimeter Road. The TFN Economic Development Corporation
boasts that "[t]he Tsawwassen Gateway Logistics Centre is expected to
become a key part of Canada's international trade through Deltaport for
the Asia Pacific, and West Coast goods handling services."[30] Reshaping
the jurisdiction governing these lands by circumscribing the assertion
of Aboriginal rights and title was essential to installing a strategic geographic transportation corridor to connect key nodes of global capital.

These new property matters are jurisdictional matters. Under the
TFN-VPA MOA, a private contract under commercial law secured the
property rights of the VPA. Under the British Columbia Treaty Process

(BCTP), First Nations exchange one regime of jurisdiction over their lands for another when they adopt the fee simple property rights system. The shift in jurisdictional organization begins upon entering into negotiation. Indigenous nations—and their territorial bases—are immediately undermined because bands, or clusters of bands, within nations may submit land claims, fragmenting national territories and further compromising governance structures. Upon settlement, bands or nations are legally reclassified as corporate entities with a limited measure of authority over a slim proportion of their traditional territory.[31] These treaty lands are chosen through an official Land Selection process, and usually include the reserve and some surrounding areas.[32] According to insiders, under the BCTP specifically, land rewards average about 5 percent of the total territorial base of the negotiating group.[33] The cash-for-land formula varies depending on the relative value of the lands in question. For example, at Tsawwassen, the amount of treaty lands awarded is actually much lower than other communities because of the value of land in the lower mainland of British Columbia. Whereas Tsawwassen members each received 2.2 hectares of land, on Nisga'a land in northern British Columbia, members received 33.49 hectares per person, Maa-nulth First Nations members on Vancouver Island received 12.275 hectares per person, and the Yale First Nation members received 12.29 hectares per person.[34] Cash settlements sound generous, reported to be in the tens of millions of dollars, but they average about $42,071 per person, and when factoring in loan repayment, the average reduces to $26,331 per person.[35]

Bands are then granted the authority to develop land-use regulations over their fee simple estates, but these lands are co-governed by the province, by virtue of constitutional allocation of jurisdiction over property and civil matters, as per section 92(13) of the Constitution Act of 1867. Under provincial jurisdiction, former reserves take on a novel municipal form, yet to be totally defined. The same holds true for Nisga'a lands: as Sari Graben describes, despite the fact that the Nisga'a have lawmaking authority over land under the Final Agreement provisions (c.11, para 59), "because provincial law applies on Nisga'a lands and the Nisga'a government has referentially incorporated a number of provincial statutes related to property, it is likely that many disputes will be adjudicated by non-Nisga'a courts in accordance with those regimes, as understood in the common law to date."[36] At Nisga'a, TFN, and in other treaty contexts, many questions remain, especially concerning how the balance of legal authority has changed. How has colonial governance been modified, and how has Indigenous law been circumscribed, by virtue of these changes in jurisdiction? Where do settler and Indigenous laws meet in this context? How do the social institutions of private property interrelate with the social institutions of Indigenous tenure regimes? Finally, when "Indians and lands reserved for Indians" are under federal jurisdiction according to section 91(24) of the Constitution Act of 1867, they accrue some measure of protection by virtue of the fiduciary duties of the federal Crown;[37] what protection from provincial legislation do they have now?[38]

Efforts to privatize reserve lands have not been limited to the CLCP. For nonnegotiating bands, a legislative process to transform Indigenous lands into fee simple lands has been in the works for years. The basic concept of the First Nations Property Ownership Act (FNPOA) is an opt-out mechanism from the reserve land system under the Indian Act of 1876. The new act would create a mechanism for an opt-in system for fee simple lands to replace the old land system, the Reserve Land Register and the Surrendered and Designated Lands Register. According to its chief proponent, Tom Flanagan, "The intended result is to enable First Nations to use their land and natural resources effectively in the modern economy. As they benefit from capitalizing on their assets, so will other Canadians; for a market economy is a wealth-creating, positive-sum game in which call [sic] can benefit from the progress of others."[39] Eagerly supported by the Conservative government, the legislation died on the order table.[40]

Although fee simple is touted by proponents of the CLCP as the solution to Indigenous poverty, echoing claims by FNPOA proponents, the lack of private property alone is not the main barrier to economic development on Indigenous lands.[41] But one does not have to take critics' word for it. The firm employed to support the contentions of FNPOA advocates produced a commissioned report in 1999 for the Indian Tax Advisory Board (now the First Nations Tax Commission) and INAC to review barriers to doing business on reserves.[42] The consultants found that project approvals took considerably longer on reserves than off them, owing to a number of factors. Interestingly, issues related directly to property rights were not the majority of reasons for delay. Rather, key problems were structural, such as administrative incapacities, lack of necessary physical infrastructure, poor connections between First Nations and business communities, and insufficient information on the part of First Nations on ways to access capital.

The integration of Indigenous peoples into the mainstream economy through new property rights has been touted in ways that are not only counterfactual, but also speak to the discriminatory society into which community members are meant to assimilate. For example, much ado was made of Tsawwassen First Nation's newly minted bus stop in the lower mainland's public Translink bus system posttreaty.[43] But, as Arthur Manuel points us, amid all this celebration no one stopped to ask what kind of racist society has until now excluded this Indian reserve from access to public transportation services. He states: "The basic key to getting 'bus service' and other services Canadians take for granted means Indigenous peoples must extinguish their Aboriginal Title through 'Modified' and 'Non-Assertion' Models like Chief Kim Baird did. The Tsawwassen Peoples are paying an exceptionally high bus fare."[44] The benefits of "economic integration" for former band members also ignores the priority that has been put all along on third-party interests, whose lands are protected from expropriation through treaty settlements, despite the fact that these private estates have less constitutional protection than Aboriginal lands ostensibly enjoy.[45] Once again, the CLCP is out of step with the courts, which are handing down decisions saying Aboriginal title exists on private land.[46] While TFN land values have doubled since the signing of the treaty,[47] time will tell who will be the beneficiaries.

Coercion at the Tables

The principal contention that Barriere Lake Algonquins have with the land claims policy is the extinguishment of their Aboriginal title. They rejected the policy because they saw it as just another land grab. As Jean Maurice Matchewan explained, "We have an agreement with Canada under the wampum belts and we don't need any other kind of agreement, especially the kind that's going to take away our rights from our land. We want to keep living the way we're living today."[48] The Algonquins continue to assert jurisdiction over their traditional territory by maintaining their hunting, trapping, gathering, and feast traditions that show respect and care for the land. Matchewan could not understand why bands would voluntarily cede jurisdiction of their lands for slim financial returns: "Well, when you look at the James Bay Agreement when it says down at the bottom that they're giving up everything that they may have, I certainly don't want to go that way. So that's why we never cared for the comprehensive claims approach, cause the government gives you all kinds of money to prove you have title, and in the end you have to give it all up with all that money that they give."[49]

First Nations debt to the CLCP hovers at more than $1.228 billion across Canada, Specific Claims included.[50] If we also include government expenditures in nonloan form, under the BCTC, "the total costs to First Nations, Canada, and BC activity in the period 1993–2008 was over $1.1 billion."[51] What is the impact of debt on negotiations? One impact is that when a band tries to pull out of negotiations, it can be pressured back to the table with the threat of exorbitant loan repayment costs.

That is exactly what happened to the Lheidli T'enneh who live on the northwest coast of British Columbia near Prince George. The Lheidli T'enneh were one of the first BC bands to join the BCTP, hoping to resolve the conflict over their lands once and for all. Instead, they found the process restricted and disempowering. As described in their submission to the UN Committee on the Elimination of Racial Discrimination (CERD), "they were negotiating from a position of dependence, relying on loan funding to be able to participate in the process and seeking ways to address the immediate needs and poverty of their people."[52] Over the course of negotiations, Lheidli T'enneh borrowed $7 million in repayable loans. But in 2007, they voted "no" against their Final Agreement, dissatisfied with the terms of settlement. Following the "no" vote, the BC Treaty Commission advised the Lheidli T'enneh band council that another vote would secure a stay in repayment of borrowed monies, which would otherwise have to be paid off over a five-year period. The CERD report highlights the coercive nature of such demands: "The Lheidli T'enneh Indian Band like most Indian Bands in Canada is poor and does not have $7,000,000 (7 million) in the bank to cover the loan and cannot afford monthly payments on the loan within the 5 year period amounting to $116,666 (without interest) a month."[53] The band ultimately capitulated because it did not have the money to repay the loans.[54] A second vote is currently being rescheduled.[55] As Peter Dexter Quaw, traditional chief of the Lheidli T'enneh, told the committee: "The Lheidli T'enneh people feel like they are in the clutches of the BC Treaty

Commission which is supposed to be neutral but instead aggressively pushes for a revote."[56]

Another example of this loan bribery can be found in the case of the Xaxli'p First Nation (formerly the Fountain Indian Band), who live in the Central Interior-Fraser region of British Columbia. This band was also an early joiner into the land claims process and it signed a framework agreement in November 1997. It spent the following two years engaged in land-use and occupancy research and an ecosystem-based plan for its traditional territory, resuming negotiations in 2000. But it had had a change of heart and no longer wanted to settle for the terms on the table. According to the band's CERD submission: "On February 27, 2007 Indian Affairs and Northern Development Canada sent a letter to the Chief and Council of the Xaxli'p First Nation stating the federal government wanted to collect '[p]ayments to satisfy a $2,430,444 debt over 5 years at 4.297% interest [that] would be $27,249 month.'"[57] Such a vast monthly payment would bankrupt the band and automatically put it in Third Party Management, which would mean that INAC could take over financial management of the band. Canada was forced to respond to CERD and they exchanged letters, the second of which reported that Xaxli'p's loan had been put in abeyance.[58] Xaxli'p had never been informed directly, however, and when Chief Arthur Adolph learned that this was the case, he says he was not necessarily relieved because Xaxli'p had never recognized, acknowledged, or confirmed that monies were owed, despite being threatened by INAC that this challenge would affect revenues distributed to the band.[59]

Chief Darrell Bob of the Xaxli'p First Nation told me in 2016 that the treaty load bills still came every month for the first eleven months after they pulled out of the treaty, but the band refused to list the debt in its audited financial statements. The band's auditors were extremely nervous, but finally agreed, adding a caveat at the bottom of Xaxli'p's financial statements that the loans had been left off. For eleven months, the federal Department of Indian Affairs refused to sign off on Xaxli'p's audited financial statements. The community and the chief and council began to get nervous, too. Finally, they submitted the audit and "lo and behold" their Contribution Funding Agreement was signed. Chief Bob told me that he got the idea to refuse to pay the loans from the fact that he had had three used cars repossessed around the time they pulled out of the treaty process. He realized that if you give back a car you can't afford, they make you pay for it. But if they repossess it, the bank has to pay. He laughed and humbly insisted that he has a grade 6 education but that he did learn some things at school. At the residential school he attended, he refused to speak English until they gave him a red sucker. He had never had candy before. After that, he learned English quickly. He said that was what the treaty process is like: you have to have something they want to get anything in return.[60]

In TFN, things went in the opposite direction. Rather than bribe bands to vote "yes" with the threat of debt repayment if they refused, a carrot was used when treaty negotiators offered band members sums of money for their "yes" vote. Community members were promised that if the majority of the band voted "yes," all members over the age of sixty would receive fifteen thousand dollars; all other members would receive one thousand dollars if the "yes" vote passed by majority. On July 25, 2007, the TFN vote on the final agreement was held and it passed with a majority vote. Checks were distributed immediately—not out of the eventual cash settlement but through a "treaty inducement package" designed specifically for such purposes.[61] Those who voted against the treaty faced the guilt of depriving elders of badly needed funds. Documented for CERD as well, the submission records then provincial Minister of Aboriginal Affairs Mike de Jong's reaction when accused of manipulating the outcome of the TFN vote through cash incentives. He answered "guilty as charged" and noted that the provincial government was unapologetic about wanting the vote to succeed.[62] It is difficult to imagine a Canadian politician being so blasé if caught bribing non-Indigenous Canadian citizens in a federal election—especially one involving a wholesale change in the country's form of governance.

Other coercive mechanisms to get bands to vote "yes" do not involve loan bribery. The average length of negotiation is fifteen years.[63] In the meantime, the treaty process does not provide mechanisms to protect land during negotiations. As mentioned earlier, the courts have said that even in the pre-proof stage of Aboriginal title assertions, governments and third parties are legally subject to engage in consultation and accommodation with First Nations.[64] However, the CLCP has failed until now to provide such protection in this regard. Recently, though, Canada responded to First Nations' demands with a solution to the lack of interim measures by introducing what it calls "incremental treaties" (also at times called "slim AIPs" [Agreements in Principle] or "pretreaty" agreements). These incremental treaties secure some benefits to bands, providing "certainty" around access to certain resources. The Tla-o-qui-aht First Nation has signed an incremental treaty, for example, securing funding and sixty-three hectares of land, in advance of treaty settlement.[65] But this land is to be "transferred in stages, as specific milestones in treaty negotiations are achieved (e.g., AIP [Agreement in Principle] signed, FA [Final Agreement] initialed, FA signed, etc.). The land becomes part of the Final Agreement, and is transferred through a First Nation company, which holds the land in fee simple until the effective date of the treaty."[66] It is a gradual incentive that keeps negotiating bands at the table. Lawyer Murray Browne asserts that from his experience the process of partial agreements is coercive "in that the governments mostly refuse to negotiate interim measures or incremental Treaties" forcing First Nations to "agree to accept government mandates and to complete a Final Treaty with everything in it."[67] But perhaps this government recalcitrance is a positive step in the final calculation. Russell Diabo warns that,

> Depending on the terms of such agreements involving natural resources and lands, these interim incremental agreements may weaken the strength of the Aboriginal title and rights of Indigenous Nations . . . to the point where the Crown governments can assert the Indigenous Nation has consented to the alienation of their rights to Aboriginal title territory and consented to infringement of their Aboriginal Rights through the terms of such agreements in the face of any section 35 legal analysis done by the Crown.[68]

In fact, a steady stream of outside treaty measures, such as Forest Consultation and Revenue Sharing Agreements, Strategic Engagement Agreements, and Economic and Community Development Agreements (such as mining revenue sharing), are all contingent upon signing Reconciliation Agreements with the Province of British Columbia. These Reconciliation Agreements allow the government to secure "certainty" for natural resource investment in the province "without prejudice" to Aboriginal title. Therefore, while Indigenous proprietary and jurisdictional interests in the land are implicitly recognized by virtue of provincial engagement and consultation, they are never recognized in terms of explicit recognition of Indigenous economic rights to their land or by explicit acknowledgment of Indigenous jurisdiction.

With the lack of interim protections, Barriere Lake saw extinguishment as embedded in the very process of the land claims policy, rather than simply in the final settlement terms. With no built-in measures to protect land over the fifteen-year period it could take to negotiate a claim, Barriere Lake's forests could have been long gone by the time they settled. Instead, Barriere Lake negotiated terms in the Trilateral Agreement to provide for interim measures to harmonize forestry with Algonquin land use while the band undertook its research and land use management plans. Prior even to the *Haida* and *Taku River* precedents on the government's "duty to consult and accommodate," Barriere Lake arranged to have their lands protected from incursion during negotiations. These measures relied on Barriere Lake's ecological knowledge to create a database from which to enable the community to respond quickly and effectively to industry and government consultation on their lands.[69] In fact, Barriere Lake used the CLCP to undertake some of this mapping before the Trilateral Agreement was signed. In 1987, Barriere Lake accepted CLCP contribution dollars to undertake research and development on Aboriginal title to their lands. They used this money to prepare two main studies: land-use and occupancy maps and a preliminary research report.[70] The land-use and occupancy maps were based on traplines and current use of the territory, and in conjunction with historical research, these maps were used as the basis for Trilateral negotiations.[71] Although Barriere Lake was undertaking research with CLCP funding, the band had no intention to negotiate under the policy. The band would only be subject to the policy if it submitted a claim, which also would have triggered loan funding to replace contribution dollars. The Trilateral Agreement ensured that research expenses would continue to be covered by the federal government. In this way, Barriere Lake would not indebt future generations or be charged to negotiate for their own lands, but they would be prepared with detailed research when state claims to jurisdiction were made on their lands.

Coercion is perhaps most subtle in the culture of land claim negotiation. The small band of K'ómoks geared up for a vote on an Agreement in Principle, the stage prior to negotiating and voting on a Final Agreement. Mary Everson, who like Bertha Williams, has taken the most vocal and outspoken stance in her community against the treaty process, described a meeting leading up to the vote on the AIP as a one-sided show: "It was just push push push push. We've never had anybody come in and say anything negative. Never."[72] Hence, it is not surprising that the community had become largely favorable to negotiations. I asked Everson if she thought that the reason people were saying "yes" was that they did not have enough information, or whether she felt the treaty was something they actually did support. She replied:

> I think that it's just that they don't have the information, and I don't think they can comprehend the information and be able to foresee the effects of a decision now could make in the future. I think a lot of people are limited in understanding that. Decisions that you make today, how that affects fifty years down the road and one hundred years down the road. What's going to happen? I'm not going to be here, so it's very important for me to make a decision for those who are going to be alive and well there.[73]

As Bertha Williams echoes, many simply do not understand what they are voting on: "There's a couple old-timers around, not many left, but one who says, 'Why did you guys vote for the treaty, you know you'd be paying taxes, land taxes—all the GST [General Sales Tax], PST [Provincial Sales Tax]?' And all they said was, 'We are.' These are the people voting on the treaty."[74] The half-million dollars spent on promoting the Tsawwassen treaty was apparently money well spent. Treaty negotiators even bused people to Nisga'a territory so that they could learn from the only other band to sign under the BCTP. But, as Williams observes, "When they got up there, there was entertainment and everything was peachy, but the people who were against the Nisga'a weren't allowed to go into these community centers, so our band members couldn't talk to them."[75] Glossy pamphlets promoting the treaty abounded, with almost no time or space dedicated to debate or counterperspectives.

Also part of the culture of negotiation is the stipulation that negotiating bands sign a confidentiality agreement agreeing not to discuss publicly the terms of the agreement while at the table.[76] This lack of transparency prevents Indigenous peoples from sharing information about their respective agreements and pooling knowledge and organizing efforts to mount collective responses to the policy. Meanwhile, the

federal government has explicit infrastructure to facilitate such information sharing between federal agencies, giving them an advantage in
negotiation and also a structure of collective maneuvering that Indigenous peoples do not share.[77]

With ninety-nine tables negotiating, perhaps the outcome seems
grim, especially if we do a quick calculation of how much Indigenous
land Canada and the provinces stand to gain. But opposition has been
baked into the process from the beginning.[78] Today, of the ninety-nine
tables counted by governments that are negotiating, how many are
actively working toward a claim? Glancing over the BCTC treaty negotiation list, we see bands "stuck" in early stages of the process for a
decade or more. Are they "stuck" or refusing to withdraw officially because they risk getting slapped with enormous treaty repayment bills?
Treaty negotiations are rife with conflict and are also sites of disruption
and national jurisdictional assertion. Recently, treaty meetings for the
Northern Secwepemc te Qelmucw (NStQ) treaty, composed of northern
Secwepmec bands (four out of seventeen bands that make up the nation),
have been disrupted by activists from the nation who have stolen ballot
boxes and refused to let meetings proceed.[79] April Thomas, who is a resident at the Sugarcane village settlement of the Williams Lake band (a
member of the NStQ) and a lead organizer with the Secwepmc'ulecw
Grassroots Movement, presented her case to the UN Special Rapporteur on the Rights of Indigenous Peoples expressing concern with the
current loan of $24 million: "There is a fear that this ever increasing
debt will decrease our capacity, further forcing the sale of our land and
resources after the treaty is finalized."[80] She also voiced grave concern
that information about the treaty was being withheld from the nation,
but also from participating band members if they expressed dissent.

Some bands are also pulling out of treaty groups, rendering the legitimacy of the process questionable. The Millbrook First Nation pulled
out of the Kwilmu'kw Maw-klusuaqn (KMK), or "Made in Nova Scotia,"
treaty process and the Algonquins of Pikwakanagan also voted "no" to
the Algonquins of Ontario Agreement in Principle, causing uncertainty
in a process where the terms of ratification do not seem to have been
clearly laid out in advance.[81] Bands have pulled out of treaty groups in
the past, but although more information accumulates about the impacts
and outcomes of treaty negotiation and implementation, this knowledge

has had trouble penetrating and circulating among communities whose bands and nations are sitting at the ninety-nine tables. This stone wall of negotiations is a central form of coercion in the land claims process.

Termination

Russell Diabo has named the CLCP a "termination" policy and he calls the ninety-nine tables negotiating under the CLCP the "Termination Tables."[82] Diabo writes that "Termination in this context means the ending of First Nations' pre-existing sovereign status through federal coercion of First Nations into Land Claims and Self-Government Final Agreements that convert First Nations into municipalities, their reserves into fee simple lands and extinguishment of their Inherent, Aboriginal and Treaty Rights."[83] The primary form of coercion that marks these policies is the simple fact that few other options are provided by the state for bands to protect their territories from unwanted exploitation and development. Bands generally cannot afford to litigate against governments, despite clear violations of domestic and international law. In this way, as Diabo puts it, "The government is taking advantage of the poverty in our community."[84] Aboriginal title can cost millions of dollars to prove. Since the *Sparrow* decision, which was the first legal case to follow the patriation of the Constitution Act of 1982 and to interpret Aboriginal rights through Section 35(1), a number of legal tests have been laid out by the courts that Indigenous peoples must meet in order to prove prior occupation. *Van der Peet* lays out the most difficult standards, introducing criteria stipulating how Indigenous peoples must show continuity in customs maintained since precontact with Europeans until the present day.[85] Diabo points out that these kinds of tests take millions of dollars to pass, involving the extensive collection of historical and cultural research. Meanwhile, the courts have simultaneously started to "limit, contain, and restrict the interpretation of Section 35 [rights]."[86] Because most bands cannot afford to sustain constitutional challenges in courts, the state takes advantage and offers communities the "opportunity" to resolve their outstanding land grievances through policy.

Litigation is expensive, its outcomes uncertain, its jurisdiction firmly grounded in state sovereignty, and the Crown's legal defense, until *Tsilhqot'in,* based on the doctrines of discovery.[87] It is no panacea.

But it has weakened the state's pretensions to innocence and bolstered the "Aboriginal fact," as plainly stated by Diabo: "Canada extended its territory and political assertions on top of pre-existing Aboriginal rights and title here."[88] Forcing Indigenous peoples to surrender jurisdiction to their lands through treaty is framed as a positive exchange of rights, but the doctrine of discovery simply plays a less public role than in the courts, never needing to be articulated before a judge or chancing repudiation by the Supreme Court, but all the while drawing the material boundaries around the terms of negotiation. As a technique of jurisdiction, the land claims policy deals with Indigenous legal orders by constraining their exercise to an exhaustively detailed list of "treaty rights," on a severely diminished land base, subject to extensive provincial oversight and regulation.

The CLCP is being challenged by dozens of bands that have chosen not to participate in the modern treaty process. One organization, the Defenders of the Land network, a grassroots, Indigenous-led coalition of people (on whose steering committee I sit as an ally), has come out strongly against the land claims policy. They state that "Canada, with Indigenous communities, jointly change the federal policies on self-government, land claims, and historic treaties to recognize Indigenous rights and Aboriginal title, including the right to self-determination and the right to exercise free, prior, and informed consent."[89] The bands, groups, and sometimes individuals representing their nations in the Defenders of the Land network have all defended their lands through so-called civil disobedience and blockades as the need arose. Bands, such as Barriere Lake, that have not signed historic or modern treaties must engage in constant struggles on the ground to protect their lands from ecological and social destruction.

But the main difficulty with resistance to the land claims policy is that so long as most other Indigenous peoples whose lands are unceded are at the negotiating table, the government has no incentive to change the policy.[90] One response to this problem has been to form a working group within the chiefs' organization, the Assembly of First Nations (AFN)—which represents negotiating and nonnegotiating bands—and deal with the federal government on a national level. This work has been organized through the AFN Comprehensive Claims Policy Reform Working Group (CCPRWG), which was mandated in 2011 through a Chiefs-in-Assembly Resolution to provoke change in the CLCP.[91] The

CCPRWG's strategy was driven at first by those unceded bands that are not currently negotiating treaties, but the committee soon turned in favor of those at negotiating tables.[92] Even given this turn, however, the AFN was unable to translate high-level meetings with the prime minister's office and the privy council office into positive change in the policy.[93]

In January 2012, an opportunity for movement on policy reform was presented in the form of the Crown–First Nations Gathering, called in response to a sudden frenzy of media attention on the northern Ontario reserve of Attawapiskat, where Chief Theresa Spence had (months earlier) called a national emergency to illicit response to the deplorable living conditions on the reserve, including an acute housing shortage and lack of potable water.[94] When attention finally turned to Attawapiskat, the government was caught in a web of neglect and Prime Minister Harper sought to appease critics by holding a nation-to-nation meeting with a select group of chiefs. Among a number of critical issues raised at the gathering, an "outcome statement" on land claims resolution was tabled that read: "The parties commit to ensuring federal negotiation policies reflect the principles of recognition and affirmation mandated by Section 35 of the Constitution Act, 1982 and advance certainty, expeditious resolution, and self-sufficiency."[95] It was a weak articulation of the AFN's 2012 First Nations' Plan, which proposed a concrete five-year plan for reforming the land claims policy and asserted that "[c]osmetic changes to process cannot mask the fundamental failure of the policy to meet its objectives."[96] In the months following the gathering, Indigenous leaders awaited signals of Harper's commitment to the outcome statements produced at the meeting. Would the civil servants at Indian Affairs continue to manage the grievances of First Nations regarding the land claims policy, or would the prime minister assign senior representatives with mandates from the prime minister's office, the privy council office, Justice and Treasury Board that had real power in federal policy and budgetary bids for cabinet consideration?[97] But there was little follow-up in either direction.

The main government response was to put Attawapiskat under Third Party Management and smear the community with allegations of financial misconduct, as had been done at Barriere Lake. Legal action swiftly followed, where the imposition of Third Party Managers was challenged, won, and subsequently repealed.[98] But conditions on the reserve remained unchanged and Chief Spence decided to fast on Parliament Hill in a final and desperate attempt to receive assistance for her community. Coinciding with her fast was the eruption of a nationwide, grassroots Indigenous resistance movement under the banner of "Idle No More" that spread like wildfire across the country, then the world, and that began to rally to her cause. Although the movement connected the deep streams of resistance that had always been running underneath the media's radar, Idle No More was originally sparked in response to the Conservative government's omnibus budget bill that included a number of acts seriously undermining environmental protection over navigable waterways and the environmental assessment process more generally. It also unilaterally changed the Indian Act and introduced "accountability" measures for First Nations finances on reserve.[99]

As the condition to end her fast, Chief Spence demanded a meeting with the prime minister and the governor general. National Chief Shawn Atleo secured a meeting with the prime minister but failed to secure the governor general's commitment. As a result, Chief Spence declined to attend the meeting and a firestorm erupted among chiefs about whether the AFN should attend the meeting without the Attawapiskat chief. Atleo chose to attend. During the January 11, 2012, meeting between the prime minister and the national chief, the AFN presented a list of eight priorities for First Nations, to which Harper declined action on most files. However, he agreed to a "higher-level" process for treaty implementation and comprehensive claims, and to provide oversight from the prime minister and the privy council office on these matters. This commitment led to the establishment of two Senior Oversight Committees (SOCs) set up to deal with these files.[100] Many First Nations critics did not have much hope in the SOCs. One of the men charged with an SOC was Jean-François Tremblay, senior assistant deputy minister, Treaties and Aboriginal Government, who was promoted to the position of deputy secretary (operations) at the privy council office. Although he was at the privy council office, he is known to First Nations as the middle-management bureaucrat who stalled any progress on the Crown–First Nations Gathering outcomes throughout most of 2012.[101]

The most recent changes to the CLCP, however, have nothing at all to do with these "high-level" meetings that tend to operate as capture mechanisms for criticism rather than vehicles of reform, but rather are the outcome of unilateral policy decisions that conform strictly to a Canadian agenda of extinguishment. First, in September 2012, a "results-based" model for comprehensive claims negotiation was introduced, designed to accelerate the pace of negotiations rather than reform substantially any of the points of opposition First Nations have been asserting for decades. This new model was meant to depend on the results of a federal assessment under way evaluating 183 bands to determine which tables are "ready" for Final Agreements. The "results-based" strategy was essentially a "take it or leave it" one: if a final settlement is offered by the government and rejected, the First Nation is rejected from the process. Diabo concludes: "It's basically blackmail."[102] The ninety-nine "Termination Tables" (comprised of those 183 bands) would be reduced to the most immediately promising bands to sign Final Agreements. Second, the Harper government hired Douglas Eyford to undertake a review of the process in the wake of the *Tsilhqot'in* decision, without ever mentioning the Supreme Court of Canada decision that found the nation had Aboriginal title to their lands—the first ever such admission in Canadian history. As discussed in chapter 5, Eyford presented no substantial modification to the policy that has persisted for nearly five decades on the basis of extinguishment of Indigenous jurisdiction. Eyford recommends a shift toward microagreements to mitigate against the failures of the policy, but also as another form of expediting resolution of competing assertions of jurisdiction. His emphasis on Section 35 rights also highlights the most potentially dangerous, unknown aspect of the *Tsilhqot'in* decision, and that is the removal of certain protections offered by 91(24) in the face of provincial legislation.[103]

But perhaps the most challenging aspect of the land claims policy is the fact that Canada uses negotiating bands as a shield against non-negotiating bands. The front line of opposition has gradually shifted focus from Indian Affairs onto Indigenous peoples themselves—between negotiating and nonnegotiating bands—making the problem with the land claims policy appear to be an internal issue between First Nations. In July 2012, for example, members of the Tla'amin First Nation blocked band members from ratifying their Agreement in Principle, which had already been voted down in 2001.[104] They claimed that many band members enrolled in the treaty process under "duress" and complained of irregularities in band membership codes that would tilt the vote toward a "yes." Coming to the defense of the treaty process were the chiefs of Tsawwassen and Maa'nulth bands.[105] What is the Canadian public to make of this Indigenous defense of a policy that other First Nations are opposing? As a result of First Nations participation in the treaty process, the federal government has shown little regard for those unceded bands protesting the CLCP who are not currently sitting at negotiating tables, such as the alliance represented by the Union of British Columbia Indian Chiefs, the Interior Alliance of BC, or even for those groups opposing their own bands' involvement in the treaty process. The land claims policy is a complicated end game that marks all Indigenous jurisdictions as collateral damage in spite of its pretensions to target only consenting bands.

It is also a flailing policy and whatever comes next may be worse. The chief commissioner of the British Columbia Treaty Commission (BCTC), Sophie Pierre, stated that if a dozen treaties are not signed in the next few years, "it's about time we faced the obvious—it isn't going to happen, so shut 'er down."[106] Provinces are now turning to new kinds of agreements to secure consent for natural resource extraction on Indigenous lands—the key objective of the land claims process in either case. The best expression of this goal can be seen in British Columbia Premier Christy Clarke's announcement in January 2011 directing her government away from treaties and toward new kinds of contracts with First Nations in order to pursue economic development.[107] Land transfers, revenue sharing, brokering between industry and First Nations—all of these "nonprejudicial" (to Aboriginal title) forms of agreements are now being aggressively pursued in order to secure economic certainty for business interests in the province, especially in the post-*Tsilhqot'in* world, which brought greater uncertainty but no new provincial commitments to institutions, resources, or processes to address Indigenous rights.[108] But this strategy will face tough opposition from Indigenous communities. A declaration signed by a coalition of Indigenous bands and issued by the Second Indigenous Assembly Against Mining and Pipelines states: "Clark's government has no jurisdiction to pursue her economic agenda without free, prior, and informed consent because we—grassroots Indigenous peoples—legally, politically, economically, spiritually, culturally, and inherently maintain Aboriginal title and jurisdiction over our territories."[109] Quick deals to gain access to Indigenous lands cannot resolve the outstanding and overlapping jurisdictional conflicts plaguing resource developers across the country. All across Canada, different kinds of access and benefit-sharing agreements are being negotiated, "giving" Indigenous peoples access to jobs and slim fractions of revenues extracted from their lands.[110] These are risk-mitigation strategies against the unsettling uncertainty of Indigenous jurisdiction and underlying Aboriginal title.

The modern treaty process has not actually failed until the ninety-nine tables are either resolved through treaty or pullout of the process. Those outside of the treaty process, such as the Algonquins of Barriere Lake, provide a stark reality check as to the devastating ordeal defending Indigenous lands can be outside of federal policies. Barriere Lake, like hundreds of other bands, have not ceded their land or jurisdiction and so they still live to fight another day, on the terms of their own legal and political orders.

Future Tense

The Trilateral Agreement never actually died. But it would take on a life of its own for the next generation. As Audra Simpson points out, "The condition of Indigeneity in North America is to have survived this ac-quisitive and genocidal process and thus to have called up the failure of the project itself."[111] The struggle for the Trilateral Agreement is one rooted in the Algonquins' need to conceive of an alternative to the land claims policy, one that would put to rest the constant attempts at domi-nation of their legal and governance systems. They sought to gain effec-tive governing control over their lands without giving up their rights to the territory. The modern land claims policy is the ultimate and most extreme abrogation of Indigenous jurisdiction. Thus, it also represents Canada's attempt to complete its unfinished sovereignty claim by elimi-nating the uncertainty of inherent Indigenous legal interests in the land. The land claims policy is Canada's claim; it is a useless attempt to hold as separate the legitimacy of Canada's legal system from that which it exists in relation to: these lands, the peoples of these lands, their laws. The land claims policy has no authority in Indigenous laws or protocols of diplomacy and negotiation. One could also make a strong argument that it has little support in Canadian law, though the logical discrep-ancies and historical implications of court decisions would have to be carefully laid out, as some legal scholars have painstakingly done.[112]

Barriere Lake remains under Third Party Management (TPM) a decade later. Calculating that the average salary accountants are paid

is two hundred thousand dollars a year, that would make the cumulative TPM intake almost twenty-two times the amount of the initial
deficit they were hired to resolve.[113] When the government introduced
the First Nations Financial Transparency Act that required all bands
to publicly post their consolidated financial audit statements, Barriere
Lake refused because they had had no control over spending for almost
a decade and felt they shouldn't be accountable for a budget over which
they had no control, and worse, which they had not seen in years, despite tireless efforts to obtain basic disclosure regarding their accounts.
Barriere Lake continues to negotiate with the province, which is still
reluctant to agree to resource-revenue sharing and other core matters.
The federal government has entirely washed its hands of the matter. In
terms of their elected council, the community selects council members
approved by elders, but they must still be held to a vote. The community
continues to discuss abandoning the Indian Act council and moving
back to the customary system. In the meantime, there are enough issues to keep them busy. At Christmas of 2015, checks came more than a
month late because of financial mismanagement by the TPM, so a fund-
raising campaign was held by BLS to feed families for the holidays. We
soon learned that someone from the government of Canada called Pay-
Pal to complain, which led to the freezing of our fund-raising account.
A Twitter campaign that reached tens of thousands of people garnered
a quick reversal by PayPal and the immediate restoral of our monies.[114]
There is always endless work to do.

What can this story of Barriere Lake tell us about where jurisdiction and sovereignty meet? One answer to this question is to parse the
meaning of Canadian sovereignty from the state's authority to govern.
Indigenous legal and political orders structure responsibility to their
relations, thus the *authority to have authority* rests in ontologies of care.
Further, Indigenous jurisdiction necessarily entails governance powers and self-determination. What marks the limits of this authority is
a relational practice to other laws. "When we meet new people," Toby
Decoursay often repeated, "we are going to shake hands." Future tense,
the grammar of Toby's lessons, prepares the listener for the ongoing
promise of the next relationship, the certainty of restoration. Perhaps
solidarity means we must engender the shared authority to speak the
law together, to find ways to become properly entangled.

Sovereignty and jurisdiction are mutually constitutive claims of the modern state. While on the surface it may seem that jurisdiction derives its authority from state sovereignty claims, the authority to exercise these claims derives in turn from the internal arrangements and organization of responsibilities carried off by jurisdictional powers. By continuing to assert their jurisdictional authority, Barriere Lake undermines the sovereignty of the Canadian state. Further, their laws are based on irrefutable logics of care and evidence of belonging. Knowledge of place structures people's understanding of it and Barriere Lake's concept and exercise of jurisdiction foregrounds the world we could inherit if we changed how laws in Canada meet. The Trilateral Agreement provides a reconstructive model for what decolonization could look like in Canada if its principles were widely adopted and implemented. All of us, Indigenous and settler, have a stake in the success of their struggle.

Acknowledgments

All that we are is all that we owe. To the Mitchikanibikok Inik I owe the greatest debt of gratitude. Thanks to everyone at the Rapid Lake Reserve who welcomed this *tchigoshii* to the community. Thanks especially to Jean Maurice Matchewan for supporting this research and providing me with access to extensive materials and resources, including sitting down to countless interviews and conversations with me over the years. I owe a special thanks to my friends Marylynn Poucachiche and Norman Matchewan for acting as liaisons, hosts, and guides to the territory. Marylynn looked after me on visits to the community despite having five children to care for, and she was never anything but generous with her time and in sharing her insights over long nights spent talking at her kitchen table. Norman Matchewan is a gifted political leader and a gracious host. His honest reflections on the community's political struggle, coupled with his infectious joy when he was out in the bush, showed me the source of the community's unwavering conviction to protect their lands.

I also deeply appreciate the support of Michel Thusky, an institution of memory for Barriere Lake and a brilliant analyst of government strategy and policy. His deference to elders and total devotion to his grandchildren exemplify the humility and kindness of the people of Barriere Lake. I will also be ever indebted to Maggie Wawatie and Rose Nottaway, dauntless community leaders who patiently explained so much to me, though admittedly Maggie did avoid me like the plague for the first couple of years. I am also indebted to the leadership, knowledge, and integrity of Tony Wawatie, who taught me a great deal about the customary system at Barriere Lake and always made himself available for long political discussions about the Anishnabe world. Thanks to Eddy and Bella Nottaway, who opened their home to me, and thanks to their son Clayton Nottaway, who is married to Marylynn, and who along with their incredible children (Lorraine, Katie, Maria, Shane, and Brennan) shared his home and his thoughts with me.

I owe a very special debt of thanks to Toby and Philomene Decoursay and to their family for hosting me on their territory and welcoming days of discussion and questions with endless patience and attention. Toby spent hours parsing spiritual knowledge that was difficult at the best of times to translate, but he took the time to explain in many different ways over the years to make sure I understood. Thanks to Angelo and Tony Decoursay for taking me hunting; to Suzanne Decoursay and her sisters for their company and their hospitality; and to everyone else who hosted me or traveled with me along the way, especially the younger generation: Sabeth and Amy Keyes, Tillis Keyes, Rachel and Randy Ratt, Monica Poucachiche, James Nottaway, Kokwetc Nottaway, Sonny Papatie, Flora Keyes, Jessica Thusky, David Papatie, and Suzette Poucachiche. You have all shown me how beautiful is the bravery that is rooted in a love of the land.

Alongside community representatives, a group of close associates to Barriere Lake also supported my research. I owe a great deal of gratitude to Peter Di Gangi, research director of the Algonquin Nation Secretariat, for guiding me through extensive banks of archival and other research, letting me hang around the office for days rifling through files, and teaching me so much about the land claims policy. Between us, Pete is a secret weapon for settler-colonial destruction. Thanks to David Nahwegahbow for always taking the time to respond to my questions and for providing valuable insights reading and commenting on drafts of this book. I first had an opportunity to see Dave at work in federal court in 2008 when he represented the Elders Council in a case against the minister of Indian Affairs. He pleaded the case by foregrounding the governance system at Barriere Lake and describing the lay of the land and its beauty. It was then I came to see the practice of Aboriginal law in light of its role: mediating encounter between Indigenous and settler legal orders. I owe an unrepayable debt to Sue Roark-Calnek for providing me with pages of notes that carefully analyzed my arguments and offered substantial resources to strengthen my claims through her considerable store of knowledge and research. She mentored me with such kindness and generosity that I can now make sense of the way Barriere Lakers who remember trailing after her in the community as children break into smiles to this day when I mention her name.

By far I am the most indebted to Russell Diabo, who started me on this path almost from the day I met him seventeen years ago. He told me that if I wanted to understand what colonialism looks like in Canada, I had to study the story of the Algonquins of Barriere Lake. Little did he know the price he would pay for putting me on this path: borrowing his books, crashing on his couch, eating his bagels, calling, texting, and e-mailing him at all hours with questions, and forcing him to read draft after draft of this work. He is my biggest supporter and my harshest critic, and to me there is no greater gift than the unwavering eye. Most of all, Russ and his wife Joanna Anaquod have treated me like a daughter and I consider them my family. They have been hard on me when I needed schooling and encouraging when I needed confidence. They have taught me about the hard road to justice and dissuaded me from expecting any rewards for pursuing it other than self-respect and integrity. Their faith that I would do the right thing with the knowledge they have entrusted to me is more than I could ever ask.

This book grew from my doctoral dissertation, and my supervisor Deborah Cowen helped bring these ideas into being. She is the most generous academic I know, both intellectually and materially. In addition to catching every nuance in an argument and knowing how to finesse it to greatest effect, she never reads a text in isolation from the broader political struggle in which it is situated, and she never misses an opportunity to support those struggles. Thanks also to my cosupervisor Scott Prudham, a razor-sharp mind whose contributions were always on point, despite his insistence that he knew nothing about what I was writing. My committee was also formative and instrumental. Jennifer Nedelsky's thought-provoking interventions went above and beyond her duties, and she continues to include me in her organizing efforts to position and practice law as a liberatory project. Many thanks to Deborah McGregor for helping to place my work within a national context of research with Indigenous peoples. It is impossible to even conceive of this project without Mariana Valverde's scholarship and intellectual fierceness, and I am ever grateful for her mentorship and friendship.

For funding this research, I acknowledge the Social Sciences and Humanities Research Council for supporting my doctoral and postdoctoral positions and thus making this research and writing possible. I also recognize the support of a very strange and wonderful grant from the University of Toronto Faculty of Arts and Science for "Funds for Study Elsewhere of Less Commonly Taught Languages for Research Purposes" that supported my application to study *anishnabemowin* in the bush at Barriere Lake. Finally, this research would not be remotely possible without the child-care subsidy program of the city of Toronto that afforded me the opportunity to finish my doctoral degree and also to write this book. Thank you truly to whomever fought for that and won.

During the writing of this book, many people had a considerable impact on my thinking. In the early writing stages, I relied heavily on Dawnis Kennedy, Amar Bhatia, and Kim Stanton. Dawnis brought us all together into a writing group, and she has taught me most of all what it means to *carry* law. For supporting or inspiring this book through conversation and exchange, thank you to my extraordinary friends and colleagues Michael Asch, Amar Bhatia, Andrée Boisselle, John Borrows, Bradley Bryan, Ravi Chimni, Charmaine Chua, Tia Dafnos, Jessica Dempsey, Nick Estes, Kanishka Goonewardena, Sarah Hunt, Marcinku Kedzior, Hayden King, Peter Kulchyski, Damien Lee, Johnny Mack, Geoff Mann, Arthur Manuel, Kent McNeil, David Peerla, Sherry Pictou, Janna Promislow, Nicole Schabus, Dayna Nadine Scott, Jakeet Singh, Heidi Kiiwetinepinesiik Stark, Martha Steigman, James Tully, Etienne Turpin, and David Wachsmuth. For reading, editing, and totally sorting me out, thank you so kindly to Gina Badger, Emma Feltes, Robyn Letson, Corvin Russell, and Andréa Schmidt. Thank you to my readers, Kevin Bruyneel and Alyosha Goldstein, for setting me on such a clear and vivid track to turn my dissertation into a book, though of course all missteps are my own. Thank you to Audra Simpson, whose heart is as big as her wit is sharp, who saw me through the prospectus process when I was at Columbia University and encouraged me since every step of the way. Then there are the people whom you write *for*: thank you to my brilliant interlocutors Glen Coulthard and Robert Nichols for keeping me sharp.

I also want to single out Arthur Manuel for his mentorship and support. He and I went on a Revolutionary Road Trip throughout the southern BC mainland and west coast of Vancouver Island meeting and talking to community members involved in the land claims process (and also gorging on fish 'n' chips). Our conversations along the way were foundational to my understanding of the power and politics of the land question in British Columbia and across the country.

Thank you to all of the incredible graduate students I met while I was living in New York City for plugging me into the field of settler-colonial studies in a way I never had been immersed before: Tamar Blickstein,

Mike Griffiths, Erick Howard, Maria John, Margaux Kristijansson, Crystal Migwans, Hayley Negrin, Leslie Sabiton, Sara Sinclair, Owen Toews, and others. I'm deeply grateful as well to my home team of grads at the University of Toronto, in particular Martine August, Martin Danyluk, Heather Dorries, Caitlin Henry, Paul Jackson, Katie Mazer, Laura Pitkanen, Jennifer Ridgley, Brett Story, Patrick Vitale, and too many others to name, for making university fun, political, and sort of irrelevant simultaneously. Thank you also to the Anti-Colonial Committee of the Law Union of Ontario for the critical, eye-opening exchanges: Sarah Colgrove, Meaghan Daniel, Mary Eberts, Emma Feltes, Christina Gray, Audrey Huntley, Mike Leitold, Crystal Sinclair, Kim Stanton, Adrienne Telford, Jessica Wolfe, and others.

To my fellow organizers in Barriere Lake Solidarity, especially Martin Lukacs and Pei Ju Wang, this book is a product of our collective learning. Thanks also to BLS members Steve Baird, Molly Churchill, Peter Haresnape, Ramsey Hart, Margaux Kristijansson, Greg Macdougall, Jamie Ross, Simone Schmidt, Kalin Stacey, Colin Stuart, and all the others. I would not be the scholar I am without the intellectual and ethical challenges I grappled with in the context of organizing in local anticolonial groups and with the national Defenders of the Land network and the Defenders of the Land–Idle No More Joint Steering Committee. Thank you to Zainab Amadahy, Tori Cress, Stefanie Gude, Audrey Huntley, Syed Hussan, Mireille LaPointe, Melina Laboucan-Massimo, Janice Makokis, Sylvia McAdams, Sheelah McLean, Heather Milton Lightening, Wanda Nanibush, Tannis Monkman Neilson, Corvin Russell, Crystal Sinclair, David Sone, Clayton Thomas-Muller, Harsha Walia, and too many others to name.

I feel very grateful to Jason Weidemann—and for the team at the University of Minnesota Press—for believing in this project from the start and for seeing it through.

The hardest people to thank are those who are most present in our lives. Thank you to all the caregivers at day cares who have watched and loved my children so I could write, especially Nancy, Felicia, Michelle, and Jen. Thanks to my mom for taking care of my kids on sick days and to my dad for joining me on a final leg of this journey, driving my daughter and me to Barriere Lake to share my finished work. To my siblings, Nellie, Maya, Sam, and Ben: I know you will be mad if your name is not in this section. Thanks to my in-laws, for all the child care and moral support they have given me over the years. Thanks to my boyfriend, Josh, whom I love to pieces, for everything, but especially for never forcing me to make any clear separation between research, activism, and life. Finally, to Lior Isadora and Amir Jude, who were born while I was writing: to you, I owe everything. May you inherit the struggle as well as the strength to fight it.

Notes

Note on Terminology

1. Evelyn Peters, "Geographies of Aboriginal People in Canada," *Canadian Geography* 45:1 (2001): 138.

Preface

1. Hussein Abu Hussein and Fiona McKay, *Access Denied: Palestinian Land Rights in Israel* (London and New York: Zed Books, 2003), 105.

2. Geremy Forman and Sandy Kedar, "From Arab Lands to 'Israel Lands': The Legal Dispossession of the Palestinians Displaced by Israel in the Wake of 1948," *Environment and Planning D: Society and Space* 22 (2004): 812.

3. Norman Bentwich, *Legislature of Palestine, 1918–25: I: Orders in Council and Ordinances* (Alexandria, Egypt, 1926), 12–13; quoted in Martin Bunton, "Inventing the Status Quo: Ottoman Land Law during the Palestine Mandate, 1917–1936," *International History Review* 21:1 (March 1999), 31.

4. Quoted in Y. Gradus, "The Emergence of Regionalism in a Centralised System: The Case of Israel," *Environment and Planning D: Society and Space* 2 (1984): 87–100; quoted in Oren Yiftachel, "Bedouin Arabs and the Israeli Settler State: Land Policies and Indigenous Resistance," in *The Future of Indigenous Peoples: Strategies for Survival and Development*, ed. I. Abu-Saad. and D. Champagne (Los Angeles: American Indian Studies Center Publication, UCLA, 2003), 28–29.

5. Oren Yiftachel, *Ethnocracy: Land and Politics of Identity in Israel/Palestine* (Philadelphia: University of Pennsylvania Press, 2006).

6. I wrote this preface in 2012, but updated this figure to reflect the most recent numbers.

7. Ahmad Melhem, "Why Israel Wants These Bedouins to Pay for Their Village's Demolition," *Almonitor*, April 16, 2016. Accessed online May 25, 2016: http://www .al-monitor.com/pulse/originals/2016/04/araqib-village-israel-demolition -palestine-land.html#ixzz49mXBQF6A.

8. Erez Tzfadia, "In the Name of Zionism," *Haaretz*, September 19, 2008; R. Khamaissi, "Mechanism of Land Control and Territorial Judaization in Israel," in *In the Name of Security: Studies in Peace and War in Israel in Changing Times*, ed. M. Al-Haj and U. Ben-Eliezer (Haifa: University of Haifa Press, 2003), 421–48 (in Hebrew).

9. Derek Gregory theorizes how geographic place-names become "cover

terms" for complex networks of people, money, ideologies, and war in *The Colonial Present: Afghanistan, Palestine, Iraq* (Malden, Mass.: Blackwell Publishing, 2004), 28.

10. For more on the production of settler space, see the hyperpoliticized frontier architecture developed in Israel, the icon of which is Homa Umigdal (Wall and Tower). This structure was erected faithfully at Nahabir by the kibbutzniks to mark their territory, but also in some fifty-seven-odd outposts between 1936 and 1957 alone. See Sharon Rotbard, "Wall and Tower (Homa Umigdal): The Mold of Israeli Architecture," in *A Civilian Occupation: The Politics of Israeli Architecture*, ed. Rafi Segal and Eyal Weizman (Tel Aviv: Babel, London and New York: Verso, 2003), 42. Homa Umigdal is a system of settlement based on fortified walls and a lookout tower; it also provides for a tiny ghetto of housing within its structure. According to Israeli architect Sharon Rotbard, this garrison-type settlement is "the fundamental paradigm of all Jewish architecture in Israel" (ibid., 46). That is because "it is more an instrument than a place" (48). An infrastructure of war, Homa Umigdal embodies a strategy of expansion as a series of fortified dots on a map, more crucial than the settlements themselves, forming together a colony of occupation. One way in which these points were important was in changing the nature of spatial and temporal organization in a region. Citing Henri Lefebvre, Rotbard theorizes that this sprinkling of Jewish settlements throughout the land transformed agrarian or nomadic time into industrial time, instilling a planning regime of modernization and European homogeneity into the Arab desert.

11. Steven Salaita, *The Holy Land in Transit: Colonialism and the Quest for Canaan* (Syracuse, N.Y.: Syracuse University Press, 2006).

12. Jodi A. Byrd, *The Transit of Empire: Indigenous Critiques of Colonialism* (Minneapolis: University of Minnesota Press, 2011), xiii.

13. Alex Lubin, "'We Are All Israelis': The Politics of Colonial Comparisons," in *Settler Colonialism*, ed. Alyosha Goldstein and Alex Lubin, *Special Edition, South Atlantic Quarterly* 107:4 (fall 2008): 677.

14. Ibid., 675.

15. Byrd, *The Transit of Empire*, xv.

16. Lubin, "We Are All Israelis," 676.

17. Noam Chomsky, "My Reaction to Osama bin Laden's Death," *Guernica*, May 6, 2011, https://www.guernicamag.com/daily/noam_chomsky_my_reaction_to_os/; accessed July 8, 2015.

18. A ripe area of recent scholarship, David Koffman attributes this interest in the role of the Indian in the Jewish imaginary in part to "the competitive appeals by both Jews and Arabs to the idea of indigeneity in Israel/Palestine and a public relations battle around the Americanization of the Holocaust and Americans' failure to rally around memorializing and nationalizing the legacy of the seismic trauma perpetrated against Native Americans" ("Members of the Tribe: Native America in the Jewish Imagination," *American Jewish History* 95:3 [2009]: 316).

19. See, for example: Stephen Katz, *Red, Black and Jew: New Frontiers in Hebrew Literature* (Austin: University of Texas Press, 2009); and Jonathan Boyarin, *The Uncovered Self: Jews, Indians, and the Identity of Christian Europe* (Chicago: University of Chicago Press, 2009).

20. Ella Shohat, *Taboo Memories, Diasporic Voices* (Durham, N.C., and London: Duke University Press, 2006), 209.

21. Ibid., 210–11.

22. Canada distinguished itself in the world by vowing "retaliation" against the Palestinian Authority for gaining—through democratic vote—"non-member observer status" at the United Nations General Assembly. See Campbell Clark, "Baird Accuses UN of Abandoning Principles by Recognizing Palestine," *Globe and Mail*, November 29, 2012; and Campbell Clark, "Canada Temporarily Recalls Palestinian UN Envoys, but Says It Isn't Breaking Off Relations," *Globe and Mail*, November 30, 2012. The new Trudeau government promises to maintain these close ties to Israel, as newspapers have reported: Mike Blanchfield, "Justin Trudeau and Benjamin Netanyahu Speak by Phone, Set New Tone," *Canadian Press*, October 30, 2015.

23. Daniel Montescru, in discussion with author, Israel–Palestine, June 23, 2009.

Introduction

1. Boyce Richardson, *Blockade: Algonquins Defend the Forest*, 1990.

2. Copper One Annual General Meeting, September 29, 2015. Norman and I attended as shareholders.

3. Cartier Resources Inc. signed a sale agreement with Copper One Inc. for $150,000 (plus shares) for the acquisition of full interest in the Rivière Doré copper-nickel project (Cartier Resources Inc., "Cartier Signs a Sale Agreement in Respect to Its Rivière Doré Copper-Nickel Project," December 1, 2011).

4. Jean Gottman, *The Significance of Territory* (Charlottesville: University Press of Virginia, 1973), 123.

5. This is a slight augmentation to Shaunnagh Dorsett and Shaun McVeigh's excellent definition of jurisdiction as the "internal arrangements for organising and exercising authority," in *Jurisdiction* (New York: Routledge, 2012), 39. For deeper discussion on how the authority of colonial and imperial legalities was established, see Shiri Pasternak, "Jurisdiction and Settler Colonialism: Where Laws Meet," *Special Issue: Law & Decolonization, Canadian Journal of Law and Society* 29:2 (August 2014): 145–61. See also Nicholas Onuf, "Sovereignty: Outline of a Conceptual History," *Alternatives: Global, Local, Political* 16:4 (fall 1991): 425–46.

6. A case could certainly be made that the terrain of settler colonial conflict between Indigenous peoples and the Crown is on the basis of competing sovereignties and not in fact centered on jurisdiction. The Haudenosaunee are the most prominent nation to explicitly assert their political status as sovereignty claims, though they are not alone. However, even the Haudenosaunee rarely express their sovereignty in settler-colonial terms—that is, as a demand for modern Western independent statehood. Mohawk scholar Audra Simpson calls Indigenous-settler political multiplicity "nested sovereignty," maintaining the autonomy of the Kahnawà:ke Mohawk, despite living within the borders of sovereign settler states. She writes that "[o]ne does not entirely negate the other, but they necessarily stand in terrific tension and pose serious jurisdictional and normative challenges to each other" (*Mohawk Interruptus: Political Life across the Borders of Settler States* [Durham, N.C.: Duke University Press, 2014], 10). It is these "jurisdictional and normative challenges" that I want to foreground here.

7. The Algonquins of Barriere Lake have rarely been "studied" by academics. With one exception, recent scholarship dealing specifically with the Algonqiuns of Barriere Lake has focused on ecological knowledge, analyzing the extensive record

produced through the mapping studies conducted in the community throughout
the 1990s. See Van Wyngaarden, "Integration of Spatial, Cultural and Toponomic
Data for First Nations Land Use and Sensitive Areas Mapping: A GIS Case Study,"
presentation at the Ninth Annual Symposium on Geographic Information Systems
in Natural Resources Management, Symposium Proceedings (1995) (Fort Collins,
Colo.: GIS World, 1995), vol. 2, 696; Scott Nickels, "Importance of Experiential
Context for Understanding Indigenous Ecological Knowledge: The Algonquins of
Barriere Lake, Quebec," dissertation, McGill University, 1999; Thom Meredith with
E. Shenkier, "The Forests at Barrière Lake: Euro-North American and Indigenous
Perception of the Natural Environment," in *Canadian Issues in Environmental Ethics*, eds. A. Wellington, Allan Greenbaum, Wesley Cragg (Toronto: Broadview Press,
1997), 67–80. The exception to these publications on recent Algonquin history is the
recent addition to the literature by Andrew Crosby and Jeffrey Monaghan, "Settler
Governmentality in Canada and the Algonquins of Barriere Lake," *Security Dialogue*
43:5 (2012): 421–38. Historian James Morrison is the most esteemed and studied
scholar in the area, but much of his work remains unpublished, as it has been commissioned specifically by the community and its intellectual property belongs to
them. Through Barriere Lake, Morrison's relevant commissioned work on the Algonquin Nation was accessible to me for research purposes. Otherwise, one can
read Morrison's chapter 2.3, "Algonquin History in the Ottawa River Watershed,"
in *A Background Study for Nomination of the Ottawa River under the Canadian Heritage Rivers System*, prepared by the Ottawa River Heritage Designation Committee,
2005. Anthropologist Sue Roark-Calnek has also undertaken extensive studies on
genealogy and social organization of Algonquin life, and though her work is also
mostly unpublished, she is regarded as a leading expert on Algonquin culture and
her work shines with intimate knowledge of the Barriere Lake language and community. Through Barriere Lake, Roark-Calnek's relevant commissioned work on
Barriere Lake was also accessible to me for research purposes. Otherwise, one can
find only the following published piece: Sue Roark-Calnek, "The Algonquin World:
Seasons, Cycles, Change: A Guide to the Exhibition" (Geneseo, N.Y.: BOCES Geneseo Migrant Center, October 18–November 2, 1991).

8. No one has done a more comprehensive job than Lisa Ford at demonstrating this, although the complex global patterns and drivers of change lie mostly
outside of her study (Lisa Ford, *Settler Sovereignty: Jurisdiction and Indigenous People
in America and Australia 1788–1835* [Cambridge: Harvard University Press, 2010]).
The language of "perfection" that I use to describe the conflation of jurisdiction,
sovereignty, and territory comes directly from her work. Of course, this pattern
may inhere in other colonial contexts, as well, but I have chosen to focus on the Anglophone colonies (with some reference to French colonialism) to limit the scope of
study, but also because Canadian political culture was shaped in relation to British
patterns of colonization.

9. Norman Matchewan, in discussion with author, May 14, 2009.

10. This inherent jurisdiction arguably is also recognized in glimpses by the
settler state through the judiciary. See Kent McNeil, "The Jurisdiction of Inherent
Right Aboriginal Governments," research paper for the National Centre for First
Nations Governance, October 11, 2007.

11. Unceded lands, according to Canadian law, are accounted for in the Royal
Proclamation of 1763 by King George III. This Royal Proclamation cemented an im-

perial property right: preemption, which is essentially the right of discovery. The royal prerogative lays out strict preemption rules making it illegal for Indigenous peoples to sell land to third parties unless they are first ceded to the Crown. Preemption is an exclusive, future right in discovered lands, what is sometimes referred to as "European title." See Royal Proclamation 1763 (U.K.), reprinted R.S.C. 1985, App. II, No.1 (hereafter "Royal Proclamation"); Robert Williams Jr., *The American Indian in Western Legal Thought, Discourses of Context* (New York: Oxford University Press, 1992), 237; cited in Dara Culhane, *The Pleasure of the Crown: Anthropology, Law and First Nations* (Burnaby, B.C.: Talonbooks), 56; Olive P. Dickason, *Canada's First Nations: A History of Founding Peoples from Earliest Times* (Toronto: McLelland & Stewart, 1994), 180–81.

12. Edward Benton-Banai, *The Mishomis Book: The Voice of the Ojibway* (Minneapolis: University of Minnesota Press, 2010).

13. On good relations as a source of authority, see Aaron Mills, "Aki, Anishinaabek, kaye tahsh Crown," *Indigenous Law Journal* 9:1 (2010): 107–213; Heidi Kiiwetinepinesiik Stark, "Respect, Responsibility, and Renewal: The Foundations of Anishinaabe Treaty Making with the United States and Canada," *American Indian Culture and Research Journal* 34:2 (2010): 145–64.

14. Val Napoleon, "Thinking about Indigenous Legal Orders," research paper for the National Centre for First Nations Governance, June 2007, 7. Napoleon also stresses the contestability of these laws and the diversity of interpretive beliefs and internal understandings within and between Indigenous communities regarding these legal orders.

15. See Taiaiake Alfred, "Sovereignty," in *Sovereignty Matters: Locations of Contestation and Possibility in Indigenous Struggles for Self-Determination,* ed. Joanne Barker (Lincoln: University of Nebraska Press, 2005), 33–50.

16. On the unique expression of discovery by the British, see Robert J. Miller, Jacinta Ruru, Larissa Behrendt, and Tracey Lindberg, *Discovering Indigenous Lands, The Doctrine of Discovery in the English Colonies* (Oxford: Oxford University Press, 2010), 89–125.

17. Technically, the Spanish kingdom was still Castilian until 1512, by which point several papal bulls had been issued dividing up the world. See L. C. Green and Olive Dickason, *The Law of Nations and the New World* (Edmonton: University of Alberta Press, 1993), 178–84; and Julius Goebel, *Struggle for the Falkland Islands* (New Haven: Yale University Press, 1927), 79–85. Thanks to Kent McNeil for these suggestions. For a poignant reflection on colonialism and Indigenous authority in this period, see Sylvia Wynter, "Unsettling the Coloniality of Being/Power/Truth/Freedom: Towards the Human, after Man, Its Overrepresentation—An Argument," *CR: The New Centennial Review* 3:3 (fall 2003): 257–337. John L. Comaroff defines *lawfare* as "the effort to conquer and control indigenous peoples by the coercive use of legal means" ("Symposium Introduction: Colonialism, Culture, and the Law: A Foreword," *Law & Social Inquiry* 26:2 [spring 2001]: 306). Other scholarly approaches to law and imperialism in the settler colonies include Lisa Ford and Tim Rowse, eds., *Between Indigenous and Settler Governance* (New York: Routledge, 2013); Irene Watson, *Aboriginal Peoples, Colonialism, and International Law: Raw Law* (New York: Routledge, 2015); and Anthony Pagden, *People and Empires: Europeans and the Rest of the World from Antiquity to the Present* (London: Weidenfeld & Nicholson, 2001).

282 NOTES TO INTRODUCTION

18. As James Sákéj Youngblood Henderson explains, underlying Crown title was a fiction invented in Britain that had no basis in any terms of actual ownership: "Ownership is not a distinct legal category or concept in British law, but a socio-political concept" (James [Sákéj] Youngblood Henderson, Marjorie L. Benson, and Isobel M. Findlay, *Aboriginal Tenure in the Constitution of Canada* [Scarborough, Ontario: Carswell, 2000], 5). The absolutist legal principle of Crown tenure—*nulle terre sans seigneur* (no land without a lord)—"informed the doctrine of tenure that asserts that all land in Britain is 'held' of the Crown, but not actually 'owned' by the Crown" (ibid.).

19. To give a brief survey of the literature, I will just highlight some of the best work on the subject that I have seen. The scholarship on the Northwest is most prolific and compelling: see, for example, H. Robert Baker, "Creating Order in the Wilderness: Transplanting the English Law to Rupert's Land, 1835–51," *Law & History Review* 17:2 (1999): 209–46; Desmond Brown, "Unpredictable and Uncertain: Criminal Law in the Canadian North West before 1886," *Alberta Law Review* 17 (1979): 497–512; Adam Gaudry, "Fantasies of Sovereignty: Deconstructing British and Canadian Claims to Ownership of the Historic North-West," NAIS 3:1 (2016): 46–74; Hamar Foster, "Long-Distance Justice: The Criminal Jurisdiction of Canadian Courts West of the Canadas, 1763–1859," *American Journal of Legal History* 34 (1990): 1–48; Hamar Foster, "Forgotten Arguments: Aboriginal Title and Sovereignty in Canada Jurisdiction Act Cases," *Manitoba Law Journal* (1991–92): 343–89; Kent McNeil, "Sovereignty and the Aboriginal Nations of Rupert's Land," *Manitoba History* (spring 1999): 37; Kent McNeil, "Negotiated Sovereignty: Indian Treaties and the Acquisition of American and Canadian Territorial Rights in the Pacific Northwest," in *The Power of Promises: Rethinking Indian Treaties in the Pacific Northwest*, ed. Alexandra Harmon (Seattle: University of Washington Press, 2008), 35–55; and Louis A. Knafla, "Treasonous Murder: The Trial of Ambroise Lépine, 1874," in *Canadian State Trials Volume III: Political Trials and Security Measures, 1840–1914*, ed. Barry Wright and Susan Binnie (Toronto: University of Toronto Press, 2009). For other historical regions and temporalities, see also Mark D. Walters, "The Extension of Colonial Criminal Jurisdiction over the Aboriginal Peoples of Upper Canada: Reconsidering the *Shawanakiskie* Case (1822–26)," *University of Toronto Law Journal* 46 (1996): 273; Katherine A. Hermes, "Jurisdiction in the Colonial Northeast: Algonquian, English, and French Governance," *American Journal of Legal History* 43:1 (January 1999): 52–73; and Sidney Harring, *White Man's Law: Native People in Nineteenth-Century Canadian Jurisprudence*, published for the Osgoode Society for Canadian Legal History (Toronto: University of Toronto Press, 1998).

20. Lauren Benton, *A Search for Sovereignty: Law and Geography in European Empires 1400–1900* (Cambridge: Cambridge University Press, 2010), 2.

21. Mariana Valverde, "Jurisdiction as Scale: Legal 'Technicalities' as Resources for Theory," *Social & Legal Studies* 18 (2009): 144.

22. Cole Harris, *Making Native Space: Colonialism, Resistance, and Reserves in British Columbia* (Vancouver: University of British Columbia Press, 2002), xvi.

23. "Other-than-human" is a profound alternative to the anthropocentric "nonhuman" used to describe human–nature relations in a range of disciplines. It comes via Zoe Todd, "Fish Pluralities: Human–Animal Relations and Sites of Engagement in Paulatuuq, Arctic Canada," *Études/Inuit/Studies* 38:1–2 (2014): 217–22.

24. Michael Asch, *Home and Native Land: Aboriginal Rights and the Canadian Constitution* (Toronto: Methuen, 1984), 30.

25. Shaunnagh Dorsett and Shaun McVeigh, "Questions of Jurisdiction," in *Jurisprudence of Jurisdiction,* ed. Shaun McVeigh (Oxford: Routledge-Cavendish, 2007), 4.

26. Ibid. However, as Jennifer Nedelsky has pointed out to me, jurisdiction does not wholly precede law in all cases, for example, in cases where the province creates municipal authority and jurisdiction. However, the foundation for these latter forms of establishing jurisdiction are premised on the initial inauguration of jurisdiction of the federal or provincial governments in the British North America Act of 1867, which adopted the common law that had been in practice in the British colonial regime and was inaugurated through the doctrine of reception.

27. Lauren Benton and Richard J. Ross, eds., *Legal Pluralism and Empires, 1500–1850* (New York and London: New York University Press, 2013), 6.

28. Benton and Ross name several kinds of obfuscation found in the field of legal pluralism studies (ibid., 4–5).

29. For an Anglophone genealogy of the idea, see Quentin Skinner, "The Sovereign State: A Genealogy," in *Sovereignty in Fragments: The Past, Present and Future of a Contested Concept,* ed. Hent Kalmo and Quentin Skinner (Cambridge: Cambridge University Press, 2010).

30. Ibid., 27.

31. James Tully, "Aboriginal Property and Western Theory: Recovering a Middle Ground," *Social Philosophy and Policy* 11:2 (June 1994): 156.

32. James (Sákéj) Youngblood Henderson, "The Context of the State of Nature," in *Reclaiming Indigenous Voice and Vision,* ed. Marie Battiste (Vancouver and Toronto: University of British Columbia Press, 2000), 16-17.

33. Skinner, "The Sovereign State," 34–36.

34. Michael Asch, "Canadian Sovereignty and Universal History," *Storied Communities: Narratives of Contact and Arrival in Constituting Political Community,* ed. Hester Lessard, Rebecca Johnson, and Jeremy Webber. (Vancouver and Toronto: University of British Columbia Press, 2011), 33.

35. Supreme Court of British Columbia, *Delgamuukw et al. v the Queen* (1991), Reasons for Judgment of the Honourable Chief Justice Allan McEachern, Number 0843, Smithers Registry. 38 B.C.L.R., 3. See also James B. Waldram, Pat Berringer, and Wayne Warry, " 'Nasty, Brutish and Short': Anthropology and the Gitksan-Wet'suwet'en Decision," *Canadian Journal of Native Studies* 12:2 (1992): 309–11.

36. Karena Shaw, *Indigeneity and Political Theory: Sovereignty and the Limits of the Political* (New York: Routledge, 2008), 9.

37. Reasons for Judgment of the Honourable Chief Justice Allan McEachern. Number 0843, Smithers Registry. 38 B.C.L.R., 224–25. So why submit to the authority of the courts at all? Because, as Haudenosaunee lawyer Aaron Detlor has stated simply, "they impact us" (Aaron Detlor, "Haudenosaunee Nationhood," *Nation to Nation Now Symposium: The Conversations, Conference, OISE, Toronto, Ontario,* March 23, 2013). As Detlor could attest, domestic courts have not necessarily been Indigenous peoples' first choice for adjudication, either. For a discussion of Cayuga leader Deskáheh's international advocacy at the League of Nations in the 1920s, see Amar Bhatia, "The South of the North: Building on Critical Approaches to International Law with Lessons from the Fourth World," *Oregon Review of International Law* 14 (2012): 131–76.

38. Archille Mbembe, *On the Postcolony* (Berkeley, Los Angeles, and London: University of California Press, 2001).

39. Sunera Thobani, *Exalted Subjects: Studies in the Making of Race and Nation in Canada* (Toronto: University of Toronto Press, 2007), 63–64.

40. David Armitage, *Declarations of Independence: A Global History* (Cambridge: Harvard University Press, 2008), 103–4; quotes in Ford, *Settler Sovereignty*, 4.

41. Ibid.

42. Ibid., 2.

43. I would argue that the same principle applies to civil law and other European legal traditions more broadly.

44. Shaunnagh Dorsett, "Thinking Jurisdictionally: A Genealogy of Native Title," dissertation, Sydney, University of New South Wales, 2005, 242–43.

45. Luana Ross, *Inventing the Savage: The Social Construction of Native American Criminality* (Austin: University of Texas Press, 1998).

46. See Heidi Kiiwetinepinesiik Stark, "Criminal Empire: The Making of the Savage in a Lawless Land," *Theory and Event* 19:4 (2016): page numbers unavailable.

47. Michael Witgen, *An Infinity of Nations: How the Native World Shaped Early North America* (Philadelphia: University of Pennsylvania Press, 2012), 327.

48. For instance, the American Revolution could not establish even a semblance of sovereignty in the northwestern region of the country until it negotiated the Jay Treaty with Great Britain in 1794. But even then, British forces did not withdraw commitment to their political alliances, continuing to dispense gifts and to trade, and the Anishnabe continued to reaffirm these relationships (ibid.). In 1812, the border had still not been precisely defined, nor was it immediately consequential, because Indigenous peoples in Canada and the United States refused to respect imperial territorial boundaries in the area.

49. Ibid., 12.

50. Ibid., 14.

51. Ibid., 28.

52. *R. v Sparrow* (1990) 1 S.C.R. 1075, 56 C.C.C. (3d) 263 (hereafter, *Sparrow*); emphasis added; cited in Foster, "Forgotten Arguments" (346), where he takes great pains to expose this statement as fabrication. Ronald Sparrow was charged under Fisheries Act for casting too large a drift net in the Fraser River in British Columbia. The court dealt with the question of whether Sparrow (as a member of the Musqueam Nation) could assert an Aboriginal right to fish that would override federal regulations requiring a fishing permit and restricting the method of fishing.

53. Ibid., 353.

54. Ibid., 354. Foster cites Johnson to John Tabor Kempe, October 7, 1765, quoted in F. Jennings, "Tribal Loyalty and Tribal Independence," in Esmond Wright, ed., *Red, White and True Blue: The Loyalists in the Revolution* (New York: AMS Press, 1976), 22–23.

55. As Michel Foucault wrote, "History was a ritual that reinforced sovereignty" (*Society Must Be Defended: Lectures at the Collège de France, 1975–76* [New York: Picador, 2003], 69). Another way of expressing the concept of the "epistemic web" is expressed best by Ludwig Wittgenstein, *Philosophical Investigations*, trans. G. E. M. Anscombe (Oxford: Blackwell, 1968), no. 115. The full aphorism reads: "A *picture* held us captive. And we could not get outside it, for it lay in our language and language seemed to repeat it to us inexorably."

56. Foucault, *Society Must Be Defended*. See also Andrew Neal, "Cutting Off the

King's Head: Foucault's *Society Must Be Defended* and the Problem of Sovereignty,"
Alternatives: Global, Local, Political 29:4 (August–October 2004): 373–98, especially
his discussion of whether Foucault succeeds, in his own terms, in cutting off the
king's head. While most criticism is focused on Foucault's ambiguous critique of
sovereignty in the juridico-philosophical register, Neal finds Foucault's engagement with sovereignty in the historico-political register to provide a productive site
of normative contestation, because history is a "ritual that reinforced sovereignty"
(Foucault, *Society Must Be Defended*, 69).

57. *Delgamuukw v British Columbia* (1997), 3 SCR 1010, paragraph 18–19.

58. As Val Napoleon notes, "When laws are broken with no recourse, the legal
order begins to break down and this has been the experience of Indigenous peoples"
("Thinking about Indigenous Legal Orders," 10).

59. Of course, sovereignty can also emerge and be maintained through banal
geopolitical practices. See Fiona McConnell, "The Fallacy and the Promise of the
Territorial Trap: Sovereign Articulations of Geopolitical Anomalies," *Geopolitics* 15
(2010): 765. For example, through public-relations stunts like the one orchestrated
by Prime Minister Stephen Harper who used the discovery of the ill-fated two
hundred-year-old ship the HMS *Erebus* to declare that the finding "laid the foundations of Canada's Arctic sovereignty" (Parks Canada, "Statement by the Prime
Minister of Canada Announcing the Discovery of One of the Ill-Fated Franklin Expedition Ships Lost in 1846," news release, Ottawa, September 9, 2014).

60. Kent McNeil, "Indigenous Land Rights and Self-Government: Inseparable
Entitlements," in *Between Indigenous and Settler Governance*, ed. Lisa Ford and Tim
Rowse (New York: Routledge, 2013), 145–46.

61. For further discussion on the doctrine of reception, see Henderson, Benson, and Findlay, *Aboriginal Tenure in the Constitution of Canada*, and for my own
discussion, in relation to jurisdiction, see "Jurisdiction and Settler Colonialism," in
particular 155–60.

62. Peter Fitzpatrick, " 'No Higher Duty': *Mabo* and the Failure of Legal Foundation," *Law and Critique* 13 (2002): 239.

63. Ibid., 247.

64. Kerry Wilkins, "Reasoning with the Elephant: The Crown, Its Counsel and
Aboriginal Law in Canada," *Indigenous Law Journal* 13:1 (2016): 55.

65. Onuf, "Sovereignty," 430.

66. Ibid.

67. Valverde, "Jurisdiction as Scale," 141.

68. Mariana Valverde, *Chronotopes of Law: Jurisdiction, Scale and Governance*
(New York: Routledge, 2015), 58.

69. Annelise Riles, "A New Agenda for the Cultural Study of Law: Taking on
the Technicalities," *Buff. L. Rev.* 53 (2005–6), 977. Riles's concept of the blueprint
describes how conflict of laws jurisprudence "locate[s] its energy in the production
of a technology, a blueprint for a thing, a set of doctrines and methods for resolving real disputes," which she flags as a crucial point for cultural theorists of law to
understand concerning the technicalities of law.

70. Chief Justice Antonio Lamer, *Delgamuukw* (1998) 1 *Canadian Native Law
Reporter* 44.

71. *Tsilhqot'in Nation v British Columbia* (2014) SCC 44 (hereafter, *Tsilhqot'in*).

72. Kent McNeil, "Aboriginal Title and the Division of Powers: Rethinking

Federal and Provincial Jurisdiction," *Saskatchewan Law Review* 61:2 (1998): 463, emphasis added. In *Delgamuukw,* after establishing that the province of British Columbia has no legislative authority to extinguish Aboriginal title owing to the constitutional divisions of power (and related matters), Lamar then shockingly grants provinces the authority to infringe on Aboriginal title, elbowing aside the painstakingly established authority of the federal government over Indians. Constitutional protections for Aboriginal title were further eviscerated in the 2014 *Tsilhqot'in* decision. Chief Justice Beverley McLachlin determined that conflicts between the federal and provincial governments regarding which law applies are not to be resolved through a heads-of-exclusive-power determination (the interjurisdictional immunity principles, to be precise). She determined that it no longer matters that the federal Crown governs Indians exclusively under 91(24). More relevant is that the constitutionality of provincial laws must be resolved pursuant to Section 35(1) constitutional protections and *Sparrow.*

73. The doctrine of paramountcy determines that federal law prevails where conflict arises with provincial law. Paramountcy developed in modern constitutions internally divided into states or provinces under a centralized government. In Canada, different theories have been presented over the years as to how and when paramountcy arises. Except for the opening words of Section 91 of the Constitution Act of 1867, which stipulate that all residual matters not governed under provincial jurisdiction fall to the federal government, the constitution is silent on federal paramountcy. The preamble to specific clauses states: "in relation to all Matters not coming within the Classes of Subjects by this Act assigned exclusively to the Legislatures of the Provinces," thereby rendering all matter not explicitly delegated to provinces to be de facto under federal jurisdiction. The Supreme Court of Canada resolved the matter by concluding that *conflict* yields paramountcy (*Smith v the Queen* [1960] SCR 776). In other words, and somewhat nonsensically, the source of ultimate federal authority is *conflict over authority.* Specifically, the courts have determined that federal law prevails where conflict arises with provincial law, rendering the latter inoperative. In this way, paramountcy doctrine creates two levels of government out of the totality of plenary power in Canada. In cases where federal or provincial law or legislation do not overlap, but rather intrude on one another's exclusive jurisdictional authority, the doctrine of interjurisdictional authority is applied. Federal paramountcy does not come into play because interjurisdictional immunity deals with the extent to which legislation is applicable when provincial or federal intrudes on another's head of power. In these cases, the principle of paramountcy is replaced by a principle of exclusivity regarding the constitutional divisions of power.

74. Valverde, "Jurisdiction as Scale," 141. Or, as Neil Brenner puts it, scale exists as an organizing logic alongside a "broader, polymorphic and multi-faceted geographic field" of spatial differentiation that orders jurisdiction ("The Limits to Scale? Methodological Reflections on Scalar Structuration," *Progress in Human Geography* 25:4 [2001]: 591–614).

75. Valverde, "Jurisdiction as Scale," 142.

76. Rebecca Aird, "Alienation of Traditional Lands through Conflicting Uses," report for the Algonquins of Barriere Lake, 1990, 10.

77. Section 109 in the British North America Act (1867), then Section 92a in the patriated constitution (1982).

78. Interjurisdictional immunity is a doctrine that dictates that one level of government's legislation is inapplicable to the extent that it intrudes on the core of

another's head of power. See, for example, *Canadian Western Bank v. Alberta* (2007) SCC 22.

79. Aird, "Alienation of Traditional Lands through Conflicting Uses," 13.

80. The exercise of this authority is accomplished through the public territory land-use plan. The Ministère des Forêts, de la Faune et des Parcs (Ministry of Forests, Wildlife, and Parks) (MFFP) has powers to promote and regulate recreational activities and forestry, which have had a substantial impact on Barriere Lake's traditional land use because they are forced to compete with tourists and loggers in the area.

81. Aird, "Alienation of Traditional Lands through Conflicting Uses," 16.

82. Ibid., 4.

83. Dorsett and McVeigh, "Questions of Jurisdiction," 5.

84. Neil Brenner, "A Thousand Leaves: Notes on the Geographies of Uneven Spatial Development," in *The New Political Economy of Scale,* ed. Roger Keil and Rianne Mahon (Vancouver: University of British Columbia Press, 2009), 38.

85. Engin Isin, "City.State: Critique of Scalar Thought," *Citizenship Studies* 11:2 (May 2007): 216.

86. Ibid.

87. Ibid.

88. Gilbert Paterson, *Land Settlement in Upper Canada, 1783–1840.* Sixteenth Report of the Department of Archives for the Province of Ontario, 1920 (Toronto: King's Printer, 1921), 26.

89. Valverde, "Jurisdiction as Scale," 144.

90. Mazan Labban, "History, Space and Nature: Building Theory from the Exception," *New Political Economy* 16:2 (April 2011): 253–59.

91. Neil Smith, *Uneven Development: Nature, Capital and the Production of Space* (Oxford: Blackwell, 1984).

92. Sarah de Leeuw, Emilie Cameron, and Margot Greenwood, "Participatory and Community-Based Research, Indigenous Geographies, and the Spaces of Friendship: A Critical Engagement," *Canadian Geographer* 56:2 (2012): 188. I also found the work of Adam Gaudry particularly good in this regard. See "Insurgent Research," *Wicazo Sa Review* (spring 2011): 113–36.

93. David Harvey, *The New Imperialism* (New York: Oxford University Press, 2003), 33.

94. Timothy Mitchell, "One: The Stage of Modernity," in *Questions of Modernity,* ed. Timothy Mitchell (Minneapolis: University of Minnesota Press, 2000), 10.

95. Ibid.

96. Stuart Banner, *How the Indians Lost Their Lands: Law and Power on the Frontier* (Cambridge: Harvard University Press, 2007); Anthony Hall, *Earth into Property: Colonization, Decolonization, and Capitalism* (Montreal: McGill-Queen's University Press, 2010); Cheryl I. Harris, "Whiteness as Property," *Harvard Law Review* 106:8 (June 1993): 1721; Joseph Singer, "Re-Reading Property," *New England Law Review* 26 (1991–92): 719; Nigel Bankes, Sharon Mascher, and Jonnette Watson Hamilton, "The Recognition of Title and Its Relationship with Settler State Land Titles Systems," *UBC Law Review* 47:3 (2014): 829–88; Pamela Palmater, "Opportunity or Temptation? Plans for Private Property on Reserves Could Cost First Nations Their Independence," book review of T. Flanagan, C. Alcantara, A. Le Dressay, *Beyond the Indian Act: Restoring Aboriginal Property Rights* (Toronto: *Literary Review of Canada,* 2010), http://reviewcandad.ca/magazine/2010/04/opportunity-or-temptation.

97. See, for example, Brian Egan and Jessica Place, "Minding the Gaps: Property, Geography, and Indigenous Peoples in Canada," *Geoforum* 44 (2013): 129–38. In this very good article about the ways in which the settler state schemes to introduce property rights for Indigenous peoples to "fix" the gaps in the nation's social, economic, and political constitution, the authors admit to struggling with a way to describe the forms of landholding Indigenous peoples aim to protect. They land on several non-Indigenous accounts of Indigenous relational ontologies, including Bradley Bryan's article, which I too lean on in my work ("Property as Ontology: Aboriginal and English Understandings of Ownership," *Canadian Journal of Law and Jurisprudence* 13 [2000]: 3–31). One notable exception to this tendency is Richard Overstall's excellent essay "Encountering the Spirit in the Land: 'Property' in a Kinship-Based Legal Order," in *Despotic Dominion: Property Rights in British Settler Societies*, ed. John McLaren, A. R. Buck, and Nancy E. Wright (Vancouver: University of British Columbia Press, 2005), 22–49. See also my review of anthropological debates in chapter 4 on whether "Indians" had "property" prior to contact.

98. *Calder v. British Columbia (Attorney General)* (1973) S.C.R. 313, (1973) 4 W.W.R (hereafter, *Calder*).

99. Russell Diabo, "Harper Launches Major First Nations Termination Plan: As Negotiating Tables Legitimize Canada's Colonialism," *Intercontinental Cry*, November 9, 2012. Accessed online May 17, 2016: https://intercontinentalcry.org/harper-launches-major-first-nations-termination-plan-as-negotiating-tables-legitimize-canadas-colonialism/.

100. Leila Abu-Lughod, "The Romance of Resistance: Tracing Transformations of Power through Bedouin Women," *American Ethnologist* 17 (1990): 41–45.

101. I want to make clear that the use of force as I describe it does not define the totality of what we could broadly term "state violence." Sarah de Leeuw insists that an overemphasis on land-based struggles in critical scholarship can ignore the daily, slow violence of colonialism. As she puts it, a focus on land, territory, or resources can eclipse the "tender geographies" of intimate and embodied spaces of Indigenous women and children (Sarah de Leeuw, "Tender Grounds: Intimate Visceral Violence and British Columbia's Colonial Geographies," *Political Geography* 52 [2016]: 14–23). Although focused on land struggle, I have tried to demonstrate the multiplicity of forms of violence deployed against the community. Here I focus on a cluster of technique we could roughly call "pacification" strategies.

102. Jeffrey Monaghan, "Settler Governmentality and Racializing Surveillance in Canada's North-West," *Canadian Journal of Sociology* 38:4 (2013): 487. The definition of settler colonialism as primarily focused on acquisition of territory and the elimination of the native is Patrick Wolfe's intellectual contribution ("Settler Colonialism and the Elimination of the Native," *Journal of Genocide Research* 8:4 [December 2006]: 387–409).

103. Labban, "History, Space and Nature."

104. "Police Standoff in the Sacred Headwaters," YouTube video, posted by Beyond Boarding, published on July 2, 2014, https://www.youtube.com/watch?v=y4_U2DRYEwA&feature=youtu.be; accessed November 10, 2015.

105. Michael Toledano, "Unist'ot'en Evict TransCanada Helicopter amid Fear of RCMP Raid," *Ricochet*, September 6, 2015.

106. *Platinex Inc. v. Kitchenuhmaykoosib Inninuwug First Nation* (2008), CanLII 11049 (ON SC), 12.

107. David Peerla, "No Means No: The Kitchenuhmaykooub Inninuwug and the Fight for Indigenous Resource Sovereignty," self-published, 2012, http://www .miningwatch.ca/sites/www.mininwatch.ca/files/No%20Means%No.pdf; accessed December 22, 2016.

108. Interview with Sarita Ahooja, "Terry Sappier, Maliseet Nation of Tobique," Isuma TV, Winnipeg. Manitoba, November 2008, http://www.isuma.tv/defenders -lanf/terry-sappier; accessed December 22, 2016.

1. Flipping the Terms of Recognition

1. See Victoria Freeman, "Indigenous Hauntings in Settler-Colonial Spaces: The Activism of Indigenous Ancestors in the City of Toronto," in *Phantom Past, Indigenous Presence: Native Ghosts in North American Culture and History,* ed. Colleen E. Boyd and Coll Thrush (Lincoln: University of Nebraska Press, 2011). Freeman cautions, however, that the "creation and migration stories in oral tradition, archaeological evidence, and linguistic analysis do not cohere to provide easy answers accepted by all concerning the question of their origins, movements, or the length of their occupation" (217).

2. Notable exceptions include Nicholas Blomley, *Unsettling the City: Urban Land and the Politics of Property* (New York: Routledge, 2004); Evelyn Peters, *Three Myths about Aboriginals in Cities* (Ottawa: Canadian Federation for the Humanities and Social Sciences, 2004); Ryan Walker, Ted Jojola, and David Natcher, eds., *Reclaiming Indigenous Planning* (Montreal: McGill-Queens University Press, 2013); and Heather Dorries, "Rejecting the 'False Choice': Foregrounding Indigenous Sovereignty in Planning, Theory, and Practice," dissertation, University of Toronto, 2012. This field of academic scholarship is growing, however, at a fast pace.

3. Victoria Freeman, "'Toronto Has No History!' Indigeneity, Settler Colonialism, and Historical Memory in Canada's Largest City," *Urban History Review* 38:2 (2010): 22.

4. Patrick Wolfe, "Settler Colonialism and the Elimination of the Native," *Journal of Genocide Research* 8:4 (December 2006): 388.

5. Ibid., 389.

6. Despite his inclusion as an advisory committee member, owing to a bout of illness he experienced during my final editing phase, I did not come to share my work with James Morrison.

7. The Honorable Mr. Justice Robert M. Mainville, *Casey Ratt et al. v Jean Maurice Matchewan et al.*, Reasons for Judgment and Judgment, Docket: T-654–09, Citation: 2010 FC 160, Ottawa, Ontario, February 17, 2010.

8. The Honorable Mr. Justice Zinn, *Harry Wawatie et al. v Minister of Indian Affairs and Northern Development*, T-462–08, Citation 2009 FC 8, Ottawa, Ontario, January 6, 2009.

9. It took almost a year from June 2010 to obtain university approval. At one point, after a third set of minor revisions were submitted to the Research Ethics Office, I waited four months for a response only to discover that these revisions had been misplaced by the office. My file had also been transferred midway through to the Innovations and Partnership Division of the university because this office processes agreements regarding access to proprietary materials or data for research purposes, referred there because of the mention of land claims research in my

application. This office then erroneously assigned a Physical Sciences, Engineering, and Information Technology Division person to my case because my co-supervisor Scott Prudham co-teaches in the Department of Environmental Studies.

10. See also Renee Pualani Louis, "Can You Hear Us Now? Voices from the Margin: Using Indigenous Methodologies in Geographic Research," *Geographic Research* 45:2 (June 2007): 130–39; and Jay Johnson, Garth Cant, Richard Howitt, and Evelyn Peters, "Guest Editorial: Creating Anti-Colonial Geographies: Embracing Indigenous Peoples' Knowledges and Rights," *Geographical Research* 45:2 (June 2007):117–20.

11. Shawn Wilson, "What Is an Indigenous Methodology?" *Canadian Journal of Native Education* 25:2 (2001): 177.

12. Deborah McGregor, Walter Bayha, and Deborah Simmons, "'Our Responsibility to Keep the Land Alive': Voices of Northern Indigenous Researchers," *Pimatisiwin: A Journal of Aboriginal and Indigenous Community Health* 8:1 (2010): 111.

13. On these colonial grounds of recognition, see Glen S. Coulthard, "Subjects of Empire: Indigenous Peoples and the 'Politics of Recognition' in Canada," *Contemporary Political Theory* 6 (2007): 437–60.

14. Albert Memmi, *The Colonizer and the Colonized,* 2d ed., trans. Howard Greenfield (Boston: Beacon Press, 1967), 38.

15. Leanne Simpson, "Oshkimaadiziig, the New People," in *Lighting the Eighth Fire: The Liberation, Resurgence, and Protection of Indigenous Nations,* ed. Leanne Simpson (Winnipeg: Arbeiter Ring Press, 2008), 14.

16. Ibid.

17. See also Derek Gregory, "(Post)Colonialism and the Production of Nature," in *Social Nature: Theory, Practice and Politics,* ed. Noel Castree and Bruce Braun (Malden, Mass.: Blackwell Publishers, 2001), 1814–25. For a more contemporary critique of the nature–society binary in the context of state–Indigenous relations in Canada, see Anna Stanley, "Wasted Life: Labour, Liveliness, and the Production of Value," *Antipode* 47:3 (2015): 792–811.

18. Juanita Sundberg and Jessica Dempsey, "Culture/Natures," in *International Encyclopedia of Human Geography,* vol. 2, ed. R. Kitchin and N. Thrift (Oxford: Elsevier, 2009), 458–63.

19. Jay T. Johnson and Brian Murton, "Re/placing Native Science: Indigenous Voices in Contemporary Constructions of Nature," *Geographical Research* 45:2 (June 2007): 127.

20. Juanita Sundberg, "Decolonizing Posthumanist Geographies," *Cultural Geographies* 21:1 (2014): 35 (internal endnotes excluded).

21. Zoe Todd, "An Indigenous Feminist's Take on the Ontological Turn: 'Ontology' Is Just Another Word for Colonialism," *Journal of Historical Sociology* 29:1 (March 2016): 4–22.

22. Glen Coulthard, Vincent Dias, J. Kehaulani Kauanui, and Robert Warrior, "Settler Colonialism and the Question of Indigenous Studies: A Position Paper and Three Responses," American Studies Association, conference, Toronto, October 8, 2015.

23. Louis, "Can You Hear Us Now?" 134.

24. Sharon H. Venne, "Treaties Made in Good Faith," in *Natives and Settlers, Now and Then: Historical Issues and Current Perspectives on Treaties and Land Claims in Canada,* ed. Paul W. DePasquale (Edmonton: University of Alberta Press, 2007), 5.

25. James (Sakej) Youngblood Henderson, "Interpreting *Sui Generis* Treaties," *Alberta Law Review* 36:1 (1997): 50.

26. Michael Asch, *On Being Here to Stay* (Toronto: University of Toronto Press, 2014), 75.

27. Ibid. For a wonderful meditation on these questions, see also the excellent work of Amar Bhatia, "We Are All Here to Stay? Indigeneity, Migration, and 'Decolonizing' the Right to Be Here," *Windsor Y B Access J* 31 (2013): 39–64, and "The South of the North," 131.

28. In a mediation judgment that dates back to 1997, Quebec Superior Court Judge Réjean Paul concluded that the Trilateral Agreement would likely be considered to be of treaty status if challenged in the courts.

29. Russell Diabo, "Canada's War on First Nations," presentation at Indigenous Sovereignty Week, Ottawa, Ontario, October 2009.

30. Frantz Fanon, *Black Skin, White Masks*, trans. Richard Philcox (New York: Grove Press, 2008), 72, where he approvingly cites Francis Jeanson.

31. For a lengthy discussion on this point, see Vic Satzewich and Terry Wotherspoon, *First Nations: Race, Class, Gender Relations* (Scarborough, Ontario: Nelson Canada, 1993).

32. Smith writes: "This way, our alliances would not be solely based on shared victimization, but where we are complicit in the victimization of others. These approaches might help us to develop resistance strategies that do not inadvertently keep the system in place for all of us, and keep all of us accountable. In all of these cases, we would check our aspirations against the aspirations of other communities to ensure that our model of liberation does not become the model of oppression for others" (Andrea Smith, "Heteropatriarchy and the Three Pillars of White Supremacy: Rethinking Women of Color Organizing," in *Color of Violence: The INCITE! Anthology, INCITE! Women of Color Against Violence* [Boston: South End Press, 2006], 69).

33. Memmi, *The Colonizer and the Colonized*.

2. How Did Colonialism Fail to Dispossess?

1. Cole Harris, "How Did Colonialism Dispossess? Comments from an Edge of Empire," *Annals of the Association of American Geographers* 94:1 (2004): 165–82.

2. Rob Nixon, *Slow Violence and the Environmentalism of the Poor* (Cambridge: Harvard University Press, 2011), 19.

3. Ibid.

4. Harvey, *The New Imperialism*, 33.

5. Aird, "Alienation of Traditional Lands through Conflicting Uses," 1.

6. Nicholas A. Brown, "The Logic of Settler Accumulation in a Landscape of Perpetual Vanishing," *Settler Colonial Studies* 4:1 (2014): 7.

7. This is the teaching of the Onakinakewin as told to me by Toby Decoursay on multiple occasions.

8. Morrison, "Algonquin History in the Ottawa River Watershed," 20.

9. Benton-Banai, *The Mishomis Book*, 3.

10. Ojibwe, Ottawa, and Salteaux belong to the Middle Tier, which is defined by linguists as a single language with mutually understandable dialects. See Carl F. Voegelin and Florence M. Voegelin "Linguistic Considerations of Northeastern North

America," in *Man in Northeastern North America, Papers of the Robert S. Peabody Foundation for Archaeology* 3, ed. Frederick Johnson (Andover: Mass. 1946): 178–94.

11. The origins of the term might derive from the Maliseet term *elakomwik*, meaning "they are our relatives (or allies)" (Morrison, "Algonquin History in the Ottawa River Watershed," 24, www.thealgonquinway.ca/pdf/algonquin-history .pdf; accessed July 12, 2010).

12. Ibid., 2.

13. Ibid., 24. Thanks are also due here to Sue Roark-Calnek for interpreting for me the connotations of these French designations.

14. Ibid.

15. Michel Thusky, in telephone discussion with author, May 28, 2012.

16. See *R. v Marshall* (1999) 3 S.C.R. 456.

17. Norman Matchewan, in discussion with the author, July 13, 2010, Barriere Lake.

18. Peter Douglas Elias, *Socio-Economic Profile of the Algonquins of Barriere Lake,* January 1996 (revised August 2002), prepared for the Algonquin Nation Secretariat.

19. Ibid., 10.

20. Toby Decoursay, in discussion with author, July 13, 2010, Barriere Lake.

21. Morrison, "Algonquin History in the Ottawa River Watershed," 28.

22. James Morrison, "Report on Treaties of 1760 to 1764," prepared for the Algonquin Nation Secretariat, March 2006.

23. Ibid.

24. John Borrows, "Wampum at Niagara: The Royal Proclamation, Canadian Legal History, and Self-Government," in *Aboriginal and Treaty Rights in Canada: Essays on Law, Equality, and Respect for Difference,* ed. Michael Asch (Vancouver: University of British Columbia Press, 1997).

25. Ibid, 163.

26. Ibid, 163–65.

27. Russell Diabo, in discussion with author, November 12, 2011. His point extends from the terms of Article 40 of the Articles of Capitulation, which read as follows: "The savages of Indian allies of his most Christian Majesty, *shall be maintained in the lands they inhabit, if they chuse to remain there*; they shall not be molested on any pretence whatsoever, for having carried arms, and served his most Christian Majesty; they shall have, as well as the French, liberty of religion, and shall keep their missionaries. The actual Vicars, General, and the Bishop, when the Episcopal See shall be filled, shall have leave to send to them new missionaries when they shall judge it necessary" (emphasis added).

28. Dickason, *Canada's First Nations,* 78.

29. Canadian Broadcasting Corporation (CBC), Transcript of wampum presentation to First Ministers Conference, television coverage of presentation of wampum belts to First Ministers Conference by Algonquin delegation, March 1987. Transcribed by Nadine Guadaur, January 26, 2004, at Timiskaming First Nation, Quebec. Edits by Peter Di Gangi, Ottawa, January 26, 2004.

30. This statement is not meant to infer that treaties actually mean land surrenders and cessions, only that this is how governments came to narrowly interpret them.

31. Aird, "Alienation of Traditional Lands through Conflicting Uses," 1.

32. Peter Di Gangi, "Algonquins of Barriere Lake: Man-Made Impacts on the Community and Fish and Wildlife, 1870–1979," prepared for the Algonquins of

Barriere Lake, March 2003, 6. On the point of epidemics, Di Gangi focuses on the 1880s, citing the following archival sources: NA RG10 Vol. 2119 File 22, 639 Reel C-11—Maniwaki Reserve—Outbreak of Smallpox (1880–85): Logue to DSGIA August 10, 1880 (RN 7966); NA RG10 Vol. 2402 File 83, 709 Reel C-11, 215—Maniwaki Agency. Correspondence regarding Dr. Joseph Comeau, Physician to the River Desert Band (1888–90): Martin to SGIA, February 25, 1888 (RN 8311); Canada, "Annual Report of the Dept of Indian Affairs for the Year ended 31st December 1889" (Ottawa: Brown Chamberlin, Queen's Printer, 1890), Part 1, 34–35: James Martin to SGIA, August 15, 1889 (RN 4837). NA RG10 Vol. 2511, File 105,670, Reel C-11,232— River Desert Agency—Request of the Chiefs of the River Desert Band for a grant or loan of $500 to pay debts incurred through sickness and death caused by various diseases during the past year (1890); Petition from Maniwaki Chiefs to Indian Affairs, April 29, 1890 (RN 7979).

33. Elias, *Socio-Economic Profile of the Algonquins of Barriere Lake*, 18.

34. Peter Di Gangi investigated contributions of the Ottawa Valley to the provincial treasury during this period. He examined Quebec's first statistical handbook, published in 1913, which, he reports, "split the province into fourteen regions for the purposes of managing the timber harvest. Two of those regions were the 'Upper Ottawa' and the 'Lower Ottawa.' Between 1870 and 1913, the Upper Ottawa generated $16,762,745.00 in provincial government revenues—48.5% of the total. In the same period timber harvesting on the Lower Ottawa contributed $3,624,026.00 to provincial coffers—10.5% of the total. Together, then, these two regions generated 59% of Quebec's revenues from timber for the period 1870–1913" ("Algonquins of Barriere Lake," 4). According to William Ryan, wood products were in third place among Quebec manufacturing industries between 1870 to 1900, foregrounding how definitively Barriere Lake lands underwrote a significant segment of Quebec's industrial development. See William Ryan, *The Clergy and Economic Growth in Quebec (1896–1914)* (Quebec City: Presses de l'Université Laval, 1966).

35. Paul-André Linteau, René Durocher, and Jean-Claude Robert, *Quebec: A History, 1867–1929* (Toronto: James Lorimer & Company, 1983), 111.

36. Di Gangi, "Algonquins of Barriere Lake," 5.

37. Linteau, Durocher, and Robert, *Quebec*, 114.

38. Ibid., 115.

39. Leigh Ogston, "Algonquins of Barriere Lake Historical Report," prepared for the Algonquins of Barriere Lake, November 1987. At page 167 she cites Anastase Roi, *Maniwake et la vallée de la Gatineau* (Ottawa: Presses du "droit," 1933), 65.

40. Ibid., 171.

41. DIA District Manager to Secretary, "Flooding at Barriere," letter, File 373/30–22–0, Vol. 1, Hudson's Bay Company, North Bay, Ontario, August 22, 1929.

42. Di Gangi, "Algonquins of Barriere Lake," 19. He cites John A. Dales, *Hydroelectricity and Industrial Development in Quebec, 1890–1940* (Cambridge: Harvard University Press, 1957), 147–48.

43. Ontario Ministry of Natural Resources, Peterborough, Land Files, Report, File 89405, "Diversion of Waters from the Ottawa River Watershed to the Gatineau River Watershed, County of Pontiac," Quebec, 1932, 1.

44. In December 1940, Quebec set aside this corridor through an Order-in-Council, designating the ten-mile strip as a "tourist reserve." This move led to bitter complaints, not only by Barriere Lake but by the Algonquins of Lac Simon and Grand Lac. See National Archives Canada, RG10 Vol. 6751, File 420–10X Pt.3, Reel

C-8106: Quebec Game Laws—Correspondence & reports re: Abitibi & Grand Lake Indian Hunting Preserves, 1938–1940, Reel C-8106–8207: Chief Nicholas Papatie, Grand Lac, to Indian Affairs, August 21, 1940 (RN 1842).

45. Chief Makakos was sent word that the community was forbidden from hunting or fishing within ten miles of the new highway owing to its designation as a tourist showcase and to help recoup costs of the highway (Di Gangi, "Algonquins of Barriere Lake"). Makokos also complained that the settlers were establishing campgrounds without consultation and without any consideration of his members' prior use of those sites.

46. Department of Indian Affairs, Public Archives Canada, Hugh Conn, Grand Lake Victoria Indian Hunting System, 1942 Annual Report, RG10 Vol. 6751, File 420–10x 5.

47. National Archives Canada (NAC), RG10 Vol. 6752, File 420–10–1, Reel C-8107: Report on Fur Conservation Projects in the Province of Quebec & maps by Hugh Conn, circa 1943 (RN 3790).

48. NAC, Report on Fur Conservation Projects in the Province of Quebec & maps by Hugh Conn, circa 1943. In chapter 4 I go into greater detail about this management regime and Hugh Conn's role in designing and implementing it.

49. NAC, RG10 Vol. 6752, File 420–10–1–3, Reel C-8107: Third Annual Report on Grand Lac Victoria Indian Hunting Reserve, 1943 (RN 3789).

50. Di Gangi cites at length from René Lévesque's patrol diary from 1947 ("Algonquins of Barriere Lake," 24).

51. Di Gangi reports that "As late as 1949 they were told by Indian Agent Baker of Maniwaki that if they did not 'make their maps' they would be 'considered as poachers and if they did not act like the others they would soon be punished for trapping illegally.'" Later that year, departmental officials reported that in 1949 the Barriere Indians "rejoined the others and seems satisfied with their results" (ibid., 26, 29).

52. See DIAND QRO File 373–23–4, Vol. 2—Report & returns, Superintendent's Semiannual Reports, Maniwaki Indian Agency (11/57–12/67): Semiannual report from Lorenzo Leclair, Superintendent, Maniwaki Indian Agency, November 30, 1957 (RN 10288); Report of June 5, 1961 (RN 10722); Semiannual report, March 28, 1967 (RN 10722).

53. Father Renaud, director general of the Commission des Œuvres Indiennes et Esquimaudes (COIE) des Pères Oblats was involved on behalf of the oblates to get land set aside for the Barriere Lake Reserve. Leigh Ogston interviewed him on the process: "No one thought about consulting the Indians there in those days. It was just a matter between the different governments. The Chiefs just wanted houses and couldn't understand why they weren't getting them. They did not understand the complicated politics going on between the federal and provincial governments" ("Algonquins of Barriere Lake Historical Report," unpaginated document).

54. QRO File 373–3–8–22, Vol. 1—Complaints & Petitions, Barriere Lake, Caughnawaga District (3/70—4/71): memo to file from C. T., Blouin, Indian Affairs, March 1970 (RN 10295).

55. Ibid.

56. Hugh Shewell, "Enough to Keep Them Alive": Indian Welfare in Canada, 1873–1965 (Toronto: University of Toronto Press, 2004), 26–27.

57. DIAND File 373/30–22–0, Vol. 1., J. Edouard Guay to Department of Mines and Resources, Indian Affairs Branch, October 26, 1945: "The Lands and Forests Act

(section 67, chapter 93, R.S.Q. 1941) gives authority to the Lieutenant-Governor in Council to 'reserve and set apart, for the benefit of the various Indian tribes of the Province of Quebec, the usufruct of public lands described, surveyed and classified for such purpose by the Minister of Lands and Forests.' Said usufruct may be 'transferred gratuitously . . . to the Government of Canada to be administered by it in trust for the said Indian tribes.' "

58. Chamber of the Executive Council, Quebec, Order-in-Council No. 1895, September 7, 1961.

59. DIAND QRO File 373/3–7-22, Vol. 1—Band Management, General, Barriere Lake Band, Montreal District (June 1964–March 1977): report on a meeting with Indian Affairs at Rapid Lake, October 20, 1970, prepared by Kermot Moore (RN 7990).

60. DIAND File E5430–31/0, Vol. 1: Joint Band Council Resolution No. 1 1b re: hunting rights in Grand Lac Preserve, April 11, 1979 (RN 3340).

61. Toby Decoursay, in discussion with author, July 23, 2009, Barriere Lake.

62. Russell Diabo, in discussion with author, November 2011.

63. Toby Decoursay, in discussion with author, July 23, 2009, Barriere Lake.

64. Timothy Mitchell, "The Limits of the State: Beyond Statist Approaches and Their Critics," *American Political Science Review* 85:1 (March 1991): 90; emphasis in original.

65. Ibid., 95.

66. Harold Innis, *The Fur Trade in Canada* (Toronto: University of Toronto Press, 1956). See also Mel Watkins, "Comment: Staples Redux," *Studies in Political Economy* 79 (spring 2007): 213–26.

67. Innis, *The Fur Trade in Canada.*

68. See Trevor J. Barnes, *Logics of Dislocation: Models, Metaphors, and Meanings of Economic Space* (New York: Guilford Press, 1996).

69. Two main schools of political economy have dominated the field in Canada and both owe some debt to the staples theory: the dependency tradition, often called the New Political Economy (NPE) of left-wing nationalism in the 1960s and 1970s, and the anti-imperial, or Marxist, tradition that emerged a bit later. For an overview of these schools of interpretation, see Glen Williams, "Canada in the International Economy," in *The New Canadian Political Economy,* ed. Wallace Clement and Glen Williams (Montreal: McGill-Queen's University, 1989); the autumn 1981 special issue of *Studies in Political Economy* 6; and Jerome Klassen, *Joining Empire: The Political Economy of the New Canadian Foreign Policy* (Toronto: University of Toronto Press, 2012).

70. Paul Kellogg, *Escape from the Staple State: Canadian Political Economy after Left Nationalism* (Toronto: University of Toronto Press, 2015).

71. Michael Howlett, M. Ramesh, and Anthony Perl, *Studying Public Policy* (Toronto: Oxford University Press, 2003), x. According to more recent statistics, this estimate might be high, though it matters how this figure is calculated. Natural Resources Canada puts the figure of Canada's natural resource economy at one-fifth of total gross domestic product (GDP) (July 2015).

72. In terms of trade, in 2014 natural resources accounted for more than half of Canada's merchandise exports (Natural Resources Canada, Key Facts and Figures of the Natural Resource Sector, http://www.nrcan.gc.ca/publications/ key-facts/16013).

73. Foreign direct investment in Canada's natural resource sectors represents 37 percent of total foreign direct investment (Natural Resources Canada, Key Facts and Figures of the Natural Resource Sector, http://www.nrcan.gc.ca/publications/ key-facts/16013). For a general overview of corporate power in Canada, see Klassen, *Joining Empire*.

74. "Canada, Left-Nationalism, and Alternatives: Paul Kellogg interviewed by Robin Chang on Escape from the Staples Trap," *The Bullet*, Socialist Project, E-Bulletin no. 1256, May 13, 2016.

75. Kellogg, *Escape from the Staple Trap*.

76. For a thorough discussion of the more general sidelining of land within critical fields of political economy, see Brett Christophers, "For Real: Land as Capital and Commodity," *Transactions* 41:2 (April 2016): 134–48.

77. Those who tend to consistently raise the alarm about the role of Indigenous peoples in the natural resource economy are often reactionary or politically conservative commentators whose ideological commitments to assimilation and marketization at least force them to acknowledge and analyze the real economic power of First Nations in Canada. See, for example, Bill Gallagher, *Resource Rulers: Fortune and Folly on Canada's Road to Resources*, self-published, 2012.

78. Although Innis believed that native people were part of highly organized societies of "primitive communism" and capable of defending their interests, in his contemporary period he ignored their presence entirely (*Problems of Staple Production in Canada* [Toronto: Ryerson Press, 1933]). See also Stanley Ryerson, *The Founding of Canada: Beginnings to 1815* (Toronto: Progress Books, 1975).

79. Frances Abele and Daiva Stasiulis, "Canada as a 'White Settler Colony': What about Natives and Immigrants?" In *The New Canadian Political Economy*, ed. W. Clement and G. Williams (Kingston, Montreal, and London: McGill-Queen's University, 1989), 240–77.

80. Leo Panitch, "Dependency and Class in Canadian Political Economy," *Special Issue: Rethinking Canadian Political Economy, Studies in Political Economy* 6 (autumn 1981): 16.

81. Brian Titley, *A Narrow Vision: Duncan Campbell Scott and the Administration of the Indian Act* (Vancouver: University of British Columbia Press, 1986).

82. There is a small but strong literature on the subject of Indigenous peoples' participation in the market economy that is interesting but not directly relevant to the argument I am making concerning the macroeconomics of Indigenous jurisdiction.

83. Karl Marx, *Capital*, Vol. 1 (New York: Penguin, 1990), chapters 26–28.

84. Roughly speaking, two schools of thought have developed regarding the historical role of primitive accumulation. Massimo de Angelis calls one the "historical primitive accumulation" or "Lenin camp" that theorizes primitive accumulation as prior to the emergence of capitalism, and the other, the "inherent-continuous primitive accumulation" or "Luxemburg camp," described in note 86 of this chapter (Massimo de Angelis, "Marx's Theory of Primitive Accumulation: A Suggested Reinterpretation," University of London, March 1999, http://http://homepages.uel .ac.uk/M.DeAngelis/PRIMACCA.htm; accessed July 11, 2012). The genealogy of the latter scholarship is more germane to my project of settler colonialism.

85. Marx, *Capital*, 876.

86. Michael Perleman emphasizes this gradual nature of primitive accumulation as well, and stresses that some degree of self-provisioning is always necessary

for capitalist development (*The Invention of Capitalism: Classical Political Economy and the Secret History of Primitive Accumulation* [Durham, N.C.: Duke University Press, 2000]). Rosa Luxemburg saw that a share of surplus value had to be reinvested in the expansion of production. She *spatialized* the dialectic, theorizing that the expansion of production relies on *non-capitalist spaces*, "as a market for its surplus values, as a source of supply for its means of production and a reservoir of labour for its wage system" (London and New York: Routledge, 2003), 348–49. As David Harvey explains, colonial policy, international trade, and war are the predominant methods of relations that Luxemburg identifies between capitalist and noncapitalist societies (*The New Imperialism*, 63–87). The expansionary tendency of capitalism—which included processes of primitive accumulation—was crucial to ongoing social reproduction.

    87. Glen Coulthard, *Red Skin, White Masks: Rejecting the Colonial Politics of Recognition* (Minneapolis: University of Minnesota Press, 2014), 13. Further theorization concerning this colonial economic dynamic is developed in Gillian Hart's and Giovanni Arrighi, Nicole Aschoff, and Ben Scully's work on postapartheid South Africa, where racial exclusion and alternative trajectories of accumulation complicate the role of proletarianization in the development of capitalism. See Gillian Hart, *Disabling Globalization: Places of Power in Post-Apartheid South Africa* (Berkeley and Los Angeles: University of California Press, 2002); and Giovanni Arrighi, Nicole Aschoff, and Ben Scully, "Accumulation by Dispossession and Its Limits: The Southern African Paradigm Revisited," *Studies in Comparative International Development* 45:4 (2010): 410–38.

    88. Robert Nichols, "Disaggregating Primitive Accumulation," *Radical Philosophy* 194 (November/December 2015): 18–28.

    89. Ibid., 21–22.

    90. Marx, *Capital*, Section 5; Mitchell, "One: The Stage of Modernity," 10.

    91. George Manuel and Michael Posluns, *The Fourth World: An Indian Reality* (Don Mills, Ontario: Collier-Macmillan Canada, 1974), 41.

3. Jurisdiction from the Ground Up

    1. Toby Decoursay, in discussion with author, July 22, 2009.

    2. Toby Decoursay, in discussion with author, July 23, 2009.

    3. Ibid.

    4. Toby Decoursay, in discussion with author and others, translators Marylynn Poucachiche and Tony Wawatie, July 18, 2009. See also Heidi Kiiwetinepinesiik Stark, "Marked by Fire: Anishnaabe Articulations of Nationhood in Treaty Making with the United States and Canada," *American Indian Quarterly* 36:2 (spring 2012).

    5. Toby Decoursay, in discussion with author, September 28, 2009.

    6. The customary code persists as an oral tradition despite the fact that the leadership laws of the Mitchikanibikok Anishnabe Onakinakewin were codified in 1996 as part of the restoration process following the reign of the Interim Band Council (IBC) facilitated by Superior Court Judge Réjean Paul.

    7. Eddy Nottaway, in discussion with author, September 30, 2009.

    8. I do recognize that care is not neutral or apolitical and depends on context for meaning. Here I try to connect care to a body of knowledge that is rooted in respect and mutual reciprocity.

    9. Sue Roark-Calnek, "Algonquins of Barriere Lake Background Reports,

Volume 3: The Social Organization of Barriere Lake Algonquin Land Use," prepared
for the Algonquin Nation Secretariat, November 2004, 58.

10. Ibid., 58–59.

11. Ibid., 58.

12. Leanne Simpson, "Land as Pedagogy: Nishnaabeg Intelligence and Rebel-
lious Transformation," *Decolonization: Indigeneity, Education & Society* 3:3 (2014): 8.

13. Marylynn Poucachiche and Clayton Nottaway, "Anishnabe Law," presentation at First Nations House, University of Toronto, November 26, 2010.

14. Scott Nickels, "Traditional Knowledge of the Algonquins of Barriere Lake,
Volume 1," report prepared for the Trilateral Secretariat, Algonquins of Barriere
Lake, August 1995. Broadly, the objectives of the Indigenous Knowledge program—
part of Phase 1 of the Trilateral Agreement—were "to document Algonquin ecological and social knowledge for incorporation into the IRMP [Integrated Resource
Management Plan] and thereby facilitate harmonization of Algonquin and non-
Algonquin land-use regimes consistent with the interest of the Algonquins of Barriere Lake." Activities of the Indigenous Knowledge program included developing
sensitive area studies (SAS) maps, Measures to Harmonize (MTH) forestry with
traditional activities of the Algonquins, toponymy studies, elders field trips, and
work with the Forest Stewardship Council on defining a workable certification for
sustainable forestry from an Algonquin perspective.

15. Sue Roark-Calnek, personal communication, September 27, 2012.

16. Nickels's report relies mainly on information collected in semidirected interviews with open-ended questions posed to as many community members as possible. Those Algonquins who proved extremely knowledgeable about the land were
often consulted repeatedly to cross-check other individuals' information. Translators played a crucial role in the process, as Nickels and the other researchers were
determined to record all aspects of traditional knowledge in the Algonquin language. Translators at times were asked to break down Algonquin terms into smaller
phonetic meanings in order to unpack and record the toponymic history embedded
in the words. Researchers wanted to correct the status quo of land management,
which until then had operated as a key method for suppressing Indigenous knowledge and culture. Affective participation meant clear translation: a premise of land
management based on Indigenous jurisdiction.

17. Nickels, "Traditional Knowledge of the Algonquins of Barriere Lake ," chapter 2, section 50.

18. Ibid., 51.

19. Toby Decoursay, in discussion with author, September 28, 2009.

20. "Widj-e-nia-mo-dwin: Walking Together for Indigenous Rights: Norman
Matchewan in Conversation with Martin Lukacs," *Canadian Centre for Policy Alternatives* (spring 2012), https://www.policyalternatives.ca/publications/ourschools
-ourselves/our-schoolsour-selves-spring-2012WT#sthash.BUBqb592.dpuf; accessed
June 7, 2016.

21. Poucachiche and Nottaway, "Anishnabe Law."

22. Ibid.

23. Ibid.

24. Ibid.

25. Nickels, "Traditional Knowledge of the Algonquins of Barriere Lake," chapter 3, section 5.

26. Roark-Calnek, "Algonquins of Barriere Lake Background Reports," 61.

27. Ibid.

28. Ibid., 63.

29. Toby Decoursay, in discussion with author, July 23, 2009, Barriere Lake.

30. Ibid.

31. Roark-Calnek, "Algonquins of Barrier Lake Background Reports," 68.

32. Sue Roark-Calnek, interview with author, Toby Decoursay and Gene-vieve Matchewan Decoursay, interview with author, interpreted by Jean Maurice Matchewan, August 15, 1994.

33. Roark-Calnek, "Algonquins of Barriere Lake Background Reports," 68.

34. Toby Decoursay, in discussion with author, July 23, 2009, Barriere Lake.

35. Roark-Calnek, "Algonquins of Barriere Lake Background Reports," 68.

36. Harry Wawatie, Helen Wawatie, Genevieve Decoursay, Louise Ratt, Pierre Ratt, and Michel Maranda, interview conducted by David Nahwegahbow, April 24, 1994, 1, translated by Michel Thusky, December 1995, Maniwaki, Quebec, Algon-quin Nation Secretariat archives.

37. Ibid., 1–10.

38. Social customs interviews, Jacob Wawatie, August 20–23, 1991; genealogy and oral history interview, Louise Wawatie Pien, August 22, 1990, Roark-Calnek, "Algonquins of Barriere Lake Background Reports," 45.

39. Peter Douglas Elias, "The Customs of the Algonquins of Barriere Lake in Respect of Leadership: An Opinion," prepared for the Facilitators to the Elders of the Algonquins of Barriere Lake, March 31, 1997, 10.

40. Ibid., 11.

41. Ibid.

42. Ibid.

43. Harry Wawatie, Helen Wawatie, Genevieve Decoursay, Louise Ratt, Pierre Ratt, and Michel Maranda, interview conducted by David Nahwegahbow, April 24, 1994, 1.

44. Ibid., 3.

45. Ibid., 12.

46. Mitchikanibikok Anishnabe Onakinakewin, Institutions of Government, 4.1 (1).

47. Harry Wawatie, Helen Wawatie, Genevieve Decoursay, Louise Ratt, Pierre Ratt, and Michel Marandal, interview conducted by David Nahwegahbow, April 24, 1994, 12.

48. Roark-Calnek, "Algonquins of Barriere Lake Background Reports," 72.

49. Ibid.

50. As a result of Canada's customary leadership intervention in 1996, the community reluctantly codified their oral law to prevent further "mix-ups" in the future. Harry Wawatie was particularly reluctant to transform these customs into a written code, feeling it was a betrayal of their way of life, and as such, would come back to haunt them. Nonetheless, the codified Mitchikanibikok Anishnabe Onakinakewin outlines the ceremony of the Leadership Assembly, as it has tended to unfold. Seats are placed in the center of the assembly area, representing the po-sitions that will be filled that day, with an equal number of seats surrounding these chairs for the spouses of those nominated to lead. The community gathers in a cir-cle around the seats as one by one the nominated candidates are escorted in by one

of the elders to the seats in the center. The spouse of the nominated candidate is also escorted to a seat by an elder. Then, the elder who nominates a candidate must address the assembly and speak to the candidate's qualities and qualifications for the position. The elder who escorted in the spouse will do the same for her. Then, the most important part of the assembly takes place: the floor opens for general discussion of the candidates, and a consensus must be reached. If it is secured, then each candidate is announced to the assembly, which continues until all seats are filled. Following selection, chiefs are closely watched for their first few years in a kind of probation period. When the chief does something wrong, he is corrected, but he can also step down or be removed in exceptional cases (Harry Wawatie, Helen Wawatie, Genevieve Decoursay, Louise Ratt, Pierre Ratt, and Michel Marandal, interview conducted by David Nahwegahbow, April 24, 1994, 17).

51. Ibid, 17.
52. Hermes, "Jurisdiction in the Colonial Northeast," 53.
53. Poucachiche and Nottaway, "Anishnabe Law."
54. Ibid.
55. Peter Douglas Elias, "Socio-Economic Profile of the Algonquins of Barriere Lake," prepared for the Algonquin Nation Secretariat, January 1996, revised August 2002, 71. Elias drew this information from an informal interview conducted by Sue Roark-Calnek with Michel Thusky.
56. Norman Matchewan, in discussion with author, June 16, 2009.
57. Michel Thusky, in telephone discussion with author, August 2, 2011.
58. Poucachiche and Nottaway, "Anishnabe Law."

4. Property as a Technique of Jurisdiction

1. Dawnis Kennedy Iminnawaanagogiizhigook, "Reconciliation without Respect? Section 35 and Indigenous Legal Orders," in *Indigenous Legal Traditions*, ed. Law Commission of Canada (Vancouver and Toronto: University of British Columbia Press, 2007), 77.
2. Ibid., 179.
3. See, for example, John C. Weaver, "Concepts of Economic Improvement and the Social Construction of Property Rights: Highlights from the English-Speaking World," in *Despotic Dominion: Property Rights in British Settler Societies*, ed. John McLaren, A. R. Buck, and Nancy E. Wright (Vancouver: University of British Columbia Press, 2005), and John C. Weaver, *The Great Land Rush and the Making of the Modern World, 1650–1900* (Montreal: McGill-Queens University Press, 2003).
4. Roark-Calnek, "Algonquins of Barriere Lake Background Reports Volume 3: The Social Organization of Barriere Lake Algonquin Land Use," 4. Subsequent references are given in the text.
5. Alexander Henry, *Travels and Adventures in Canada and the Indian Territories between the Years 1760 and 1776, Originally Published in 1809* (Edmonton: M. Hurtig, 1969), 23.
6. Roark-Calnek, "Algonquins of Barriere Lake Background Reports, Volume 3," 39.
7. Ibid., 33. Free areas could be found at key junctions on the territory, such as main camping sites and nearby the reserve at Cabonga. They were to be used by those who could not travel because of infirmity or age or otherwise inaccessible

family hunting grounds. In the course of my own research, I also noted that key transportation routes such as highways were considered commons, though logging roads near people's bush cabins were considered family territories and consent needed to be obtained to gain access in these places.

8. Ibid., 38.

9. Bryan, "Property as Ontology," 16. The shift toward modern conceptions of property took place during a period when Anglo-Norman England was rationalizing its governing structure away from the feudal mode toward a more Lockean model of "use" and "exchange" tailored to the market economy. Property is still not about accumulation, but rather self-preservation, through mixing one's labor to acquire the right to private property. This idea gradually shifted to reflect not who owns the property and what they have done to earn it, but what it is worth: "The 'use' value of a thing disappears because property becomes understood in terms for which it can be bargained, i.e., in contract" (ibid., 13).

10. Ibid., 16.

11. The concept of *fictitious commodity* is used by Karl Polanyi, who observed that land, labor, and money could never be wholly subsumed under the all-prevailing market logic of buying and selling. This "crude fiction" by which the substance of society is subordinated to the needs of the market *disembeds* people from their social and ecological economies, as common lands are enclosed and people are forced into wage labor. These grounded economies are then replaced by "an institutional setting controlled and regulated more than ever by social authority," paradoxically endorsed as economic "freedom" (*The Great Transformation: The Political and Economic Origins of Our Time* [Boston: Beacon Hill Press, 1957], 73 and 67).

12. David Harvey, *The Limits to Capital* (London: Verso, 2007), 338.

13. Polanyi, *The Great Transformation*. Karl Marx doesn't use the language of "fictitious," but in *Capital*, volume 3, in the section called "The Trinity Formula," he describes ground rent in related terms, where rent is fetishized as a source of value in capitalism, though the process of commodification begins much earlier historically, as described in volume 1 of *Capital* in the section called "So-Called Primitive Accumulation" (Karl Marx, *Capital: A Critique of Political Economy*, vol. 3 in *Karl Marx: Selected Writing*, ed. David McLellan (Oxford: Oxford University Press, 2000), 530–44.

14. Brett Christophers, "For Real: Land as Capital and Commodity," *Transactions* 41:2 (2016): 134–48.

15. Toby Decoursay, in discussion with the author, July 24, 2009, Barriere Lake.

16. Elias, "Socio-Economic Profile of the Algonquins of Barriere Lake," 22.

17. Hugh Conn, *Grand Lake Victoria Indian Hunting System, 1942 Annual Report*, submitted to the Department of Indian Affairs, Public Archives Canada (RG 10, vol. 6751, file 420–10x 5).

18. The same case was to be found in the beaver preserves set up in James Bay Cree territory. As Toby Morantz explains: "[Quebec's] role in the beaver preserves followed along these lines: the government passed orders-in-council designating the territories but provided no funding or management. It was federal government personnel in the fur supervisor division of Indian Affairs that oversaw the running of the beaver sanctuaries and the sale of fur—individuals such as Hugh Conn, a looming figure in the north, judging by the correspondence" (*White Man's Gonna Getcha: The Colonial Challenge to the Crees in Quebec* [Montreal: McGill-Queen's University Press, 2002], 221).

19. July 28, 1931: Memorandum and map from HJ Bury, Lands & Timber Branch, DIA to Deputy Minister, DIA . LAC RG10 Vol. 6751 File 420-10X Pt.1, Reel C-8106: Quebec Game Laws—Corresp & reports re: Abitibi & Grand Lake Indians Hunting Preserves, 1928–1935.

20. Elias, "Socio-Economic Profile of the Algonquins of Barriere Lake," 25.

21. Anastase Roi, *Maniwake et la vallée de la Gatineau* (Ottawa: Presses du droit, 1933), 65; cited in Leigh Ogston, *Algonquins of Barriere Lake Historical Report*, prepared for the Algonquin Nation Secretariat, November 1987, pages unnumbered.

22. Quebec Hydro Archives—citation incomplete: W. B. Hutchison to Major W. Blue, Gatineau Power Company, June 2, 1928 (RN 11214). Also Hutchison to Blue, August 25, 1929 (RN 11219), cited in Di Gangi, "Algonquins of Barriere Lake," 18.

23. A notice on "Special Regulations" to Indian residents of the Grand Lake Victoria Trapping Reserve from Indian Affairs officials in Canada and Quebec prohibits big-game hunting (Article 2) by Indians *and* others "at all times." In case there was any misunderstanding that the preserve was for the exclusive benefit of Indians, an example of provincial priority is showcased in the new regulation that Indians could no longer camp where it would be a "nuisance" to tourists (Article 4). See "A Notice to Indian Residents of the Grand Lake Victoria Trapping Reserve: Special Regulations," May 15, 1941, from Harold W. McGill, director, Indian Affairs Branch, Department of Mines and Resources, Dominion of Canada, and L. A. Richard, deputy minister, Department of Game and Fisheries, Province of Quebec, Public Archives of Canada, Indian Affairs (RG 10, vol. 6751, file 420–10X 6).

24. Peter Di Gangi, "The Barriere Lake Band: Claims Research," October 1986, 5; cited in Leigh Ogston, "Algonquins of Barriere Lake Historical Report," November 1987, document unnumbered.

25. Not *the* René Lévesque (founder of the Parti Québécois).

26. Harvey A. Feit, "Re-cognizing Co-management as Co-governance: Visions and Histories of Conservation at James Bay," *Anthropologica* 47:2 (2005): 278.

27. Ibid., 273.

28. Ibid.

29. Ibid.

30. Ibid.

31. As a field report from the local game warden confirms: "August 22. Friday, fair. Left at 8 am for Rapid lake and Barriere to see the Indians about their beaver maps, but when out there I found out they were all over the country and the few I could see would not cooperate because [Jules] Sioui had told them they almost own Canada and that the white men did not have anything to do with them also that they could trap where and when they felt like it" (August 1947: Diary of field investigation from René Lévesque, Quebec Game Warden, Senneterre. NA RG10, Vol. 6753 File 420–10–4GR-1: Quebec Fur Conservation—Correspondence re: the Grand Lac Victoria Preserve of the Maniwaki Agency [Maps] 1947–1950). Jules Sioui was a Huron-Wendat activist from Quebec who was a founding member of the North American Indian Brotherhood. See Hugh Shewell, "Jules Sioui and Indian Political Radicalism in Canada, 1943–1944," *Journal of Canadian Studies* 34:3 (fall 1999): 211–42. He came around and radicalized some of the Barriere Lake men during this period. Community members at Barriere Lake, such as Eddy Nottaway, still carry their North American treaty card that Sioui issued and distributed to represent members' status as sovereign Indigenous people.

32. Continuing from reports in 1947, the next year, game warden René Lévesque reported on ongoing noncompliance by the Algonquins to map their territory: "The Barriere Indians as usual have declined to make their maps and as they have not been issued any beaver tags, they cannot trap beaver on the reserve. If the trap line system had been well organized in Pontiac we could seize every beaver without a tag in their possession, but if they declare that they have trapped the beavers they may have outside the reserve there is not very much we can do. The only way to catch these Indians is to find them trapping on the Reserve and this can only be done by using airplane to cover their old grounds. Many trips were made during the summer and fall to get their cooperation but without any success. I have not lost hope yet because by this contact with the Grand Lake Indians they might realize that we are working for their own benefit. A great help to get the cooperation of the Indians was the 25 dollars checks issued in the favor of the ones who made their maps and if they receive a 50 dollars one this year it will mean more cooperation from them" (1948: Annual Report for Grand Lake Victoria Hunting Reserve, 1948 from René Lévesque, Quebec Game Warden to Indian Affairs, NA RG10 Vol. 6752 File 420–10–1-3 Reel C-8107; NA RG10 Vol. 6754, File 420–10–4GR3—Grand Lac Victoria Annual Report 1950).

33. The full report documents events of November 6, 1947: "Thursday, rain. Left Forbes Depot at 7 am for Larouche and High Portage which was the best place to watch for these Indians. When they arrived around 4 pm we tried to search every bag they had but as these Indians went wild (the squaws pointed guns at us) we might have missed one where the fur was. As the squaws start to hit us with paddles and whatever they could find I pulled out my revolver which kind of scared them a little. I have been in some mix-up with Indians but never seen the like of this trouble we had. We did the very best we could to find the beaver pelts but as there was 15 Indians and only four of us with only one revolver (mine) we had to be very careful not to get hurt. I was lucky to see one squaw who was getting ready to hit Cont [Constable] Christe [Christie] with an axe and stopped her. Finally after they had left by canoe, we search both sides of the portage and found a small bag containing part of the meat of one beaver, some moose and 6 muskrat pelts not yet dried" (November 1947: Diary of field investigation from René Lévesque, Quebec Game Warden. NA RG10 Vol. 6753, File 420–10–4GR-1: Quebec Fur Conservation—Correspondence re: the Grand Lac Victoria Preserve of the Maniwaki Agency [Maps] 1947–50).

34. Diary of field investigation from René Lévesque, NA RG10 Vol. 6753, File 420–10–4GR-1; emphasis added.

35. January 22, 1948: Letter #2 from René Lévesque, Quebec game warden, to Hugh Conn, Fur Supervisor, Indian Affairs, NA RG10 Vol. 6753, File 420–10–4GR-1: Quebec Fur Conservation—Correspondence re: the Grand Lac Victoria Preserve of the Maniwaki Agency (Maps) 1947–50.

36. Ibid.

37. The registered trapline regulations were introduced in 1945 by a Quebec Order-in-Council and were meant to be a source of revenue for Quebec to recoup costs of the Mont Laurier-Senneterre Highway. See #3235 (August 17, 1945); #3440 (August 28, 1946); #1636 (June 14, 1967); and 1559–72 (June 6, 1972).

38. Di Gangi, "The Barriere Lake Band," 13. To recoup millions of the highway costs, Quebec took advantage of preserve for tourist purposes. No commercial fishing would be allowed.

39. Morantz, *White Man's Gonna Getcha*, 221.

40. NAC RG10 Vol. 6752 File 420–10–1-3, Reel C-8107: Report on Fur Conservation Projects in the Province of Quebec maps by Hugh Conn, circa 1942 (RN 3790).

41. Ibid.

42. Sue Roark-Calnek, "Barriere Lake Algonquin Family Narratives," a report to the Algonquin Nation Secretariat, Mitchikanibikok Inik, Algonquins of Barriere Lake. November 11, 2004, 21.

43. As Stu Herbert notes: "Plans showing the location of the territory were to be submitted for each license. The license could be lost if the territory was not trapped each year or if the trapper failed to follow the regulations. An annual inventory and report was required from each trapper (see: #1641 [14 Sept 67])" (Summary of Quebec Orders-in-Council [1928–1980], September 16, 1988, 6).

44. George Nottaway, Harry Wawatie, Trapline Map Identifications, interviewed by Sue Roark-Calnek and Terry Tobias; interpreter: Maggie Wawatie, February 7, 1993, BL Band Office, Maniwaki.

45. Adrian Tanner believes that the fur trade simply brought to light variations in the degree of *recognition* for pre-standing Algonquin tenure systems. He attributes the uneven application of recognition of Indigenous tenure regimes to the fact that the imposition of jurisdiction itself is subject to extremely uneven application, because of economics, resistance, monopoly, and relationship between industry and trade ("Algonquin Land Tenure and State Structures," *Canadian Journal of Native Studies* 3:2 [1983]: 311–20).

46. Hugh Conn, *Grand Lake Victoria Indian Hunting System 1942, Annual Report*.

47. This pithy definition comes from Mignolo's blog, http://waltermignolo.com/on-pluriversality/ (accessed April 6, 2016), but to read a scholarly book on this subject, see Walter D. Mignolo, *Local Histories/Global Designs: Coloniality, Subaltern Knowledges, and Border Thinking* (Princeton, N.J.: Princeton University Press, 2000).

48. Hugh Conn, *Grand Lake Victoria Indian Hunting System, 1942, Annual Report*. Roark-Calnek notes this interpretation of Conn's interaction with Barriere Lakers in discussion with the author (September 27, 2012).

49. Fabian Muniesa, Yuval Millo, and Michel Callon, "An Introduction to Market Devices," *Sociological Review* 55, supplement s2 (October 2007): 2.

50. Simpson, *Mohawk Interruptus*, 67.

51. Frank Speck, *Family Hunting Territories and Social Life of Various Algonkian Bands of the Ottawa Valley*, Canada Department of Mines—Geological Survey—Memoir 70 No. 8, Anthropological Series (Ottawa: Government Printing Bureau, 1915).

52. Ibid., 4.

53. Frank G. Speck, "The Family Hunting Band as the Basis of Algonkian Social Organization," *American Anthropologist* 17 (1915): 290.

54. Lowie writes: "We cannot content ourselves with a blunt alternative: communism versus individualism. A people may be communist as regards one type of goods, yet recognize separate ownership with respect to other forms of property" (*Primitive Society* [New York: Boni and Liverlight, 1920], 210).

55. D. S. Davidson, *Family Hunting Territories in Northwestern North America* (New York: Museum of the American Indian, Heye Foundation, 1928); John M. Cooper, "Is the Algonquin Family Hunting Ground System Pre-Columbian? *American Anthropologist* 41 (1939): 66–90; and Lowie, *Primitive Society*.

56. Tanner, "Algonquin Land Tenure and State Structures," 312.

57. Eleanor Leacock, *The Montagnais Hunting Territory and the Fur Trade*, American Anthropological Association, Memoir no. 78, 1954.

58. See, for example, Diamond Jenness, "Origin of Copper Eskimos and Their Copper Culture," *Geographical Review* 13:4 (1923): 540–51. Another early and influential critic of Speck was Alfred G. Bailey, *The Conflict of European and Eastern Algonkian Cultures, 1504–1700: A Study in Canadian Civilization* (Sackville, New Brunswick: Tribune Press, 1937). For a good overview of this literature more generally, see Charles A. Bishop and Toby Morantz, "Who Owns the Beaver? Northern Algonquian Land Tenure Reconsidered," *Anthropologica* 28:1–2 (1986): 7–9.

59. Edward Rogers, *The Hunting Group-Hunting Territory Complex among the Mistassini Indians*, National Museum of Canada Bulletin (Ottawa: Department of Northern Affairs and National Resources, 1963), 195. For a deeper discussion of these debates, see Siomonn Pulla, "A Redirection in Neo-Evolutionism?: A Retrospective Examination of the Algonquian Family Hunting Territories Debates," *Histories of Anthropology Annual* 7 (2011): 170–90. See also Harvey Feit, "Les territoires de chasse algonquiens avant leur 'découverte'?" *Recherches Amerindiennes au Québec* 34:3 (2004): 5–21.

60. Flanagan in fact cites a derivative source rather than referencing Leacock directly. His secondary source also refrains from mentioning Leacock by name, but the correlation is obvious, though Flanagan reads back her conclusions about the emergence of post-fur-trade property regimes in Indigenous societies as evidence of the fundamental nature of Indigenous societies as protocapitalist: "There has been much scholarly debate over the extent to which eastern forest hunters developed institutions of collective and individual control over land in response to the incentives of the fur trade. European fashions for beaver and other pelts raised their value and certainly encouraged Indians in the direction of exercising control over trapping grounds. A modern author describes how the Montagnais of Labrador and Quebec assigned trapping rights in the eighteenth century: 'It was a highly sophisticated system. The Montagnais blazed trees with their family crests to delineate their hunting grounds, practiced retaliation against poachers and trespassers, developed a seasonal allotment system, and marked beaver houses'" (Robert J. Smith, "Resolving the Tragedy of the Commons by Creating Private Property Rights in Wildlife," *Cato Journal* 1 [1981]: 452; in Tom Flanagan, Christopher Alacantra, and André Le Dressay, *Beyond the Indian Act: Restoring Aboriginal Property Rights* [Montreal: McGill-Queen's University Press, 2010], 38–39). The ideological purpose of Flanagan's book is to promote the First Nations Property Ownership Act, a bill proposing the privatization of reserve lands.

61. Adrian Tanner, "The New Hunting Territory Debate: An Introduction to Some Unresolved Issues," *Anthropoligica* 28:1–2 (1986): 28.

62. Ibid., 21–22.

63. Robert Nichols, "Indigeneity and the Settler Contract Today," *Philosophy and Social Criticism* 39:2 (2013): 175.

64. Ibid. *Dominion* and *imperium* are Roman distinctions, respectively, between the rule over things by the individual and the rule over all individuals by the prince.

65. Ibid., 168.

66. Ibid., 175.

67. Di Gangi, "The Barriere Lake Band."

68. Toby Decoursay, in discussion with author, July 24 2009, Barriere Lake.

69. Di Gangi, "The Barriere Lake Band" (Informant #8, #170, interviewed by Sue Roark-Calnek, August 24, 1990, at "Romance Lake" bush camp).

70. Peter Douglas Elias summarizes Scott Nickels's primary research in his sweeping research profile covering the socioeconomic history of Barriere Lake: "Elders stated that winds live at the ends of the earth in each of the primary directions. The four wind beings are kîwedinok, 'north wind,' câwanok 'south wind,' nigabîyanok, 'west wind,' and wâbanok, 'east wind' . . . The winds are known and encountered by Algonquin on a daily basis" ("Socio-Economic Profile of the Algonquins of Barriere Lake," 101).

71. Peter Di Gangi, "Barriere Lake Leadership: Excerpts from Oral History and HBCo Records," prepared for the Algonquin Nation Secretariat, 1996. The feast baskets they refer to here presented food offerings for bush spirits associated with game renewal and change of seasons, customs of the Onakinakewin.

72. Dorsett and McVeigh, "Questions of Jurisdiction," 15.

73. Harris, "How Did Colonialism Dispossess?" 175. For another succinct article, see Matthew Sparke, "The Map That Roared and an Original Atlas: Canada, Cartography and the Narration of Nation," *Annals of the Association of American Geographers* 88:3 (1998): 463–95. But for more sustained discussions of colonial cartographies and Indigenous countermapping in the context of North America, see Byrd, *The Transit of Empire,* and Mishuana Goeman, *Mark My Words: Native Women Mapping Our Nations* (Minneapolis: University of Minnesota Press, 2013).

74. Jean Maurice Matchewan, in discussion with author, July 26, 2009, Rapid Lake.

75. Feit, "Re-cognizing Co-management as Co-governance," 282.

76. Ibid., 281.

77. Jean Maurice Matchewan, in discussion with author, July 26, 2009, Rapid Lake.

78. Bryan, "Property as Ontology," 5.

79. Paul Nadasdy, "The Case of the Missing Sheep: Time, Space, and the Politics of 'Trust' in Co-Management Practice," in *Traditional Ecological Knowledge and Natural Resource Management,* ed. Charles R. Menzies (Lincoln: University of Nebraska Press, 2006), 144.

80. Ibid., 130.

81. Peter Usher, Robert Galois, and Frank Tough, "Reclaiming the Land: Aboriginal Title, Treaty Rights and Land Claims in Canada," *Applied Geography* (1992): 12; emphasis added.

82. Kim Tallbear, "An Indigenous Reflection on Working beyond the Human/ Not Human," *GLQ: A Journal of Lesbian and Gay Studies* 21:2–3 (June 2015): 235.

83. The reference to "objects" and "forces" as living is from Tallbear, "An Indigenous Reflection on Working beyond the Human/Not Human," and the phrase "ecologies of intimacy" was borrowed from Leanne Simpson, "Anishnabe Nationhood," *Nation to Nation Now: The Conversations,* Symposium, Toronto, March 23, 2013. Simpson uses this phrase in her talk to describe Indigenous nationhood.

84. Jean Maurice Matchewan, in discussion with author, July 16, 2009, Rapid Lake.

85. Billy-Ray Belcourt, "Animal Bodies, Colonial Subjects: (Re)Locating Animality in Decolonial Thought," *Societies* 5 (2015): 1–11.

86. Scott Lauria Morgensen, "The Biopolitics of Settler Colonialism: Right Here, Right Now," *Settler Colonial Studies* 1 (2001): 52.

87. Ibid., 56.

88. Toby Decoursay, in discussion with author, August 28, 2010.

89. Vanessa Watts, "Indigenous Place-Thought and Agency amongst Humans and Non-humans (First Woman and Sky Woman Go on a European World Tour!)," *Decolonization: Indigeneity, Education and Society* 2:1 (2013): 23.

90. Ibid., 21.

91. Ibid., 23.

92. Ibid.

93. Norman Matchewan, in discussion with author, June 2, 2010.

5. "They're Clear-Cutting Our Way of Life"

1. See the affidavit of Patrick Wabamoose at 7 in the Motion for Provisional Interlocutory Injunction Motion for Interlocutory Injunction for a Permanent Injunction and Declaration. Applicant: Jean-Maurice Matchewan, March 30, 1990; see also line 11 of the Motion.

2. Russell Diabo, in discussion with author, November 12, 2011.

3. Jean Maurice Matchewan, in discussion with author, February 18, 2009, Rapid Lake.

4. Russell Diabo, in discussion with author, November 12, 2011.

5. Jean Maurice Matchewan, in discussion with author, February 18, 2009, Rapid Lake.

6. Rebecca Aird. "Quebec's New Forestry Policy: Its Implications for the Algonquins of Barriere Lake and for Nature and Wildlife Conservation in Quebec," presentation to the annual meeting of the Canadian Parks and Wilderness Society, October 1988, 4. Subsequent references are given in the text.

7. Mike Blanchfield, "Indians Block Hwy. 117 to Protest Building of Power Line on Reserve," *Ottawa Citizen*, July 28, 1988.

8. Sarah Cox, "Natives Leave Island Protest," *Ottawa Citizen*, September 23, 1988.

9. Blanchfield, "Indians Block Hwy. 117."

10. Anne Tolson, "Natives Occupy Island to Protest Land Use," *Ottawa Citizen*, September 20, 1998.

11. Cox, "Natives Leave Island Protest."

12. Pat Bell and Charles Lewis, "Mounties Throw Camping Natives off Hill," *Ottawa Citizen*, September 29, 1988.

13. Russell Diabo, in discussion with author, November 12, 2011.

14. Bell and Lewis, "Mounties Throw Camping Natives off Hill."

15. Ibid.

16. Algonquins of Barriere Lake, "Barriere Lake Algonquins Angered by Superior Court Decision," press release, April 10, 1990, Ottawa.

17. Ibid.

18. Clifford Lincoln, e-mail communication with author, May 8, 2011.

19. "Barriere Lake: Algonquins Vow to Continue Blockade of Logging Roads," *Ottawa Citizen*, August 17, 1990.

20. Russell Diabo, in discussion with author, November 12, 2011.

21. Personal communication between Ellen Gabriel (spokesperson for the Mohawks during the reclamation) and journalist Martin Lukacs, Amnesty International Annual General Meeting, September 2008, as conveyed to the author by Lukacs on June 10, 2010.

22. Janis Hass, "Discontent Will Spread, Indians Say," *Ottawa Citizen,* July 15, 1990. Hass quotes Barriere Lake's lawyer stating that the federal government "is provoking an Indian war. And I'm not just talking about Mohawks. They're provoking all native people across Canada to stand united." The article reports that a contingent from Barriere Lake, including Chief Matchewan, was barred from entering Oka by the military. In a letter to Quebec Premier Robert Bourassa, Matchewan issued the following warning: "We ask you to believe us when we say that you are making a terrible mistake in confronting the Mohawks in their legitimate demands and that you and your government will be sorry . . . We will show no less determination in defending ourselves than the Mohawks of Kanesatake have shown."

23. "Algonquin Indians End Road Blockade," *Toronto Star,* August 21, 1990, A11.

24. Rhoda Metcalfe, "Quebec Offers Barriere Lake Natives Plan for Wildlife Reserve," *Ottawa Citizen,* September 6, 1990.

25. Ibid.

26. Ibid.

27. Ibid.

28. See Rhoda Metcalfe, "Algonquins Give Logger Tentative Approval to Cut Wood on Reserve," *Ottawa Citizen,* September 21, 1990.

29. Ibid.

30. Rhoda Metcalfe, "Ciaccia to Take Algonquin Case to Quebec Cabinet," *Ottawa Citizen,* August 22, 1991.

31. Ibid.

32. Ibid.

33. Rhoda Metcalfe, "Lumberman Willing to Negotiate with Indians," *Ottawa Citizen,* August 27, 1991.

34. Leasehold rights are, as Christopher Essert writes, "transferable or alienable rights, good against the world, that others not perform some action without the owner's permission" ("Property in Licenses and the Law of Things," *McGill Law Journal* 59:3 [2014]: 565).

35. Minister of Supply and Services Canada, "Enhancing the Forests of Indian Lands: Forest Management Program of Indian Lands," Forestry Canada, 1989. However, no methodology is provided for arriving at this figure.

36. Ibid.

37. Secretariat of the Assembly of the First Nations of Quebec and Labrador, "The Occupation of Forest Land in Quebec and the Constitution of Forest Management Corporations," presented to the Commission de l'économie et du travail, October 22, 2008, 7; emphasis added.

38. Boyce Richardson, *Strangers Devour the Land: The Cree Hunters of the James Bay Area versus Premier Bourassa and the James Bay Development Corporation* (Toronto: Macmillan, 1975).

39. In 1989, Prime Minister Brian Mulroney brought the First Ministers to the table to deal with the outstanding issue of Quebec's exclusion from the Constitution Act of 1982. Indigenous peoples had not opposed recognition of Quebec as a distinct society in what became known as the Meech Lake Accord, but the agree-

ment only served to amplify their own lack of distinct status within the Canadian state. Provincial legislatures had to unanimously ratify the Meech Lake Accord, but in the Manitoba legislature, Elijah Harper, an Oji-Cree from Red Sucker Lake and the only Indigenous member of the legislature, managed to delay the vote, forcing the accord to fail on the grounds of time expiration. The Meech Lake ratification vote came on the heels of three years of failed First Ministers' Conferences, promising to develop self-governance provisions extending from rights enshrined, but not defined, in the Constitution Act of 1982. By the third (and final) meeting between Indigenous leaders and provincial authorities in 1987, state commitments were weak and halfhearted. It was in this context that Quebec was granted distinction and special authority within the Meech Lake constitutional talks and Harper laid down his feather (Dickason, *Canada's First Nations,* 409).

40. Jean Maurice Matchewan, "Presentation of the Committee to Examine Matters Relating to the Accession of Quebec to Sovereignty," Quebec City, Quebec, February 4, 1992.

41. In 1990, the largest military standoff on Canadian soil was mobilized against a group of Kanehsatà:ke Mohawks protecting a sacred pine grove from a golf course expansion. See Leanne Simpson and Kiera Ladner, *This Is an Honour Song: Twenty Years since the Blockade* (Winnipeg: Arbeiter Ring Press, 2010).

42. Mary Ellen Turpel, "Does the Road to Quebec Sovereignty Run through Aboriginal Territory?" in *Negotiating with a Sovereign Quebec,* ed. Daniel Drache and Roberto Perin (Toronto: James Lorimer & Company Publishers, 1992), 93.

43. Ibid., 94.

44. Ibid., 97.

45. Ibid., 94.

46. See, for example, Article 1 of the United Nations International Covenant on Civil and Political Rights (1966), which reads: "All people have the right of self-determination. By virtue of that right they freely determine their political status and freely pursue their economic, social and cultural development."

47. Erick Duchesne, Munroe Eagles, and Stephen Erfle, "Constituency Homogeneity, Economic Risk and Support for Quebec Sovereignty: A Research Note," *Canadian Journal of Political Science/Revue canadienne de science politique* 36:3 (July–August/juillet–août 2003): 643–56.

48. Metcalfe, "Ciaccia to Take Algonquin Case to Quebec Cabinet."

49. The exact sum derived is $56,534,540 (Cogesult, "Quantification de la valeur économique des industries de la forêt, du tourisme, des loisirs et des autres industries et activités dans la région de l'Outaouais et le secteur couvert par l'entente trilateral, Rapport Final," March 1996, ix).

50. This estimate was provided in a commissioned study by consulting firm Ottawa Engineering for Barriere Lake, 1993.

51. Cogesult, "Quantification de la valeur économique des industries," ix.

52. Sylvia Massicotte and Gilles Carpentier, "Principal Economic Indicators for the Quebec Forestry Sector—Presentations and Analysis," Forestry Canada: Quebec Region, Information Report LAU-X-104E, 1993.

53. C. McLaren, "Wonders of the Unknown Woods: Saving the Boreal Forest," *Equinox* 53 (September/October 1990): 51.

54. Robert Beauregard and Luc Bouthillier, "Crisis in the Quebec Forest Industry: Problems and Possible Solutions," *Forestry Chronicle* 69:4 (August 1993): 407.

55. Ibid., 406–8.

56. Ibid., 407.

57. *Calder v. British Columbia (Attorney General)* (1973) S.C.R. 313, (1973) 4 W.W.R (hereafter, *Calder*).

58. Thomas R. Berger, *A Long and Terrible Shadow: White Values, Native Rights in the Americas, 1492–1992* (Vancouver and Toronto: Douglas & McIntyre, 1991). See chapter 11, "Native Claims and the Rule of Law."

59. Ibid., 154.

60. Canada, Indian and Northern Affairs, *Statement of the Government of Canada on Indian Policy* (Ottawa: Department of Indian and Northern Affairs, 1969), http://epe.lac-bac.gc.ca/100/200/301/inac-ainc/indian_policy-e/cp1969_e .pdf; accessed May 1, 2013. Trudeau's line is quoted in J. R. Miller, "Great White Father Knows Best: Oka and the Land Claims Process, *Native Studies Review* 7:1 (1991): 38. The full quote ends with the phrase "when we did the white paper." The "white paper" of 1969, introduced by Trudeau's government, attempted to erode Indigenous peoples' distinct status in Canada, for example, by scrapping the Indian Act and reserve system, under the auspices of liberal equality.

61. Johnny Mack, "Hoquotist: Reorienting through Storied Practice," in *Storied Communities: Narratives of Contact and Arrival in Constituting Political Community*, ed. Hester Lessard, Rebecca Johnson, and Jeremy Webber (Vancouver: University of British Columbia Press, 2011), 299.

62. Department of Indian Affairs and Northern Development, "Statement Made by the Honourable Jean Chrétien, Minister of Indian Affairs and Northern Development on Claims of Indian and Inuit People," communiqué, August 8, 1973. The policy was reaffirmed in Government of Canada, *In All Fairness: A Native Claims Policy—Comprehensive Claims*, Department of Indian Affairs and Northern Development, Ottawa, 1981.

63. Paul Rynard, "'Welcome In, but Check Your Rights at the Door': The James Bay and Nisga'a Agreements in Canada," *Canadian Journal of Political Science* 33:2 (June 2000): 211–43.

64. James Bay and Northern Quebec Agreement, Section 2: Principal Provisions, 2.1; emphasis added; www.gcc.ca; accessed May 1, 2013.

65. Government of Canada, *In All Fairness*; emphasis added.

66. Department of Indian Affairs and Northern Development (DIAND), *Living Treaties: Lasting Agreements—Report of the Task Force to Review Comprehensive Claims Policy*, Ottawa, 1985. The Coolican Task Force was a five-member task force chaired by Murray Coolican and appointed by then Minister of Indian Affairs David Crombie.

67. The group organized under the banner of the "Comprehensive Claims Coalition." At the table were the Dene-Metis, Council of Yukon Indians, Conseil Attikamek-Montagnais, Tungavit Federation of Nunavit, Taku River Tlingit, and Nisga'a. See Terry Fenge and Joanne Barnaby, "From Recommendations to Policy: Battling Inertia to Obtain a Land Claims Policy," *Canadian Arctic Resources Committee* 15:1 (January–April 1987), http://carc.org/pubs/v15no1/4.htm; accessed May 1, 2013.

68. Ibid.

69. Legislative Session: 1st Session, 36th Parliament Select Standing Committee on Aboriginal Affairs Transcripts of Proceedings 1996, (Hansard) Victoria, Thursday, April 24, 1997, Issue No. 35; Tim Koepke (Indian and Northern Affairs

Canada), the chief government negotiator for Yukon claims, describes to the committee the background of the comprehensive claims policy.

70. Algonquin First Nations Comprehensive Claims Policy Reform Regional Discussion Forum Roll-up Report, March 28, 2012, 2. Keith Penner, the Liberal Opposition critic on Indian Affairs, provided the most scathing review of the Conservative reform under McKnight. He summarized what he saw as the government's disdain for the reality of Aboriginal title: "The difficulty with the new claims policy, as with the old, is that it stems from a premise narrow in scope and fragile in structure, that is, that aboriginal title involves traditional use and occupancy which continues in certain respects up to the present. This so-called title as the Government sees it is an annoyance" (*Hansard),* House of Commons Debates, December 18, 1986, 2232, cited in Fenge and Barnaby, "From Recommendations to Policy").

71. DIAND, *Living Treaties,* 30.

72. Indigenous peoples gained constitutional recognition in the Constitution Act of 1982: under section 35(1), Aboriginal and treaty rights were "recognized and affirmed" (Schedule B to the Canada Act, 1982, [U.K.] 1982 c. 11), Part II: "Rights of the Aboriginal Peoples of Canada." Subsections 35(1) and (2) read: (1) The existing aboriginal and treaty rights of the aboriginal peoples of Canada are hereby recognized and affirmed; (2) In this Act, "aboriginal peoples of Canada" includes the Indian, Inuit and Métis peoples of Canada.

73. *Sparrow,* at 1119.

74. *Delgamuukw,* at paragraph 166.

75. Under the CLCP, third-party interests are protected. This means the negotiating group must consent to the alienation of Aboriginal title territory and give up all right to compensation for past infringements.

76. Rynard, " 'Welcome In, but Check Your Rights at the Door,' " 220.

77. For a sharp and deeply pessimistic view, see Gordon Christie, "A Colonial Reading of Recent Jurisprudence: Sparrow, Delgamuukw and Haida Nation," *Windsor Yearbook of Access to Justice* 23:1 (2005): 17–54.

78. Canada voted twice against the UNDRIP, once as a member of the United Nations Human Rights Council on June 26, 2006, and once at the UN General Assembly on September 13, 2007. However, Canada endorsed the declaration on March 3, 2010, in Prime Minister Stephen Harper's "Speech from the Throne," then issued a statement of support endorsing the UNDRIP on November 12, 2010. Previous Canadian governments had made clear that the UNDRIP is viewed as "a non-legally binding aspirational document" that can only be supported "in a manner fully consistent with Canada's Constitution and laws" (Aboriginal Affairs and Northern Development Canada, "Canada's Endorsement of the United Nations Declaration on the Rights of Indigenous Peoples," http://www.aadnc-aandc.gc.ca/eng/1309374807748/1309374897928; accessed March 7, 2013). However, the government of Prime Minister Justin Trudeau vowed to respect Canada's obligations under the protocol (Joanna Smith, "Canada Will Implement UN Declaration on Rights of Indigenous Peoples, Carolyn Bennett Says," *Toronto Star,* November 12, 2015). In addition to UNDRIP, Canada is also a signatory to the International Labor Organization's Convention 169, the UN Committee on the Elimination of Racial Discrimination, the International Covenant on Economic, Social and Cultural Rights, and the Convention on Biological Diversity, all of which recognize the right of Indigenous peoples to self-determination.

79. Concluding observations of the Committee on Economic, Social and Cultural Rights: Canada 10/12/98, E/C.12/1/Add.32 (Concluding Observations/Comments), principal subjects of concern.

80. See Arthur Manuel, spokesperson for Indigenous Network on Economies and Trade, *Report on Canada's Self-Government and Land Rights Policies at the Root of Canada's Opposition to the UN Draft Declaration on Indigenous Rights,* submitted to Rodolfo Stavenhagen, UN Special Rapporteur on the Situation of Human Rights and Fundamental Freedoms of Indigenous Peoples, October 1, 2006.

81. Canada, Fifth Periodic Report, International covenant on civil and political rights, General, CCPR/C/CAN/2004/5, November 18, 2004, Consideration of Reports Submitted by States Parties under Article 40 of the Covenant [October 27, 2004]. As Aboriginal Affairs and Northern Development further explains, certainty over ownership is a key goal of the CLCP. To accomplish this task, modification and nonassertion clauses are necessary: "Under the modified rights model, aboriginal rights are not extinguished, but are modified into the rights articulated and defined in the treaty. Under the non-assertion model, Aboriginal rights are not extinguished, and the Aboriginal group agrees to exercise only those rights articulated and defined in the treaty and to assert no other Aboriginal rights" (Canada, Resolving Aboriginal Claims, 2003).

82. Committee on Economic, Social and Cultural Rights, Presessional Working Group, May 16–20, 2005, Implementation of the International Covenant on Economic, Social and Cultural Rights, list of issues to be taken in connection with the consideration of the fourth periodic report of CANADA concerning the rights referred to in Articles 1–15 of the International Covenant on Economic, Social and Cultural Rights (E/C.12/4/Add.15).

83. Para 2.23 of Nisga'a Final Agreement reads: "This Agreement *exhaustively* sets out Nisga'a section 35 rights, *the geographic extent of those rights, and those limitations to those rights,* to which the parties have agreed, and those rights are: a. the aboriginal rights, including aboriginal rights, *as modified by this Agreement,* in Canada of the Nisga'a Nation and its people in and to Nisga'a Lands and other lands and resources in Canada; b. the jurisdictions, authorities, and the rights of Nisga'a Government; and c. the other Nisga'a section 35 rights"; emphasis added.

84. Carole Blackburn, "Searching for Guarantees in the Midst of Uncertainty: Negotiating Aboriginal Rights and Title in British Columbia," *American Anthropologist* 107:4 (December 2005): 592.

85. Ibid., 593.

86. The last policy revision was released by the federal government in 1993, and was not updated since despite widespread changes to the political landscape and to the policy itself, such as the inclusion in 1995 of self-government policies. See https://www.aadnc-aandc.gc.ca/eng/1408631807053/1408631881247.

87. Eyford, for context, was the author of "Building Partnerships," a report he was previously commissioned to write by the Conservative government to make recommendations on West Coast energy infrastructure in 2013 (https://www.nrcan.gc.ca/sites/www.nrcan.gc . . . /ForgPart-Online-e.pdf). The Eyford report spelled out Canada's priority: the need to "capitalize" on global energy demands, therefore "to construct pipelines and terminals to deliver oil and natural gas to tidewater." Eyford recommends that Indigenous peoples standing in the way of this development should be brought on as partners wherever possible. The possibility of Indigenous refusal is not seriously contemplated or envisaged.

88. Douglas R. Eyford, *A New Direction: Advancing Aboriginal and Treaty Rights,* commissioned by Aboriginal Affairs and Northern Development Canada, February 20, 2015, 12.

89. Russell Diabo and Shiri Pasternak, "Harper v. First Nations: The Assimilation Agenda," *Ricochet,* October 21, 2014; https://ricochet.media/en/125/harper -first-nations-assimilation-agenda; accessed April 8, 2016.

90. Judith Sayers, "Treaties and Tsilhqot'in-Treaties at Risk?" *First Nations in British Columbia Portal,* July 4, 2014; http://fnbc.info/blogs/judith-sayers/treaties -and-tsilhqot-treaties-risk; accessed April 8, 2016.

91. The Nisga'a Final Agreement recognized 200,450 hectares of Nisga'a's traditional territory as modern treaty lands. The total lands claimed by Nisga'a, however, amounted to 2,200,000, which meant that only 8 percent of total lands claimed were rewarded, or that British Columbia received 92 percent of Nisga'a's traditional land base (Union of BC Indian Chiefs, "Plain Language Guide to the Nisga'a Agreement," 1998, 8).

92. The exact data behind this figure is difficult to obtain because the British Columbia Treaty Commission (BCTC) does not disclose the amount of lands claimed by each negotiating group. In addition, because negotiating groups are not required to provide land surveys of their total land base, First Nations themselves do not necessarily possess these figures (e.g., Tsawwassen's land office did not have this exact figure). But most negotiators for First Nations I spoke with informally were told by government negotiators that 5 percent of a group's territory was the average land settlement they would be awarded.

93. AFN, Comprehensive Claims Policy Reform Regional Discussion Forum Roll-up Report, March 28, 2012, 2; emphasis in original.

94. AANDC, "Fact Sheet: A Results-Based Approach to Treaty and Self-Government Negotiations," September 4, 2012.

95. INAC, "Negotiating Tables," http://www.aadnc-aandc.gc.ca/eng/134678232 7802/1346782485058; accessed April 19, 2016.

96. See INAC's website for a full listing of negotiations (ibid.); accessed April 19, 2016.

97. Rudolph C. Rÿser, *Indigenous Nations and Modern States: The Political Emergence of Nations Challenging State Power* (New York and London: Routledge, 2012), 85.

6. The Trilateral Agreement Is Born

1. Coulthard, "Subjects of Empire," 439; emphasis in original.

2. United Nations Convention on Biological Diversity, September 30, 1997. The UNCBD statement was issued in response to a 1995 presentation made by Jean Maurice Matchewan at an intersessional meeting on Indigenous Peoples (Russell Diabo, in discussion with author, November 5, 2011).

3. Claudia Notzke, "The Barriere Lake Trilateral Agreement," a report prepared for the Royal Commission on Aboriginal Peoples—Land, Resource and Environment Regimes Project (Barriere Lake Indian Government—October 1995), 21.

4. Ibid.

5. For further critical reading on comanagement arrangements between Canada, the provinces, territories, and First Nations, see Paul Nadasdy's account of how the broader political context of comanagement between Indigenous people

and state bureaucrats perpetuates unequal power relations ("The Case of the Missing Sheep," 127–51). See Harvey A. Feit for a brilliant illustration of the ways in
which state jurisdiction came to be exercised over the James Bay Cree through comanagement conservation schemes that sought to complete Canada's unfinished
sovereignty claims in the north ("Re-cognizing Co-management as Co-governance,"
47, 2). See also Nancy Peluso, who shows how comanagement conservation ideology
has been used as an excuse for states to justify coercion against local populations
("Coercive Conservation? . . . ," *Global Environmental Change* 3:2 [1993]: 199–218).
Finally, see Roderick Neumann, who suggests that many "community-friendly"
forms of conservation are closely linked to forms of disciplinary power ("Disciplining Peasants in Tanzania," Nancy Lee Peluso and Michael Watt, eds., *Violent
Environments* (Ithaca, N.Y.: Cornell University Press, 2001).

 6. The Honorable Réjean F. Paul, "Mediation Report," Longeuil, September 14,
1992, 4.

 7. See Nickels, "Importance of Experiential Context for Understanding Indigenous Ecological Knowledge," and Elias, *Socio-Economic Profile of the Algonquins of
Barriere Lake*.

 8. "The Trilateral Agreement," August 22, 1991, 2.

 9. Algonquins of Barriere Lake, "Declaration and Petition," November 26,
1992. See also letter from Clifford Lincoln (special representative, ABL) to André
Lafond (special representative, Quebec), February 6, 1992, Algonquin Nation Secretariat archives, Ottawa, Ontario. In this letter, Lincoln holds Lafond to account
for breach of sensitive area zones, despite repeated requests for an ABL monitoring
role to be accepted. He also cites the fact that the volume of cut allowed for per the
agreement with ABL was exceeded by Quebec. Lincoln urges mediation by Judge
Paul to move forward. According to Lincoln's letter, in response to these concerns,
Quebec repeatedly pleads that it cannot circumvent its own laws.

 10. Clifford Lincoln (special representative, ABL) letter to Secrétaire général
associé, Secrétariat aux Affaires autochtones, March 22, 1992, Algonquin Nation
Secretariat archives.

 11. Clifford Lincoln (special representative, ABL) letter to André Lafond, February 11, 1992, Algonquin Nation Secretariat archives.

 12. Christos Sirros (Quebec minister of Indian Affairs) letter to Jean-Maurice
Matchewan (chief, ABL), June 22, 1992, Algonquin Nation Secretariat archives.

 13. Jean-Maurice Matchewan (chief, ABL) letter to Christos Sirros (Quebec
minister of Indian Affairs) July 2, 1992, Algonquin Nation Secretariat archives.

 14. Ibid.

 15. Ibid.

 16. David Nahwegahbow (acting special representative for Barriere Lake Algonquins) letter to André Lafond (Quebec special representative) and Frank Vieni
(Canada special representative), April 21, 1992, Algonquin Nation Secretariat
archives.

 17. A Funding Mechanism Document that had been negotiated the previous
year precisely to avoid such restrictive funding and financial roadblocks to accomplish critical tasks was ignored.

 18. Christos Sirros (Quebec minister Indian Affairs) letter to Jean-Maurice
Matchewan (chief, ABL), July 22, 1992, Algonquin Nation Secretariat archives; emphasis added.

 19. In my Conclusion, however, I discuss how in 1987 Barriere Lake used non-

tied contribution dollars under the CLCP to undertake some preliminary research and traditional land-use mapping before the Trilateral Agreement was signed.

20. Paul, "Mediation Report," 1992, 8; emphasis added.

21. Boyce Richardson, in collaboration with Russell Diabo, "Canadian Hunters Fight for the Forest: The Algonquins Striving for Territory and Good Management," in *Forests for the Future: Local Strategies for Forest Protection, Economic Welfare and Social Justice,* ed. Paul Wolvekamp (London: Zed Books, 1999), 209.

22. Paul, "Mediation Report," 1992, 5.

23. Ibid., 9–10.

24. Richardson and Diabo, "Canadian Hunters Fight for the Forest," 209.

25. Christos Sirros (Quebec minister Indian Affairs) letter to Jean-Maurice Matchewan (chief, ABL), April 28, 2003.

26. François Gagnon, title unknown, *Le Droit,* April 30, 1993; my translation.

27. Ibid.

28. Assembly of First Nations, Media Advisory, April 30, 1993, Ottawa.

29. Notzke, "The Barriere Lake Trilateral Agreement," 2.

30. Richardson and Diabo, "Canadian Hunters Fight for the Forest," 210.

7. Coup d'État in Fourth-World Canada

1. Shiri Pasternak, "They're Clear-Cutting Our Way of Life: Algonquins Defend the Forest," *Upping the Anti* 8 (2009): 79.

2. See J. S. Milloy, "The Early Indian Acts: Development Strategies and Constitutional Change," in *Sweet Promises: A Reader on Indian–White Relations in Canada,* ed. J. R. Miller (Toronto: University of Toronto Press, 1991); NA, RG 10, vol. 239, part 1, Rev. T. Hurlburt letter to R. J. Pennefather, December 22, 1867. Milloy writes that "Hurlbert's letter also brings forward the department's solution" (153).

3. Richard H. Bartlett, "The Indian Act of Canada," *Buffalo Law Review* 27 (1977–78): 593.

4. Ibid. But, as Bartlett points out, this may have been the theory, but in practice the government negotiated seven of the numbered treaties from 1871 to 1877 with hereditary chiefs because only they held the authority to speak for their nations (608).

5. The full name of the act is "An Act for the Gradual Enfranchisement of Indians, the Better Management of Indian Affairs, and to Extend the Provisions of the Act 13st Victoria, Chapter 42."

6. Milloy, "The Early Indian Acts," 150–51.

7. Sessional Paper No. 3 (1871), at 4–7; emphasis added; cited in Bartlett, "The Indian Act of Canada," 594.

8. Ibid., 597–98.

9. Further amendments to the Indian Act in 1880 bolstered the role of the elective system, challenging the term of "life chiefs" and abolishing their powers with the introduction of the elective system, under the now absolute discretion of the Governor in Council (ibid., 596).

10. The transition to the election system had by no means meant the obliteration of customary orders throughout the country—bands adapted in a number of ways, including the establishment of parallel governments (e.g., Six Nations) or through maintaining their traditional roles as law carriers in the new office (e.g., Kitchenuhmaykoosib Inninuwug).

11. The band council institution itself, whether customary or elective, holds the power to subordinate Indigenous leadership under the massive administrative burden the leadership must carry. This technocratic system of governance and its attendant problems could be the subject of another lengthy book.

12. Russell Diabo, in discussion with author, November 5, 2011.

13. Joseph Junior Wawatie (spokesperson for Provisional Government) letter to Guy McKenzie (director general, Indian Affairs Canada), April 20, 1994, Algonquin Nation Secretariat archives.

14. Jérôme Lapierre (associate director general, Indian and Northern Affairs Canada) letter to Joseph Junior Wawatie (spokesperson for Provisional Government), April 25, 1994, Algonquin Nation Secretariat archives.

15. Ronald Irwin (minister of Indian and Northern Affairs Canada) letter to Joseph Junior Wawatie (spokesperson for Provisional Government), April 30, 1994, Algonquin Nation Secretariat archives.

16. A Senate Standing Committee Report on First Nations governance lays out the legalities of customary bands. To avoid confusion here, it is helpful to point to a distinction the Senate report makes between two separate legal categories of custom bands. The first kind pertains to Barriere Lake—a band that has never been governed under the Indian Act election provisions—and the second kind pertains to bands that were once under the Indian Act election process but then "reverted" to custom by meeting requirements of federal policy under the Conversion to Community Election System Policy. In the first case, bands are not governed under the regulatory oversight of the Department of Indian Affairs, whereas in the latter case, under the conversion to custom policy, bands' election protocols are considerably shaped by department rules. See Senate Standing Committee on Aboriginal Peoples, "First Nations Elections: The Choice Is Inherently Theirs," *Report of the Standing Senate Committee on Aboriginal Peoples,* May 2010.

17. See, for example, Denis Chatain (director general Quebec, Indian and Northern Affairs) letter to chief and councillors at Barriere Lake, December 22, 1994, or Gregor MacIntosh (direct general, Registration, Revenues and Band Governance, Indian and Northern Affairs) letter to the Algonquins of Barriere Lake, November 4, 1994, Algonquin Nation Secretariat archives.

18. Charlie Angus, "Algonquins of Barriere Lake: Against All Odds," *Highgrader Magazine,* November/December 2001.

19. Barriere Lake Indian Government, "Press Release: SQ Keeps Harassing Rapid Lake Community," October 27, 1994.

20. Ibid.

21. Angus, "Algonquins of Barriere Lake."

22. Ibid. Angus worked with the community in a number of roles over the years. He began as a journalist with *Highgrader Magazine,* then became an adviser to the Algonquin Nation Secretariat during the Adams Mine fight to stop a Toronto garbage site, and was also a communications adviser and trainer for the Algonquins of Barriere Lake Trilateral team in 2005–6. He went on to become MP for Timmins-James Bay as a member of the New Democratic Party, a post he holds until this day.

23. Carrie Buchanan, "Barriere Lake: Reserve Grapples with Report of Abuse; Counsellers Sent to Aid Young Victims," *Ottawa Citizen,* May 5, 1995, C7, final edition.

24. Mike Shahin, "Analysis: Indifference, Politics Hinder Reserve's Effort to

Heal Wounds of Child Sex Abuse; Report Recommends Barriere Lake Algonquin Use Healing Circles, Not Imprisonment," *Ottawa Citizen*, December 19, 1995, B1, final edition.

25. Ibid.

26. Ibid.

27. I would hasten to add that this would not be the first incident of a settler-colonial government using sexual abuse allegations for political purposes against Indigenous peoples. In 2007, in the Northern Territory of Australia, the Board of Inquiry into the Protection of Aboriginal Children from Sexual Abuse produced a report called *"Ampe Akelyernemane Meke Mekarle*, Little Children Are Sacred." The report, which alleged an unsafe and failed Indigenous society for women and children, prompted the Australian government to launch the Northern Territory National Emergency Response in 2007. The suite of legislation included the Northern Territory National Emergency Response Act 2007, the Families, Community Services and Indigenous Affairs (Northern Territory Emergency Response and Other Measures) Act 2007 and the Social Security and Other Legislation Amendment (Welfare Payment Reform) Act 2007, which were collectively referred to as the "NTER legislation." This emergency response warranted "separate legal measures and administration" because a state of "juridical exceptionalism" was deemed necessary to deal with Aborigines (e.g., the Racial Discrimination Act 1975 was suspended and criminal courts were banned from taking into account cultural consideration for Aborigine offenders) (Peter Billings, "Juridical Exceptionalism in Australian Law, Nostalgia and the Exclusion of 'Others,'" *Griffith Law Review* 20:2 [2011]: 279). As Billings explains: "Perceived emergencies—broadly, border (in)security and physical (in)security—have resulted in the creation of legal spaces in which 'Others' are constituted within and without the juridical order by the sovereign: simultaneously subject to law's commands and constraints while often beyond its protective reach" (272). The National Emergency Response has now been replaced by the Stronger Futures Policy, 2011.

28. David Nahwegahbow (acting special representative for Barriere Lake Algonquins) letter to Gliberte Lavoie (special representative for Canada), October 31, 1994, Algonquin Nation Secretariat archives.

29. Department of Indian Affairs and Northern Development (DIAND), "Overview of the Situation at Barriere Lake," Protected Security Classification, approved by Denis Chatain (July 4, 1995), 4, Algonquin Nation Secretariat archives.

30. Interim Band Council (IBC) letter to Denis Chatain (director general Quebec, Indian and Northern Affairs), November 23, 1995, Algonquin Nation Secretariat archives.

31. DIAND, Strategic Communication Planning, Communications Branch, "Advice to Minister: Former Barriere Lake Chief and Council Present Community Petition Supporting Their Reinstatement" (January 30, 1996).

32. Ibid.; and DIAND, Strategic Communication Planning, Communications Branch, "Advice to Minister: Various Developments at Barriere Lake" (January 30, 1996).

33. Two briefings—on December 20, 1995, and January 10, 1996, approved by Denis Chatain, the regional director general of the Quebec Region of INAC—reveal important new developments in the department's thinking. Whereas in December the issue posed in the ministerial briefing was, "Should DIAND recognize the

results of the election petition of November 23, 1995, thereby confirming the choice of the new band council?" by January it was, "How is DIAND Quebec Region, going to minimize impacts of its decision to recognize the interim Band Council as the legitimate Band Council of Barriere Lake?" (DIAND, Lands, Revenues and Trusts, "Recognition of New Council Elected according to Custom at Barriere Lake," internal file, briefing, approved by Denis Chatain, December 20, 1995, and DIAND, Lands, Revenues and Trusts, "Recognition of New Council Elected according to Custom at Barriere Lake," internal file, briefing, approved by Denis Chatain, January 10, 1996).

34. DIAND, "Recognition of New Council," press release, January 10, 1996; emphasis added.

35. Martia Freeman, director and general counsel, Administrative Legal Section, Ken Katz, counsel, Administrative Legal Section, and Ryan Rempel, counsel, Administrative Legal Section, to Yves Cazelas, counsel, DIAND Legal Services, "Algonquins of Barriere Lake—Request by 'Interim Band Council' for Recognition," memorandum, protected: solicitor-client, December 1995.

36. Ibid.; emphasis added.

37. Jean Maurice Matchewan (chief, ABL) letter to Ronald Irwin (minister of Indian Affairs), January 29, 1996, Algonquin Nation Secretariat archives. In this letter Matchewan states that that community was prepared to hold a referendum on community leadership "as per the January 14, 1996 Council Resolution we presented to you."

38. Barriere Lake Indian Government, "Response to the Department of Indian Affairs Document Entitled 'Backgrounder.'" See also Jean Maurice Matchewan (chief, ABL) to David Nahwegahbow (ABL legal counsel), December 7, 1995, where Matchewan faxes twenty-four typed and signed statements of individuals who came into the band office to complain to Matchewan that they had no knowledge that their signatures were used for the IBC petition, Algonquin Nation Secretariat archives.

39. Jean Maurice Matchewan (chief, ABL) letter to Ronald Irwin (minister of Indian Affairs), January 29, 1996, Algonquin Nation Secretariat archives.

40. David Nahwegahbow (ABL legal counsel) letter to Christos Sirros (Quebec minister of Indian Affairs), Re: *Algonquins of Barriere Lake, the Interim Band Council of Barriere Lake, et al. v The Attorney General of Canada, et al.*, Federal Court of Canada, File No. T-2590–95, January 23, 1996, Algonquin Nation Secretariat archives.

41. *Mitchikanibikok Inik v. Michel Thusky, et al.*, Federal Court of Canada, T-1761–98, September 8, 1999, at paragraphs 5 and 6.

42. Cross-examination of Pierre Nepton, Questions 293—325 and 300. Regarding *Mitchikanibikok Inik v. Michel Thusky, et al.*, Federal Court Trial Division, Docket T-1761–98, September 8, 1999, paragraph 6. The Algonquin group followed the department's counsel and circulated a petition on- and off-reserve proclaiming themselves to be the IBC.

43. Jean Chrétien (prime minister of Canada) letter to Michel Gratton (special representative for Barriere Lake), August 29, 2002, Algonquin Nation Secretariat archives.

44. Marc Perron, "Report by Special Ministerial Representative to the Algonquins of Barriere Lake," submitted to the Honorable Chuck Strahl, minister of Indian and Northern Affairs Canada, December 20, 2007, 5; emphasis added. See also Martin Lukacs, "Top Diplomat's Report to Minister Laid Out Strategy for

Government Subversion of Algonquin Community," *Znet,* August 21, 2009, http://www.zcommunications.org/top-diplomat-s-report-to-minister-laid-out-strategy-for-government-subversion-of-algonquin-community-by-martin-lukacs; accessed February 24, 2010; and Martin Lukacs, "Minister's Memo Exposes Motives for Removing Algonquin Chief," *Dominion Paper,* March 27, 2009, http://www.dominionpaper.ca/articles/2560; accessed February 24, 2010.

45. Clifford Lincoln, in discussion with author, April 26, 2011.

46. James Bikerton, "Deconstructing the 'New Federalism,'" *Canadian Political Science Review* 4:2–3 (June–September 2010): 58–59.

47. An Originating Motion for Provisional Interlocutory Injunction, Interlocutory Injunction and Declaration, For Permanent Injunction was submitted to the Quebec Superior Court on April 5, 1994, by the Algonquins of Barriere Lake against Gerard Guay (No. 550–05–000492–945). A decision was rendered on May 9, 1994, by the Honorable Mr. Justice Jean-Pierre Plouffe, who granted the motion for provisional interlocutory injunction, determining that Gerard Guay could not represent the Provisional Government, could not come onto Barriere Lake territory, and must return all files, documents, and records belonging to the band.

48. Alex Roslin, "Long, Cold Days Spent on the Barricades," *Wind Speaker,* January 1, 1997.

49. Originating Notice of Motion, Federal Court of Canada, Trial Division, T-2590–95, Interim Band Council of the Algonquins of Barriere Lake, Lisa Chief, Henry Nottaway, Archie Ratt, Patrick Ratt, and Marie-Claire Wawatie, as Council and Representatives of the Algonquins of Barriere Lake, applicants; and the Attorney General of Canada, Jean Maurice Matchewan continuing to act of Chief, Jean Paul Ratt continuing to act as councilor, and Michel Thusky continuing to act as Band Administrator of the Algonquins of Barriere Lake Band, respondents [hereafter, *IBC v Matchewan*], December 8, 1995. The case was set to challenge the status quo of the 1980 chief and council. The year 1980 was the time of Jean Maurice Matchewan's council's original customary selection.

50. Nahwegahbow makes note of the nature of this conflict of interest in his affidavit for the case in paragraph 9. He cites paragraph 4 of the Notice of Motion (ibid.), which requests a mandatory interlocutory requiring the respondents, their servants, and their agents "to surrender up to the applicants all items and records necessary to act as the duly constituted government of the Algonquins of Barriere Lake."

51. Ibid.

52. Federal Court of Canada, Trial Division, T-2590–95, *IBC v Matchewan*; reasons for order delivered orally from the bench at Ottawa, Ontario, on Thursday, February 8, 1996. Whereas the courts determined the legality of the ministers' recognition in terms of the Indian Act, the Matchewan council asserted their case in terms of Indigenous rights. This intervention, Barriere Lake maintained, was a violation of the band's self-government, a contravention of the Department of Indian Affairs' own policies, and the move failed to recognize the inviolability of custom bands, so was also an abrogation of Section 35 protection of Aboriginal rights in the Constitution Act of 1982.

53. Ibid.; emphasis added.

54. Barriere Lake Indian Government, "Response to the Department of Indian Affairs Document Entitled 'Backgrounder: Barriere Lake Leadership Issues,'" February 19, 1996.

55. Although in July 1994, the Provisional Government accused community leaders of designing the Trilateral Agreement to "sell off the territory," by April, they were promising to "protect" and "improve" the agreement (Kitiganik Anicinabek Provisional Government, "Community Notice," April 23, 1994).

56. The auditor-general included criticisms of the policy in her 2006 audit, noting that communities under third-party management have no way to dispute decisions made on their behalf, have no input in the selection of their managers, do not receive any actual training to develop management or finance skills, and have no recourse to any formal evaluations of the manager's work or an independent process to regain control over their finances. In addition, there is ample and discouraging evidence to support concerns that the policy has systematically abused the process to police First Nations bands with which it has disagreements. Barriere Lake features among these bands, but see also the case of Pikangikum First Nation in Manitoba and the Peigan Tribe, part of the Blackfoot Confederacy, in Alberta.

57. Rosalee Tizya, press conference transcript, January 23, 1996, city hall, Hull, Quebec.

58. Former principal of the Rapid Lake school, Jonathan Robinson, explains that an education committee in the community was finally permitted to take over control of education. An Algonquin-speaking education assistant was placed in each classroom, a proper play structure was built, a Head Start program was initiated to encourage kindergarten participation, and suddenly, student enrollment jumped and classroom participation livened up, with the assistance of Algonquin-speaking instructors. He stated: "What this means is for the first time in a generation a child can go into the school in Rapid Lake and speak their own language and what this means is that over the next 4 or 5 years, when they gain proficiency in Algonquin, they will then learn the French and English they haven't been able to learn in the past 20 years" (Jonathan Robinson, press conference transcript, January 23, 1996, city hall, Hull, Quebec). This community-driven education committee was disbanded with the recognition of the IBC.

59. Russell Diabo, in discussion with author, November 5, 2011.

60. Harry Wawatie, Barriere Lake chief, letter to the Honorable Doug Young, minister of Human Resources Development, Canada, and the Honorable Ethel Blondin-Andrew, secretary of state for youth and training, Quebec, April 16, 1996, Algonquin Nation Secretariat archives.

61. This loyalty partially drew from the partnership the community had established with educators, which was no accident. The community had established a careful and lengthy process to hire staff to rebuild their school. They received several hundred applications, interviewed twenty people, and hired six to support their vision. These six teachers worked hard with the parent committee to ensure that the quality of education met and exceeded provincial standards, while maintaining a strong connection to Algonquin culture and language. The IBC tried to coerce the teachers into supporting it, and issued bizarre directives such as "oaths of allegiance" to the council and prohibiting teaching staff from speaking to the media. See Stephen Pearson, teacher at Rapid Lake Federal School, letter to the Honorable Jean Charest, leader of Progressive Conservatives, Re: Educational Services in the Native Community of Rapid Lake, March 8, 1996, Algonquin Nation Secretariat archives.

62. Denis Chatain, regional director general Indian Affairs, Quebec Region, let-

ter to Stephen Pearson, teacher at Rapid Lake Federal School, May 7, 1996, Algonquin Nation Secretariat archives.

63. Even officials within the department found these grounds insupportable. See Harold Gideon, letter to internal department staff (undisclosed), re: docket response—letter to Jonathan Robinson, Barriere Lake, March 25, 1996, Algonquin Nation Secretariat archives, in which he states that the department constantly deals with community members and has never limited itself to discussion with the "governing council." He is responding to a draft response to Robinson circulated for feedback.

64. Jonathan Robinson, principal Rapid Lake Federal School, letter to Ron Irwin, minister of Indian Affairs, March 20, 1996, Algonquin Nation Secretariat archives.

65. Truth and Reconciliation Commission of Canada, "Truth and Reconciliation Commission of Canada: Calls to Action," 2015, 2.

66. Carrie Buchanan, "The Bitterness at Barriere Lake," *Ottawa Citizen,* February 3, 1996.

67. Ibid.

68. Denis Gratton and Julie Lemieux, "Clan War Continues among Algonquins of Barriere Lake: The Children Are Caught in the Crossfire," *Le Droit,* January 31, 1996.

69. Angus, "Algonquins of Barriere Lake."

70. Marylynn Poucachiche, in discussion with author, January 21, 2009.

71. Alex Roslin, "Algonquins to Extend Barriere Lake Blockade—13 Logging Companies Targeted in Dispute over Ancestral Lands—Mediator Quits," *Montreal Gazette,* January 16, 1997.

72. Michel Gratton, "Ottawa's Barriere Lake Move Was Undemocratic," *Montreal Gazette,* February 4, 1997, B.3, final edition.

73. Roslin, "Algonquins to Extend Barriere Lake Blockade."

74. Ibid.

75. Ibid.

76. Algonquins of Barriere Lake, Band Council Resolution, 97–05, April 23, 1997.

77. The Honorable Réjean Paul, "Mediation Report," January 28, 1997.

78. Ibid.

79. Tony Wawatie retold his uncle Harry's prophesy, in discussion with author, February 1, 2011.

80. Department of Indian Affairs, "Questions and Answers—Barriere Lake," January 24, 1996.

81. Government of Quebec and Algoquins of Barriere Lake, "Agreement on Approach and Process for Completing Phases Two, Three and Undertaking Negotiations under The Trilateral Agreement," Quebec, May 22, 1998.

82. For example, the World Wildlife Fund petitioned Indian Affairs Minister Robert Nault to plead for reinstatement of the Trilateral process (Angus, "Algonquins of Barriere Lake"). As well, other First Nations were learning about the Trilateral, and the cutting-edge documentation and mapping the community was producing, and were contacting Barriere Lake advisers to learn more (Russell Diabo, in discussion with author, April 4, 2010). A presentation on the Trilateral Agreement was made at the United Nations Fourth Forum on Forests held in Geneva, Switzerland, in May 2004. Other presentations on the Trilateral Agreement approach were

made to the National Aboriginal Forestry Association, Sustainable Forest Managment Network, Forest Stewardship Council of Canada, Natural Resources Canada, Manitoba Model Forest Network, Interior Alliance of First Nations, Carrier-Sekani Tribal Council, Ulkatcho First Nation, Neskonlith Indian Band, Adams Lake Indian Band, Union of B.C. Indian Chiefs, and Spallumcheen Indian Band (*Trilateral Secretariat Communications Newsletter* 2:3 [September 2006]).

83. Harry Wawatie (chief, ABL) letter to Guy Chevrette (Quebec minister of Natural Resource and minister Responsible for Native Affairs), August 24, 2001, Algonquin Nation Secretariat archives.

84. See Algonquins of Barriere Lake, "Press Release: Complete Shutdown of Logging in La Vérendrye Park Region Begins," August 9, 2001, in which Chief Harry Wawatie states: "At a meeting . . . on July 16, 2001 . . . the federal representative Sophie Lise Ratt indicated that we should use our community's capital project budget, meaning that urgently needed housing for our people would be partially sacrificed to compensate for the refusal of the Department of Indian Affairs to honour its financial obligations under the terms of the Trilateral Agreement. In light of the serious situation of over-crowding on our reserve, of course our people rejected the idea."

85. Between December 4, 2002, and April 30, 2003, Health Canada undertook a series of inspections of the housing on the Rapid Lake Reserve at the request of its community health representative. Health Canada's inspections revealed widespread mold contamination—at medium and elevated levels of risk to residents' health—as well as rotting walls, faulty electricity, deteriorating fixtures, walls, and windows, overcrowding, and, in one case, lack of heating on the first floor of a house. In at least two cases, previous Health Canada inspections from November 2000 were cited in which elevated health risks owing to mold contamination and respiratory illness were urgently flagged but had never been resolved and where conditions had only worsened. Health Canada issued a series of reports from January 9, 2003, to June 3, 2003, based on inspections at Rapid Lake on December 4, 2002, and April 30, 2003. The results of these inspections are conveyed in letters of correspondence between Health Canada's environmental health officer and Robert Smith, director of finance for the Algonquins of Barriere Lake, between January 9, 2003, and June 3, 2003.

86. Harry Wawatie (chief, ABL) letter to Jerome Lapierre, September 7, 2001, Algonquin Nation Secretariat archives.

87. Marc Lefrenière (deputy minister of Indian Affairs) letter to Harry Wawatie (chief, ABL), September 25, 2001, Algonquin Nation Secretariat archives.

88. In addition, the regional DIA office had not even begun to comply with the MOMI for an entire year after signing the agreement, leaving the band with only two years to undertake an ambitious restoration plan for the tiny, impoverished community.

89. INAC, "Statement Regarding the Situation with the Barriere Lake First Nation," press release, September 26, 2001.

90. Four Arrows E-Newsletter, "The Algonquins of Barriere Lake: A Case Study in How to Kill Opportunity," newsletter, March 17, 2002.

91. Michel Gratton, in discussion with author, April 9, 2011.

92. Harry Wawatie (chief, ABL) letter to Guy Chevrette (Quebec minister Indian Affairs), September 17, 2001, Algonquin Nation Secretariat archives.

93. Algonquins of Barriere Lake, "Termination of Federal Funding Forces Complete Shutdown of Logging in La Vérendrye Park," August 13, 2001.

94. Quoted in Four Arrows E-Newsletter, "The Algonquins of Barriere Lake." Chief Harry Wawatie also quotes this letter in a press release on August 15, 2001, titled "Domtar's Intervention Welcomed by Algonquins."

95. Giovanni Arrighi, *The Long Twentieth Century* (London: Verso, 1994), 34.

96. Ibid.

97. Deborah Bird Rose, *Hidden Histories* (Canberra: Aboriginal Studies Press 1991), 46.

98. Timothy Mitchell, "The Stage of Modernity," in *Questions of Modernity*, ed. Timothy Mitchell (Minneapolis: University of Minnesota Press, 2000), 7. Ironically, though, this space–power relationship has been one of the key indictments of Michel Foucault's studies of modernity by postcolonial scholars. As critics contend, for Foucault, the very knowledge forms that produce the genealogies of modernity are always centered in European nations; the rest of the world is rendered as a periphery, producing a temporal world set by the pace and standards of modernity within Europe. (See ibid., 5–7.)

99. CJOH-TV News, "Coon Come Joins Algonquins' Protest on Victoria Island," October 3, 2001, Ottawa.

8. The Government Must Fall

1. Under the Indian Act provisions on governance, Section 2(1) defines the band council to mean, either (a) in the case of a band to which Section 74 applies, the council established pursuant to that section, or (b) in the case of a band to which Section 74 does not apply, the council chosen according to the custom of the band, or, where there is no council, the chief of the band chosen according to the custom of the band. The Algonquins of Barriere Lake fall under the (b) provisions: a customary band that is not governed under the election provisions of Section 74, but rather where the leadership is chosen according to the customs of the band.

2. *The Annotated Indian Act and Aboriginal Constitutional Provisions* (Scarborough, Ontario: Carswell, 1998).

3. The Haudenosaunsee are a confederacy of Six Nations—the Seneca, Cayuga, Tuscarora, Onondaga, Oneida, and Mohawk nations—bound together by a peaceful alliance known as "Kaianerakowa," or Great Law of Peace. Until 1924, the confederacy was the only governing body for the whole community of six nations. The Canadian government ordered the removal of the Haudenosaunee government using Section 74 of the Indian Act. For more on the events of 1924 at Six Nations, see Grace Li Xiu Woo, "Canada's Forgotten Founders: The Modern Significance of the Haudenosaunee (Iroquois) Application for Membership in the League of Nations," *L., SOC. JUST. & GLOBAL DEV. J.* (April 30, 2003). Since that time, two bands in Manitoba were subject to Section 74 impositions in the 1980s—Dakota Tipi and Sandy Bay; however, both bands had been previously governed under Section 2(1) (a) of the Indian Act, that is, under band council elections. Both bands reverted to custom using the INAC Conversion to Community Election System Policy, so the situation was not strictly the same as at Barriere Lake, where the band's leadership selection had never been under the Indian Act and where their Indigenous law was still the primary and unbroken source of their Aboriginal rights, title, and jurisdiction to their lands.

4. See, for example, the excellent book by Hugh Shewell, *"Enough to Keep Them Alive": Indian Welfare in Canada, 1873–1965* (Toronto: University of Toronto

Press, 2004). For other reports that highlight more contemporary fiscal relations, see AFN, "Fiscal Transfers, Programs and Services: The End of the Line? A Brief Survey of Crown–Indian Fiscal Relations," September 17, 1996; Sharon Venne, "The Difficulties of Shedding a Colonizers' Burden: A History of 'Devolution' in the 'Indian Affairs' Regime, or Why There Are 'Contribution Agreements,'" prepared for Thunderchild First Nation, May 19, 2012; and, Judith Rae, "Program Delivery Devolution: A Stepping Stone or Quagmire for First Nations?" *Indigenous Law Journal* 7:2 (2009): 10–11.

5. Chief Harry Wawatie resigned on July 10, 2006. In his letter of resignation, he regretfully submits that under his leadership, he failed to get the federal government back to the negotiating table to implement the 1997 MOMI or the 1991 Trilateral Agreement. He writes that at his age, he has neither the stamina nor the health to continue fighting with the government. His comments are cited in the Honorable Réjean Paul, Superior Court Justice Mediator's Report, "The Algonquins of Barriere Lake, Prepared for the Algonquins of Barriere Lake and the Authorities of the Quebec City Office of Indian and Northern Affairs Canada," Montreal, May 15, 2007.

6. Following Chief Wawatie's resignation, Resolution # 03–08–06 of the Council of Elders was adopted on August 3, 2006, stating that the "Council of Elders hereby confirm, that the following people were selected as our new customary Chief and Council during a Leadership Assembly on July 24th 2006 and confirmed in a Community Meeting on August 1st 2006 in accordance with our First Nation's Mitchikanibikok Anishnabe Onakinakewin (Customary Governance Code), and they represent a broad consensus of our Eligible Community Members": Jean Maurice Matchewan as chief, with Benjamin Nottaway, Moise Papatie, Jean Paul Ratt, and David Wawatie as councillors.

7. William Nottaway's council consisted of Patrick Ratt, Hector Jerome, Thomas Ratt, and Emmett Papatie.

8. On the failure of Indian Affairs to attach the Special Provisions (explaining the deficit) to the 2007 Contribution Agreement, see paragraph 140 in the Application for Judicial Review, Federal Court File No. T-1514–06 between the Elders' Council of Mitchikanibikok Inik and minister of Indian Affairs and Northern Development, August 10, 2006. It reads: "After the disputed 2006 appointment of a TPM to the ABL, DIAND executed a Contribution Agreement with the TPM which excluded the Special Provisions for the first time since 1996. This Contribution Agreement was executed between the TPM and DIAND, without the approval of the Chief and Council."

9. Judge Réjean Paul was mandated on January 23, 2007, to examine the situation at Barriere Lake and to make appropriate recommendations to the minister of Indian Affairs. He lost the support of George Nottaway, who led the dissident council, and therefore stepped down from his official role as mediator, but he prepared a final mediator's report that was submitted on May 15, 2007 ("The Algonquins of Barriere Lake: Mediator's Report," 2007).

10. Ibid., 4.

11. Back on Parliament Hill in June 2007, Jean Maurice Matchewan met with the Deputy Minister of Indian Affairs Michael Wernick. Wernick only agreed to the meeting because Barriere Lake had camped out on Parliament Hill just days before Canada Day celebrations would be held there and the minister sought to avoid their embarrassing presence at the national party.

12. Marc Perron, "Report: Special Ministerial Representative to the Algonquins of Barriere Lake," 14.

13. Chuck Strahl (minister of Indian Affairs) letter to Benjamin Nottaway (acting chief), January 29, 2008, Algonquin Nation Secretariat archives.

14. As a result of extensive wrangling, the ABL special representative, Clifford Lincoln, and the Quebec special representative, John Ciaccia, were given a mandate in 2005 to come up with a series of recommendations to resume negotiations. "The Ciacca–Lincoln Joint Recommendations," as they came to be known, are seven articles of consensus for moving forward toward comanagement of the territory. They include recognition of the Trilateral Agreement territory and the development and implementation of final Integrated Resource Management Plans on forestry, wildlife, fish, and social indicators that would bring in measures to harmonize Algonquin subsistence with long-term plans for resource development in the territory. Ciacca and Lincoln also provided recommendations for institutionalizing Algonquin participation in the management of renewable resources, as well as revenue sharing, housing, and infrastructure improvements, and electrification of the Rapid Lake Reserve. Many articles that first appeared in the 1998 bilateral agreement between Quebec and the band now applied more broadly to federal and provincial governments. But the implementation was spotty at best.

15. Harry Wawatie, chief, Algonquins of Barriere Lake, letter to Rémy Trudel, minister responsible for Native Affairs, April 18, 2002, Algonquin Nation Secretariat archives.

16. These charges were eventually cleared on May 2, 2013, Algonquin Nation Secretariat archives.

17. Casey Ratt letter to Chuck Strahl (minister of Indian Affairs), January 31, 2008, Algonquin Nation Secretariat archives.

18. Harry Wawatie (on behalf of Mitchikanibikok Inik Council of Elders) letter to minister of Indians Affairs (Canada federal office and Quebec regional office), February 4, 2008, Algonquin Nation Secretariat archives.

19. The court worker had second thoughts himself about the validity of his testimony regarding the legitimacy of Ratt council election: "After reading the report that I had sent you in regards to the above mentioned subject, I realized that my last sentence: 'To the best of my knowledge, it was in accordance with the Mitchikanibikok Anishnabe Onakinakewin', could cause confusion. This statement reflects only the way in which the candidates were nominated during the review and the choice of candidates by the members of Barriere Lake. It does not confirm that all other Leadership review regulations were observed. I cannot swear that Article 8.11 (2)(3)(4)(5) and (6) was observed because I only had access to the list of persons voting and the Mitchikanibikok Anishnabe Onakinakewin. I cannot guarantee therefore that the Elder's [sic] Council was advised or that proper notification for a leadership review was carried out according to the regulations, that is to say, if everyone eligible to vote for Chief and Council had been duly notified" (Laurier Riel letter to Minister Chuck Strahl, "Re: Leadership Review at Barriere Lake," February 10, 2008, Algonquin Nation Secretariat archives). Riel furthermore had no expertise in the community's customary code, in Anishnabe law, or even in Canadian law. His confirmation of the leadership selection in the capacity of a court worker raises serious questions about why the government ignored Nottaway and Wawatie's claims that the Ratt council was not elected according to the Mitchikanibikok Anishnabe Onakinakewin.

20. Martin Lukacs, "Minister's Memo Exposes Motives for Removing Algonquin Chief," *Dominion*, March 27, 2009.

21. Harry Wawatie on behalf of Elders Council letter to Minister of Indian Affairs Chuck Strahl, Re: New Mitchikanibikok Inik Leadership Selection Process, March 31, 2008, Algonquin Nation Secretariat archives.

22. Ibid.

23. *Harry Wawatie, et al. v Minister of Indian Affairs and Northern Development*, Application Notice under section 18.1 of the Federal Courts Act, March 25, 2008.

24. As Justice Zinn states in paragraph 10: "The Prothonotary accepted the respondent's submission that the Minister was not acting as a federal board, commission, or other tribunal within the meaning of section 18.1 of the *Federal Courts Act* and thus there was no decision that was reviewable in this Court" (*Harry Wawatie et al., in Their Capacity as Members of the Elders Council of Mitchikanibikok Inik v Minister of Indian Affairs and Northern Development*, the Honorable Mr. Justice Zinn, Reasons for Order, Ottawa, Ontario, January 6, 2009).

25. Justice Zinn accepted plaintiffs' submission of the Crown's duty to consult with First Nations articulated in *Haida Nation v British Columbia (Minister of Forests)*, 3 S.C.R. 511, 2004 SCC 73 at paragraph 25: "Whether the duty to consult can be said to arise in the present circumstances is not without question. This appears to be an area of evolving jurisprudence. In this respect, the observations of Justice Hugessen in *Shubenacadie Indian Band v Canada (Attorney General)*, 2001 FCT 181, at paragraph 5, made in the context of a motion to strike an action involving aboriginal law, are apt: . . . 'If there is in a pleading a glimmer of a cause of action, even though vaguely or imperfectly stated, it should, in my view, be allowed to go forward' (*Wawatie et al.*, Reasons for Order).

26. In paragraphs 14–17, Justice Zinn lays out his reasoning for rejecting the Prothonotary's grounds based on Justice McGillis's decision in *Barriere Lake* (Federal Court of Canada, Trial Division, T-2590–95, *Interim Band Council et al., v The Attorney General of Canada, et al.*, Reasons for Order). Zinn notes that McGillis's ruling was not based on Indian Affairs' legal jurisdiction to determine the proper leadership at Barriere Lake, but rather on the *method* by which this determination could be scrutinized, as in the present case (*Wawatie et al.*, Reasons for Order).

27. Ratt council, Barriere Lake press release, October 6, 2008.

28. Ibid. In addition, a controversial school closure had also caused a major breech between families in the community. The reserve elementary school closure began in February 2008 was initiated by the Mitchikanibikok Inik Education Authority (MIEA) to assert pressure on Quebec and Canada, which had been non-committal on MIEA's request for greater control over curriculum (i.e., reinstating Algonquin curriculum) and community input on educational affairs at the school (Mitchikanibikok Inik, *Widmadwin*, Algonquins of Barriere Lake Community Newsletter, February 18, 2008, 1).

29. One example of the projects the Ratt council committed to is demonstrated by its win in December 2008 when the Algonquins of Barriere Lake picked up the Community Team of Year Award at the Dialogue for Life Suicide Prevention Conference in Montreal for their plan to identify, develop, and implement priority action plans to remedy social issues on the reserve—although it is unclear if this project ever developed further. But in terms of their actual community accountability and legitimacy, members of the Ratt council did not live in the community, and, like the

IBC, were also a government in exile based in Maniwaki, meeting with government officials off-reserve for negotiations.

30. Keith Penner, Facilitator's Report on the Leadership Selection Process in Accord with the Mitchikanibikok Anishnabe Onakinakewin (the Barriere Lake Customary Governance Code), Article VII Nikanikabwijik (the Council) Wasakawegan (the process for selecting leaders) s. 8.6 to s. 8.9, June 24, 2009, 8.

31. Ibid.

32. In fact, this application was a revived lawsuit of the injunctions Swinwood attempted to serve during the leadership selection process. There were some changes to the original Swinwood application, for example, David Nahwegahbow, on behalf of his clients, managed to have Keith Penner and the Algonquin Nation Secretariat struck from the suit.

33. These discussions took place at a case conference held on November 9, 2009, before Prothonotary Mireille Tabib. Details of this case conference are included in the following communication: David Nahwegahbow to Michael Swinwood, Re: Clarification of the Decision of Justice Zinn in *Wawatie v Canada (Indian Affairs and Northern Development)*, FC 8 (January 6, 2009), March 26, 2009.

34. Justice Mainville found that the leadership selection undertaken to appoint Casey Ratt chief was in violation of the Mitchikanibikok Anishnabe Onakinakewin because the conveners did not follow the proper protocols of a leadership review process. Key here for Justice Mainville was that they neglected to invite the sitting chief and council to their meeting and in effect deposed the entire council because of a grievance with the appointment of Benjamin Nottaway as acting chief (*Casey Ratt, et al. v Jean Maurice Matchewan, et al.* The Honorable Mr. Justice Mainville, Reasons for Judgment, 2010 FC 160, February 17, 2010, at paragraph 119).

35. There were a number of inconsistencies in Justice Mainville's decision. For example, he found that the purpose of the June 24, 2009, leadership selection process was simply a ruse to dislodge the Ratt council and restore the Matchewan council. However, he chastised the Ratt council later in his judgment for refusing to participate in this leadership selection process, in effect, recognizing the efforts of the Matchewan–Nottaway council to pursue a path of reconciliation with the Ratt council.

36. According to Matchewan, Quebec's Ministry of National Resources (MNR) sent one set of documents to Matchewan and one set to Ratt for approval. For example, one document they both received was a "*Permis d'intervention, pour l'approvisionnement d'une usine de transformation*" (management permit for the supply of a wood-processing plant) on June 2, 2010, advising of logging cut requests from Bois Nobles Ka'N'Enda Itée and Louisiana-Pacific Canada Ltd., with dozens of additional forestry industry beneficiaries listed as such in the permit request.

37. A good example of the negotiations under way during this period can be found in a letter to the Quebec minister of Natural Resources and Aboriginal Affairs, written on June 1, 2010, and signed by Jean Maurice Matchewan. In the letter, Matchewan reminds the minister that the community had been waiting for four years for a response to implement the joint recommendations submitted to the Quebec government on July 13, 2006, by their special representatives, Clifford Lincoln and John Ciaccia. Referring to a recent letter sent on May 26, 2010, by the minister, Matchewan points out that they fell short of their Crown obligations under the law to consult and accommodate the Algonquins through negotiation of

just settlement *(Haida)* in good faith *(Sparrow, Mikisew)*. He reminds the minister that the legal obligations in this case burdened the Crown to deal with the joint recommendations, the bilateral agreement, and the Trilateral Agreement provisions.

38. See the Ratt group's press release of November 12, 2010, where it states that "Barriere Lake members . . . refuse to concede to the decision of the Department of Indian Affairs to do away with their Customary Governance." The title of the press release is "Barriere Lake Assert Right to Self-Determination," and the last line states: "The community is demanding the Canadian Government to respect their rights to self-determination."

39. See Norman Matchewan and Casey Ratt letter to Anita Decoursay and Wanda Thusky, October 27, 2010, Algonquin Nation Secretariat archives, in which Matchewan and Ratt reference numerous open meetings held throughout 2009 where Section 74 was unanimously rejected and the Mitchikanibikok Anishnabe Onakinakewin affirmed.

40. Resolution of the Elders, Re: Rejection of Minister of Indian Affairs Plan to Impose Section 74 Elective System, December 14, 2009; Community Resolution, Re: Support of Elders Resolution to Reject Minister of Indian Affairs Plan to Impose Section 74 Elective System, December 15, 2009.

41. Norman Matchewan, Crystal Ratt, Donat Thusky, and David Wawatie letter to Pierre Nepton, May 26, 2010, Algonquin Nation Secretariat archives.

42. Chuck Strahl (minister of Indian Affairs) letter to Casey Ratt council and Jean Maurice Matchewan council, October 30, 2009, Algonquin Nation Secretariat archives.

43. *Bone v Sioux Valley Indian Band No. 290 Council,* [1996] 3 C.N.L.R. 54 at 65 (F.C.T.D).

44. David Nahwegahbow letter to Mitchikanibikok Inik Customary Council, Re: Impact of a Decision by the Minister to Put ABL into Indian Act Elections, November 10, 2009, Algonquin Nation Secretariat archives.

45. See *R. v Van der Peet* (1996) 2 S.C.R. 507 at paragraph 74: "In considering whether a claim to an aboriginal right has been made out, courts must look at both the relationship of the aboriginal claimant to the land and at *the practices, customs and traditions arising from the claimant's distinctive culture and society,*" and reiterated in *Delgamuukw v British Columbia* (1997) 3 S.C.R. 1010 at 141; emphasis added.

46. See, for example, *Delgamuukw,* where the court states that the Crown must demonstrate a compelling and substantive legislative objective to justify an infringement of Aboriginal title. See also *R. v Sparrow,* (1990) 1 S.C.R. 1075, and *R. v Marshall (No. 2),* (1999) 3 S.C.R. 533 (hereafter, *Sparrow*).

47. See Section 3.2, Ministerial Order under SubSection 74(1), in the Custom Election Dispute Resolution Policy: "As a last resort, in a situation where a community is in chaos and it is impossible to get agreement to mediation or arbitration from the parties, the option exists to bring the First Nation under the *Indian Act* for election purposes through the use of a ministerial order under Subsection 74(1). Such an action by the Minister is the antithesis of self-government and would be viewed very negatively as an intrusion into the affairs of the First Nation. However, there may be situations where the dispute is so volatile that no other option is viable."

48. Pierre Nepton, "Notice of Information to the Algonquins of Barriere Lake," flier, April 6, 2010.

49. Denis Chatain (INAC director general, Quebec Region) to Scott Serson

(deputy minister) and Shirley Serafini (associate deputy minister), "Recognition of New Council Elected according to Custom at Barriere Lake," protected briefing, December 20, 1995. Chatain writes that "Recourse to Section 74 of the *Indian Act* could also be had to put the band back on the track, pending the definition of its electoral custom."

50. Camil Simard (director, Negotiations, Governance and Individual Affairs, Quebec Region, INAC) and Jean Boucher (senior negotiator, INAC), "Barriere Lake Impact Scenarios Acknowledging the New Band Council," information prepared for minister and deputy minister, March 3, 2008. Scenario 1 identifies this option.

51. Chuck Strahl (minister of Indian Affairs) letter to Casey Ratt, Ricky Decoursay, Roger Jerome, Wayne Papatie, Donat Thusky, Jean Maurice Matchewan, Benjamin Nottaway, Eugene Nottaway, Joey Decoursay, David Wawatie, and Mitchikanibikok Inik, October 30, 2009.

52. Indian Country Today Media Network (ICTMN) Staff, "Indian Affairs Calls Indian Act Council 'Temporary Measure,'" *Indian Country Today,* December 27, 2010.

53. Norman Matchewan, in discussion with author, December 16, 2009.

54. Benjamin Nottaway, Eugene Nottaway, Joey Decoursay, David Wawatie, Jean Maurice Matchewan, chief and council, Barriere Lake Algonquins, and council, letter to Pierre Nepton, regional director general, Indian and Northern Affairs Canada, Re: Notice of Information to the Algonquins of Barriere Lake, January 13, 2010, Algonquin Nation Secretariat archives.

55. Pierre Nepton to Algonquins of Barriere Lake, "Notice of Information to the Algonquins of Barriere Lake concerning the Community Public Assembly of December 15, 2009," December 18, 2009, Algonquin Nation Secretariat archives.

56. Benjamin Nottaway, Eugene Nottaway, Joey Decoursay, David Wawatie, Jean Maurice Matchewan, chief and council, Barriere Lake Algonquins, and council letter to Pierre Nepton, regional director general, Indian and Northern Affairs Canada, Re: Notice of Information to the Algonquins of Barriere Lake, January 13, 2010, Algonquin Nation Secretariat archives.

57. Resolution of the Mitchikanibikok Inik, Re: Support of Elders Resolution to Reject the Minister of Indian Affairs Plan to Impose Section 74 Elective System, No. 12–15–09 B.

58. As Barriere Lake communicated to Nepton: "Only one is between our Council and the Casey Ratt group, and that was heard by the Federal Court on February 1 and 2, 2010" (Jean Maurice Matchewan, Benjamin Nottaway, Eugene Nottaway, Joey Decoursay, and David Wawatie letter to Pierre Nepton, Re: Second Notice of Information to the Algonquins of Barriere Lake, February 10, 2010, Algonquin Nation Secretariat archives).

59. Ibid.

60. These communications provided ample evidence that the community had the capacity to resolve issues on their own without the department's interference. On May 13, 2010, Barriere Lake sent a letter to Nepton informing him of actions taken by the community to resolve the leadership dispute. The letter outlines a process of internal consultation initiated for reviewing the customary code and a plan to establish a working group mandated to conduct community consultation. The purpose of the working group, as Barriere Lake explained it, was to facilitate a practical working relationship between the community and the governments, and it would actively engage all segments of the community, particularly youth, in the consultation process. But the letter also warned that healing times for

reconciliation cannot be artificially expedited. This correspondence echoed earlier community resolutions communicated to the department, such as the community resolution dated May 17, 2010, with 150 signatures from all segments of the community supporting a motion for their elders to protect their Onakinakewin and customary laws.

61. Pierre Nepton, "Notice to the Algonquins of Barriere Lake, Concerning Recent Correspondence Received by Indian and Northern Affairs Canada from Community Members," June 18, 2010.

62. Algonquins of Barriere Lake, "Barriere Lake Set Up Peaceful Blockade to Stop Unconstitutional Attack on Their Customary Government; AFN Passes Emergency Resolution Condemning Minister Strahl," July 22, 2010.

63. Ibid.

64. Courtney Kirkby and Jamie Ross, "Indian Affairs Confronted by Mitchikanibikokinik (Barriere Lake Algonquins," August 12, 2010, http://vimeo.com/14121623; accessed December 5, 2010.

65. This information was contained in confidential surveillance documents gained by an Access to Information and Privacy (ATIP) request. The INAC report states: "As the Indian Act election process allows for nominations to be made through the mail, despite the meeting not taking place, the Electoral Officer was in receipt of five valid written nominations (one for Chief and 4 for Councillor positions). As the number of persons nominated did not exceed the number to be elected, the Electoral Officer acclaimed the five individuals as Chief and Councillors" ("Barriere Lake First Nation—Protest—Governance," INAC Emergency and Issue Management Weekly Summary, for the week ending August 13, 2010).

66. Casey Ratt letter to Pierre Nepton, Re: Letter to Decline Nomination, August 20, 2010.

67. INAC Council to Algonquins of Barriere Lake, letter, September 8, 2010. The letter acknowledges that not everyone in the community is supportive of the changes, but says that they were encouraged nonetheless by the community to focus on two principles during their two-year term: "1. Develop a Reconciliation Process based on the revision and ratification of the ABL Customary Code of Governance; and 2. Continue to provide or improve, as deemed appropriate, new or current basic programs and services." No one whom I spoke to in the community knew anything about this consultation meeting taking place.

68. Minister of Indian Affairs Chuck Strahl used this concept of restoring democracy to the community in his letter informing them of his decision to impose a Section 74 order on the community: "At this point, I see the establishment of a transparent, democratic and accessible leadership selection process as the only viable option available to address the long-standing governance disputes in the community and to ensure the well-being of the residents and members of Barriere Lake" (Chuck Strahl letter to the Algonquins of Barriere Lake, October 30, 2009, Algonquin Nation Secretariat archives).

69. Algonquins of Barriere Lake, "Barriere Lake Set Up Peaceful Blockade to Stop Unconstitutional Attack on Their Customary Government."

70. Assembly of First Nations, "Support for Algonquins of Barriere Lake and Development of National Framework on First Nation-Driven Elections," July 20–22, 2010, Winnipeg, Manitoba.

71. National Chief Shawn Atleo met with Casey Ratt, Tony Wawatie, Jessica

Thusky, and Crystal Ratt in Montreal at the AFN fall 2010 Policy and Dialogue Forum, November 8–9, 2010.

72. Algonquins of Barriere Lake Elders Council (on behalf of the Algonquins of Barriere Lake) letter to Minister of Indian Affairs Chuck Strahl, Robert Nicholson, minister of Justice and Attorney General of Canada, Pierre Corbeil, Quebec minister of Aboriginal Affairs, and Jacques Dupuis, minister of Public Security, Re: Threat to Our Customary System of Governance by Illegitimate Federal and Provincial Decisions & Actions, August 25, 2010, Algonquin Nation Secretariat archives.

73. Joseph Boyden, "Why We Try to Protect Our Land: Lessons from Barriere Lake," *Globe and Mail*, December 13 2010; AFN, "Assembly of First Nations Supports Algonquins of Barriere Lake in Their Call for Canada to Respect Their Traditional Governance," December 13, 2010.

74. ICTMN Staff, "Indian Affairs Calls Indian Act Council 'Temporary Measure.'"

75. Ibid.

76. *Casey Ratt et al. v Jean Maurice Matchewan et al.*, Reasons for Judgment, FC 160, February 17, 2010, at paragraph 10.

77. Also, when the ANS could no longer represent Barriere Lake following the Mainville decision of February 2010, the research director of ANS had sealed all of the records pertaining to Barriere Lake and sent them to Nahwegahbow's office in Rama, Ontario, where they awaited resolution.

78. David Nahwegahbow, in discussion with author, October 9, 2010.

79. A conflict of interest motion failed to remove Swinwood from the case when members Casey Ratt's council refused to endorse the motion (Michel Thusky, in discussion with author, September 14, 2012).

80. The INAC council put out a notice to the community on May 2, 2011, regarding the Trilateral Agreement files, stating that it had initiated a fact-finding process on November 10, 2011, with Pierre Nepton and Lucien-Pierre Bouchard (Quebec), "by requesting clarification on the Trilateral Agreement Contribution funds" distributed to the Barriere Lake Algonquins. Since then, the INAC council reports, they have been dealing with the matter through the courts, following Nahwegahbow's filing his application.

81. Terms of Reference: For Discussion Purposes, the Algonquins of Barriere Lake Reconciliation Process, July 7, 2011, Algonquin Nation Secretariat archives.

82. The Report on the Preliminary Directed Audit by Lindquist Avey Macdonald Baskerville, commissioned by the Quebec Regional Office of INAC, stated that one of the main reasons for the audit was that thirty-two allegations were brought to its attention by this individual. The political credibility of this individual was never called into question, despite the well-known machinations of the dissident group operating within Barriere Lake's community. See Algonquins of Barriere Lake, Resolution of the Customary Council No. 01–14, Re: Retaining of Clayton Ruby (Ruby & Edwards) as Legal Counsel, August 28, 2001, Algonquin Nation Secretariat archives.

83. Ibid.

84. Jean-Claude Sarrazin, an employee of INAC, contacted Nahwegahbow and requested he waive solicitor–client privileges in respect of an RCMP investigation in connection with "certain communications we purportedly had between April 1994 and June 1999"; to which Nahwegahbow responded: "I must admit to finding it strange that the RCMP would inquire through you about my involvement

in these matters when my records show clearly over 3 years ago, on June 2, 1998, I spoke with Corporal Bacon of the RCMP, when he called me, regarding an investigation of the First Nation leadership. At the time, Corporal Bacon said he was putting the investigation 'on ice' when I informed him that the First Nation was in the middle of a political conflict with the federal government. I have not heard from Corporal Bacon or anyone else from the RCMP since" (David Nahwegabow letter to Jean-Claude Sarrazin, August 23, 2001, Algonquin Nation Secretariat archives).

85. Algonquins of Barriere Lake, Resolution of the Customary Council No. 01–14, Algonquin Nation Secretariat archives.

86. Brett Popplewell, "The Algonquins of Barriere Lake and Their Battle with Indian Affairs," *Toronto Star*, October 29, 2010.

87. I have in my possession two letters addressed to the attorney general of Canada from Barriere Lake forwarding serious grievances regarding health delivery on the reserve by Atmacita Hartel Financial Management. One letter is from Michel Thusky, dated July 21, 2011. He writes: "My daughter, Mel Thusky, has an urgent appointment in Montreal on Tuesday, July 26, 2011 and I have not been able to obtain the resources necessary and entitled to our family to travel to her hospital appointment. We do not have the necessary funds for gas, food, or accommodations—*if we do not obtain this funding immediately, my daughter's health is at serious risk . . . Neither Health Canada nor Lemieux Nolet will provide these necessary funds, nor take responsibility for helping to obtain the funds, to travel to Montreal on Tuesday.* I have done my best to resolve this situation on my own accord and with my own limited resources, but have only reached dead-ends. Over the last two weeks, I have made repeated phone calls to Health Canada, but they do not return my calls. The Third Party Managers are on holidays and I cannot get through to anyone with the authority to release these funds." On December 6, 2011, the Elders Council at Barriere Lake sent a letter on behalf of the community to the attorney general. The following is a telling excerpt: "Tonight a community meeting was held on the reserve where people shared dozens of stories of mistreatment and neglect regarding access to medical services at our Health Clinic on the Rapid Lake Reserve. The grievances expressed by community members ranged in kind, from failure to secure medical transportation to obtain necessary medical care at the nearest hospital, 150 km away in Maniwaki, to inadequate dental care on the reserve. We are concerned that the source of some of this mistreatment may be politically motivated, since the current band council, which the community does not support, is based out of the Health Clinic, and may be informing medical practitioners' decisions about who to treat."

88. Michel Thusky, in discussion with author, April 23, 2013.

89. Michel Thusky stated to me that though the community has a strong case for challenging the imposition and ongoing extraction of Third Party Managers of their band funds, he knows the conditions for doing so would involve major political concessions to which the community is unwilling to submit (ibid.).

90. The auditor general of Canada has reported on precisely this problem. Assessing Third Party Management, she writes: "The region we visited had no results-based management and accountability framework in place" (Canada, Minister of Public Works and Government Services, "Report of the Auditor General of Canada," November 2003, paragraph 10.32, 10).

91. Norman Matchewan and Casey Ratt letter to Anita Decoursay and Wanda

Thusky, Re: Recap of October 23, 2020, Discussions and Recommendations, October 27, 2010, Algonquin Nation Secretariat archives.

92. The cover letter for the information package was dated April 27, 2011. According to community members, later that year, the INAC council also compiled all the affidavits submitted for the Trilateral case and distributed these as an information package to the community at large.

93. ICTMN Staff, "Indian Affairs Calls Indian Act Council 'Temporary Measure.'"

94. Marketwire, "Cartier Selects 35 Priority Targets for First Drill Program on Its Copper-Nickel Rivière Doré Project," May 26, 2011.

95. Barriere Lake Band Council letter to Algonquins of Barriere Lake, Re: Report on Meeting with Cartier Resources on March 17, 2011, April 27, 2011, Algonquin Nation Secretariat archives.

96. Barriere Lake Solidarity, "Solidarity Update on the Algonquins of Barriere Lake," March 23, 2011.

97. Mitchikanibikok Inik Council of Elders letter to Nathalie Normandeau (minister of Natural Resources and Wildlife), Geoffrey Kelley (minister of Native Affairs) and Serge Simard (minister for Natural Resources and Wildlife), Re: Opposition to Natural Resource Exploitation within Trilateral Agreement Territory, May 2, 2011, Algonquin Nation Secretariat archives.

98. Mitchikanibikok Inik Council of Elders letter to Nathalie Normandeau, April 13, 2001, Algonquin Nation Secretariat archive.

99. Pierre Corbeil (minister responsible for Aboriginal Affairs) and Nathalie Normandeau (minister of Natural Resources) letter to Casey Ratt and Jean Maurice Matchewan, May 26, 2010.

100. Jean Maurice Matchewan, in discussion with author, July 26, 2010.

101. Cartier Resources Inc., "Cartier Suspends Work on Rivière Doré Project," press release, July 8, 2011.

102. The mining stake on Barriere Lake lands is far from over. Cartier Resources Inc. signed a sale agreement with Copper One Inc. for $150,000 for the acquisition of full interest in the Rivière Doré copper-nickel project (Cartier Resources Inc., "Cartier Signs a Sale Agreement in Respect to Its Rivière Doré Copper-Nickel Project," December 1, 2011). Insiders say the speculative gambles are only just beginning.

103. Barriere Lake Band Council letter to the Algonquins of Barriere Lake, Re: Algonquins of Barriere Lake Band Council's Position concerning Forestry, June 13, 2011, Algonquin Nation Secretariat archive.

104. Mitchikanibikok Inik Council of Elders letter to Nathalie Normandeau, Geoffrey Kelley, and Serge Simard, Re: Opposition to Natural Resource Exploitation within Trilateral Agreement Territory, April 13, 2001, Algonquin Nation Secretariat archive.

105. Traditional Council of Elders of the One Nation, "Notice to Cease All Ongoing or Planned Activities on Algonquin Territory That Have Not Been Agreed by the Council of Elders of the Algonquin Nation," Rapid Lake, Algonquin territory, May 18, 2011.

106. Barriere Lake Band Council letter to the Algonquins of Barriere Lake members, Re: Algonquins of Barriere Lake Band Council's Position concerning Forestry, June 13, 2011, Algonquin Nation Secretariat archive.

107. Ibid.

108. Norman Matchewan, in discussion with author, September 30, 2011. Matchewan and others interrupted meetings in August, verifying that these parties were present, and reminding those present at the Maniwaki meeting that they had no authority to negotiate on the community's behalf over land.

109. Mitchikanibikok Inik Council of Elders, Letter to Whom It May Concern, December 7, 2011. At the time the Algonquins drafted the letter, they were not even sure to whom it should be addressed, since they had not been informed of the logging in the territory.

110. Norman Matchewan, e-mail to author, June 30, 2012.

111. Tim McSorely, "Montreal Rallies in Support of Algonquin of Barriere Lake: Hundreds Protest Unsanctioned Clear-Cutting on Unceded Territory by Resolute Forest Products," *Montreal Media Co-op,* July 20, 2012.

112. Margaux L. Kristjansson, e-mail to author, May 3, 2016. Kristjansson is a member of Barriere Lake Solidarity who did substantial legal and court support for community members from 2012 to 2013.

113. Quebec Superior Court, *Jugement Rectifié: PF Résolu Canada v Wawatie,* Montreal 2012, at paragraph 44; Margaux L. Kristjansson, "They're Not the Boss— They're Just Visitors: The Algonquins of Barriere Lake and Settler Law, from the Bush to the Courtroom," MA thesis, McGill University, August 16, 2014, 76. The judge's statement is translated by Kristjansson from the French, where she stated: "Au contraire, le Tribunal est d'avis que l'ordonnance doit viser tout le monde, d'autant plus que Résolu ne connaît pas le nom de tous les membres de ABL susceptibles d'entraver leurs travaux."

9. Security, Critical Infrastructure, and the Geography of Indigenous Lands

1. Martha Steigman, director, "Barriere Lake Anishnabe Kachigwasin," video, 2008.

2. Ibid.

3. Norman Matchewan, "Barriere Lake Indians Set Up Blockades as Last Resort: It Was the Only Way to Get Governments to Listen to Us, Algonquins Say," *Montreal Gazette,* October 8, 2008.

4. Ibid.

5. Jorge Barrera, "Ontario Chiefs Criticize Quebec Police Action in Blockade," *Canwest News Service,* October 11, 2008. Barrera reports that while the SQ confirmed that the police fired canisters containing a chemical irritant into the crowd, tear gas was not in fact used. Also, although Barrera reports that Algonquins communicated to him that a three-year-old girl was hit with a tear-gas canister, reports on the ground alleged that a band councillor member had been hit in the chest and hospitalized.

6. Steigman, "Barriere Lake Anishnabe Kachigwasin."

7. According to journalist Martin Lukacs, who obtained this information through an Access to Information request, the Quebec Ministry of Public Security figures on general police costs for 2008 amounted to approximately a million dollars allocated for the policing operation on Barriere Lake's territory.

8. Barrera, "Ontario Chiefs Criticize Quebec Police Action in Blockade." The Ontario Provincial Police (OPP) killed Dudley George, an unarmed protester who

was defending his lands at Ipperwash Provincial Park from expropriation, leading to the Ipperwash Inquiry and a series of recommendations to avoid violent confrontations between Indigenous peoples and armed forces in the future.

9. The Honorable Sidney B. Linden, commissioner, *The Ipperwash Inquiry, Recommendations,* vol. 1, Investigation & Findings, May 31, 2007. See recommendations 9 and 1, respectively.

10. Algonquins of Barriere Lake, Community Newsletter, March 2008.

11. Barriere Lake Solidarity, "Quebec Judge Imprisons Algonquin Chief for Two Months for Peaceful Protest: Crown Asks for One Year to Send 'Clear Message' to Impoverished Community," press release, December 10, 2008.

12. See note 101 to the Introduction.

13. Monaghan, "Settler Governmentality and Racializing Surveillance in Canada's North-West," 487. The definition of settler colonialism as primarily focused on acquisition of territory and the elimination of the native is Patrick Wolfe's intellectual contribution ("Settler Colonialism and the Elimination of the Native," *Journal of Genocide Research* 8:4 [December 2006]: 387–409).

14. Monaghan, "Settler Governmentality and Racializing Surveillance in Canada's North-West," 423.

15. Andrew Crosby and Jeffrey Monaghan, "Settler Governmentality in Canada and the Algonquins of Barriere Lake," *Security Dialogue* 43:5 (2012): 421–38.

16. Mark Neocleous, "'A Brighter and Nicer New Life': Security as Pacification," *Social & Legal Studies* 20 (2011): 191–208.

17. Adrian Smith, "Pacifying the 'Armies of Offshore Labour' in Canada," *Socialist Studies* 9:2 (winter 2013): 82.

18. George Rigakos, "'To Extend the Scope of Productive Labour': Pacification as a Police Project," in *Anti-Security,* ed. Mark Neoceleous and George Rigakos (Ottawa: Red Quill Books, 2011), 62. For sharp parallel scholarship on surveillance and criminalization within the migrant labor sector, see Smith, "Pacifying the 'Armies of Offshore Labour' in Canada."

19. The quoted phrase is from Robert Nichols, "The Colonialism of Incarceration," *Radical Philosophy Review* 17:2 (2014): 454.

20. Labban, "History, Space and Nature."

21. The Emergency Management Assistance Program (EMAP) was established by INAC in 2007 to monitor "civil unrest." Its mandate was expanded at this time from monitoring emergencies mostly concerning floods and fires (Tia Dafnos, "Pacification and Indigenous Struggles in Canada," *Socialist Studies* 9:2 [winter 2013]: 68).

22. Russell Diabo and Shiri Pasternak, "Canada Has Had First Nations under Surveillance: Harper Government Has Prepared for First Nations Unrest," *First Nations Strategic Bulletin* 9:1–5 (January–May 2011): 1–23.

23. INAC monitoring is conducted out of a national headquarters, with on-the-ground surveillance done by ten regional operation centers. These regional centers feed intel to the central body, as well as to other departments and agencies such as the RCMP and the Integrated Threat Assessment Centre, which is run by the Canadian Security and Intelligence Service (CSIS) and was established as part of the federal National Security Policy. The ten regional hubs also engage in extensive information sharing with local security forces and third parties (Dafnos, "Pacification and Indigenous Struggles in Canada," 69).

24. See, for example, Shawn McCarthy, "'Anti-Petroleum' Movement a Growing Security Threat to Canada, RCMP Say," *Globe and Mail,* February 17, 2015; Greg Weston, "Other Spy Watchdogs Have Ties to Oil Business," CBC News, January 10, 2014; Tim Groves, "Canada's Spy Groups Divulge Secret Intelligence to Energy Companies," *Dominion,* October 10, 2012; and Martin Lukacs, "Alberta, Ottawa, Oil Lobby Formed Secret Committee," *Toronto Star,* March 12, 2012. In terms of government sharing across departments and ministries, an RCMP presentation to CSIS lists the following "key partners" for sharing information: INAC, CSIS, Ontario Provincial Police, SQ, Canadian Border Services Agency, Department of National Defence, Natural Resources Canada, Transport Health, and Department of Fisheries (RCMP, "RCMP Operational Response to Aboriginal Occupations and Protest," presented by Superintendant Shirley Cuillierrier to CSIS, April 3, 2007).

25. INAC, "Aboriginal Hotspots and Public Safety," slide presentation to RCMP, March 30, 2007, 5.

26. INAC, "Final Report—Evaluation of the Emergency Management Assistance Program" (2010), 39, http://www.aadnc-aandc.gc.ca/eng/1100100011392/1100100011397; accessed March 12, 2012.

27. Russell Diabo and Shiri Pasternak provided the Canadian Broadcasting Corporation (CBC) with the ATIP request documents in June 2011 verifying the Hot Spot Reporting program. Tia Dafnos provided us with the original documents and her research is fundamental to this chapter more generally. See her dissertation: Democratia Dafnos, "Negotiating Colonial Encounters: (Un)Mapping the Policing of Indigenous Peoples' Protests in Canada," York University, Toronto, September 2014.

The statement quoted by INAC was made by Michelle Yao, director of communications in the office of John Duncan, minister of Aboriginal Affairs and Northern Development, claiming that the safety of citizens was at stake and that First Nations are not being targeted (CBC News, "Monitoring of First Nations Beefed Up in '06: Documents Aboriginal Affairs Minister's Office Says First Nations Not Only Public Safety Areas Targeted," June 13, 2011).

28. INAC, "Aboriginal Hotspots and Public Safety," March 30, 2007. See also the 2006 report by Michael Hudson, assistant deputy attorney general of the Aboriginal Affairs portfolio, *Aboriginal Civil Disobedience, Lessons Learned,* which states: "A common driver are the long-standing disputes between the Crown and First Nations about traditional land or resources" (6, cited in Holman B [2007] *Final Report: Formative Evaluation—Indian and Northern Affairs Emergency Management Assistance Program,* Ottawa: Indian and Northern Affairs Canada, 18 and 29 INAC ATI request #A-2011-01156). The next line is redacted, but the citation remains, summarizing the underlining land disputes at Oka/Caledonia, Burnt Church, and Gustafsen Lake.

29. RCMP, "RCMP Operational Response to Aboriginal Occupations and Protest," 5–6.

30. The Government Operations Centre (GOC) "was established as a centralized hub for federal situational awareness relating to critical infrastructure. Its reports are disseminated widely to government, police, intelligence agencies as well as the US Department of Homeland Security" (Tia Dafnos and Shiri Pasternak, "The Criminalization of Aboriginal Protests in Recent History and the Implications

for Sovereignty Summer," *For the Defence: Criminal Lawyers' Association Newsletter* 34:3 [August 2013]: 15–23).

31. Max Paris, "Energy Industry Letter Suggested Environmental Law Changes," CBC News, January 9, 2013.

32. INAC, Update on Algonquins of Barriere Lake (Information for Deputy Minister), unclassified—QC135, August 5, 2008.

33. Dorsett and McVeigh, "Questions of Jurisdiction," 4.

34. Nicholas Blomley, "Law, Property, and the Spaces of Violence," *Annals of the Association of American Geographers* 93:1 (March 2003): 132.

35. Security agencies also define their roles in part by producing these boundaries of law. For example, the RCMP Criminal Intelligence Aboriginal Joint Intelligence Group (JIG) was tasked with monitoring signs of potential Indigenous disruption in 2009–10. By stating that "[t]he scope of the report does not cover lawful protest or legitimate dissent," the JIG determined the bounds of acceptable Indigenous assertions of jurisdiction and action that may be taken. It monitored Indigenous groups in the run-up to the G8 and G20 meetings, as well as the 2010 Vancouver Olympics. The Aboriginal JIG was created in January 2007 and comprises members of the RCMP Criminal Intelligence and RCMP's National Security Criminal Investigations. Its "primary mandate is to collect and analyse information, and produce and disseminate intelligence concerning conflict and issues associated with Aboriginal communities" (Aboriginal Joint Intelligence Group, RCMP Criminal Intelligence, "Aboriginal Communities Issue, Events and Concerns 2009/2010," June 2009).

36. INAC, Emergency and Issue Management Directorate (EIMD), Notification 1, "Protest at Bowater Forestry Site 'Matchewan Clan')," September 1, 2009.

37. RCMP Corporal L. W. Russett, Aboriginal and Ethnic Liaison Officer, NCO i/c Outreach Program A—Division National Capital Region communicates—E-mail; recipient unknown.

38. Martin Lukacs, in discussion with author, April 16, 2010. See also Joe Friesen, "CSIS Probes Potential for Violence on Quebec Reserve," *Globe and Mail,* August 23, 2012.

39. Kenneth Jackson, "Undercover Help in Arrests," *Ottawa Sun,* July 15, 2010.

40. The Ipperwash Inquiry recommendations were produced in the wake of Dudley George's killing in 1995 by Ontario Provincial Police offers. See Sydney Linden, *Ipperwash Inquiry Report, Volume 2,* taken offline by May 6, 2016; cited in Dafnos, "Pacification and Indigenous Struggles in Canada," 6.

41. RCMP, Criminal Intelligence, Aboriginal and Public Safety Community Public Safety Situation Report, "National Issues: Indigenous Sovereignty Week, October 25–31, 2009," September 30, 2009, 4. Defenders of the Land is a national network of Indigenous land defenders and their allies. See www.defendersoftheland.org.

42. CSIS, Canada: Bi-Annual Update on the Threat from Terrorists and Extremists, November 14, 2008; cited in Jeffrey Monaghan and Kevin Walby, "Making Up 'Terror Identities': Security Intelligence, Canada's Integrated Threat Assessment Centre and Social Movement Suppression," *Policing and Society* 10 (2011): 1–19.

43. Monaghan and Walby, "Making Up 'Terror Identities,'" 1–19. Take also, for example, the introduction of the drift net cast by the antiterrorism Bill C-51

(introduced in 2015) that applies to any activity that "undermines the sovereignty, security or territorial integrity of Canada," which can be exercised to tamp out or reassign Indigenous law and rights to an insurrectionary danger.

44. I would like to acknowledge here Tia Dafnos's ATIP research, which she has generously shared with me and which includes files on Barriere Lake from various departments within INAC, CSIS, and the RCMP.

45. See Shiri Pasternak, Sue Collis, and Tia Dafnos, "Criminalization at Tyendinaga: Securing Canada's Colonial Property Regime through Specific Land Claims," *Canadian Journal of Law and Society* (May 2013): 1–17.

46. The exact sum is $56,534,540 (Cogesult, "Quantification de la valeur économique des industries de la forêt, du tourisme, des loisirs et des autres industries et activités dans la région de l'Outaouiais et le secteur couvert par l'entente trilateral, Rapport Final," March 1996, ix).

47. This estimate was provided in a commissioned study by the consulting firm Ottawa Engineering for Barriere Lake, 1993 (ibid.).

48. The summons, served on April 29, 2011, stated: "Between September 1st and 8, 2009, at the Parc de la Vérendrye, in Abitibi, at the km 200, junction 29, prevented, interrupted or disturbed abitibi bowater in the use [*jouissance* in the judicial system also means use], or legitimate exploitation of a good which value is superior to 5000$: the 'Esden' site and its access, thus committing a criminal crime under article 430 (1) d) (3) a) of the criminal code."

49. As Norman's legal counsel, Jared Will, explained: "The indictment . . . was a bit vague because it alleged that between September 1 and September 8, 2008, that he had committed this act of mischief, and the evidence that was disclosed to us talked about a couple of different incidents. One where Norman and a few others had met some loggers who were actually working, which occurred on the night of August 31, technically September 1, where they told them to leave and they left. And another incident where a supervisor or foreman came back on the morning of [September] 2 and was told to leave and left. And then another incident where somebody came and wanted to inspect the machinery and he was told he could inspect the machinery and do nothing else. And then there were sort of descriptions of this roadside camp they set up. And I asked the Crown to specify what exactly they were alleging to be the mischief, or the crime, and it was kind of veiled, but the answer was basically 'all of it.' They refused to specify" (Jared Will, in discussion with author, June 11, 2012).

50. Ibid.

51. According to Will, these anomalies in consultation consisted of the fact that there was a leadership dispute taking place at the time that the logging permit was issued. Because Norman Matchewan and others in the community genuinely believed that the Ratt council was not the legitimate governing authority, serious questions were raised about which entity had decision-making powers in the community at that time (ibid.).

52. In the Perron Report, the former diplomat states that "The leadership of the ABL and their councilors will continue to want to breathe life into this unbelievable illusion [that the Trilateral Agreement could be restored]. It's their basic right." He recommends "that under no circumstances should INAC or any other Federal instances contribute to perpetuate this utopia" ("Report: Special Ministerial Representative to the Algonquins of Barriere Lake," document submitted to the Hon-

orable Chuck Strahl, minister of Indian Affairs and Northern Development Canada, December 20, 2007, 5).

53. *R. v Matchewan, QCCP* (Provincial Court of Quebec) 615. 2012 06 04; quoted in Kristjansson, "They're Not the Boss of Us, They're Just Visitors."

54. Jared Will, in discussion with author, June 11, 2012.

55. *R. v. Matchewan, QCCP* (Provincial Court of Quebec) 615. 2012 06 04. Court notes taken by Margaux Kristjansson and reported in Kristjansson, "They're Not the Boss of Us, They're Just Visitors." I adjusted the French translation here.

56. Jared Will, in discussion with author, June 11, 2012.

57. Vincent Larin admitted, after first claiming that the cutting permits could not be altered once they were electronically signed and entered in the ministry's computer system, that he presented the Court with a cutting permit that was substantially different from the version that had been disclosed to the defense.

58. INAC Emergency and Issue Management Directorate (EIMD) Notification 1—Protest at Bowater Forestry Site ("Matchewan Clan"), September 1, 2009. The source of reporting is recorded as INAC Quebec Region, filed by Silvie MacDonald, EIM program adviser. It turned out that Domtar was bringing out wood harvested the year before.

59. Ibid.

60. Ibid.

61. Ibid.

62. INAC, EIMD for the week ending March 25, 2011, Hot Spot summary, NCR#3542780, 1.

63. I have noted several such reports in earlier chapters. In addition, see, for example, Algonquins of Barriere Lake Leadership Selection (Decision by Minister), Protected B-QC154, August 11, 2009, which states under the heading "Next Steps": "Ensure collaboration and co-ordinate actions with other federal departments, law enforcement agencies and the Government of Quebec."

64. This picture is even bleaker when deaths in custody are considered. For example, Gerald Papatie from Barriere Lake was killed in prison in 2005, and the community is acutely aware of potential fatalities of incarceration. See Sherene Razack, *Dying from Improvement: Inquests and Inquiries into Indigenous Deaths in Custody* (Toronto: University of Toronto Press, 2015).

65. Neocleous, "'A Brighter and Nicer New Life,'" 193.

66. For two excellent examples of this kind of work, see Heather Dorries, "Rejecting the 'False Choice'"; and Michael McCrossan, "Contaminating and Collapsing Indigenous Space: Juridical Narratives of Canadian territoriality," *Settler Colonial Studies* 5:1 (2015): 20–38.

67. Anna Zalik, "Protest-as-Violence in Oilfields: The Contested Representation of Profiteering in Two Extractive Sites," in *Accumulating Insecurity: Violence and Dispossession in the Making of Everyday Life*, ed. S. Feldman, C. Geisler, and G. Menon (Athens: University of Georgia Press, 2011), 264.

68. For a good overview of the principles of consultation outlined in *Haida* (2004) 3 S.C.R. 511. 210 and *Taku River Tlingit First Nation v British Columbia* (2004) 3 S.C.R. 550, see John Borrows, "Crown and Aboriginal Occupations of Land: A History and Comparison," Ipperwash Inquiry (2005), 66–67.

69. In *Politics as a Vocation*, Max Weber defines the state as a "human community that (successfully) claims the monopoly of the legitimate use of physical force

within a given territory" (*From Max Weber: Essays in Sociology*, trans. and ed. H. H. Gerth and C. Wright Mills [New York: Oxford University Press, 1946], 1).

70. Norman Matchewan, in discussion with author, May 13, 2012.

71. The date of this stop was July 8, 2010. The community police contract expired in April 2010, and with no clear leadership in place to renew the contracts, the Barriere Lake police service was retired and the SQ returned to patrol the tiny community.

72. The date of Katherine Keyes's funeral was July 9, 2010.

73. Norman Matchewan, in discussion with author, August 29, 2010. The event occurred several days prior to this conversation.

74. This list of charges and assaults was provided to me by Norman Matchewan. Matchewan and others also recounted a long string of conflicts between factions in the community biased toward the dissidents. Because I cannot verify these accounts and the personal risk to people's safety is much higher in naming individuals than SQ officers, whose anonymity is protected by their uniforms, I have chosen to leave these out. Among these incidents, however, is an unprovoked SQ beating. Other fatal tragedies occurred that might have been avoided. On July 9, 2008, community members rallied in front of the Barriere Lake police station. Elder Jackie Keyes had a stroke and was rushed down the road to the Rapid Lake Health Clinic. Both the SQ and Barriere Lake community police refused, for some reason, to provide assistance. Perhaps they thought it was a ruse. Keyes succumbed to the stroke and the community still blames the neglect of the police for his death. Such incidents need not speak to the politically motivated nature of the SQ—it certainly did not receive direct orders from Canada or Quebec to let Keyes die that day, in front of friends and family—but they do speak to the general atmosphere of mistrust, and the consequence of years of racism, discrimination, and harassment. In another incident, on July 17, 2008, Terry Matchewan was assaulted by the Gatineau police in Gatineau, Quebec. He was charged for his beating. Few bother to file complaints at all these days.

75. Chief Jean Maurice Matchewan and the people of Algonquins of Barriere Lake (written on their behalf by Benoit Tremblay, lawyer, Waswanipi Cree First Nation) letter to SQ Commissaire, Ottawa, August 23, 1993, Algonquin Nation Secretariat archives.

76. Jean Maurice Matchewan, customary chief, letter to the Honorable Claude Ryan, minister of Public Security, August 8, 1993, Algonquin Nation Secretariat archives.

77. Martha Steigman for Barriere Lake Solidarity, "House Arrest," unpublished, 2010. Subsequent references are given in the text.

78. Jean Maurice Matchewan, in discussion with author, July 12, 2010.

79. The superior court heard the appeal in mid-January and his legal aid was denied again.

80. Information on these protests is relatively scarce, but see Monique Manatch, "Grandmother Mary Whiteduck Assaulted by Quebec Provincial Police SQ Agents and Is Now Hospitalized," August 31, 2000, http://rabble.ca/babble/environmental-justice/grandmother-mary-whiteduck-assaulted-quebec-provincial-police-sq-agents; accessed December 20, 2016.

81. The message was posted, for example, on the message board of Cultural

Foundation Native Expressions, Rabble.ca, and a support group was established on Facebook that has since been removed.

82. For more on racialized policing in Aboriginal communities, see Ross, *Inventing the Savage*; Sherene Razack, *Dying from Improvement: Inquests and Inquiries into Indigenous Deaths in Custody* (Toronto: University of Toronto Press, 2015); Blomley, *Unsettling the City*; Elizabeth Comack, *Racialized Policing: Aboriginal People's Encounters with the Police* (Winnipeg: Fernwood Publications, 2012); and Penelope Edmonds, "Unpacking Settler Colonialism's Urban Strategies: Indigenous Peoples in Victoria, British Columbia, and the Transition to a Settler-Colonial City," *Urban History Review* 38:2 (spring 2010): 4–20.

83. Clayton Nottaway, "Stop Canada's Cultural Genocide at Barriere Lake," Ontario Institute for Studies in Education, University of Toronto, November 1, 2010.

84. Arthur Manuel, *Unsettling Canada: A National Wake-Up Call* (Toronto: Between the Lines, 2015), 172.

85. Ibid.

86. Borrows, "Crown and Aboriginal Occupations of Land," 20–21.

87. Blomley, "Law, Property, and the Spaces of Violence," 121 and 124.

88. Canadian Press, "Quebec, Natives Reach Agreement," June 15, 1991. The article recounts Matchewan's arrest in October 1989 when the chief was arrested for blocking logging trucks from entering the wildlife reserve.

89. See, for example, J. R. Miller, *Skyscrapers Hide the Heavens: A History of Indian–White Relations in Canada,* 3d ed. (Toronto: University of Toronto Press, 2000), 221–22, 274–76 especially, but important historical insights can be found throughout the book. Specifically related to commercial interests, a 1905 treaty commissioner statement attests to the importance of reserve geography, explaining that reserves "have been selected in situations which are especially advantageous to their owners, and where they will not in any way interfere with railway development or the future commercial interests of the country. While it is doubtful whether the Indians will ever engage in agriculture, these reserves, being of a reasonable size, will give a secure and permanent interest in the land which the indeterminate possession of a large tract could never carry," *The James Bay: Treaty No. 9 (Made in 1905 and 1906) and Adhesions Made in 1929 and 1930,* Ottawa, November 6, 1905; reprinted from the edition of 1931 by Roger Duhamel, F.R.S.C. [Fellow of the Royal Society of Canada], Queen's Printer and Controller of Stationery, Ottawa, 1964. The treaty commissioner nobly imagines that the country unburdened native peoples from the "indeterminate possession" of their traditional territories, which had secured Indigenous economic well-being for centuries, in favor of smaller tracts that could be more manageably cultivated because of their "permanence." The settlers could now intervene to maintain the commercially viable parts of the territory.

This was a process established with the early numbered treaties (*A Narrow Vision: Duncan Campbell Scott and the Administration of the Indian Act*, Vancouver: University of British Columbia Press, 1986, 10). The ambition of the nation in its accumulative zest to secure possession of the land's resources through treaties was not as unilateral as scholars often depict, however. Settlers could not access Indigenous lands west of the Great Lakes, for example, without these treaties because the Salteaux and Cree recognized their own riches and sought to bargain for reciprocal access to white wealth in the form of farming equipment and seeds (Tobias, "Canada's Subjugation of the Plains Cree," 520). Reserves and treaty annuities figured into treaty agreements, but were not perceived by Indigenous peoples as land surrenders or imperial conquest, though they later came to be interpreted this way by the Crown.

90. Nichols, "The Colonialism of Incarceration," 454. See also Deborah Cowen, *The Deadly Life of Logistics: Mapping Violence in Global Trade* (Minneapolis: University of Minnesota Press, 2014), 5.

91. Nichols, "The Colonialism of Incarceration," 454.

92. Wendy Brown, *Walled States, Waning Sovereignty* (New York: Zed Books, 2010), 7–8; cited in ibid., 451.

93. Cindy Holmes, Sarah Hunt, and Amy Piedalue, "Violence, Colonialism, and Space: Towards a Decolonizing Dialogue," *ACME: An International E-Journal for Critical Geographies* 14:2 (2014), 550. See also Lee Maracle, *I Am Woman* (North Vancouver: Write-On Press, 1988); Sarah Hunt, "Decolonizing Sex Work: Developing an Intersectional Indigenous Approach," in *Selling Sex: Experience, Advocacy and Research on Sex Work in Canada,* ed. Emily van der Meulen, Elya M. Durisin, and Victoria Love (Vancouver: University of British Columbia Press, 2013); Mary Hampton, Wendee Kubik, and A. Anderson, eds., *Torn from Our Midst: Voices of Grief, Healing and Action from the Missing Indigenous Women Conference, 2008* (Regina: University of Regina Press, 2010); Evelyn J. Peters, "'[W]e Do Not Lose Our Treaty Rights outside the . . . Reserve': Challenging the Scales of Social Services Provision of First Nations Women in Canadian Cities," *GeoJournal* 65 (2006): 315–27; Native Women's Association of Canada (NWAC), *What Their Stories Tell Us: Research Findings from the Sisters in Spirit Initiative,* published by NWAC, 2010; Amber Dean, *Remembering Vancouver's Disappeared Women: Settler Colonialism and the Difficulty of Inheritance* (Toronto: University of Toronto Press, 2015); Rauna Kuokkanen, "Globalization as Racialized, Sexualized Violence: The Case of Indigenous Women," *International Feminist Journal of Politics* 10:2 (June 2008): 216–33; Shawna Ferris, "'The Lone Streetwalker': Missing Women and Sex Work-Related News in Mainstream Canadian Media," *West Coast Line* 41:1 (spring 2007): 14–24; Sherene Razack, "Gendered Racial Violence and Specialized Justice: The Murder of Pamela George," *Canadian Journal of Law and Society* 15:2 (2000): 91–130; Christina Heatherton, "Policing the Crisis of Indigenous Lives: An Interview with Red Nation," in *Policing the Planet: Why the Policing Crisis Led to Black Lives Matter,* ed. Jordan T. Camp and Christina Heatherton (New York: Verso Books, 2016), 109–19; and Luana Ross, "Inventing the Savage: The Social Construction of Native American Criminality," *Canadian Woman Studies* 19:1–2 (1999): 216–17.

94. Patricia Monture-Angus, "Women and Risk: Aboriginal Women, Colonialism, and Correctional Practice," *Canadian Woman Studies* 19:1–2 (spring/summer 1999): 26.

95. See Heidi Kiiwetinepineziik Stark, "Criminal Empire."

96. Native Youth Sexual Health Network statement to National Energy Board regarding Line 9 Pipeline Proposal, October 18, 2013, http://www.nativeyouthsexual health.com/october182013.pdf; accessed June 28, 2016.

97. Regulation pertaining to mineral extraction on reserves is jurisdiction-specific, though, with British Columbia and Ontario, for example, allowing for

staking on reserve lands (Natural Resources Canada, *Exploration and Mining Guide for Aboriginal Communities,* Her Majesty the Queen in Right of Canada, 2013).

98. Although one might anticipate that these geographic proximities reflect a general rural–urban divide in the Canadian population, the spatial dispersion pattern of Indian reserves is actually unique compared to non-Indigenous settlement throughout Canada, tending to be much more rural than the Canadian population, and covering every region from coast to coast. More than half of First Nations people with registered status live on a reserve (Statistics Canada, *Aboriginal Peoples in Canada in 2006: Inuit, Métis, and First Nations,* 2006 Census, catalog no. 97–558-XIE). Compare this to the non–First Nation population, where 81 percent of the population is urban (Statistics Canada, *Population, Urban and Rural, by Province and Territory,* 2011).

99. Aboriginal Joint Intelligence Group, RCMP Criminal Intelligence, "Aboriginal Communities: Issue, Events and Concerns, 2009/10," June 2009, 3.

100. Ibid., 7. The concern expressed in the RCMP's 2009–10 report is that disruption to critical infrastructure will be used to leverage national and international attention to grievances and conflicts with the government at high-profile national and international events such as the 2010 Olympic Games in Vancouver and G8 Summit in Toronto.

101. Dafnos, "Pacification and Indigenous Struggles in Canada," 66.

102. See World Bank, *Connecting to Compete 2010: Trade Logistics in the Global Economy: The Logistics Performance Index and Its Indicators,* 2010. But more generally, see Cowen, *The Deadly Life of Logistics.*

103. See Canadian Trucking Alliance, "Trucking in Canada." Accessed online May 28, 2013: http://www.cantruck.ca/iMISpublic/Content/NavigationMenu2/CTAIndustry/TruckinginCanada/default.htm; accessed May 28, 2013. Thanks to Deborah Cowen for this source.

104. Nicholas Blomley, "First Nations Blockades in British Columbia, 1984–1995," *BC Studies,* no. 3 (autumn 1996): 20.

105. See http://unistoten.camp/.

106. Danos and Pasternak, "The Criminalization of Aboriginal Protests in Recent History and the Implications for Sovereignty Summer," 15–23.

107. Government of Canada, *Risk Assessment Blockade of TransCanada Proposed Pipeline in North-Western British Columbia,* April 1, 2015, RDIMS No.: 30191, ATIP # A-2015–00104, 4; emphasis added.

108. Ibid. Unfortunately, the impact assessment of the resistance camp on the national interest is redacted.

109. RCMP, *Briefing Note to Deputy Commissioner,* June 4, 2007. Obtained through an ATIP request to the RCMP, no. GA-3951-3-00060/11; cited in Dafnos, "Pacification and Indigenous Struggles in Canada," 85.

110. *Critical 5: Role of Critical Infrastructure in National Prosperity, Shared Narrative,* October 2015, 5; emphasis added.

111. Ibid., 6–7.

112. See Shiri Pasternak and Tia Dafnos, "How Does a Settler State Secure the Circuitry of Capital?" *Environment and Planning D: Society and Space,* forthcoming, spring 2017.

113. Arthur Manuel and Nicole Schabus, "Indigenous Peoples at the Margin of

the Global Economy: A Violation of International Human Rights and International Trade Law," *Chapman Law Review* 8:222 (2005): 222–52.

114. Cowen, *The Deadly Life of Logistics*, 10.

115. Saskia Sassen, "When Territory Deborders Territoriality," *Territory, Politics, Governance* 1:1 (2013): 25; quoted in ibid.

116. On geoeconomics, see Matthew Sparke, "Geopolitical Fears, Geoeconomic Hopes, and the Responsibilities of Geography," *Annals of the Association of American Geographers* 97:2 (2007): 338–40.

117. Wolfe, "Settler Colonialism and the Elimination of the Native," 388.

Conclusion

1. Order-in-Council Executive Chamber Council, Number 1637, *Concerning Regulations Applicable in Beaver Reserves*, Quebec, June 14, 1967. As in the original 1928 Order-in-Council, the 1967 one also provides exclusive use of provincially created beaver reserves to the natives: "Only Indians and Eskimos may trap or hunt fur-bearing animals in the reserves in New Quebec, Fort Georges, Vieux Comptoir, Rupert, Nottaway, Abitbiti, Mistasinni, Grand-Lac Victoria, Roberval and Bersimis."

2. As Peter Usher explains, the courts have interpreted the rights of Aboriginal peoples on lands that they have used and occupied very restrictively, but at the very least, this land interest means the right to hunt, trap, fish, and gather in traditional areas of use and occupancy (Peter Usher and N. D. Bankes, *Property: The Basis of Inuit Hunting Rights* [Ottawa: Inuit Committee on National Issues, 1996]).

3. Unfortunately, I do not have sufficient space to unpack the related self-government policy here and the ways in which it relates to assertions of inherent Indigenous jurisdiction.

4. Peter Russell, in discussion with author, September 8, 2011.

5. Harold Johnson, *Two Families: Treaties and Government* (Saskatoon: Purich Publishing, 2007).

6. Arthur Manuel, "Federal Comprehensive Land Claims Policy," e-mail, August 8, 2010. For a non-Indigenous approach to this matter, Michael Asch makes this case movingly in *On Being Here to Stay*.

7. *Tsilhqot'in Nation v British Columbia* (2014), for example, dismisses the Crown's claim that the doctrine of *terra nullius* ever applied in Canada, but the Supreme Court never offers an alternative ground for how Canada came to legitimately claim sovereignty over Indigenous peoples "who occupied and used the land prior to European arrival" (at paragraph 69).

8. For a sample of this, see Canadian Chamber of Commerce (CCC), "Ready for Business: Canada's Aboriginal and Non-Aboriginal Businesses as Equal Partners," December 2010. The report recommends "That the federal government work with the First Nations Tax Commission, interested First Nations communities, the provinces and other stakeholders to develop a voluntary legal framework and support structure to enable First Nations to have access to full, unrestricted fee simple ownership of their reserve lands" (8). It also warns against "Jurisdictional chaos" which has been identified by CCC members who do regular business with Indigenous peoples as a source of "major frustration for them and their Aboriginal partners" (10).

9. Canada has a number of different property registration systems, which are governed under provincial jurisdiction. The western provinces use the Torrens system, and in the Atlantic and Quebec provinces a deed system is used; however, in the Atlantic region this is shifting toward a land registry system. Ontario has both a land title and a deed registration system, the latter of which it is phasing out.

10. Aboriginal Affairs and Northern Development Canada Assessment of Negotiations: Template Questionnaire, Core Data, Confidential, undated.

11. See the TFN Final Agreement here: http://www.gov.bc.ca/arr/firstnation/ tsawwassen/down/final/tfn_fa.pdf. The third treaty is with the Maa-nulth First Nations and it came into effect April 1, 2011, though the Final Agreement was signed two years earlier on April 9, 2009. The treaty was negotiated between Canada, British Columbia, and the Huu-ay-aht, Ka:'yu:'k't'h'/Che:k'tles7et'h', Toquaht, Uchucklesaht, and Ucluelet First Nations, whose lands are on the west coast of Vancouver Island.

12. Indigenous Network on Economies and Trade, press release, Geneva, Switzerland, February 19, 2009.

13. See, for example, Williams's advocacy in Sandor Gyarmati, "Treaty Process Criticized: As Another First Nation Signs a Treaty, Some Are Speaking Out against B.C.'s Processes," *Delta Optimist*, August 24, 2012. Williams does have support outside of TFN. The Union of British Columbia Indian Chiefs (UBCIC) remain a critic of the British Columbia Treaty Process and, led by Grand Chief Stewart Phillip, the UBCIC demonstrated outside of the provincial legislature when the Tsawwassen deal was signed officially into treaty.

14. Bertha Williams and Arthur Manuel, in discussion with author, April 29, 2011. See the Land Act Summary that outlines these regulations on the TFN website: http://www.tsawwassenfirstnation.com/pdfs/TFN-Laws-Regulations-Policies/ Laws/Summaries/FINAL_Summary_Land_Act.pdf.

15. Colin Ward, e-mail to author, October 20, 2011. The Tsawwassen Land Act can be accessed here: http://www.tsawwassenfirstnation.com/tfnlaws/land_act .php.

16. Ibid.

17. According to the city of Vancouver, "The Regional Context Statement demonstrates how the City's existing plans and policies support the goals, strategies and actions identified in the Metro Vancouver Regional Growth Strategy, titled 'Metro Vancouver 2040—Shaping Our Future'" (http://vancouver.ca/ home-property-development/regional-context-statement.aspx; accessed May 17, 2016). However, TFN's submissions process is unique compared to other municipalities, as laid out in chapter 17 of the TFN Final Agreement, according to Tom McCarthy, TFN acting chief administrative officer, communication with author, May 14, 2013.

18. Bertha Williams and Arthur Manuel, in discussion with author, April 29, 2011.

19. Russell Diabo, "Harper Launches Major First Nations Termination Plan: As Negotiating Tables Legitimize Canada's Colonialism," *Intercontinental Cry*, November 9, 2012, https://intercontinentalcry.org/harper-launches-major-first-nations -termination-plan-as-negotiating-tables-legitimize-canadas-colonialism; accessed May 17, 2016.

20. Bertha Williams, e-mail to author, October 10, 2011. Each member of the

TFN who held a certificate of possession interest prior to the treaty has now been replaced with a TFSI. Pretreaty band lands continue to be owned by the nation in fee simple.

21. Tsawwassen First Nation, Land Act, Section 6, April 3, 2009.

22. TFN Economic Development Corporation, "Backgrounder: Location, Location, Location," June 2011.

23. Cowen, *The Deadly Life of Logistics*, 178.

24. Canadian Environmental Assessment Registry: 04–03–3734, http://www.ceaa.gc.ca/052/details-eng.cfm?pid=3734; accessed May 20, 2016. For a counterfactual to the Canadian Environmental Assessment Agency (CEAA) assessment, see Boundary Bay Conservation Committee, *Deltaport Third Berth Expansion Project: Response to Comprehensive Study Report*, submitted to the Canadian Environmental Assessment Agency, September 1, 2006.

25. Boundary Bay Conservation Committee, *Deltaport Third Berth Expansion Project*.

26. Tsawwassen First Nation (TFN) and Vancouver Port Authority (VPA) (Collectively The "Parties") Roberts Bank Development Memorandum of Agreement, November 2004.

27. Port Vancouver, "Vancouver Port Authority and Tsawwassen First Nation Sign Memorandum of Agreement," press release, November 10, 2004.

28. Tsawwassen First Nation (TFN) and Vancouver Port Authority (VPA) (Collectively The "Parties") Roberts Bank Development Memorandum of Agreement, November 2004, Section 8.1.b., 19.

29. Port Vancouver, "Vancouver Port Authority and Tsawwassen First Nation Sign Memorandum of Agreement."

30. TFN Economic Development Corporation, "Backgrounder," June 2011. However, Bertha Williams and another TFN Member filed against the construction of the South Perimeter Road in the BC Supreme Court. Maintaining responsibility over their traditional lands, thus exercising their jurisdiction despite the extinguishment of their Aboriginal title, these community members are fighting to protect the sacred and spiritual St. Mungo area where the road would pass through a native burial site (Mike Bothwell, "Tsawwassen Band Oppose New Road," Delta/CKNW [AM980], Radio, May 25, 2011).

31. For further analysis of the nonnegotiable terms and outcomes of the CLCP, see Isabel Altamirano-Jiménez, *Indigenous Encounters with Neoliberalism: Place, Women, and the Environment in Canada and Mexico* (Vancouver: University of British Columbia Press, 2013); Peter Kulchyski, "Trail to Tears: Concerning Modern Treaties in Northern Canada," *Canadian Journal of Native Studies* 35:1 (2015): 69–81; Paul Rynard, "'Welcome In, but Check Your Rights at the Door': The James Bay and Nisga'a Agreements in Canada, *Canadian Journal of Political Science* 33:2 (2000): 211–43; Colin Samson, "The Dispossession of the Innu and the Colonial Magic of Canadian Liberalism," *Citizenship Studies* 3:1 (1999): 5–25; Peter J. Usher, "Environment, Race and Nation Reconsidered: Reflections on Aboriginal Land Claims in Canada," *Canadian Geographer* 47:4 (December 2003): 365–82; and Andrew Woolford, *Between Justice and Certainty: Treaty Making in BC* (Vancouver: University of British Columbia Press, 2006). See also the campaign site for Idle No More and Defenders of the Land: http://www.idlenomore.ca/turn_the_tables.

32. See item 5 ("Land Selection") under the policy, published online in 2003. The

policy instructs that while an Agreement in Principle is being negotiated, the following tasks should commence simultaneously: "production of a map demarcating all the lands claimed by the Aboriginal group; full legal description of the boundaries to be surveyed; survey of the adjacent lands to the claimed area; municipal lands within the claimed settlement area must also be demarcated" (Resolving Aboriginal Claims—A Practical Guide to Canadian Experiences, Ottawa, 2003, http://www.aadnc-aandc.gc.ca/eng/1100100014174/1100100014179#selpr; accessed May 7, 2013).

33. This figure is more difficult to ascertain through calculation because the total hectares of lands claimed is an unknown figure for each of the modern treaties signed. Lands are not formally surveyed in preparation for a land claim but are drawn roughly on maps to convey land use and occupation. Much conflict has ensued as a result, when negotiating groups claim "use" lands that were often shared with other communities. The lack of time and resources committed to this early stage of land selection in the Statement of Intent is also a significant factor in overlap disputes. We do know, however, that Nisga'a obtained roughly 8 percent of their lands claimed, and that Tsawwassen received 0.1 percent. The Northern Secwwepemc te Qelmucw (NStQ) have circulated the figure 0.465 percent of total lands claimed. All of these figures require further research and corroboration.

34. These figures are drawn from the Final Agreements of these signatories to the modern treaty process.

35. These figures are taken and averaged from five signed Final Agreements: Nisga'a, Maa-nulth, Tsawwassen, Yale, and Tla'amin. These figures are just an indication of how far cash settlements would go if allocated on a per capita basis, but they are not necessarily distributed this way posttreaty.

36. Sari Graben, "Lessons for Indigenous Property Reform: From Membership to Ownership on Nisga'a Lands," *UBC Law Review* 47:2 (2014): 437.

37. See *Guerin v The Queen* (1984) 2 SCR 335 (hereafter, *Guerin*), where the Supreme Court of Canada confirmed that the federal government has a special duty to act in the best interests of Indigenous peoples.

38. See the critical discussion in chapter 5 regarding Section 35 as a protection of Aboriginal rights posttreaty.

39. Flanagan, Alacantra, and Le Dressay, *Beyond the Indian Act*, 29.

40. The Liberal Party of Canada, under Prime Minister Justin Trudeau's leadership, has committed to review all legislation affecting Aboriginal rights that was passed and impending during the previous Conservative regime (2007–15). The legislation could conceivably be resurrected by the Liberals or subsequent governments.

41. For a more comprehensive critique of the claim that private property on reserves is a form of poverty alleviation, see Shiri Pasternak, "How Capitalism Will Save Colonialism: The Privatization of Reserve Lands in Canada," *Antipode* 47:1 (2015): 179–96.

42. Fiscal Realities Economists, *Expanding Commercial Activity on First Nation Lands: Lowering the Costs of Doing Business on Reserve*, November 1999. It is notable that the report is also cited in the 2003 November Report of the Auditor General of Canada, chapter 9, Exhibit 9.2, though the auditor general qualifies its inclusion, stating, "We did not reconfirm the analysis of the project undertaken by Fiscal Realities Economists."

43. See the original announcement here: Translink, "Bus service comes to Tsawwassen First Nation," press release, December 31, 2008, http://www.translink .ca/en/About-Us/Media/2008/December/Bus-service-comes-to-Tsawwassen-First -Nation.aspx; and see the celebration here: Nancy Macdonald, "Going Out on Their Own: Are First Nations Groups in B.C. Ready for Independence?" *Macleans*, March 17, 2010, http://www2.macleans.ca/2010/03/17/going-out-on-their-own/; accessed May 7, 2013. The article cites TFN Chief Kim Baird explaining how the Translink stop is the first, tangible benefit of the modern treaty.

44. Arthur Manuel, e-mail to author, March 18, 2010.

45. To add insult to injury, while Indigenous treaty rights benefit from constitutional protection under Section 35(1) of the Constitution Act of 1867, Canadians enjoy none of these legal protections, yet apparently all of the privileges. The Charter of Rights and Freedoms (1982) contains no express protection of private property rights. Unlike the American Bill of Rights (Amendments 5 and 14) and the European Convention on Human Rights (Article 1 of Protocol No. 1), and also the International Convention on Civil and Political Rights (Article 17–1), Canada chose not to carry over the protection of property rights from the 1960 Canadian Bill of Rights. For discussion on why property rights were not included in the patriated constitution, see Roy Romanow, John Whyte, and Howard Leeson, *Canada . . . Notwithstanding: The Making of the Constitution, 1976–1982* (Toronto and New York: Carswell/Methuen, 1984), 216–62. The Bill of Rights is an ordinary statute, which arose against a background of egregious racial discrimination that denied Chinese, Japanese, and Hutterite communities rights of employment, land, and home ownership, and it is still in effect, but rife with problems that make the courts reluctant to enforce, and is generally underused. For discussion on the ongoing relevance of the Bill of Rights, see Philip W. Augustine, "Protection of the Right to Property under the Canadian Charter of Rights and Freedoms," *University of Ottawa Law Review* 18 (1986): 61–66. The Charter does contain two provisions in Section 7—the right to security and the right to liberty—that have been interpreted as potentially protecting economic and property rights, but because property is not explicitly mentioned, these rights could be interpreted otherwise, for example, as protecting bodily integrity or privacy.

46. Kent McNeil, "Reconciliation and Third-Party Interests: Tsilhqot'in Nation v. British Columbia," *Indigenous Law Journal* 8:1 (2010): 7–25. See also *Hupacasath First Nation v British Columbia (Minister of Forests) et al.* (2006) 1 CNLR 22, where the Crown's position on the incompatibility between Aboriginal title and fee simple was called into question.

47. Gerry Bellett, "Valuation of Tsawwassen Band's Land Doubles," *Vancouver Sun*, September 16, 2010, http://www.vancouversun.com/business/Valuation+ Tsawwassen+band+land+doubles/3532219/story.html; accessed May 8, 2013.

48. Jean Maurice Matchewan, in discussion with author, July 26, 2009.

49. Ibid.

50. Aboriginal Affairs and Northern Development Canada (AANDC) does not distinguish in their accounts between CLCP and Specific Claims. See AANDC, financial statements for the year ended March 31, 2015 (unaudited), Section 7: Settled Claims: https://www.aadnc-aandc.gc.ca/eng/1445002892771/1445002960 229#07; accessed May 31, 2016; and Section 12: Loans receivable: https://www .aadnc-aandc.gc.ca/eng/1445002892771/1445002960229#12; accessed May 20, 2016.

51. Mark Milke, "Incomplete, Illiberal and Expensive: A Review of 15 Years of Treaty Negotiations in BC and Proposals for Reform," published by the Fraser Institute, Studies in Aboriginal Policy (Vancouver: Fraser Institute, July 2008), 63. Also, James M. Lornie, special representative to the minister of Aboriginal Affairs and Northern Development Canada (AANDC), reported that for BC bands at the negotiating table, debt hovered at around $400 million (for figures for BC, see James M. Lornie, "Final Report: The Minister of Aboriginal Affairs and Northern Development," November 30, 2011, http://www.bctreaty.net/files/pdf_documents/Lornie-Report_30Nov2011.pdf; accessed March 7, 2013).

52. Indigenous Network on Economies and Trade, on behalf of Chief Darrell Bob, Xaxli'p Indian Band; Dexter Quaw, hereditary chief of the Lheidli T'enneh people; Bertha Williams of the Tsawwassen people; and the Skwelkwek'welt Protection Centre: In Relation to Canada, Request for Urgent Action under Early Warning Procedure to the Committee on the Elimination of Racial Discrimination (CERD) of the United Nations, February 9, 2009, 16, at paragraph 55.

53. Ibid., at paragraph 62.

54. Arthur Williams, "Lheidli T'enneh Treaty Itself Is the Problem," *Prince George Free Press*, November 23, 2010, http://www.bclocalnews.com/bc_north/pgfreepress/opinion/110207189.html; accessed May 9, 2013.

55. Lheidli T'enneh First Nation, "Treaty," website: http://www.lheidli.ca/Treaty/index.php; accessed May 17, 2016.

56. CERD, 17, at paragraph 63.

57. Ibid., 19, at paragraph 70.

58. Government of Canada, "International Convention on the Elimination of All Forms of Racial Discrimination Nineteenth and Twentieth Reports of Canada, Covering the Period June 2005–May 2009," submission to CERD, at paragraph 114: "Canada will also seek to ensure that loan funding offered to Aboriginal groups to permit their unfettered participation in the treaty process is property understood as a mean to facilitate the achievement of constitutionally protected treaties for Aboriginal groups as well as a new relationship between federal and provincial governments and Aboriginal groups. In regard to the Xaxli'p First Nation, the Xaxli'p First Nation accepted loan monies to participate in the Treaty process and elected to withdraw from Treaty negotiations in 2001. Canada restates that Canada has written to the Xaxli'p First Nation to state that the obligation to repay the loan amount has been placed into abeyance and thus loan repayment is not being sought by Canada."

59. Arthur Adolph, in discussion with author, May 13, 2013.

60. Chief Darrell Bob, in discussion with author, Secwepemc Territory, February 15, 2016.

61. Bertha Williams, in discussion with author, April 29, 2011.

62. CERD, 11, at paragraph 37. On this point, the CERD report cites Brian Lewis, "Funds Flow to Ensure Yes Vote on Treaty Deal," *The Province*, July 12, 2007.

63. This figure is by AANDC's own admission. See Aboriginal Affairs and Northern Development Canada, Comprehensive Land Claims," September 12, 2012, http://www.aadnc-aandc.gc.ca/eng/1100100016296/1100100016297; accessed May 8, 2013.

64. For the key cases on the Crown's duty to consult and accommodate, see *Haida Nation v British Columbia (Minister of Forests)* (2004) S.C.J. No. 70, 2004 SCC

73 and *Taku River Tlingit First Nation v British Columbia (Project Assessment Director)* (2004) S.C.J. No. 69, 2004 SCC 74. For a good legal analysis of these cases, see Kent McNeil, "Aboriginal Rights, Resource Development, and the Source of the Provincial Duty to Consult in Haida Nation and Taku River," *Supreme Court Law Review* 29 (2005): 447–60.

65. Tla-o-qui-aht Incremental Treaty Agreement, November 13, 2008, http://www.gov.bc.ca/arr/treaty/down/tla_o_qui_aht_ita_final_for_signing_premier_nov0608.pdf; accessed May 8, 2013.

66. BC Treaty Commission, "Financial and Economic Impacts of Treaty Settlements in BC," *Price Waterhouse Cooper,* November 2009, 45.

67. Murray W. Browne, "Fair or Foul? Legal Issues in BC Treaty Negotiations," prepared for the Continuing Legal Education Society of British Columbia, May 2007, 1.1.15.

68. Russell Diabo to Algonquin Nation Secretariat, "Briefing Note: Aboriginal Title/Rights v. Federal Comprehensive Claims Policy," February 11, 2013, 4.

69. Martin Lukacs, "Elusive Co-Management? The Barriere Lake Algonquin's Trilateral Agreement," unpublished manuscript.

70. Russell Diabo, in discussion with author, April 19, 2013.

71. The area defined as "Annex 1" of the Trilateral Agreement drew a line demarcating about seventeen thousand square kilometers of current use. Quebec found this area excessive and pushed successfully for a second, smaller area to be demarcated as a "study area" to pursue harmonization measures. This smaller area is "Annex 2" in the Trilateral Agreement. Barriere Lake knew that the northwestern area that was left out of Annex 2 had recently been clear-cut and that it would take at least a generation for the forest to regenerate, so, after consultation with the families of this excluded region, they agreed to Quebec's proposed changes. However, in the preamble to the Trilateral Agreement, the language stipulates that both areas be considered for protection: "Whereas Quebec and the Algonquins of Barriere Lake wish to ensure, on the territory currently used by the latter and included in Annex 1 and in Annex 2, the rational management of renewable resources in view of making possible, with a concern for conservation, their versatile utilization, and the pursuit of the traditional activities by the Algonquins of Barriere Lake."

72. Mary Everson, in discussion with author, May 2, 2011.

73. Ibid. Everson has also been critical of the content of the AIP, arguing that five thousand hectares currently being offered represents an extremely diminished proportion of the community's traditional lands: "That's seven square miles. That's nothing. We used to utilize five thousand square miles gathering food, harvesting . . . seven square miles is nothing." The only people who will benefit, she contends, are those who will service the isolated, nonserviced area, with a sewer system, roads, and other amenities. She also worried, like Barriere Lake, that her people would not be able to afford the rising cost of living when the new taxes imposed by treaty begin to kick in.

74. Bertha Williams, in discussion with author, April 29, 2011.

75. Ibid.

76. AFN, Comprehensive Claims Policy Reform Regional Discussion Forum Roll-up Report, March 28, 2012, 2.

77. See Aboriginal Affairs and Northern Development Canada, "Guide for Fed-

eral Implementation of Comprehensive Claims and Self-Government Agreements," Government of Canada, May 2011, at 5.2: "Information Sharing."

78. See Manuel, *Unsettling Canada,* 46.

79. Throughout February and March 2016, several treaty meetings were "disrupted" by members of the nations who posed questions and expressed their opposition to the treaty process. In a letter dated April 20, 2016, Chief Patrick Harry, on behalf of the Northern Shushwap Treaty Society, sent a letter to all chief and councils of the Secwepmec Nation specifically noting that no information can be shared outside of the treaty members because of a confidentiality agreement between NStQ, Canada, and British Columbia (Chief Patrick Harry letter to chief and councils of the Secwepmec Nation, Re: Secwepemc Unity, April 20, 2016).

80. April Thomas, presentation to the UN Special Rapporteur on the Rights of Indigenous Peoples, Victoria Tauli-Corpuz, March 31, 2015, Westbank, B.C., Sylik Territory.

81. See Maureen Googoo, "Millbrook Second NS First Nation to Leave Mi'kmaq Rights Initiative," *Kukukwes,* May 20, 2016; and Jorge Barrera, "Key Algonquin Chief Wants Tighter Rules on Who Can Be Part of Massive Ontario Modern Treaty," APTN National News, February 27, 2016.

82. Russell Diabo, "Harper Launches Major First Nations Termination Plan: As Negotiating Tables Legitimize Canada's Colonialism," *First Nations Strategic Bulletin* 10:7–10 (June–October 2012): 1–9.

83. Ibid., 1.

84. Russell Diabo, "Canada's First Nation Termination Plan," Nation to Nation Now Symposium, Toronto, March 23, 2013.

85. *R. v Van der Peet* (1996) 2 S.C.R. 507 (hereafter, *Van der Peet*).

86. Diabo, "Canada's First Nation Termination Plan."

87. See note 7.

88. Diabo, "Canada's First Nation Termination Plan."

89. See www.defendersoftheland.org.

90. This precise sentiment is expressed to Arthur Manuel by the minister of Indian Affairs. See Robert Nault (minister of Indian Affairs) letter to Arthur Manuel (chair of Shushwap Tribal Council), "Re: Changes to Comprehensive Claims Policy," July 18, 2000.

91. The following mandates passed at the Assembly of First Nations Annual General Assembly in 2010: Resolution 71/2011—Comprehensive Claims Policy Reform Initiative—focusing on the Crown–First Nation Gathering held in January 2012, and emphasizing the need to advance CLCP reform as a part of this event; Resolution 17/2011—Specific Claims Tribunal Act Timelines—concerning Canada's inappropriate use of timelines to limit negotiations; and Resolution 14/2011—Additions to Reserve (ATR) and Economic Development and 70/2011 Improving the Additions to Reserve Policy and Process—both confirming the need to reform the ATR policy and process.

92. This is not unprecedented. The efforts of the Delgamuukw Implementation Strategic Committee (DISC) were derailed from inside as well when two AFN committees worked at cross-purposes to ultimately sabotage the efforts of DISC.

93. See Manuel, *Unsettling Canada,* 201–3, for a more detailed account of this process.

94. See Shiri Pasternak, "The Fiscal Body of Sovereignty: To 'Make Live' in Indian Country," *Settler Colonial Studies* 6:4 (2016): 1–22.

95. AFN, "Crown–First Nations Gathering Next Steps," February 2012, http://www.afn.ca/uploads/files/cfng/cfng_next_steps_-_february_2012.pdf; accessed May 8, 2013.

96. AFN, "First Nations Plan: Honouring Our Past, Affirming Our Rights, Seizing Our Future," January 23–24, 2012, 38.

97. Russell Diabo, "Crown–First Nations Gathering: The Harper Government and AFN Politics," *First Nations Strategic Bulletin* 10:1–3 (January–March 2012): 3.

98. Meagan Fitzpatrick, "Attawapiskat Handed Victory by Federal Court: Judicial Review Says a 3rd-Party Manager Was 'Unreasonable' Fix to Housing Crisis," CBC News, August 1, 2012.

99. To pick just one of a number of excellent summaries of the movement's demands, see Wab Kinew, "Idle No More Is Not Just an 'Indian Thing,'" *Huffington Post Canada*, December 17, 2012.

100. Jody Wilson-Raybould, "Regional Chief's Quarterly Report to the Chiefs of BC," British Columbia Assembly of First Nations, March 1, 2013.

101. Aboriginal Affairs and Northern Development Canada, Announcement, e-mail, April 23, 2013.

102. Diabo, "Canada's First Nation Termination Plan."

103. Nigel Bankes and Jennifer Koshan, "Tsilhqot'in: What Happened to the Second Half of Section 91(24) of the Constitution Act, 1867?" ABlawg.ca, July 7, 2014.

104. Ariel Fournier, "Sliammon Protesters Seek Injunction to Halt Upcoming Treaty Vote," thetyee.ca, July 6, 2012. This article provides a link to concerned Sliammon members' press release explaining why they were blocking the vote.

105. See Maa-nulth First Nations, "Maa-nulth First Nations Support Sliammon Voting Process," press release, Vancouver, June 26, 2012; and Tsawwassen First Nation, "Tsawwassen First Nation Supports Tla'amin First Nation's Right to Vote on Their Future," press release, June 22, 2012.

106. Justine Hunter, "Head of BC Treaty Commission Suggests Shutting It Down," *Globe and Mail*, October 12, 2011.

107. Justine Hunter, "Clark Seeks Non-treaty Deals with Natives," *Globe and Mail*, November 4, 2011.

108. Judith Sayers, "Chiefs Win Face-Off, Premier Barely in the Game: Critique of What Didn't Happen in Chiefs/Cabinet Summit Sept. 11," First Nations in BC Knowledge Network, October 6, 2014.

109. Statement of the Second Indigenous Assembly against Mining and Pipelines, November 6, 2011, http://noii-van.resist.ca/?p=4533; accessed May 9, 2013. Signed by Sliammon, Secwepemc, Wet'suwet'en, St'at'imc, Tsimshian, Dakelh, Carrier, Nuxalk, Tla-o-qui-aht, Haida Gwaii, Nak'azdli, Nlaka'Pamux, Siksika, Ahousaht, Ktunaxa, and Sayisi Dene.

110. See, for example, Courtney Fidler and Michael Hitch, "Impact and Benefit Agreements: A Contentious Issue for Environmental and Aboriginal Justice," *Environments Journal* 35:2 (2007): 45–69; and Guillaume Peterson St-Laurenta and Philippe Le Billon, "Staking Claims and Shaking Hands: Impact and Benefit Agreements as a Technology of Government in the Mining Sector," *Extractive Industries and Society* 2 (2015): 590–602.

111. Audra Simpson, "Settlement's Secrets," *Cultural Anthropology* 26:2 (2011): 205.

112. Kent McNeil's body of legal scholarship could be held here to exemplify this painstaking project. More than any other scholar of Aboriginal law, McNeil has rigorously analyzed the jurisprudence to find legal mechanisms to support Indigenous self-determination and jurisdictional authority over their lands, resources, and communities. See, for example, Kent McNeil, "The Jurisdiction of Inherent Right Aboriginal Governments," research paper for the National Centre for First Nations Governance, October 11, 2007; Kent McNeil, "Aboriginal Title and the Supreme Court: What's Happening?" *Saskatchewan Law Review* 69 (2006): 281–308; Kent McNeil, "Aboriginal Title as a Constitutionally Protected Property Right," in *Beyond the Nass Valley: National Implications of the Supreme Court's Delgamuukw Decision,* ed. Owen Lippert (Vancouver: Fraser Institute, 2000), 55–75; and Kent McNeil, "Sovereignty and the Aboriginal Nations of Rupert's Land," *Manitoba History* 37 (spring 1999): 2–8.

113. Shiri Pasternak, "Barriere Lake Sues Aboriginal Affairs and Third Party Managers," *Two Row Times,* February 4, 2015.

114. Barriere Lake Solidarity, "Communiqué: Barriere Lake Solidarity PayPal Account Frozen Due to Harper Government," press release, February 23, 2015.

Index

Blomley, Nicholas, 226, 240, 242
British Columbia, 14, 17, 29, 33–34, 38,
    55, 141, 145, 243, 248–51, 255–56, 258;
    treaty process, 149, 252, 255, 260, 267
Brundtland report, 28, 131
bureaucracy/bureaucrats, 19, 93, 108, 120,
    128, 170–71, 173, 225, 265

Calder v. British Columbia, 29, 141–42
care, 28, 56, 71, 161, 254; legal order /
    labor of, 77, 81–88, 105, 120–24, 270;
    ontology of, 6, 27, 104; reciprocity
    of, 84, 95, 101; space of, 100. *See also*
    supply
cartography. *See* maps
Chrétien, Jean, 171–74
Christianity, xxiv, xxv, 61, 62, 292n27;
    anti-Christian, 71; Catholicism, 69–71
codification of custom, 21, 92, 168–71,
    181–82, 192, 250
coercion, 23, 31, 115, 161, 190–91, 222, 229,
    246, 255–62
colonialism: acquisition, 11, 32, 56, 73,
    187, 222, 288n102; economics, 26, 52,
    73–75, 297n87; imaginary, xxii, 37, 46,
    278n18, 341–42n89; law, 10, 15, 33, 35,
    99, 279n5, 281n17; policy, 23, 45, 140,
    176, 297n86; power, 12, 14, 17, 118,
    140; property, 100, 104, 124–25, 176,
    226; subject, 33, 123, 150, 241; violence,
    8, 12, 33, 288n101, 335n12. *See also*
    economics; jurisdiction; state power;
    violence
complicity, in systems of oppression,
    xxvi, 52, 113, 291n32
Conn, Hugh, 67, 111–13, 121
consent, 14, 44, 49, 150, 159, 217, 231,
    234, 263, 267; coerced, 246, 258; pro-
    ceeding without Indigenous, 2, 136,
    197, 220, 225, 233. *See also* coercion;
    consultation
Conservative Party of Canada, xxv, 115,
    173–74, 209, 253, 265, 311n70, 312n87,
    347n40
Constitution Act of 1982, 9, 61, 99, 134,
    202, 252–53, 262, 264
consultation, 128, 152, 154, 181, 195, 199,
    203, 211, 214, 217, 225, 232–33; duty to,
    234–35, 251, 257, 259. *See also* consent;
    Haida Nation v. British Columbia
containment. *See* spatial
Copper One Inc., 2–3, 214
corruption, 31, 124, 190, 196, 227

Coulthard, Glen, 75, 150
court, 1, 8, 12, 13, 32–35, 42, 104, 130–32,
    152, 173, 178, 182, 195, 198, 210, 230–31,
    238, 247, 252, 254, 257, 262, 268; High
    Court of Australia, 13, 16; kangaroo,
    32, 229; Ontario Superior, 210–11;
    Quebec Superior, 130, 134, 152, 156–57,
    168, 181, 192, 218; Supreme Court of
    British Columbia, 11, 141. *See also* Paul,
    Superior Justice Réjean; Supreme
    Court of Canada
Cree, 43, 58, 209, 214, 247; James Bay,
    111, 142; lawsuit, 136, 142; territory,
    108–9, 119
criminalization, 8, 31–32, 52, 185, 190,
    222, 226, 231, 233–39, 241; criminality,
    13, 137, 190, 227, 242; violent crime,
    13, 236
customary leadership. *See* governance;
    government; Indigenous law

death, xviii, xxiv, 38, 65, 70, 103, 176, 240
decentralization, 67, 69; society, 53, 89,
    108, 114
decolonization, 24, 25, 44–47, 270
Decoursay, Philomene, 79–80
Decoursay, Toby, 39, 43, 51, 61, 63, 70–71,
    77–79, 90–91, 105, 117–18, 123, 166,
    200, 208, 269
Defenders of the Land. *See* land
Delgamuukw v. British Columbia, 11, 17,
    135–36, 144
democracy, 45; failure of, 11; imposition
    of, 207–9
de/reterritorialization, 21, 55, 241
Diabo, Russell, 24, 38, 41, 51, 147, 166–67,
    185, 191, 196, 250, 258, 262–63, 266
Di Gangi, Peter, 41–42, 93
dispossession, 26, 55, 71; absolute, 25, 64;
    capitalism, 72–76, 241; Indigenous, 12,
    51, 55–56, 109, 113, 123–24, 145, 225,
    237; resisting, 9, 119. *See also* aliena-
    tion; social reproduction
divide and conquer tactics, 30, 172,
    195–96, 219
Domtar, 126, 174–75, 180, 186, 232–33, 239
Dorsett, Shaunnagh, 10, 12–13, 21, 118,
    226
drum, 71, 79, 89, 92

eagles, 91, 106, 159
earth, xxvii, 50, 57, 78–79, 84, 106
ecological: destruction, 5, 107, 127, 151,

Shiri Pasternak is assistant professor in the School for the Study of Canada at Trent University in Nogoiowanong (Peterborough), Ontario. She holds a PhD from the Program of Planning and Geography at the University of Toronto.